ISBN 978-1-5280-4033-4
PIBN 10926453

1 MONTH OF
FREE
READING

at

www.ForgottenBooks.com

By purchasing this book you are eligible for one month membership to ForgottenBooks.com, giving you unlimited access to our entire collection of over 1,000,000 titles via our web site and mobile apps.

To claim your free month visit: www.forgottenbooks.com/free926453

English
Français
Deutsche
Italiano
Español
Português

www.forgottenbooks.com

Mythology Photography **Fiction**
Fishing Christianity **Art** Cooking
Essays Buddhism Freemasonry
Medicine **Biology** Music **Ancient
Egypt** Evolution Carpentry Physics
Dance Geology **Mathematics** Fitness
Shakespeare **Folklore** Yoga Marketing
Confidence Immortality Biographies
Poetry **Psychology** Witchcraft
Electronics Chemistry History **Law**
Accounting **Philosophy** Anthropology
Alchemy Drama Quantum Mechanics
Atheism Sexual Health **Ancient History**
Entrepreneurship Languages Sport
Paleontology Needlework Islam
Metaphysics Investment Archaeology
Parenting Statistics Criminology
Motivational

Historic, archived document

Do not assume content reflects current
scientific knowledge, policies, or practices.

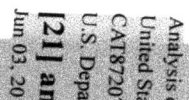

State Agricultural Experiment Stations

History of Research Policy and Procedure

Miscellaneous Publication 904
Cooperative State Experiment Station Service
United States Department of Agriculture

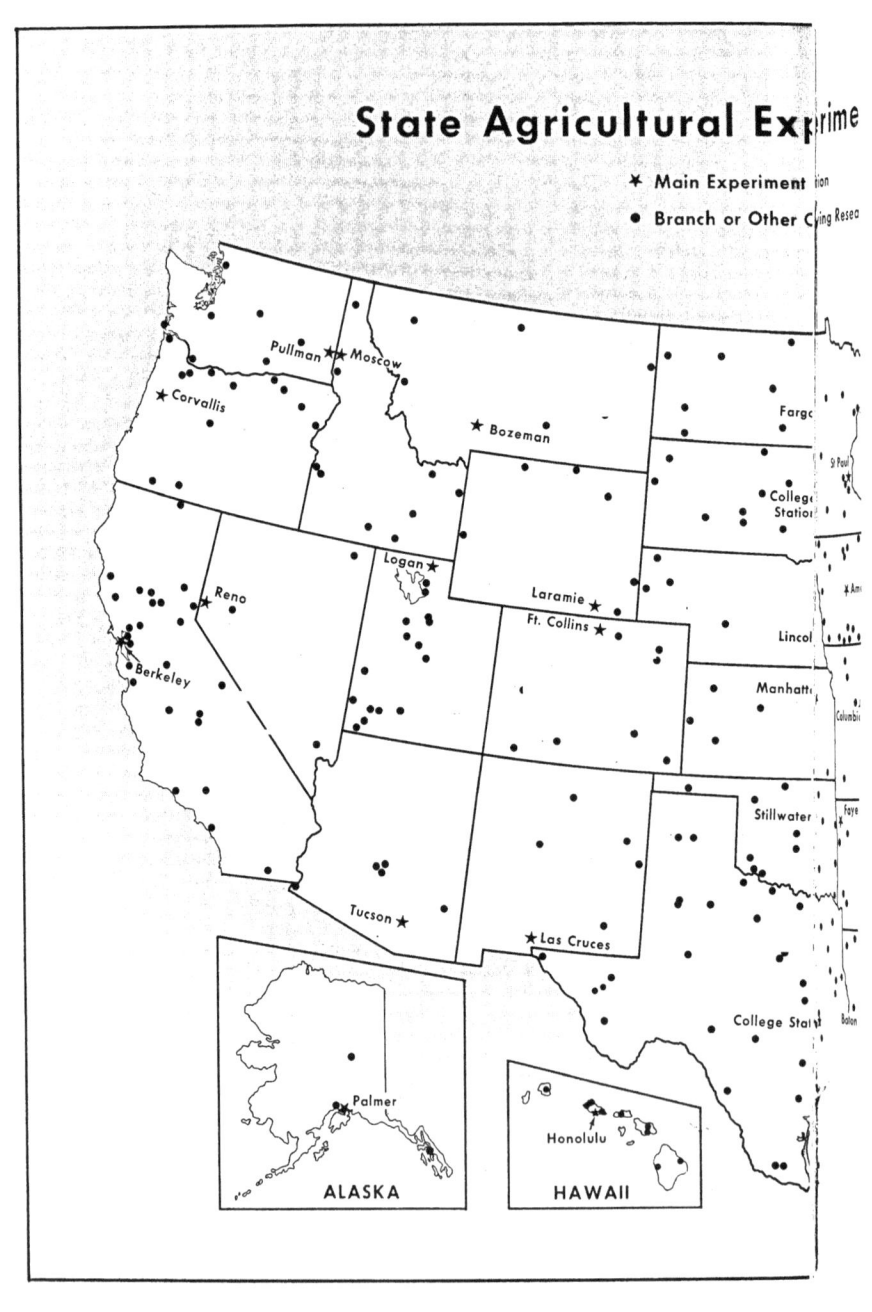

State Agricultural Exprime

★ Main Experiment tion

● Branch or Other C ing Resea

Pullman ★ ★ Moscow

★ Corvallis

★ Bozeman

Fargo

St Paul

College
Station

Logan ★

Laramie ★

★ Reno

Ft. Collins ★

Lincol

★ Berkeley

Manhatt

Columbi

Stillwater

Faye

Tucson ★

★ Las Cruces

College Stat

Balon

Palmer

ALASKA

Honolulu

HAWAII

riment Station System

ion

ing Research Location

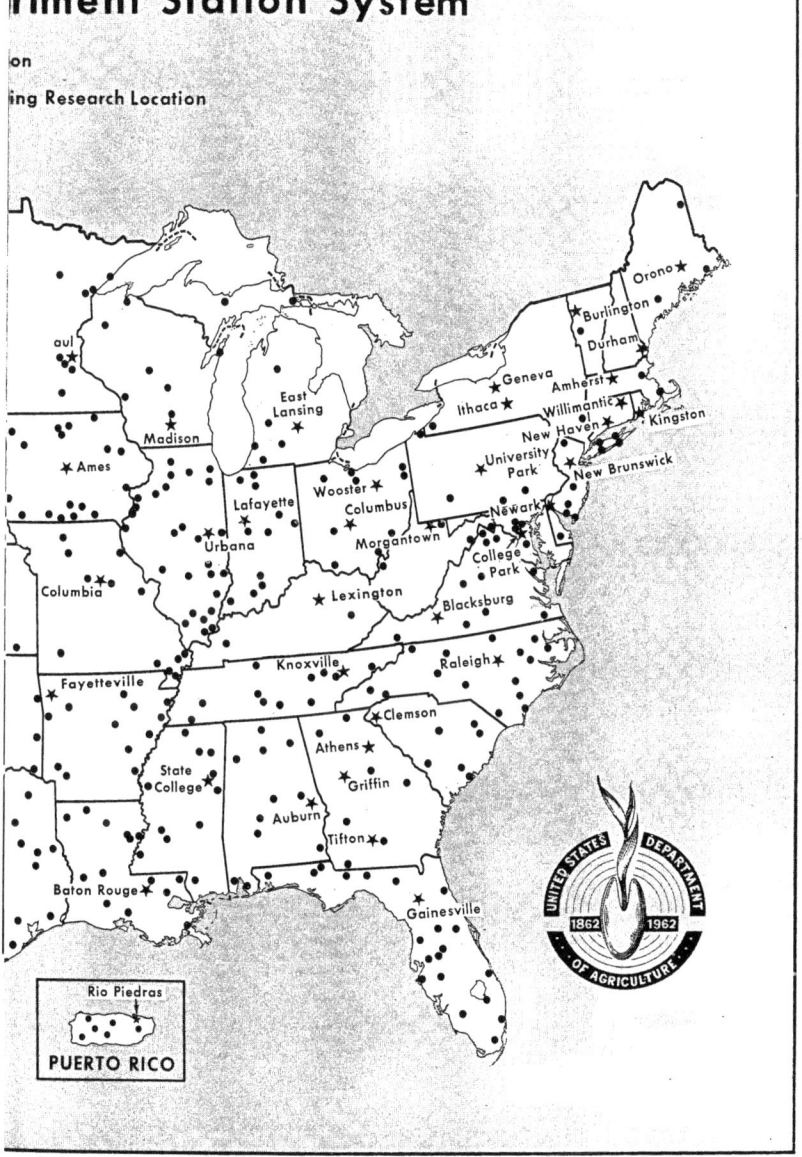

State Agricultural Experiment Station System

★ Main Experiment Station

● Branch or Other Outlying Research Location

Bozeman

Laramie ★
rt. Collins ★

College
Station ●

Fargo

Manhattan ★

Lincoln ●

★ Ar

Columbia ★

New Brunswick ★

State

Agricultural

Experiment

Stations

A History of Research Policy and Procedure

Authors

H. C. Knoblauch   E. M. Law   W. P. Meyer

Contributing Authors

B. F. Beacher   R. B. Nestler   B. S. White, Jr.

Issued May 1962   Miscellaneous Publication No. 904

UNITED STATES DEPARTMENT OF AGRICULTURE

This Volume Is Published
In Observance of the
USDA—Land-Grant College
Centennials, 1962

CONTENTS

	Page
PREFACE	iv
Chapter 1—AGRICULTURAL SCIENCE EMERGES	1
Chapter 2—EUROPEAN BACKGROUND FOR THE STATION IDEA	5
Chapter 3—AMERICAN BEGINNINGS	19
Chapter 4—THE HATCH MOVEMENT: Winning Federal Support for the Land-Grant College Station	29
Chapter 5—ASSOCIATION AND THE ADMINISTRATION OF RESEARCH	55
Chapter 6—TOWARD BASIC RESEARCH—THE ADAMS ACT	81
Chapter 7—THE STATE STATIONS AND THE DEPARTMENT OF AGRICULTURE: Consultation and Cooperation	111
Chapter 8—PUBLISHING RESULTS OF RESEARCH: Information, Communication, and Public Relations	143
Chapter 9—ORGANIZED SELF-APPRAISAL: The Project System, Improved Procedures, and Consolidated Legislation	159
Chapter 10—FEDERAL-GRANT PROGRAMS IN MARKETING RESEARCH, 1940–60	175
Chapter 11—BROADENING THE SCOPE OF INVESTIGATION: Regional Approach to Research Problems	191
Chapter 12—MOVING FORWARD: The Stations as a Force for Progress	207
APPENDIX	217
Basic legislation authorizing establishment of and Federal grant payments to agricultural experiment stations	217
USDA policy letters concerning Federal grant payments to State programs	236
USDA policy statements concerning Departmental organization affecting relations with experiment stations	243
Some major policy recommendations made by directors of agricultural experiment stations	247
SUBJECT INDEX	253
NAME INDEX	

PREFACE

Successful modern-day agriculture in the United States reflects in considerable part a century of effective cooperative relations between the land-grant colleges and the United States Department of Agriculture. In 1962 we will commemorate the signing by Abraham Lincoln on May 15, 1862, of "An act establishing the United States Department of Agriculture," and on July 2, 1862, of "An act donating public lands to the several States and Territories which may provide colleges for the benefit of American agriculture and the mechanic arts."

With the approaching centennials in mind, the Experiment Station Committee on Organization and Policy of the Association of Land-Grant Colleges and State Universities (ESCOP), in 1958 expressed a desire for a document that would provide a record of experiment station policy developments. The Committee suggested an annotated publication with an index for quick reference.

In the hundred years that have passed since they were established, the Department of Agriculture, as a Federal agency, and the land-grant colleges, as State-administered institutions supported in part by Federal grants, have carried on many interdependent and cooperative programs. Together they have contributed much to the growth of American farm technology. In 1860, 2 years before the organic acts were passed, one farmworker supported only 4.53 persons. In 1890, 3 years after the Hatch Experiment Station Act of 1887 became law, one farmworker supported 5.77 persons.

Since then there has been a steady increase in each decade. In 1960, one farmworker supported 26 persons. Credit for this increase in productivity must go to many individuals and institutions. Important influences were favorable farm and home environment, traditional American beliefs in public education, credit opportunities, significant shifts from manpower and horsepower to mechanical power and machines.

Research administrators and directors of experiment stations recognize that prior and parallel developments had much to do with the growth of modern farm technology. They fully acknowledge the effective contributions of industrial agencies and organizations in making American agriculture more productive. McCormick and his reaper, the steel plows, the cream separator, tractors, combines, and many more recent mechanical developments have brought tremendous acceleration. Their successful development was encouraged by the gradual evolvement of a workable system whereby scientific research was directed toward continuous improvement of farm practice. The organized agricultural research and closely related educational programs extended new knowledge from the scientific laboratory and experimental plots to the farmer. The land-grant colleges and the U.S. Department of Agriculture provided the cooperative frame-

iv

Analysis o
United Sta
CAT87207
U.S. Depar
[21] an
Jun 03, 201

work. Thus the twin centennials of the organic acts creating the Department and the land-grant institutions present an appropriate occasion for this review.

The purpose of this volume is to document and evaluate administrative and policy developments in the operations of the State agricultural experiment stations. Growth of the agricultural experiment station concept as part of the land-grant college system reveals an historical epoch in bringing search for knowledge in closer relationship with teaching at institutions of higher learning. Cooperation among the individual land-grant colleges and between them and the Federal Department of Agriculture provides a unique pattern that can well be regarded as a model for effective State–Federal cooperation in many scientific endeavors.

State agricultural experiment stations as divisions of the land-grant colleges, responsible only to their parent institutions and State governments, have through the years been closely related to the Federal Department of Agriculture because of the Federal-grant support for agricultural research, first authorized in the Hatch Act of 1887. The U.S. Department of Agriculture is charged with the administration of the Hatch Act and subsequent amendatory legislation providing for support of agricultural research at the State stations.

The pattern for the conduct of agricultural research evolved gradually during the past 100 years. Following passage of the Land-Grant Act, some of the farm leaders and government officials questioned whether experiment stations should be a part of the academic institutions. At the same time others urged that research was a vital part of seeking the scientific knowledge essential for the "improvement of agriculture."

Interests of farmer, educator, scientist, and legislator occupied the stage at various times for a phase of activity that contributed to the progressive development of the American system of agricultural research organization, administration, and development.

The first part of this publication presents important background information that relates to origin of the concept of a tax-supported experiment station. Included are brief reviews of the historical development of the experiment station idea in Europe and the experiences of American agricultural leaders in promoting the establishment of experiment stations in the United States. .

Early activities in research administration and policy development reveal the dedication of experiment station leaders to the research ideal. Examples include the early efforts to make stations independent institutions; the persistent attempts to create a national association of station workers; the continuing effort to maintain balance between Federal Department of Agriculture research programs and State station programs, with full recognition of the responsibility of the States within their respective jurisdictions; efforts to reduce teaching loads and extension assignments in order to free investigators for research; and the periodic movements to obtain additional funds for station research.

The historical review reveals occasional conflict in viewpoints within the station movement itself and concerning other institutions with which the stations have historically established interdependent relationships. These could have produced continuing antagonisms and friction. But, as men of dedicated purpose and good will, the station leaders consistently negotiated compromises that promoted the public interest. To this policy we may attribute much of the progress in the successful operation of interdependent research units in a complex system of Federal–State tax-supported research.

Both farm and urban populations have gained from the many research accomplishments of the State experiment stations. Their findings have contributed immensely to the growth and welfare of the respective States. Their research, together with that of the closely associated Federal Department of Agriculture, provides a pattern of science organization that is unique in history.

This publication traces the developments. Early chapters draw richly on historical records searched and established by Ernest M. Law, historian and professor of history at Boston University. Subsequent chapters rely in part on "A History of Agricultural Experimentation and Research" by the late A. C. True, on the Proceedings of the American Association of Land-Grant Colleges and State Universities, and on records of ESCOP meetings contributed by Dean and Director Emeritus R. E. Buchanan of Iowa State University. The appendix includes official records and policy statements available in the Department of Agriculture.

The reader is cautioned not to consider this volume as a history of agricultural experiment station accomplishments, but rather a history of cooperative research procedure and policy development under the dually administered system of publicly supported agricultural research of the State Experiment Stations and the U.S. Department of Agriculture. In addition to historical photographs, some pictures have been included to provide glimpses of current activities underway at many stations.

The writers are indebted to Associate Director Noble Clark of the Wisconsin Agricultural Experiment Station for his review of the manuscript and for his many helpful criticisms and suggestions. Grateful acknowledgment is made for the cooperation given over the years by the directors of agricultural experiment stations and present and former members of ESCOP, many of whom played major roles in the development of an established State–Federal cooperative system that has stood the test of time.

Chapter One—
AGRICULTURAL SCIENCE EMERGES

Modern society places considerable confidence in science and technology as the solvers of major problems that confront the world. In the course of human history, no problem seems to have been more real to more people than that of hunger. So it is not surprising that, in an age when science is splitting atoms and conquering distance and time, more and more people all over the world look expectantly to science for a solution to the hunger problem.

This hope, this image of the ultimate goal of science, has become fixed in the minds of millions. It has grown from the practical recognition that food abundance is a reality in the United States. This development, stimulated largely through science and education, is now recognized as perhaps the greatest step forward in the history of civilization.

Many centuries and many ages contributed to the scientific knowledge we are now putting to work in American agriculture. As far back as the 13th century, a Franciscan friar named Roger Bacon (1214–92) advocated the demonstration of fact through experiments. He repeated the same experiments many times until there could be no reasonable doubt of effect following cause. Although a prisoner of medieval thought, he recognized a principle that later became the basis for all scientific research.

Several centuries later another Bacon—Francis Bacon (1561–1626)—proposed a "House of Salomon" to be manned by a company of scholars that would acquire new knowledge by observation and experiment, knowledge that would lead to practical results and advancement.

Experimentation as proposed by the Bacons began being applied to agriculture in England and the American colonies as early as the 17th century. During the 1600's, experiments in growing mulberry trees and silkworms were underway in Virginia and the Carolinas. In 1630, Parliament provided funds to Georgia for experiments to encourage indigo growing. James Logan, Secretary to William Penn, sought agricultural improvements in Pennsylvania through scientific observations on the botanical nature of maize. These were so accurate in the light of present knowledge that Logan is often credited with being America's first scientific agriculturist. In 1733, Jethro Tull (4)[1] reported experiments with cultivation of soil between plants that brought increased yields.

"These few examples," wrote R. W. Trullinger in 1952 (3), "illustrate that the agricultural revolution had well begun by the middle

---

[1] Italic numbers in parentheses refer to Literature Cited, p. 4.

of the 18th century. Experimentation, the making of scientific inquiry and the systematic probing of practice, was destined to become the new tool whereby man would enlist the cooperation of nature for the advancement of human welfare. This trend was helped greatly in the late 18th and early 19th centuries when there were rapid developments in the field of science. These came under the influence of scholars with a practical bent, like Joseph Priestly, Lavoisier, Sir Humphrey Davy, Jean G. Boussingault, and Justus von Liebig. Their work established some of the basic principles of chemistry.

"The years of the industrial and agricultural revolutions were marked by a spirit of discovery and invention on the part of many practical men . . . they appreciated the value of the knowledge that could be contributed by the scholars and students of science toward speeding progress in industry. Societies at the meetings of which the philosophies of the scholars and practical suggestions in the field of science could be discussed became organized in both England and the United States.

"The Royal Society of London was incorporated in 1662. Its American counterpart was the American Philosophical Society, organized in Philadelphia in 1743 under the leadership of Benjamin Franklin. Since colonial interests were to a considerable extent rural, scientific inquiries and discussions in the American Philosophical Society frequently turned to agriculture. This no doubt had much to do with Franklin's active part in organizing the Philadelphia Society for the Promotion of Agriculture in 1785."

NEED FOR EXPERIMENTATION

Thus the 17th and 18th centuries reflected a growing consciousness of the need for experimentation in farming. The early agricultural societies, of which men like Washington and Jefferson were active members, are links in the sequence from which grew the subsequent establishment of the U.S. Department of Agriculture, the land-grant colleges, and the State agricultural experiment stations. The New Jersey Society for the Promotion of Agriculture, Commerce, and Art was formed in 1781. The Philadelphia Society, referred to above, and the South Carolina Society for Promoting Agriculture were organized in 1785. Others were formed in the following order: New York in 1791, Massachusetts in 1792, and Connecticut in 1794.

Following the pattern of the pioneer societies, many State and county agricultural societies came into being during the early decades of the 19th century. Meetings were held, usually in the wintertime. These meetings featured papers and talks aimed at bringing about agricultural improvements in the States and counties. By 1852, approximately 300 such societies were active in 31 States and 5 territories. By 1860, 2 years before the organic acts creating the U.S. Department of Agriculture and the land-grant colleges were signed, there were more than 900 societies. Proceedings reflect that as early as the 1840's the establishment of agricultural colleges was prominent in the public mind.

The agricultural societies also had a profound effect on the movement that led later to the development of agricultural experiment stations as they became organized under the Hatch Act. The mass

2

effect of wide discussion of the need for improving agriculture in the societies has been ably described by Carstensen (*1*) :

Behind this dramatic development lay a long period of groping. For more than a century the notion had been propounded again and again—from lecture platforms, editorial offices and even pulpits—that the farmer not only could but should improve his craft; that he could and should become more productive. Thus, for example, the Massachusetts Agricultural Society, in its petition to the General Court in 1792 asking for corporate powers, underscored the need for an organization that would itself make experiments aimed at improving agriculture and would invite others to do so. Moreover, the petitioners claimed that they had funds with which to reward "men of enterprise who have, by their inquiries, made useful discoveries and communicated them to the public." Similiarly, the Albemarle Agricultural Society, as conceived by Thomas Jefferson, proposed to obtain "A succinct report of the different practices of Husbandry in the district inhabited by the members . . . including the bad as well as the good. . . . It is believed that a judicious execution of this article alone might nearly supercede [sic] every other duty of the society, inasmuch as it would present every good practice which has occurred to the mind of any cultivator of the state for imitation and every bad one for avoidance; and the choicest processes culled from every farm would compose a course probably near perfection.

This idea lay at the base not only of the agricultural societies and the 19th century farmers' clubs, but it provided the justification for many other activities : the organization of agricultural fairs, the launching of farm journals, the creation of state and federal departments of agriculture, and the many experiments with agricultural education. In large measure this faith provided the basis for the Morrill Act of 1862. Editors, educators, politicians and self appointed farm spokesmen never tired of reminding each other and the public that improvement was the motto of the age, that agricultural progress was both necessary and inevitable.

RESEARCH SYSTEM ESTABLISHED

The Act of May 15, 1862, "establishing the United States Department of Agriculture," and the Act of July 2, 1862, "donating public lands to the several States and Territories which may provide colleges for the benefit of American agriculture and the mechanic arts," became the first Federal, legal authority under which the cooperative features of today's nationwide agricultural research system was to develop. In the framework thus established it became possible to cultivate further the concept that the problems of farming were primarily problems of man understanding nature. To do the latter required scientific knowledge. And to acquire and interpret scientific knowledge in the light of the many localized farm problems, required a new kind and quality of education. The land-grant institutions were established to provide such education and training. Although they were intended primarily to aid agriculture, the pattern of higher education developed by them, combining laboratory research and classroom training, became the model now used in most areas of preparation for a career in science and technology.

"As early as 1835, the first chemical laboratory for student instruction had been started at the University of Pensylvania," wrote Eddy (*2*). "By 1868, the Massachusetts Institute of Technology offered the first laboratory work in physics. But up to 1872 only six colleges in the country taught either chemistry or physics by the laboratory method. The early use of the method, then, was scattered and purely experimental. It remained for the land-grant colleges to assist in a development born of necessity rather than design."

The necessity confronting the land-grant colleges was the solution of agricultural problems. Here, on a new continent, the spirit of frontier had fathered a new kind of government "of the people, by the people, and for the people." For many years farmers had heard the word "experimentation."

The modern type of agricultural experiment station, although of European parentage, as later chapters will show, was perfected in the United States under the USDA–land-grant system. It represents a combination of systematic research carried on by qualified scientists in a laboratory, combined where necessary with intensive and repeated field trials, and wide dissemination of findings through scientific publication and demonstration of new practices accruing from the research. This organizational pattern of experiment stations grew out of the discussions of the agricultural societies and subsequently out of the debates and trials of the early land-grant institutions.

LITERATURE CITED

(1) CARSTENSEN, VERNON.
    1960. THE GENESIS OF AN AGRICULTURAL EXPERIMENT STATION. Agr. Hist. 34(1) : 13–20.
(2) EDDY, E. D.
    1957. COLLEGES FOR OUR LAND AND OUR TIME; THE LAND GRANT IDEA IN AMERICAN EDUCATION. 328 pp. Harper & Bros., New York.
(3) TRULLINGER, R. W.
    1952. THE ROOTS FROM WHICH OUR FARM SCIENCE GREW. County Officer Magazine 17(5) : 128–134, 144, illus.
(4) [TULL, JETHRO.]
    1733. THE HORSE-HOING [SIC] HUSBANDRY . . . 269 pp., illus. London.

Chapter Two—
EUROPEAN BACKGROUND FOR THE STATION IDEA

The movement to establish the State agricultural experiment stations in the United States drew its first inspiration from European experience in founding successful institutions for scientific research in agriculture.

In the mid-19th century young American students of a new science, agricultural chemistry, traveled to the countries of Western Europe, notably Scotland and Germany. There they spent many months of apprenticeship in the laboratories of scientists who were building careers and reputations in a new profession; namely, the application of science to agriculture.

The Scots in the 1840's and the Saxons in the 1850's pioneered in providing an administrative structure for putting the scientist to work to improve agriculture. They could not avoid dealing with the intrinsic problems of policy and procedure in the organization and work of their new ventures. What should be, for example, the functions and duties of an agricultural laboratory? Where should lie the responsibility for administrative direction and for financial support? Under what authority—and for what constituency— should the laboratory operate? These questions were identical with those that subsequently confronted administrators in the United States in the land-grant college and experiment station movement there. In their studies abroad, Americans learned lessons on-the-spot from the European attempts to introduce improved techniques in research.

SCOTLAND PIONEERED IN FARM SCIENCE

Scotland in 1840 was a country of earnest and serious-minded farm improvers, well adjusted to a changing farm technology, and long accustomed to a system of deliberate innovation supervised by the Highland and Agricultural Society. For a half-century this Society—which traced its origins to 1784, its Royal charter to 1787, and its Parliamentary subsidy to 1789—had sought diligently to discover a methodology that would increase production in its thin-soiled homeland.

In 1789 the Society introduced a plan for accumulating agricultural information. It published a premium list offering medals, monetary awards, and honorary prizes for reports of farming accomplishments and for essays on prescribed topics. Numerous contestants responded.

5

Annually thereafter the Committee of Directors examined Scotland's farm economy, selected for investigation its weakest features, and compiled a premium list accordingly. Volunteers in the farm population regularly supplied data and explanations, the yearly harvest of prize essays multiplied in the Society's published *Transactions*, and the Directors constructed a countrywide improvement program on the cornerstone of the premium lists.

Emphasizing the theme of farm experiments in the 1830's, the Society strove to spread throughout Scotland a spirit of agricultural improvement. Via its premium lists it stimulated and partially rewarded farm experimenters; it hoped to make home trials a national habit. It proposed to produce a race of self-reliant investigators continually exerting themselves to become better farmers (*5*).[1] Farmers who regularly conducted the trials would, the Directors believed, in time become responsive to new ideas, alert to find them, and ready to apply them; farmers who experimented would, in short, catch the vital spirit of improvement. Thus the success of the Society's campaign for improvement hinged on the popularity of home experiments. In December of 1840 the Directors congratulated themselves on their efforts to make the Scottish farmer experiment-conscious.

Convinced that farmer experiments were concurrently bettering agricultural practices, the Directors decided to tap another source of information. They added to the premium list a section on the "Science of Agriculture," requesting essays that would explain on "scientific principles" enumerated problems of soil fertility and vegetable growth (*4*). They anticipated that chemists and vegetable physiologists, working at their own expense and in their own laboratories, would investigate subjects on the premium list and submit results useful to farmers. In 1841 the scientific section was moved to the head of the premium list, subjects requiring chemical analyses as the basis of proof were included, and the prize money was increased (*5, pp. 506–507*).

Had the Society hit upon the most effective arrangement for the efficient use of a scientist's services? A Scottish professor of chemistry, James F. W. Johnston, raised his voice in dissent. Well known in Edinburgh, Johnston had emerged in 10 years of study to a position of scientific prominence. In 1833 the newly founded Durham University appointed him to a faculty post in chemistry and mineralogy (*3*). By 1840 new discoveries in organic chemistry, publicized by Justus von Liebig's report to the Association turned the attention of the Association to the prospect of applying science to agriculture (*16*).

Professor Johnston sharply criticized the Society's program on two counts. First, he charged, the home trials were not producing accurate and reliable results because farmers had not learned how to experiment correctly. Second, the premium system did not sufficiently encourage chemists to perform agricultural research in a serious and steady manner. For each deficiency Johnston proposed a remedy. Farmers, he urged, should receive written instructions which explained the objectives and procedural details of worthwhile experiments. Furthermore, he contended, chemists should undertake "analytical researches of various kinds . . . in the laboratory, at the

[1] Italic numbers in parentheses refer to Literature Cited, p. 17.

cost, under the direction, and for the immediate benefit of the practical agriculturist, and for the direct advancement of his art" (*13, p. 208*).

JOHNSTON SET THE PATTERN

Johnston in this way directly proposed that the farmers learn experimental techniques from scientists and, in addition, subsidize laboratory research; indirectly he recommended that the Society establish and maintain an institution for laboratory research. The Directors did not disapprove the former idea, but they stubbornly opposed the latter. Clinging to the precedent that the Society should stimulate others to experiment but should not itself be the experimenter, they considered a centralized research agency a menace to the continued operation of farm experiments. Farmers would rely on the centralized research, feeling that trials at home were no longer necessary, and thus the incentive for improvement would be destroyed. The Society pleaded that its treasury could not pay the expenses of a research establishment (*5, pp. 497–498*).

Particularly anxious to teach the farmers the proper methods of experimentation, Johnston in 1841 circulated a small tract, *Suggestions for Experiments in Practical Agriculture*. For several years thereafter he issued periodic revisions of this pamphlet and appended current numbers to a text he had written, *Lectures on Agricultural Chemistry and Geology* (*12*), and to a simplified version of that text, *Elements of Scientific Agriculture and Geology*, published especially for farmers.

Johnston also began an intensive study of fertilizers at his Durham Laboratory. This was at a time when there was widespread suspicion among farmers of the newly introduced "special manures" or commercial fertilizers. In volunteering to provide farmers with methodologies, Johnston realized that the scientists could rely on the farmers' findings only when the farmer complied with the scientist's standard for accuracy. He formulated his *Suggestions* accordingly. He reiterated in these releases his faith that farm trials were essential for improvements as he set forth his recipes for fertilizers and his instructions for testing them. He pointed out the laboratory worker's inability to perform field trials. He similarly stressed the field experimenter's contribution to the improvement of agriculture (*12*). Thereby he skillfully persuaded both farmers and the Directors to cooperate in what amounted to a new step forward in scientific agriculture. Farmers could not avoid the conclusion that a chemist was superintending a new kind of improvement. Johnston's successful efforts in demonstrating the immediate usefulness of fertilizer and soil analysis rapidly popularized among Scottish farmers the concept of a laboratory for the investigation of farm problems.

In the spring of 1842 the Directors, noting that farmers were accepting the idea of soil and fertilizer analysis, moved one step nearer to Johnston's goal, a Society-sponsored laboratory. They appointed a committee to consider the problem of hiring a chemist as a Society officer. On July 5, 1842, the committee reported in favor of the project but stressed its inability to find ways for raising the minimum salary that a first-class chemist would demand (*6*). The only possible method, it concluded, was some form of popular subscription. The Directors accepted the report but took no further action.

During the next 3 weeks, however, several tenant farmers in the Edinburgh area assumed the initiative. Searching for a way to obtain analyses of their own soils and fertilizers at the cheapest possible prices, they drew up and submitted to the Directors on July 25 a simple scheme whereby the Society would hire a chemist to give lectures and perform at cut rates the two types of analyses, and each farmer would pay for his own analyses (7). When this was turned down by the Directors, the disappointed but resourceful tenants determined to get a chemist's services at low cost to themselves. In the following week 67 of their tenant brethren and 30 proprietors joined in a subscription movement. For 5 months the subscription list grew; soon it contained the names of prominent Society members and influential landholders.

AGRICULTURAL ASSOCIATION FORMED

On December 12, 1842, the proprietors and tenants gathered in an Edinburgh hotel and by resolution created the *Agricultural Chemistry Association of Scotland*. They set a subscription goal of 500 pounds and named a committee on Association-Society relations. Within a month this committee worked out a bargain with the Directors. The Society agreed to contribute 50 pounds per year and rooms in its new museum for the meetings of the Association; the latter agreed in return that the Society should appoint three of its own members to the nine-man Committee of Management and should have the exclusive right to publish the Association's *Proceedings* in its *Transactions* (6). The Committee of Management organized itself in January 1843, prepared a prospectus of the chemist's duties and the subscribers' privileges (7), advertised for a chemist, and in July elected Professor Johnston.

The Association placed a heavy load on Johnston's shoulders (7), but in doing so it recognized the contribution his ideas had made to its formation. Interpreting improvement to mean a search for new knowledge and the search, in turn, to involve the technique of applying selected sciences to agriculture, the charter set up a research agency comprising a chemical laboratory and a system of farm experiments. It gave Johnston a key role in formulating and executing a research program: the chemist should suggest experiments for laboratory and field and should explain the results to scientist and farmer.

The charter did not define the nature of the new knowledge for which Johnston should search. Did performance of routine analyses for individual members satisfy the charter's insistence on "the enlargement of our present knowledge," or did research require additional effort? The Committee of Management supplied the answer. It decreed that the research program should aim "to establish general principles" and not confine itself to "analyses for immediate profit" (7).

News of the Johnston appointment traveled across the Atlantic to Benjamin Silliman, Sr., Professor of Chemistry, Mineralogy, and Geology at Yale College. Known abroad as the founder and editor of the *American Journal of Arts and Sciences*, Silliman dated his scientific training to graduate work at English and Scottish universities in 1805–06. Since that time he had kept in touch with British scientists and their work. Famous at home as Yale's lecturer on science, Silliman had become a suave speaker and a deft demonstrator of experiments in the classroom and on the public lecture platform. A faculty member since 1802, he had attained stature as an influential figure at Yale and as an American authority on science.

In 1840 there appeared in Silliman's lecture hall John Pitkin Norton, an 18-year-old lad who was determined to become a well instructed farmer and to assume the management of his wealthy father's Connecticut estate. Sharply curious about chemical analysis, young Norton acquired during his year under Silliman an appetite for advanced work in chemistry. He thereupon spent the following year, 1841–42, in study at Silliman's private laboratory on the Yale campus. Norton returned to New Haven in 1843, this time reporting to the private laboratory of Silliman's son and professional assistant, Benjamin, Jr. By the spring of 1844 Norton was bent on acquiring "a thorough knowledge of analytical chemistry as applied to agriculture" (17). Silliman, Sr., pleased with Norton's skill, urged that his protege go abroad to gain further proficiency; he arranged for Norton to become a pupil of Professor Johnston (15). Norton arrived at Johnston's quarters in May of 1844 and settled down to an 18 months' stay.

NORTON APPLIED SCIENTIFIC METHODS

In June 1844, Johnston escorted Norton to Edinburgh and set him to work as one of three assistants in the laboratory of the Agricultural Chemistry Association. There Norton applied methods for analyzing the numerous samples of soils, manures, minerals, and water which the subscribers submitted; he also began, at his teacher's urging, an extended analysis of oat proteins, a project for which the Society had announced a substantial premium. He learned the details of Johnston's new technique for controlling the price and quality of fertilizers on the market. He participated in the detection of serious adulteration in samples of some new commercial fertilizers. From the many procedures he saw his mentor establish, the young scientist acquired both scientific and practical experience (13, 17).

The American apprentice also saw another side of the Association's work. In July of 1844, soon after his introduction to the routines of the Edinburgh laboratory, he accompanied Johnston, the ambassador of improvement, on the latter's first annual tour of Scottish farming districts. For several weeks the pair visited marketplaces, towns, and fairs. At each stopping point Norton listened to his teacher's lectures before groups of farmers who had assembled for the occasion; at each gathering he paid close attention to the chemist's explanations of the ways science could solve local problems.

The enthusiastic response of "dirt" farmers to Johnston's lecturing convinced Norton that the Chemistry Association was exerting an "immense increasing influence . . . on the prosperity of Scotland" (17). His admiration for the Association—and for Johnston's skill as a teacher and an advice-giving savant—grew as the months slipped past. The Association in his view provided a praiseworthy organization whereby the scientist and the farmer could blend "scientific researches" with "practical experience" so as to achieve the ultimate goal, "a system of scientific agriculture" (18).

9

ships—one for Norton in Agricultural Chemistry and Vegetable and Animal Physiology, the other for Silliman, Jr., in Practical Chemistry. In 1847 the Yale Corporation created a Department of Philosophy and the Arts, a framework within which Norton and his associate, "Young Ben" Silliman, were enabled to organize on the Yale Campus their School of Applied Chemistry (2). To accomplish the school's educational objective, the partners set up a course of laboratory work for students wishing to study pure science, applied science, or techniques of teaching. To pay for the upkeep of the Analytical Laboratory, they announced their readiness to conduct all kinds of commercial analyses.

As supervisor of the school's agricultural program, Norton selected for imitation a cluster of features from his Scottish experience. Specializing in soil analysis, that part of the Edinburg laboratory's work which had attained the greatest popularity with the Scottish farmers, he encouraged farmers to submit samples of their soils and fertilizers. To each sample-sender he penned a report of the analyst's findings and priced his services according to the time, labor, and materials used in the analysis.

Early in 1848 he went beyond the Johnstonian precedent when he introduced a 2 months' course of lectures, designed especially for practicing farmers and based on Johnston's texts (19). To the professional farmer he directed the course's theme: Understand the relationship between science and farming and unite theory with practice. Thus, winter lectures for practical farmers, commercial analyses of substances important in the farmers' business, and laboratory instruction to prospective agricultural chemists comprised Norton's version of a competent agricultural school.

NORTON PROMOTED AGRICULTURAL COLLEGES

Once started, however, on a program of administering an infant school and shaping a proper curriculum, Norton soon became engrossed in the widening movement to establish State agricultural colleges. In 1850 he announced a plan calling for primary, secondary, and collegiate instruction in agricultural science and proposing that public and private schools in each State cooperate to provide an integrated course of study. At the top of his three-level system he placed "one grand central State institution, and Agricultural College," equipped with an experimental farm and staffed by professors well trained in science (20, p. 18). The graduates of the college, he urged, should form the faculties of numerous private academies and normal schools, which in turn should train teachers for primary schools. No longer did he intend to reach only the mature, practicing farmer with part-time education via the Analytical Laboratory; now he proposed to concentrate on undergraduate students in a scientific curriculum and a degree program.

Familiar with the varied proposals preached by the enthusiasts for farm schools, Norton became disturbed because the plans made no clearcut provision for the conduct of research. Such provision he believed essential if the college were to be the source of scientific knowledge for the entire State.

Emphatically he warned that the projected heavy schedules of teaching and administration would smother a research program. He advocated that college authorities adopt a positive method for the accomplishment of research projects.

"There should be every facility for original research, and experiment," he said (20), "so that this might not only be a great centre for instruction, but afford also a rich harvest of discoveries, whereby science should be advanced in every direction."

His plea that a chemist whose sole responsibility would be research should be appointed to the college staffs brought into the open a difficulty which Johnston had continually faced: the competition between research and nonresearch activities for the scientist's time. By guaranteeing his "branch for the pursuit of chemistry as connected with agriculture" a secure place within the collegiate structure, Norton attempted to eliminate an incipient conflict between teaching and research. For teaching, he contended, appoint a full-time teacher; for research, appoint a full-time researcher. This conclusion seemed to provide a solution to the problem which the Chemistry Association had only partially solved.

The problem of securing endowment funds from a State treasury for putting a college into operation, however, worried Norton and other planners far more than did that of reaching a decision regarding the relative roles of teaching versus research. The rural majorities in the State legislatures of New England repeatedly rejected bills granting stipends for founding an agricultural college. The legislative refusals deeply disappointed Norton because they revealed to him the presence of a deep-seated belief among farmers that scientists could not make a useful contribution to farm improvement (21).

Attributing the farmers' attitude to the home-style education the average farmer had received, Norton described that manual labor system as "a species of close corporation, which attaches men to old habits, renders them jealous of innovations, and does not encourage independent thought" (20, p. 7).

He might explain rural conservatism but he could not overcome it. Farmers trained at home not only believed their own educational experience to be the best possible preparation for farming, but they also resisted every attempt to change the system. They especially opposed the efforts of educators to introduce schemes that required boys to leave home and learn farming in schools. They denounced book farming, and Norton could return their fire only by advocating more book farming. Thus the professor faced a problem having no immediate solution. In order to combat conservatism he first had to change the educational system; but to change the system he first had to conquer conservatism.

Norton could see no escape from the predicament. He resigned hope of introducing a system of scientific agriculture into New England. He turned instead to New York State, a "newer country" where farmers perhaps might appreciate the advice of scientists, and in 1851 put his willpower and his overtaxed physique into a movement for a State university there (22). That campaign halted his missionary work; he encountered a frustration more decisive than discouragement and disillusionment: death in 1852 at the age of 30.

When death ended Norton's career, did it also end Norton's influence? He died 5 years before Michigan founded the Nation's first agricultural college, and 10 years before the Federal Government approved the Morrill Land Grant College Act. He did not live to

13

witness the difficulties that the administrators and the teachers in the forthcoming institutions experienced as they struggled in later decades to make their agricultural colleges popular. Yet during his short-lived career he collided with the same set of serious issues that persistently would vex them. In his training and his thinking about the conduct of research, Norton traveled to the doorstep of the idea of the college-connected experiment station, in function if not in name.

Norton's unfulfilled ambitions for establishing an agricultural college and an agency for agricultural experimentation became the property of his small band of students in the Yale Analytical Laboratory. One of these enthusiasts, Samuel William Johnson, dedicated his career, for the remainder of the century, to finding a solution to the difficulties obstructing the creation and the successful operation of an institution for scientific investigation in agriculture.

GERMAN EXPERIMENT STATION MOVEMENT

Samuel W. Johnson spent a lifetime searching for the most effective ways to institutionalize research in agriculture. Entering the Analytical Laboratory in 1850, he absorbed Professor Norton's ideas and enthusiasm. Later he studied science in German laboratories and personally observed the German experiment station movement in its infancy. He became America's first advocate calling for a similar movement in the United States.

"There have been lately established in Germany" he wrote in 1855 (11, p. 80), "especially in Saxony, a number of so-called Experiment Stations, or experimental farms, with laboratories in connection, for the exclusive object of promoting scientific agriculture. These are intended to make science practical, and practice scientific, and no agency can be desired better adapted for these important purposes."

Support for Johnson's concept of an agricultural experiment station came from many of the young men, once students of Norton and Johnson at New Haven, who subsequently became leaders in the land-grant agricultural college movement. Johnson's first success in his ardent advocacy is reflected in the establishment in 1876 of America's pioneer experiment station—The Connecticut Agricultural Experiment Station.

More earnestly and persistently than any other scientist during the latter half of the 19th century, Johnson developed and publicized the standards which in his judgment ought to prevail permanently in the organization and the operation of a center for agricultural research. From his student days in the 1850's to his directorship at New Haven after 1877, Johnson steadily elaborated his concept of the proper administrative setting for the conduct of significant research. His thinking during this period produced America's first example of a regularly organized station, one chartered and financed by the State legislature for the sole purpose of investigation and experiment.

In 1851, after he had become Norton's chief analyst, Samuel Johnson detected, as Norton had done previously under Johnston in Edinburgh, misrepresentations on the part of some fertilizer people. After Norton's death Johnson resolved to check false claims by using fearlessly in the public interest the analytical techniques he had mastered. Analyzing and comparing samples he had collected in market channels, he published his findings in 1853 in a farm magazine whose crusading editor encouraged the chemists' purpose (23). This technique of periodic analyses, evaluation, and publication Johnson made peculiarly his own in his ensuing long career devoted to demonstrating the usefulness of applying science in the consumers' interest.

JOHNSON ADVOCATED AGRICULTURAL COLLEGES

During his first year in Norton's laboratory, Johnson accepted Norton's solution to the problem of institutionalizing research in agriculture in the most effective way; he agreed that a well-endowed State agricultural college with an experimental farm should employ teachers for diffusing knowledge and researchers for enlarging it (9). Convinced by the summer of 1851, however, that legislators would continue to balk at bills for a State college, he turned to the county agricultural societies for aid in subsidizing a noncollegiate form of laboratory research and rural education.

Johnson proposed that American farmers ignore their slow-moving State legislatures and, instead, convert their local agricultural societies, already established as features of farm life, into copies of the pace-setting British societies—the Scottish Highland Society and the Royal Agricultural Society.

Each county society, urged Johnson, should recruit a large membership with a minimum of 2,000 dues-payers, incorporate itself as a "Scientific Institution," adopt a constitution, and elect officers, a board of directors, and "one or more professors of agricultural science"; it should construct a building containing lecture rooms, a library, and in particular an analytical chemistry laboratory.

This Agricultural Institute, as Johnson carefully designed it, clearly recognized the chemist as "the chief means of the Society's usefulness." The heavy responsibility required of the scientist a special capacity and an unusual preparation; the appointee could qualify for his post, Johnson advised, only if his inclination and specialized training fitted him for research and only if, in addition, he understood practical farming. Having made the research scientist the central figure in the Institute, Johnson then placed at his convenience every available resource.

The British technique for subsidizing the agricultural scientist, transmitted by way of Norton's laboratory, Johnson accepted as his model during his 3-year apprenticeship in New Haven. Having finished his studies there, however, he sailed for Europe in the spring of 1853 to begin 2 years of study in German laboratories. Ardently he wished to receive instructions from Professor Justus von Liebig, whose influential book (16) had prodded Professor Johnson into energetic action in Scotland.

The ambitious American managed to make his wish come true although, finding it impossible to enter Liebig's laboratory for some months after arriving in Germany, he spent a period of time at a laboratory in Leipzig. Johnson's stay in the Saxon city proved profitable because it enabled the young chemist to examine a new type of research center differing in several features from the plan for an Agricultural Institute. To the village of Moeckern, lying on the outskirts of Leipzig, went Johnson on a February day in 1854 to visit a new institution, not yet 2 years old, which its founders called an "Agricultural Experiment-Station" (10).

The station at Moeckern was the Saxon answer to the search, stirring in the German provinces since the publication of Liebig's treatise in 1840, for methods of applying science to agriculture. Though that volume had evoked considerable discussion among German landowners, 5 years passed before a group of volunteers emerged to urge a proposal for employing an agricultural chemist. In 1845, after the Germans had learned of the Scottish success in operating the Chemistry Association, Friedrich Riessner and his associates submitted a petition to the Saxon government. They requested that their state appoint "an able young chemist" for each circuit district. This chemist should analyze soils and fertilizers when farmers in his district submitted samples; he should travel through his district familiarizing himself with the problems of the practical farmer and giving scientific advice to troubled farmers; he should lecture on agricultural chemistry; he should make the rural population experiment-conscious and improvement-minded (*1*).

The Moeckern plan maintained, in short, that Saxony should use tax moneys for the hiring of a number of scientists to perform the same type of duty which the Scottish tenants had demanded in 1842. Dispensing with intervening agricultural societies and an Association, it would make the chemists direct employees of the State.

The Saxon governmental officials, skeptical of the capacity of ignorant farmers to benefit from the proposed innovation, denied the petition. They did, however, decide before long to appoint Adolph Stockhardt to a professorship of chemistry at the Royal Academy of Agriculture and Forestry at Tharand. Stockhardt, going far beyond the call of duty, attempted to carry out by himself the activities envisioned in the Riessner petition and to do for the Saxons what Professor Johnston had done for the Scots. He analyzed samples, gave lectures at the meetings of farmers' clubs, and edited a journal of agricultural chemistry. He also conducted some laboratory experiments, though he complained that he could not perform field experiments because Tharand had no farm available.

In 1851, a wealthy landowner named Crusius conveyed a portion of his estate near Moeckern to several cooperating societies for the purpose of fitting out a scientific laboratory on an experimental farm. Thereupon he, Professor Stockhardt, and the societies created a board of directors representing the sponsoring groups. They drafted a charter, which the Saxon government legalized by statute. They secured an annual appropriation from the government and proceeded to appoint a brilliant young chemist as the station director and an experienced farmer as the superintendent of the 120-acre farm (*10*). The enterprise opened its doors in 1852.

The organization and functioning of the Moeckern station deeply impressed Samuel Johnson when he visited there in 1854. He took the trouble to translate into English the pertinent statutory provisions authorizing the new institution to conduct scientific research in agriculture. These details he immediately sent home for publication in the farm press:

Under the title "Ag(ricultural) Experiment-Station, upon the farm of the Leipsic Ec(onomical) Society, and the adjoining lands of Dr. Crusius," is founded an institution to be devoted to the advancement of agriculture by means of scientific investigation carried on in close connection with practical experiment. This object shall be prompted by the co-operation of a practical farmer and a man of science. The investigations and experiments they shall institute, shall be mainly directed to the following particulars:

1. The growth of plants—the conditions affecting it generally; and in particular, the influence of the constituents of the atmosphere, of the soil, of manures, and of the preparation of the soil upon it; and also the various hindrances to vegetable development.

2. The ingredients of plants and their action on the animal organism. The various kinds of feeds, their composition and their valuation for the production of flesh, milk, wool, etc.

3. Meterological observations.

4. The cultivation of plants here little known, and the determination of their value.

5. Testing of ag(ricultural) implements and machines.

6. The construction of authentic tables of comparative numbers, having references to all branches of agriculture, as for example, tables of the relative value of feed.

The conduct of these investigations is under the care of a practical farmer, and of a scientific man, and the institution falls therefore into two divisions—that of *practical agriculture* and that of *natural science.*

The Saxon statute revealed clearly that the German system for subsidizing the agricultural scientist, though it had evolved more slowly than the British system, had introduced a greater number of significant refinements by 1852 than had its Scottish counterpart. That statute established a specialized institution operating under its own charter and separated organically from an agricultural society, although on its board of control there sat representatives from several societies.

As a state-chartered station for experimental research, the Moeckern station drew some of its funds directly from the tax revenues of the state. It concentrated in one location all necessary facilities for the conduct of research in the laboratory and in the field; the availability of its farm eliminated the chemist's need for cooperative experiments. Its founders, not leaving to chance the interpretation of the station's research function, carefully designated the broad areas of investigation. Its charter directed the station to concentrate on research as a profession. It eliminated "diffusion", the duty which in the British experience had been a companion feature with the "enlargement of knowledge."

Both the Scottish and the Saxon movements to subsidize science started with simple demands from farmers for a service agency; yet the Saxons, though starting later than the Scots, proceeded much more speedily and directly to the establishment of a station designed solely for research.

LITERATURE CITED

(1) CALDWELL, G. C.
    1882. THE EXPERIMENT STATION AS AN EDUCATOR OF THE FARMER. *In* Convention of Agriculturists Proc. U.S. Dept. Agr. Rpt. 22, 204 pp.
(2) CHITTENDEN, R. H.
    1928. HISTORY OF THE SHEFFIELD SCIENTIFIC SCHOOL OF YALE UNIVERSITY, 1846–1922. (2 v.) v. 1, pp. 37–41.
(3) DICTIONARY OF NATIONAL BIOGRAPHY.
    1908. JOHNSTON, JAMES FINLAY WEIR. v. 10, pp. 953–954. Oxford Univ. Press, London.

(4) THE HIGHLAND AND AGRICULTURAL SOCIETY OF SCOTLAND.
     1839. SCIENCE OF AGRICULTURE. Highland and Agr. Soc. Scotland Trans.
            6 (n.s.) : 28–29.
(5) ———
     1841. [REPORT ON THE ESTABLISHMENT OF AN EXPERIMENTAL FARM.]
            Highland and Agr. Soc. Prize-Essays and Trans. 7 (n.s.) 1839–
            1841 : 497–507.
(6) ———
     1845. PRELIMINARY NOTICE. Highland and Agr. Soc. Scotland Trans.
            (n.s. 3) July 1843–March 1845 : 9–11.
(7) ———
     1845. PROCEEDINGS OF THE AGRICULTURAL CHEMISTRY ASSOCIATION OF
            SCOTLAND. Highland and Agr. Soc. Scotland Trans. 1 (n.s. 3)
            July 1843–March 1845 : 459–469.
(8) ———
     1849. [REPORT BY THE DIRECTORS ON THE PROPOSED CHEMICAL ESTABLISH-
            MENT.] Highland and Agr. Soc. Scotland Trans. 3 (n.s. 3) July
            1847–March 1849 : 335–344, 484–485.
(9) JOHNSON, S. W.
     1851. COUNTY AGRICULTURAL INSTITUTES. The Cultivator 8 (n.s.) : 263–
            265.
(10) ———
     1854. FOREIGN CORRESPONDENCE. The Country Gentleman 3 (17) : 261–
            262.
(11) ———
     1856. LECTURE, "ON THE RELATIONS THAT EXIST BETWEEN SCIENCE AND
            AGRICULTURE." N.Y. State Agr. Soc. Trans. (1855) 15:[73]–95.
(12) JOHNSTON, J. F. W.
     1844. LECTURES ON AGRICULTURAL CHEMISTRY AND GEOLOGY. app. no. 1,
            — pp. Edinburgh.
(13) ———
     1848. THE PRESENT STATE OF AGRICULTURE IN ITS RELATION TO CHEMISTRY
            AND GEOLOGY. Roy. Agr. Soc. England Jour. 9 : 200–236.
(14) ———
     1850. LECTURES ON THE GENERAL RELATIONS WHICH SCIENCE BEARS TO
            PRACTICAL AGRICULTURE. 221 pp. New York.
(15) [LARNED, W. A.]
     1852. JOHN PITKIN NORTON. New Englander 10 (n.s. 4) : 614–616.
(16) LIEBIG, JUSTUS VON.
     1840. ORGANIC CHEMISTRY IN ITS APPLICATIONS TO AGRICULTURE AND
            PHYSIOLOGY. 387 pp., illus. London.
(17) NORTON, J. P.
     1844–45. LETTER FROM EUROPE. [No. I.] The Cultivator 1 (n.s.) : 204 ;
            —No. II. 1 (n.s.) : 245–246 ; —No. V. 1 (n.s.) : 364 ; 2 (n.s.) :
            139, 171.
(18) ———
     1844–45. MR. NORTON'S LETTERS—NO. IX. The Cultivator 2 (n.s.) : 121.
(19) ———
     1847. LECTURES ON AGRICULTURE. The Cultivator 4 (n.s.) : 324–325.
(20) ———
     1850. ADDRESS DELIVERED BEFORE THE ONTARIO CO. AGRICULTURAL SOCIETY.
            25 pp. Canandaigua, N.Y.
(21) ———
     1850. LETTERS FROM PROF. NORTON—NOS. 9 AND 10. ON THE IMPORTANCE
            OF EXTENDED CHEMICAL INVESTIGATIONS. The Cultivator 7 (n.s.) :
            296–297 ; 323–324.
(22) ———
     1851. NOTES OF A TOUR IN CENTRAL NEW-YORK. The Cultivator 8 (n.s.) :
            74–76.
(23) OSBORNE, E. A.
     1913. FROM THE LETTER-FILES OF S. W. JOHNSON. 292 pp., illus. New
            Haven.
(24) TRUE, A. C.
     1929. A HISTORY OF AGRICULTURAL EDUCATION IN THE UNITED STATES,
            1785–1925. U.S. Dept. Agr. Misc. Pub. 36, 436 pp., illus.

Chapter Three—
AMERICAN BEGINNINGS

A hundred years ago the exploration and settling of a largely underdeveloped continent presented many practical, physical problems. They appeared minor, indeed, in the face of the war that was being waged between the States. And they were minor when compared with many facing the world today. Yet their magnitude and urgency, as viewed by many in those years, provided a fertile seedbed for the idea of solving problems by gearing science and education to the objective. The Land Grant Act, like its Federal counterpart, the Act creating a Department of Agriculture, was passed midway during the war. Both helped formalize the programs for "improvement" discussed by the agricultural societies for many years.

As the agricultural colleges became physical realities, the professors of those colleges continued to grope for scientific subject matter that could be taught so as to provide practical methods for the improvement of agriculture. Little such subject matter was available. Moreover, the great variations in climate, soils, topography, and other natural conditions required a variety of interpretation of such knowledge in the sciences fitted to a particular area. In the discussions that were to ensue for the next 25 years among college presidents and professors, those with experience abroad enjoyed an advantage. Samuel Johnson, the young chemist who had observed the pilot operation at Moeckern, was one of the group that made their influence felt in the discussions and policy formulation that took place between 1862, when the Land-Grant Act was passed, and 1887, when the Hatch Experiment Station Act became law.

JOHNSON ADVOCATED LABORATORIES

On his return from Germany in August 1855, Samuel Johnson accepted an assistantship in the Analytical Laboratory at New Haven as a temporary base of operations from which to explore the possibilities for initiating a station. Convinced that a prominent agricultural society must make the first move, he renewed his contacts with the New York State Society, which in 1849 had first hired a chemist's services and had therefore prepared itself, he felt, to subsidize a larger laboratory and to concentrate on a project of scientific research. Securing an invitation to address that group at its annual meeting in February of 1856, Johnson there presented a major essay (6).[1] In it he urged the Society to sponsor an agricultural laboratory patterned according to proposals which he proceeded to set forth. First of all, however, he attempted to familiarize his audience with the procedures

---

[1] Italic numbers in parentheses refer to Literature Cited, p. 28.

for research that he had acquired in his 6 years of diligent study. "The method of investigation," he declared, ". . . must be the method of science" and the investigator, dedicated to eliminating the guess-work omnipresent in farm practice, "must multiply facts . . . by observation and experiment."

Research, Johnson emphasized, was a highly complex process requiring, above all, the trained talents of a competent researcher. Meaningful research had its source in the schooled mind of the scientific personality who, knowing how to deal with the technical data which even the sharp eye of the practical farmer would find meaningless, followed the strict methods of scientific experimentalism. Johnson explained at length the careful way in which the skilled experimenter contrived an experiment and then used a closely reasoned analysis in order to demonstrate the validity or falsity of a given hypothesis. A series of experiments, "if rationally devised and skilfully [sic] executed, . . . must reveal a truth," he asserted.

To his mind, moreover, the properly equipped researcher should have a training and a scientific interest extending considerably beyond chemistry alone. He proceeded to recommend the type of research activity which in his judgment a competent agricultural scientist should undertake. He urged the merits of an integrated program of laboratory and field experiments. Realizing that the Society members would tend to see value in field trials but not appreciate the research in the laboratory, he boldly ventured to downgrade the field tests and upgrade the laboratory work. He dismissed as useless most field experiments undertaken without laboratory supervision. "The mere field trial," he declared flatly, "cannot lead to definite conclusions." To the laboratory he assigned a higher place because there, unaided by the field test, the scientist could find answers to a number of problems.

Johnson, with his European training, unquestionably believed activity in the laboratory outweighed that in the field; nevertheless he did concede that the field trial, if carried out according to the scientist's prescription, would perform an essential function because "it especially shows whether any plan or procedure be *remunerative*, and draws the line between what is theoretically possible, and that which is actually practicable." Johnson thereupon pointed out that an interdependent relationship did in fact exist between the laboratory analyses and the field tests; therefore, a combination of the two types of investigation would operate more effectively than either one treated independently.

Thus Johnson presented to the New York State Agricultural Society the great lessons he had learned in his lengthy scientific apprenticeship. First, he contended, an effective policy for agricultural research must coordinate efforts in the laboratory and in the field in order to achieve maximum gains. Second, the wisest policy would recognize that the heart of the research program lies in the laboratory.

Johnson did not expect, of course, that the Society would immediately establish a Moeckern-type station. He did propose, however, that the Society appoint a capable chemist, supply him with a well-appointed laboratory, permit him to use that laboratory for the exposure of fraud in the sale of commercial fertilizers, andyauthorize him to conduct "a plan of inquiry into the special conditions which most favor the production of our usually cultivated plants" (*6, p. 89*).

SETBACKS ENCOUNTERED

The Society proved unresponsive to Johnson's plea. Although it published his essay in its *Transactions*, it did not offer to employ him nor to subsidize his program of research. He resumed his duties at New Haven and subsequently accepted a professorship of analytical chemistry at the Scientific School. Thereupon he revived his earlier practice of evaluating the quality of commercial fertilizers sold on the open market, arousing the interest of the newly formed Connecti. cut Agricultural Society. The Society employed Johnson in 1857 to continue his analyses as a service in the farmers' interest. This new venture, a primitive yet encouraging beginning from which a station could eventually emerge, crumbled when war came in 1861.

The war years eliminated any possibility of founding a station. They took Johnson's students and interrupted his anti-fraud campaign in the fertilizer trade (7, *pp. 107–134*). After Appomattox, when students appeared again on the campus, Johnson concentrated on building a scholar's career in the classrooms and laboratories of Sheffield. During the sixties his pen produced pioneer texts in plant nutrition and earned for him a widening recognition as a first-rate scientist.

Did Johnson's increasing absorption in collegiate concerns dull the edge of his enthusiasm for imitating the Moeckern precedent? Had he followed the trend of Norton's short-lived career as an agricultural educator, he would have become so engrossed with collegiate responsibilities, so intent on building a research unit within a collegiate framework, that he would have put aside indefinitely—or perhaps discarded—any hopes or plans for institutionalizing agricultural research of the Moeckern type, completely disassociated from a college context.

Johnson won in later years a reputation as the American "Nestor of Agricultural Chemistry." He and his colleague, William Henry Brewer, fulfilled the ambitions of Professor Norton by making Sheffield a widely known center for the teaching of agricultural science. He and Brewer in time personified the efforts of Sheffield and the Connecticut legislature to subsidize the teaching of agriculture as authorized by the Federal funds from the Morrill Act of 1862. He exerted his frail physique and his strong will in order to evangelize agricultural education throughout Connecticut among a farming population perennially indifferent to appeals from bookfarmers. He collided repeatedly with the local variety of the hardy rural conservatism that had vexed Norton. He spent a busy lifetime as an agricultural educator and a college professor. Despite these many scholastic achievements, Samuel Johnson never lost sight of his fundamental objective, namely, the founding of a government-subsidized, extra-collegiate institution devoted solely to agricultural research.

SUCCESS FINALLY CAME

Johnson persevered in bringing about formation of a State Board of Agriculture in 1866, secured an appointment as its official chemist, and in the late sixties renewed under its jurisdiction his technique of publishing his evaluation of marketed fertilizers. Patiently he groomed a small corps of graduate students including Wilbur Olin Atwater, Henry Prentiss Armsby, and Edward Hopkins Jenkins.

Persistently he propagandized the American need for an experiment station. His earnestness attracted a band of like-minded devotees of the station cause, and success finally came in the turbulent 10 years from 1872 to 1882.

The complex movement to found a station in Connecticut ended in triumph for Johnson's formula for station organization. In 1875 the State Board of Agriculture drew up a legislative bill which proposed to place the station under the jurisdiction of the Board and, furthermore, to make it responsible for "investigation and experiments; (and) diffusion of useful knowledge" (9). The agricultural committee of the General Assembly, however, convinced that farmers neither needed nor desired a station, shelved the bill.

The situation soon changed when Orange Judd, farm-paper publisher and a former student at the Analytical Laboratory, also a trustee of Wesleyan University at Middletown, intervened with the agricultural committee and proposed a simple substitute for the Board's project. If the legislature would contribute $2,800 per year for 2 years, Wesleyan University would supply laboratory space and the services of a chemist-director, and Judd personally would contribute $1,000 to the cause. The legislature accepted and passed a simple measure granting the stipulated sum to Wesleyan University "to be used in employing competent scientific men to carry on the appropriate work of an agricultural experiment station" (5).

Thereupon, Wesleyan University trustees organized a station at Judd Hall on the campus at Middletown. To the directorship they appointed Wilbur O. Atwater, a new professor of chemistry at Wesleyan and a former protege of Sheffield's Johnson.

A host of pressures beset the directorship during the 2-year trial period of the Middletown station.[2] These soon prompted Atwater and other earnest advocates of administrative changes to recommend a different format as they carefully drafted a new bill for establishing a permanent station. Becoming law in 1877, the revised arrangement created The Connecticut State Agricultural Experiment Station, to be governed by a board of control and financed by a continuing annual appropriation of $5,000 from the State treasury. The State charter severed organic connection with a university and explicitly assigned to the station a single duty: the conduct of "scientific investigation and experiments" (5).

The new governing board immediately proceeded to put the statute into effect. It ended the Middletown experiment, elected Johnson to the directorship, and leased temporary quarters at Sheffield, which were occupied until 1882 when the State legislature authorized purchase of a small private estate with buildings adaptable for laboratories in suburban New Haven.

The administrative organization of the relocated station demonstrated by 1882 that it had faithfully reproduced Johnson's three major requirements for an ideal station: (1) a State charter and subsidy, (2) research as a sole function, and (3) extra-collegiate self-government. It also exhibited two additional features which Johnson championed: (1) the absence of a farm, and (2) a suburban location. These latter characteristics obviously contradicted the original John-

---

[2] LAW, E. M. THE AGRICULTURAL EXPERIMENT STATION MOVEMENT IN CONNECTICUT, 1840–1900. 255 pp. (Unpublished doctoral dissertation, Yale University Library, 1951) pp. 117–128; 136–143.

sonian model at Moeckern in 1854, yet they harmonized with similar changes introduced by the Germans themselves in later years. The scientists at Moeckern in the seventies, for example, preferring small trial gardens and plant houses conveniently near the laboratory, largely ignored the farm acreage which in the fifties had appeared essential.

Sympathizing with the views of European plant scientists who had come to the conclusion that only small plots were needed for their field experiments, and that an experiment station should not attempt operating a model farm in competition with farmers, Johnson advocated a suburban site for the Connecticut station (3). There, he announced in 1881, the necessary facilities for research could be concentrated in a limited area. There, for example, the scientist could make efficient use of the laboratory, library, greenhouses, and test plots; he would have handy the important facilities of post, telegraph, and express offices, and public utilities.

ATWATER AIDED PLAN

The Johnsonian formula for station organization owed its triumph in no small way to the evangelical efforts of the young chemist, Wilbur Atwater, who in 1873 had begun a professorial career at Wesleyan after earning his doctorate in Johnson's laboratory in 1869 and spending 2 additional years in post-graduate work at German experiment stations. Filled with a ministerial zeal for spreading the gospel of German agricultural science, Atwater volunteered his pen and his voice in the station campaign in Connecticut. Energetically in the midseventies he publicized his firsthand knowledge concerning the work and current organization of the German stations. His definition, a product of his recent apprenticeship at the German stations, coincided with Johnson's and underlined the central significance of basic research.

The American observer, Atwater explained, should note carefully the distinctions between an authentic experiment station and other types of institutions conducting research in agriculture. Initiated by private individuals and societies, subsidized and chartered by Government, entitled to expend its income from whatever source as it alone saw fit, the station operated as a self-managed entity administratively separate from any other institution. A topnotch scientist filled the administrative post of director and served as the executive officer responsible for conducting the research authorized by the board of control.

Atwater (1) emphasized that not every laboratory automatically constituted an experiment station. For example, he pointed out, Liebig's university laboratory at Munich did not constitute an experiment station; neither did Stockhardt's laboratory at the agricultural school at Tharand; nor, elsewhere in Europe, did Boussingault's laboratory on his private estate in France; nor did Sir John Bennet Lawes' privately endowed laboratory-on-a-farm at Rothamstead, England.

What setting, according to Atwater's analysis, had European experience shown to be most suitable for the efficient operation of the station? Contrary to their first assumptions 25 years earlier, German scientists discovered that they did not need farms for experimental work and could work more effectively if their stations were located in a different

23

environment. Realizing that such a view would surprise and easily antagonize the American farmer, Atwater quickly observed:

"It must not be understood . . . that farm-experience and the use of farm-appliances are unnecessary to the work of experiment-stations, but rather that immediate connection with scientific men, books, and appliances is of more importance than immediate connection with a farm."

Atwater sought to account for the changed attitude of German scientists relative to location as follows:

". . . profiting by the results of long experience, the founders of new stations are locating them in the cities, and, so far as practicable, in connection with large universities. In fact, paradoxical as it may seem, the abstract researches which bring the most practical benefit to farming are made, not on a large scale in the country, upon the farms, but in the towns, where individual or small numbers of plants and animals can be experimented upon, with the aid of such close, patient, and thorough investigation as can be furnished only with the aid of the best scientific appliances and talent, and these are most easily secured in cities and in connection with scientific institutions."

Did Atwater mean to advocate physical incorporation or administrative amalgamation of the experiment station with a university, or an agricultural school, or similar body? No. He reasoned that station scientists could most profitably use the benefits coming from their varied contacts with the personnel and scientific resources of a nearby academic institution; yet they must not pay the penalty of involving themselves in the multiple problems of any organization devoted to numerous interests other than research in agricultural science.

Atwater's emphasis on institutional separatism of the experiment station mirrored an awareness of subtle difficulties that can obstruct meaningful research in agriculture. Always difficult to accomplish, research in any science required constant and assiduous encouragement, which a scientific community and perhaps a university attachment could best provide. Research *in agriculture*, thus far the newest and least developed type of scientific effort, especially needed the maximum measure of protection and cultivation. This devoted attention and secure environment the American university, even when attuned to science, could not guarantee to provide.

Atwater agreed with Johnson's conviction that there would come from research in a university unoriented to agriculture only "gratuitous and accidental drippings" for farmers. They did not, however, reach the simple conclusion that the contemporary agricultural colleges offered a haven for an experiment station. If a scientific but not agricultural atmosphere endangered the proper growth of research in agriculture, likewise an agricultural but not scientific concentration jeopardized research in science. The small agricultural colleges, struggling to stay alive on a tiny income, frequently lacked the facilities attractive to scientists.

Basic in Atwater's attitude lay a deep-seated doubt that an agricultural college could unfailingly provide, any more surely than any other type of college or institution, the environment in which agricultural scientists could single-mindedly concentrate on their research with the least possible interference from all other concerns. Safety for fundamental scientific research, then, prompted both Atwater and Johnson, America's pioneer pair of station directors in the seventies, to insist on a specific set of administrative features which, constituting in total a clearly defined system of self-management for a station enterprise, permitted an uninterrupted absorption in the research process.

24

FEDERAL DEPARTMENT PROPOSED

The three decades following the midpoint of the 19th century, which produced the Johnson-Atwater philosophy of administration for a State-sponsored station, gave simultaneously to the Federal Government a remarkable opportunity to conduct scientific research in agriculture. The Committee on Agriculture of the House of Representatives favorably reported in August of 1856 a bill proposing the establishment of a Department of Agriculture. This bill provided for the severance of the Patent Office from the Department of the Interior and recommended the promotion of the enlarged Patent Office to the status of a "Department" under a Commission of noncabinet rank.

The House Committee in its accompanying report urged Congress to subsidize the study of agricultural science and to make scientific research in agriculture a major assignment for the proposed department. The Federal Government ought to accept the new responsibility, the Committee contended, because that Government, unlike the State and local agricultural societies whose attempts at research had proved unsatisfactory and unproductive, could supply sufficient means and administrative capacity to employ a force of experimenters, to coordinate the efforts of experiment-minded personnel in the States, and, in short, to accomplish the necessary research activity (11).

The committee stressed the technical function of their "economical, practical, and scientific department." They specified that under no circumstances should a politician fill the Commissioner's chair. Responsible for the active direction of his department, the Commissioner should have the competence to select and direct a group of assistants including among others "four men of sufficient scientific and practical qualifications to prosecute . . . investigations in agricultural science and rural economy. . . ." Though the committee did not limit the Commissioner's duties solely to the administration of scientific research, they clearly revealed their intention to encourage the emerging scientific bent of the Agricultural Division in the Patent Office, which recently had added an entomologist and a chemist to its staff.

Thus there appeared in 1856, the same year in which Johnson aired his station philosophy in New York, the beginnings of a Congressional sympathy for a federally subsidized laboratory concentrating on agricultural research. The desired department, however, did not appear in 1856. Despite the approval of the Committee on Agriculture, the bill lay on the table in the busy House for the remainder of the session.

The movement to institutionalize experimentation on a formal and practical basis at Federal expense gathered momentum during the following 6 years. In 1862 the sponsors of a revised proposal successfully guided through the Federal Congress a bill establishing a Department of Agriculture. The House bill of 1862 specifically directed the Commissioner "to acquire and preserve in his Department all information concerning agriculture which he can obtain by means of books and correspondence and by practical and scientific experiments (accurate records of which experiments shall be kept in his office), by the collection of statistics, and by any other appropriate means within his power . . ." (12). Although this provision did not insist on the exclusive use of techniques of experimentation in the Commissioner's

25

dutiful and comprehensive search for information, another provision did emphasize the importance of scientific research when it empowered the Commissioner to employ, when Congress so provided, "chemists, botanists, entomologists, and other persons skilled in the natural sciences pertaining to agriculture."

The House Committee on Agriculture in February of 1862 stoutly contended, furthermore, during the floor discussion of the duties to be assigned to the proposed commissionership, that scientific experimentation would constitute an essential duty of the new Federal agency because that research, in turn, would provide a needed service (13).

The Committee insisted that a separate Federal Department of non-cabinet status should shoulder complete responsibility in the United States for the study of agricultural science and the discovery of new facts useful to farming. Their insistence not only reaffirmed the views of the Committee of 1856; it resolutely maintained in effect that the Federal Government should immediately and determinedly enter a field of activity which thus far the State governments had refused to enter. The House, not quarreling with this position, passed the Committee's bill without significant change.

RIVAL GROUPS BATTLED

The Senate, however, subjected the House bill to the pressures of opposing amendments. One Senatorial group objected to the creation of a separate department. Convinced that the Commissioner ought to head a Bureau of Agriculture and Statistics within the Department of the Interior, this bloc favored a type of fact-gathering which in practice would pertain more to commerce and manufacturing than to farming. Assuming that a search for "information . . . valuable in relation to the mode of cultivation, renovation, and drainage of the soil" would give satisfactory scope to the Commissioner's investigatory duties for agriculture, their substitute measure eliminated all indications that the new Bureau should have power to conduct scientific research (4). A rival group battled for a separate department of four bureaus, each of which should concentrate by direction on a clearly defined area of investigation in agricultural science and technology (14). This proposal urged the empty-pocketed Congress in wartime to authorize a large and expensive department devoted exclusively to scientific research.

This pair of contradictory attitudes demonstrated the extent to which the Senators grappled with the central question implicit in the assignment of duties to a Federal administrator, namely, whether the Federal Government should limit its activities to the collection of assorted statistics or, instead, specialize in laboratory research in agriculture. The rival viewpoints neutralized each other. The Senate finally agreed to accept the original House bill which directed the new Department "to acquire . . . useful information on subjects connected with agriculture in the most general and comprehensive sense of that word. . . ." It did not require the Department to concentrate exclusively on the conduct of "practical and scientific experiments;" it enumerated additional duties of a nonscientific nature.

Nowhere did the spokesmen for the act of 1862 announce an intention to build an experiment station within the Department, nor did they disclose any tangible familiarity with the European movement or with Johnsonian proposals. The House Committee in February 1862, observed that European "experimental stations" were conducting precise experiments in animal and plant nutrition. Content with this vague allusion, the committeemen did not thereupon advocate that the Department should become an American station; instead they used their brief reference to European institutions only as one of many arguments that the American Federal Government should subsidize the study of agricultural science and publish the results of experimentation, as the European governments already had done. Behind the scenes, the United States Agricultural Society, practically from its birth in 1852 a prime mover in the effort to secure a separate Department of Agriculture (2), did not lobby for a Federal station. Though favoring the increase of scientific knowledge for farming purposes, it remained unresponsive to the station idea as an effective technique for the administration of agricultural investigation.

EARLY POLICIES SET

The Department of Agriculture received from its organic act ample powers and opportunity, nevertheless, to accommodate admirably in the following years the emerging Johnson–Atwater formula for an ideal research institution. Located by law in the District of Columbia, the Department erected its buildings on a nonfarm plot in a suburban environment. Administratively, it was independent and free from the ties of either an agricultural society or an agricultural college. Authorized to employ scientists and directed to acquire facts pertaining to agriculture, the Department appeared ready to function as a scientific institution. Only in two respects, apart from the substitution of Federal for State sponsorship, did the new agency show significant departures from the high standard of Johnson and Atwater. The act of 1862 did not require or intimate that the Commissioner must be a scientist, nor did it designate scientific research as his sole duty. That act specified, in fact, that the Department not only must acquire information but also must "diffuse" it.

While passage of the 1862 legislation gave the Department of Agriculture a scientific reputation, its early Commissioners were unfamiliar with the intricacies of scientific research. There was a tendency in those early years to become preoccupied with other responsibilities outlined in the Act. Many problems combined in delaying until the late 1880's crystallization of any clear departmental research policy based on "long continued experiments" (8).

Slow progress in developing the Department as a national experiment station served as an incentive in the States to go ahead with State stations. Atwater's labors, given recognition in the establishment of the first regularly organized experiment station at New Haven in 1877, encouraged legislatures in other States to grant subsidies for station purposes. North Carolina, New Jersey, New York, Ohio, Massachusetts, and Maine initiated the Johnson–Atwater format and established "independent" institutions during the station-founding decade 1877–87 (10, pp. 82–106). The precise format, however, did not characterize the administrative origins of every American experiment station emerging in that period.

27

An assertive movement, rooted in a native American philosophy of agricultural education, secured generous Federal aid for station purposes in the years preceding passage of the Hatch Experiment Station Act. This movement deeply influenced the succeeding development of the station story in the United States, and it compelled the introduction of significant revisions in the administration of station research.

LITERATURE CITED

(1) ATWATER, W. O.
     1876. AGRICULTURAL-EXPERIMENT STATIONS IN EUROPE. U.S. Dept. Agr. Rpt. 1875: 517–524.
(2) CARRIER, LYMAN.
     1937. THE UNITED STATES AGRICULTURAL SOCIETY, 1852–1860. Agr. Hist. 11(4) : 278–288.
(3) CONNECTICUT BOARD OF AGRICULTURE.
     1882. EXPERIMENT STATION. Conn. Bd. Agr. Ann. Rpt. (1881–82) 15: 264–270.
(4) FOSTER, [L. S.]
     1862. DEBATE ON H.R. 269. Cong. Globe, 37th Cong., 2d Sess., pp. 1755–1757 ; 2017.
(5) HUBBARD, R. D., and BREWER, W. H.
     1878. REPORT OF THE BOARD OF CONTROL. Conn. State Agr. Expt. Sta. Ann. Rpt. 1877: [7]–11.
(6) JOHNSON, S. W.
     1856. LECTURE, "ON THE RELATIONSHIPS THAT EXIST BETWEEN SCIENCE AND AGRICULTURE." N.Y. State Agr. Soc. Trans. (1855) 15: [73]–95.
(7) OSBORNE, E. A.
     1913. FROM THE LETTER-FILES OF S. W. JOHNSON. 292 pp., illus. New Haven.
(8) ROSS, E. D.
     1946. THE UNITED STATES DEPARTMENT OF AGRICULTURE DURING THE COMMISSIONERSHIP. Agr. Hist. 20(3) : 129–143. See also: DUPREE, A. H. SCIENCE IN THE FEDERAL GOVERNMENT. 460 pp., 1957. Cambridge.
(9) THE HARTFORD DAILY *COURANT*.
     1875. THE FARMERS' EXPERIMENT STATION. The Hartford Daily Courant 39(134) : 2. June 4, 1875.
(10) TRUE, A. C.
     1937. A HISTORY OF AGRICULTURAL EXPERIMENTATION AND RESEARCH IN THE UNITED STATES, 1607–1925. U.S. Dept. Agr. Misc. Pub. 251, 321 pp., illus.
(11) UNITED STATES CONGRESS, HOUSE COMMITTEE ON AGRICULTURE.
     1856. REPORT H.R. 321, TO ACCOMPANY H.R. 550, ON THE DEPARTMENT OF AGRICULTURE. Cong. Globe and app., 34th Cong., 1st Sess., pp. 8–10.
(12) ——
     1862. H.R. 269: A BILL TO ESTABLISH A DEPARTMENT OF AGRICULTURE. Cong. Globe, 37th Cong., 2d Sess., p. 855.
(13) ——
     1862. A REPORT TO ACCOMPANY H.R. 269. Cong. Globe, 37th Cong., 2d Sess., pp. 855–856.
(14) WRIGHT, [J. A.]
     1862. DEBATE ON S. 249. Cong. Globe, 37th Cong., 2d Sess., pp. 1690–1692.

Chapter Four—

THE HATCH MOVEMENT: Winning Federal Support for the Land-Grant College Station

Collegiate experimentation in agriculture appeared very early in the agricultural colleges founded in the mid-19th century. The first States to institute the new schools explicitly directed, either by charter provision or by separate enactment, that the collegiate governing bodies initiate and maintain a program of experiments (*21, pp. 71–75*).[1] These directives did not authorize, however, or imply the establishment of experiment stations. The pioneer agricultural colleges of the fifties did not immediately provide for organizing stations, nor did the legion of institutions endowed by the Land-Grant College Act of 1862. Nevertheless, the colleges assumed the responsibility for research. That duty immediately placed an unavoidable and heavy burden on the college staff, for it compelled those college officers charged with research duties to find effective procedures of administration at a time when the conventional system of experimenting, relying heavily on empirical field and livestock tests, had not yet incorporated laboratory techniques.

The governing board of the Michigan Agricultural College, recognizing by 1862 that productive experimentation called for the talents of professional scientists, gave to its academic professors full responsibility for selecting and conducting all experiments; it authorized a laboratory-and-field approach, and appointed a faculty member to superintend the departmental programs (*21, p. 74*). This practice, a notable improvement over customary practices in sister institutions, gave early promise that Michigan would steadily develop specialized routines of administration and before long refine its system of research into a distinct stationlike organization which, in function, in budget, and in position, would approximate the well-established stations of Europe. Despite this promising beginning, a distinct station did not develop at this pace-setting college during the following quarter century.

Similarly, in broad expanse of the Mississippi Valley, college-sponsored stations appeared only after long and disappointing delay. Prior to the passage of the Hatch Act in 1887, only three Valley colleges voluntarily launched station ventures: Tennessee in 1882, Wisconsin by direction of the State legislature in 1883, and Kentucky in 1885 (*21, pp. 100–105*). Elsewhere in the Nation the governing boards of the land-grant colleges proved almost equally hesitant to organize stations. Customarily until the mid-eighties they accepted as satisfactory the State legislative actions which founded and subsidized stations operating independently of college control. Only in California did the University trustees act at an early date (1875) to encourage a station movement and, aided by a subsidy from the State

---

[1] Italic numbers in parentheses refer to Literature Cited, p. 52.

legislature, to give broad authority (by 1880) to a station director (*21, p. 87*).

The first campaign to awaken an awareness that each agricultural college needed an experiment station took form, soon after the ending of the Civil War, at the newly founded Illinois Industrial University. The State charter of this land-grant institution required that the corresponding secretary of the board of trustees administer a state-wide program of farmer-conducted tests of specified field crops. This arduous assignment further expected the trustees' agent to select particular experiments for home trial, to prepare instructions for volunteer experimenters, to publish the meaningful results, and, in short, to follow techniques similar to those used in Scotland by the Highland and Agricultural Society during the early years of the century. Willard C. Flagg undertook this duty in 1867.

FLAGG ADVOCATED EXPERIMENT STATION

Energetic and enterprising, Flagg earnestly attempted to devise experimental routines of scientific accuracy. He promptly collided with the manifold complexities implicit in agricultural research and, discerning the crudeness of the system he had engaged himself to supervise, determined to find administrative methods for concentrating the professional scientific training of the college faculty on the problems of research (*21, p. 80*). For the utilization of this faculty talent, taking his cue from Sheffield's Professor Johnson (*8, p. 254*), Flagg decided by 1870 that an experiment station would provide the best administrative organization in Illinois.

This decision clarified Flagg's thinking but it did not solve his immediate and urgent problem of devising more comprehensive arrangements, even if informal and temporary ones, than yet existed to involve college teachers of science in permanent experimentation on farmers' problems. Assuming that experiment-minded men at other agricultural colleges faced a similar situation, Flagg discussed the matter with Professor Manly Miles of the Michigan faculty. The two men agreed that it would be possible to draft a set of simple and economical field experiments which cooperating college officers could conduct conjointly, all experimenters to follow uniform procedures at their own institutions. Convinced that the time had come for an intercollegiate discussion and an action program, Flagg then persuaded President John M. Gregory of Illinois University to participate in the project. Thereupon Gregory addressed a call to the presidents and the professors of the agricultural colleges. Representatives from 12 land-grant institutions met in Chicago on August 24 and 25, 1871.

President Gregory chaired this convention of "Friends of Agricultural Education" (*8*), but Flagg's leadership on the floor gave direction and purpose to the discussions and activity at the 2-day sessions. Flagg introduced a series of resolutions containing his recommendations for accelerating experimental investigations and for improving administrative methods. The convention after frank discussion adopted his major propositions. It directed chairman Gregory to appoint a committee of five members to report "a set of experiments recommended for trial at the agricultural colleges in the various States, with detailed statements of the methods of performing them, so as to insure all possible uniformity of conditions at each point." That committee under Flagg's leadership reported to the convention an enumeration of the types of investigation which "our colleges founded on the national grant" ought to pursue:

I. Meterological observations.

II. Mechanical experiments.

III. Experiments in physics, especially in the effects of different degrees of light, heat and electricity and moisture on vegetable life.

IV. Experiments in industrial chemistry, such as analysis of clays and other earths used in the arts; of coal, lime, and building rocks, minerals, manures, plants and their products, and animal products.

V. Experiments in mining and metallurgy.

VI. Experiments with soils in their drainage, pulverization by different implements and their compaction; the application of different fertilizers; the variation of soils in adjoining plots, then continuous cropping without manure and other irrigation.

VII. Experiments in special culture with different varieties of grasses, grains, roots, plants, trees, etc. with variations in the time, distance and depth of planting, modes of cultivation, harvesting, manuring, modes of propagation; and with insects and diseases affecting plants.

VIII. Experiments in the breeding and fattening of domestic animals, comparing difference, breeds and species, then diseases, etc.

After presenting these comprehensive recommendations to the convention, the committee report went on to account for the exceptional length, breadth, and depth of the program:

We enumerate these [classes] to give those who have not given the subject special attention, some idea of the immensity of the labor to be performed. To a large extent, of course, these experiments must be tried by each State, for its own people, according to its peculiar wants and capabilities. To a large extent, however, experiments may be tried in common or repeated all over the country. Especially this is true of the culture of certain widely grown plants, such as corn, wheat and other cereals. Accordingly we submit herewith two or three simple experiments of primary importance and inexpensive character, which we hope to have begun next year at a large number of our agricultural colleges, and prosecuted to final results.

The format of this report clearly revealed the quality of Flagg's generalship. The recommendations did not limit themselves to the formulation of a small set of simple field tests, though the committeemen showed keen interest in these practical experiments and Flagg soon secured the appointment of a subcommittee charged with putting them into operation. The recommendations, by stressing "the immensity of the labor to be performed", deliberately laid heavy initial emphasis on the long-range objectives of research. The fields of investigation, most of which implicitly made laboratory research mandatory, further disclosed Flagg's skill in steering the convention away from an easy assumption that adequate research included only empirical trials.

FLAGG REPORT ADOPTED

The statesmanlike comprehensiveness of the report adopted by the convention evidenced an even more significant triumph for Flagg. The report professed to present areas suitable for immediate investigation via the techniques of conjoint experimentation. Yet it openly recognized the inadequacy of an approach which relied on collating the results of experiments conducted in dissimilar physical environments; effective research would not occur, the report admitted, until each State initiated experimentation "for its own people, according

31

to its peculiar wants and capabilities." The committeemen concluded that the informal cooperation of volunteer experimenters at widely scattered colleges, though useful as a preliminary step, could not accomplish in the long run the research program which in their judgment the agricultural colleges ought to undertake.

What additional action, then, should the convention take as it sought to select the most useful procedure for research? Flagg set the goal early in the session when he announced, "It is one of my ideals that . . . we shall establish at each of our agricultural colleges an agricultural experiment station, similar to those of Europe. I think that is absolutely necessary to agricultural advancement." Thus at Flagg's urging the "Friends" turned their thinking toward the prospect of founding experiment stations at the colleges.

The convention members promptly discovered, however, that bothersome obstacles lay in their path. Unfortunately for them, Senator Morrill in his Act of 1862 had not clearly indicated his ambitions concerning the nature and extent of research activity in the land-grant colleges. When he introduced his college bill in April 1858 he confidently, predicted that his proposed "thoroughly scientific institutions" could make "a careful, exact, and systematized registration of experiments . . .;" he intimated that faculty members were to "collate" the results of empirical tests and prepare "tables" as preliminary procedures for making "a rational induction of principles upon which we may expect to establish a proper science [of agriculture]" (16).

These enigmatic remarks presumably anticipated that each college would administer in its State a system of cooperative experimentation in which a large number of participating farmers would volunteer the data secured in home trials. Perhaps he intended an interstate form of conjoint experimentation; yet he did not indicate that this type of investigation would involve laboratory work, nor that the college should perform the functions of an experiment station.

Justin Morrill did refer, nevertheless, to the German station movement in his Senatorial remarks in 1858. "In Saxony," he observed at one point, "they have a number of experiment stations, or experimental farms, with laboratories attached. . . ." (16). He used this brief reference, however, only as one of several examples to demonstrate the desirability of governmental support for agricultural education. This Saxon innovation did not give him the same inspiration that it had given 4 years earlier to Samuel Johnson.

The Morrill bill itself, which Congress enacted into law in 1862, made only two references to the research function. The act provided that a sum not to exceed 10 percent of the initial endowment could be used to purchase lands "for sites or [for] experimental farms;" it further stipulated that the annual report should record any "experiments made, with their cost and results" (16). Thus the philosophy of research voiced by Senator Morrill permitted the endowed colleges to conduct a simple form of experimentation. Yet the indistinct nature of the research authority in the Act of 1862, compared to the emphatic assignment of a teaching mission to the new colleges, prompted the first generation of college administrators to doubt that the Act of 1862 required the colleges to experiment, except as an aid in the instruction of students.

President Gregory, at the convention of 1871 (8), called attention to the seemingly incidental role which the phraseology of the Morrill Act had unfortunately allotted to the research function. His presidential colleagues, he pointed out, seriously questioned the view that the Morrill Act obligated the colleges to experiment and, he discreetly noted, "it has not been uniformly accepted that the agricultural colleges are to be experiment stations." Thus the Morrill Act provided no strength for a station movement; nor did the well-known European practice of founding independent stations offer persuasive precedents for an integration of college and station which the convention contemplated. Nevertheless, Gregory heartily sympathized with the sentiment of the convention that the colleges must immediately find ways to press forward with research activity. Conjoint experimentation appealed to him because it would put faculty investigators at a number of colleges simultaneously to work on a few selected problems, an arrangement promising to produce solutions more speedily than if each college faculty followed an independent course.

A tone of urgency sounded in Greogory's words when he observed that the need for a well-developed system of research had become "a very serious practical question." Farmers, beset with problems they could not solve, were bringing to the college staff pointed questions that could be answered only by astute, continuous, and productive experimentation. The infant colleges, depending for their existence on the public purse and public confidence, could not afford to ignore the public need; neither could they afford to mislead the farm population by giving it incorrect advice lest the potent suspicion of "book-farmers" deepen into scorn. Gregory's concern led him to declare:

We know this, that the country is demanding of the institutions that they shall conduct experiments. They are constantly calling, through the agricultural press, at agricultural conventions and otherwise, upon these colleges to help them to settle questions relating to agriculture. Whatever might have been claimed at the outset to be the duty of these colleges, I trust we shall fulfill a public demand and duty by instituting experimentation.

ROLE OF COLLEGES BROADENED

For this reason Gregory openly encouraged the convention to take action, in addition to approving immediate conjoint experimentation, which would initiate "combination and cooperation" among the college faculties as a means of accelerating and amplifying research of top quality. He urged the convention to decide "how far [the land-grant colleges] . . . can be made experiment stations, how far their forces and funds can be diverted . . . and used for this purpose." This encouragement provided Willard Flagg with an opportunity. He introduced, toward the close of the discussions on the second day, the following resolutions which the convention approved:

Resolved, That the very strong commendation that the agricultural experiment stations of Europe have received from such persons as Johnson and Liebig as a source of a large amount of agricultural science and practical progress, as well as our own examinations into the subject, make us believe the establishment of not less than one such station in each of the several States of the Union, would be eminently beneficial to the agricultural interests of the country.

Resolved, That a committee, consisting of one from each of the several States in which an institution founded on the national grant has been organized, be appointed by the President [Gregory], whose duty it shall be to memorialize

Thus the conventioneers of 1871 in their thinking and their action stressed three major convictions. First, they affirmed that the faculties of the agricultural colleges must assume in the public interest the urgent duty to conduct productive research in agriculture. Second, they decided that the experiment station, a specialized and specific administrative institution, could best accomplish comprehensive experimentation. Third, they resolved that the stations must appear *soon*.

The convention recognized, in addition, a most troublesome handicap, namely, the inability of the hard-pressed colleges to pay the necessary expenses of founding and maintaining a station establishment. Accordingly, the convention delegates determined to seek support from the State legislatures, and the Federal Government as well. This decision answered Gregory's searching question as to "how far . . . [the colleges] can be made experiment stations." The Morill funds should not be "diverted" from the college's teaching function; instead, additional and separate Government funds should support the station movement. This action signified more than a realistic concession to expediency; it revealed the convention's realization that research in station form, so fundamental a role in land-grant education would it play, deserved separate and substantial tax support. Moreover, the distinctive function of the proposed stations entitled the movement to the special attention of lawmakers.

The committeemen appointed by President Gregory to memorialize their legislative bodies presumably began their campaigning after the convention adjourned in August. Presumably, too, they must have encountered a vexing problem which the late convention had not discussed, that is, the preparation of a plan containing specific proposals for the founding of stations at public expense. Yet no plan emerged from this committee during the following 6 months.

Meanwhile, the station cause received sudden encouragement from an unexpected quarter. Frederick Watts, the Commissioner of Agriculture, took an unprecedented step shortly before Christmas in 1871; he invited representatives from the land-grant colleges, numerous agricultural societies, and State boards of agriculture to a National Agricultural Convention, to be held in Washington, D.C., in mid-February of 1872 (*17*).

The Commissioner used the unusual device of convention-calling to deal with an urgent problem. He hoped to stimulate a sense of united purpose, in the interest of nationwide agricultural improvement, among agricultural organizations receiving governmental subsidies; especially he wished to forge bonds of understanding between his Department, supported completely by Federal funds, and the land-grant colleges, endowed by the Morill Act. Immediately, however, the Commissioner wished the delegates to mobilize support behind Senator Morrill's renewed campaign for an enlarged Federal appropriation for the Morill Act colleges (*17, pp. 18–19*). On Judge Watt's agenda, moreover, there appeared the following item: "The subject of establishing experimental farms and stations for the promotion of agricultural knowledge."

STATIONS COMMITTEE FORMED

President Gregory and several other members of his station committee appointed by order of the Chicago convention, attended the Watts Convention of 1872. Gregory quickly called a meeting of his skeleton force, but his group produced no proposals for the February conventioneers to discuss. The Watts Convention promptly took independent action. It created a new Committee on Experimental Stations and to it appointed five of its own members, including S. W. Johnson (*17, p. 25*). A sixth figure, W. O. Atwater, assisted this committee at its invitation and delivered the committee report to the convention.

The report of this station committee revealed in every paragraph the influence of the Johnson–Atwater thinking (*17, pp. 62–63*). It urged the convention members to make a cluster of features axiomatic in their deliberations about station-founding. Define a station, so the report advised, as a specialized institution "for the exclusive purpose of carrying on experimental investigations for the benefit of the farmer"; distinguish between the "spasmodic, imperfect, inadequate" efforts at research thus far made in the United States, and the new professional, full-time, permanent research activity identified with the station form of administration; accept the necessity for employing personnel highly trained in the methods of experimental research, including laboratory procedures; also accept the necessity for understanding the European experience in station research, in order to profit by borrowing European discoveries and by avoiding the repetition of work already done; require and enable the American stations to attain a high standard of productivity from the moment of establishment; understand that a station, never financially self-supporting, must have a regular and adequate income.

Thus the report succinctly restated the Johnson–Atwater formula for station-founding; it announced a set of characteristics which all American stations should incorporate and exhibit; it implicitly stressed the serious obligations that station makers would assume when they volunteered to initiate a station movement; it dispelled any quick assumptions that makeshift stations of indistinct character would effectively answer the farmers' need for research of high quality, or that station-making would be an easy or incidental process. "Make haste slowly," that report in effect advised.

The strength of the committee's work lay in the clear depiction of the features, functions, and objectives of the proposed stations; the weakness lay in the absence of specific proposals for establishing the desired institutions. How, for example, should the stations be financed? The committee contented itself with the comprehensive observation that the State legislatures should "aid in their establishment and maintenance," that agricultural societies should contribute liberally, that each landholder should "add his subscription," that the Department of Agriculture should "aid" the project, that Congress should provide "direct support."

Urging contributions from all possible sources, the committee did not distinguish between private and public, nor between State and Federal monetary sponsorship. It did not submit a plan of action specifying that a particular agency ought to provide to a station organization a specified sum of money at stated times for prescribed purposes; neither did the committee propose any pattern of station administration, nor define the relationship between the financing authority and the station officers. The committee did not, despite Johnson's longstanding familiarity with the details of European station organization and Atwater's recent apprenticeship in the German stations, submit a procedure upon which the convention could act, nor did the committee deliberately omit specific proposals in the expectation that the convention would originate them. The committee report recommended, on the contrary, that the convention should merely continue the committee and authorize it to prepare and issue at a later date a report discussing "the character, value, and practicability of experimental stations . . . ."

MOVEMENT PROGRESSED SLOWLY

The surprising reluctance of the committee to press ahead with the station movement revealed in part a belief, typically Johnsonian, that too few of the American spokesmen for agriculture grasped the significance of a clear-cut concentration on research; accordingly the committee chose to bide its time and publicize the objectives of the station cause, thereby not inviting the risk of premature defeat.

The failure to submit a program for establishing the stations indicated much more clearly, however, that the committee of 1872, like its Gregory-led predecessor of 1871, had met an impasse. It could not devise a satisfactory plan which would guarantee adequate governmental support to stations at the land-grant colleges. No practical precedents existed on which a claim could be based for continuous State or Federal appropriations for scientific research in agriculture. No State had thus far founded a station. The Department of Agriculture operated on a small budget and, impeded by Congressional indifference, could offer no encouragement to the emerging station movement. Moreover, no precedent existed, except for the pioneer attempt of Commissioner Watts in the current convention, for a plan of cooperation between the colleges and the Department, even if that agency could secure an increased Federal appropriation. The land-grant colleges traced their support to Federal and State law; nevertheless, few State legislatures provided adequate support, the Morrill endowment proved disappointingly small, the colleges as a group desperately needed substantial increases in revenue (*17*, *p. 46*), and Congress consistently refused for a quarter century after 1862 to regard the Morrill Act as a compelling precedent for increasing the Federal support of the colleges. Had Congress increased the college income in the seventies, undoubtedly the colleges would have used the increase for general expenses rather than for station purposes.

The station committee of 1872 encountered other difficulties, as well. It could find no way to integrate with the land-grant college the Johnson–Atwater format of the independent station. Did not a station have value, moreover, primarily because it served a local area? Accordingly, should not a station be a State rather than a Federal institution, and operate on income from the State and not the Federal treasury?

The committee accepted the principle of joint support from the State and Federal governments, yet it did not thereby suggest Federal legislation for the creation of stations on the principle used by the

Morrill Act for the colleges. The committee presented no bill for submission to Congress, and it did not refer in any way to the prospect of lobbying campaigns in the States. It did not attempt, in short, to solve the political problem of winning governmental subsidies for the desired stations. The Watts Convention followed the recommendations of the report and, having decided to hold a similar convention in February of 1873, continued the station committee.

The possibility that a practical plan might emerge from future conferences faded, however, when Commissioner Watts at the last moment canceled the Convention of 1873 and thereafter refused to call another. Though the Commissioner did not announce the reasons for his decision, his action indicated that he no longer considered conventions to be a helpful device for winning Federal appropriations for the land-grant colleges; the Convention of 1872 had disappointed him, for example, when a lack of unanimity there prevented him from authorizing a committee to request Congressmen for an enlarged collegiate endowment (*17, pp. 34–52*).

A greater discouragement for land-grant fortunes lay in a stiffening Congressional determination to curtail its expenditures and to disapprove bills requesting federal subsidies, no matter how worthy the cause. During the seventies, too, the concept of land-grant support for collegiate education met an equally vigorous competitor in the movement to secure land-grant funds for common schools (*2*). Accordingly, Senator Morrill, the perpetual champion of collegiate "land-grantism", failed repeatedly in his attempts at bill-passing. The onset of the serious depression in 1873, and the feverish competition between the two major political parties, spelled doom for college and for station subsidies in the seventies.

STATE SUBSIDIES SOUGHT

The inability to secure Federal support left only one course of action open to station-minded men, namely, local campaigns in the individual States. Station advocates in Connecticut and several of her sister States along the East coast succeeded in persuading their respective State legislatures to subsidize independent stations. This activity in the late seventies established the principle and practice of State support and State control.

Not all research-minded professors in the eastern land-grant colleges, however, followed the Connecticut precedent. Faculty members at the Massachusetts Agricultural College instituted, when aided by sympathetic trustees, a college station in 1878 (*21, pp. 92–93*). An equally determined panel of professors at Cornell, without the benefit of assistance from the trustees, collected private funds to organize a station at the college in 1879 (*21, p. 74*). In neither State did the State legislature grant a charter, or appropriate funds, or participate in the station-making procedure. In both States the consequent lack of an adequate and permanent income soon imperiled the new enterprises. The State legislature rescued the Massachusetts venture by converting it to a State station in 1883. The Cornell station could expect no similar assistance from the New York legislature, which already had established its station at Geneva; luckily, however, the college trustees, having financial resources which made Cornell the envy of her impecunious land-grant sisters, adopted the station in the early eighties.

The eastern experience in station-founding offered small encouragement, therefore, to college researchers who desired a college-sponsored station. To win a legislative subsidy, the interested individuals on the college staff had no choice but to develop and lead a difficult political campaign in each State. The hard-won victory in such a campaign usually meant that the station would operate under legislative, not collegiate, direction. Even where the State located its station on the college campus, the station remained a separate institution providing opportunities for research only to the very small number of professors who could gain employment there. The governing boards of the colleges, on the other hand, seemed unable or disinclined to sponsor and subsidize the college-controlled station. Thus in the early eighties the outlook for establishing permanent stations under college direction appeared, if not bleak, distant and uncertain.

NEW ASSOCIATION FORMED

Nevertheless, the movement for college stations soon renewed its vigor. Research-minded professors from a number of midwestern land-grant colleges assumed the initiative in 1880 and volunteered to restate the case for formalizing research efforts in station form at public expense. They gathered at the University of Illinois in June 1880; there they formed an association known as the Teachers of Agriculture, and agreed to hold an annual regional conference, a practice which the earlier Convention of 1871 had urged but had been unable to make permanent. This new association at its organizational meeting appointed a committee to study during the following year the procedures for conducting conjoint experiments and to recommend "a plan for united and systematic experimentation" (20). Thus this new association, reaffirming its faith in the goal first announced in the Gregory–Flagg convention, tackled anew the problem of administering research precisely at the point where circumstances had compelled the men of 1871 to leave it.

The Committee on Conjoint Experimentation submitted its report to the next meeting of the Teachers held at Michigan Agricultural College in 1881 (20). That report postulated the purpose of systematic experimentation: "the discovery or verification of new truths in agricultural science;" it summarized the European efforts during the preceding 75 years to achieve an identical goal; it recognized that European administrators had proceeded more rapidly than had Americans in the search for the most effective procedures; it praised the European acumen in developing experiment stations as clearly-defined institutions for research; and it concluded that European and American experience alike had shown the station to be the most useful format for administering permanent and continuous research in the science of agriculture. The report did not recommend, therefore, further attempts at conjoint experimentation; instead it pleaded only for the establishment of stations.

The committee then proceeded to define the features and facilities of a station best adapted to the American environment and especially suited to midwestern needs, as follows:

38

To answer the knotty questions that beset the American farmer, it is essential that a farm be attached to every experimental station, and that the farm shall have pastures and meadows, crops of all kinds, and all kinds of stock, and fences, buildings, implements, teams and laborers. Suitable buildings are indispensable, such as propagating or plant-houses, in which the temperature can be controlled, not only for the growth of plants, but for the testing of commercial fertilizers. There must be rooms for weighing and measuring, for drying and storage, and also for chemical laboratory. . . . Experimental work requires money for the purchase of materials such as seeds and fertilizers and for laboratory expenses, and to compensate experts. . . . Still more is money needed to compensate the large amount of careful labor which all experimental work necessarily involves. . . . Well qualified men are also necessary to successful experimentation. The direction of a station may rest with a Board or upon a single individual. If under the control of one person, he must be familiar with all forms of agricultural industry, or in such intimate relations with each that he will understand the wants of all. And he must command the assistance of . . . [specialized scientists].

The Teachers' committee, having thus given its detailed formula for an ideal American station, pointed out with equal care the reasons why that station should be attached to an agricultural college. The land-grant college already possessed, and therefore could most economically supply, the resources essential for the proper operation of a station. It could at minimum cost provide abundant farm land, the laboratory of "an associate educational institution," and the services of the scientific specialists on the teaching staff. The availability of this scientific talent, the committee emphasized, "is the great reason for attaching experiment stations in the United States to agricultural colleges."

At the same time the committee predicted a benefit for the college, as well as for the station, in a college-connected center for research. "The original research of an experiment station," it observed, "has great value to students as a means of practical education." More significantly, however, the Teachers clearly understood that the station, if administered according to their prescription, would establish an intimate relationship between the farm population, beset with "knotty questions," and the land-grant institutions, dedicated to an educational philosophy of service. The Teachers' policy of research stipulated that the college-connected station must prepare itself from its inception to accommodate "the various interests [the dairyman, the grain-raiser, the stockman, the fruit grower, and others] which will be certain to present problems for solution." The college-attached station, so ran the tenor of the Teachers' thinking, would establish with the public the popularity which college personnel had sought for two decades to achieve.

The Teachers' formula of 1881, the first detailed proposal for a college-attached station, provided the competitive answer to the earlier Johnson-Atwater formula for an independent station. The Teachers thus supplied an idea-pattern which solved, by adapting the station to a land-grant setting, one of the practical problems confronting the conventioneers of 1871 and 1872. The Teachers also simplified the question of finance; they placed the responsibility for station support squarely and exclusively on each State legislature.

Wise public policy, they asserted, should not only take notice of the inability of the individual farmer to solve his problems without the stations' help; it should also recognize that improved agricultural production benefits the entire population, not solely the producers on the farms. "If the States," the Teachers observed in conclusion, "will take up the work which Congress began [via the Morrill Act of 1862], and will now endow well-appointed experiment stations in connection with all of these colleges, a most valuable combination of teaching with research will be secured."

USDA BECAME INTERESTED

The cause of the college station soon received opportune encouragement from the Department of Agriculture. In July of 1881 the newly appointed Commissioner, George Bailey Loring, officially invited delegates from the agricultural colleges to convene in Washington, D.C., early in January of 1882 for the purpose of discussing the current problems confronting agricultural education (5). Determined to cultivate the good will of the influential agricultural organizations across the Nation, Commissioner Loring revived the Watts' principle of holding conventions; he hoped especially to bring the colleges "into a close connection with . . . [the] department of agriculture" (5, p.5).

The director of the new station in New Jersey, George Hammell Cook, and the director of the new venture at Cornell, George Chapman Caldwell, seized the opportunity to publicize the value of a college-connected station (5, pp. 7–12; 20–25). Slated to present papers dealing with education, they described the experiment stations as institutions specializing in educating the practical farmer. "The experiment station takes up the work where the agricultural college leaves it," said Professor Cook; "the two institutions work together admirably." The speakers emphasized, in tones reminiscent of J. P. Norton 30 years earlier, that the teaching functions of the station and the college would blend smoothly, and that the station work had already demonstrated its educational value to appreciative farmers. Thereupon the Convention of 1882, buzzing with enthusiasm for the station project during the 2-day sessions, devoted its discussions to the problem of institutionalizing experimentation.

The outcome of the convention, nevertheless, did not immediately advance the station cause beyond the point reached by the Teachers in 1881. The convention did agree that "scientific investigation is as much a part of the duty of the agricultural college as teaching" (5, p. 37). Yet it hesitated to pass resolutions urging the establishment of college stations; instead it authorized Commissioner Loring to administer a new series of conjoint experiments among the colleges and stations volunteering to participate (5, p. 61). This decision in part reflected the esteem of the group for Professor Atwater, who for 5 years had administered an interstate program of conjoint experiments and had reported his work to the convention (5, pp. 27–55).

Commissioner Loring himself, however, played the decisive role in the vote favoring conjoint experiments rather than station-founding. Having called the convention in order to mobilize land-grant support behind his new administration, Loring wished the delegates to endorse a program enabling the Department to strengthen its bid for increased appropriations from Congress.

The station movement, advocated as a collegiate attachment by its professional champions, thus far did not involve the Department in any way; therefore it could not accommodate the Commissioner's purpose. Accordingly, the convention at Loring's special request (5, p.

62) diverted its support from station-founding to conjoint experimentation, an activity which Loring could administer by employing
Atwater as his technical assistant. The convention formally requested
that the Commissioner "take measures to become the medium of communication between all parties engaged in systematic agricultural experimentation in this country, and endeavor to secure general cooperation in this work . . ." (*5, p. 61*). It further requested that Loring
apply to Congress for the funds necessary to operate the program and,
in addition, to prepare a digest of the discoveries already made in the
European stations.

HILGARD TOOK ACTIVE PART

The intervention of the Commissioner, though it temporarily side-
tracked the station advocates at the Convention of 1882, soon prompted
a significant resurgence of the station movement. Shortly after adjournment of the January meeting, Professor Eugene Woldemar
Hilgard of the University of California prepared a forceful essay,
"Progress in Agriculture by Education and Government Aid" which
the *Atlantic Monthly* published in May 1882 (*12*).

German born and trained, Hilgard had held since the midseventies
the directorship of the California station at Berkeley, the oldest college-created station in continuous operation in the United States
(*21, p. 87*). This stalwart chemist, who had taken an active part
in the Conventions of 1871 and 1872, could no longer restrain his
impatience with the repeated delays in establishing college stations.
Commissioner Loring's deflection of the station project disappointed
the Californian and inclined him to the view that the current Commissioner, like his predecessors, neither understood the significance
of the station's role in agricultural improvement nor grasped the
waiting opportunity to cooperate with the colleges in a more elaborate
program of research.

A broader problem of public policy, however, disturbed Hilgard
much more deeply. His irritation spilled over when he contrasted, on
the one hand, the "pittance" currently allotted by the State legislatures
to the few stations in existence and, on the other hand, the "millions . . . wasted" by the professional politicians in the spoils system.
Hilgard's eye, equally as sharp as his tongue, observed the accumulating surplus in the Federal treasury. "I am beginning to feel aggressive on the subject," Hilgard wrote to S. W. Johnson in March
of 1882 (*18*).

Director Hilgard presented in his *Atlantic* article a vigorous proposal for establishing and maintaining college stations at Federal expense. The Federal Government, Hilgard urged, ought no longer to
leave the problem of collegiate agricultural research solely to the jurisdiction of the individual State legislatures. It should recognize an
unfortunate situation of nationwide dimension, namely, that the States
most in need of the improved technology that only a local station
could provide had stingy legislatures and penniless colleges. The
Federal Government, then, should follow a corrective policy of "enlightened intervention" and supply "substantial aid" to each land-
grant college for the specific purpose of operating a station.

The precedents for Federal action, Hilgard pointed out, lay immediately at hand. Congress could follow the principle of the Morrill

41

Act and provide "additional endowments," or it could increase its annual appropriation to the Department of Agriculture which by "direct cooperation" with the land-grant colleges would operate a station in each State. Hilgard preferred the latter alternative because it would enable the linkage of two great potentials: the scientific capacity of a Federal research center at the Nation's capital, and the existing collection of talents awaiting formal organization at the agricultural college in each State. This combination of resources, Hilgard declared, would produce a "radiating network" of scientific research.

The director's line of reasoning, though forthright in its plea for Federal funds, encountered several intrinsic obstacles. Why, for example, should Congressmen, acutely aware of the historic distinctions between Federal powers and States' rights, intervene in the responsibilities of the State governments in order to do what the State legislatures had not done? Why should Congressmen, politically accustomed to a Federal Government of strictly limited functions, activate at this time the rudimentary precedents which for 20 years had lain dormant? If, furthermore, American farmers desperately needed the benefits of experimentation, why had not the farmers, comprising a substantial majority of the American citizenry, insisted long since that stations be established?

In his article, Hilgard attempted an answer to these implicit objections by pointing reprovingly to a longstanding omission in the administrative policies of the Department of Agriculture and the agricultural colleges. Both institutions had neglected, he charged, "to appreciate adequately, and to minister to, the strongly-felt want of the American farmer for more information directly to the point . . . upon the problems immediately before him, and bearing within them the alternative of success or failure, crops or no crops."

Hilgard particularly regretted the administrative attitude of the Commissioners, who had permitted the smallness of the Congressional appropriations since 1862 to discourage them from developing their Department into a technical agency for scientific research. This policy, Hilgard asserted, did not accord with the intent of Congress in founding the Department; for Congress in 1862 had charged the Department with a mission, "the usual and well-understood work of an agricultural experiment station." Had the Commissioners developed the Department into a Federal station, their handiwork would have emitted a nationwide "impulse" so strong that "local stations" would have appeared "in every State." So little interest had the Commissioners shown in this matter, however, that they had even neglected to "stimulate" the colleges "into active cooperation."

Hilgard did not bypass the college administrators in his outspoken critique; they, too, had followed a shortsighted course when they ignored on the one hand, the farmers' need for the practical results of station research, and failed, on the other hand, to grasp the benefits which the stations would bring to the colleges. The college administrators should acknowledge, Hilgard continued, that the influence of the colleges in improving farm technology "has not been marked, *except in the case of those which have assumed to some extent the functions of experiment stations*, and as such have rendered assistance in the solution of practical agricultural problems." [2] If the colleges would mend their ways and cease to regard the college stations as

---

[2] His italics.

"step children," the college authorities would thereby solve the vital problem of attunement to the agricultural public.

The director's rebuke in public print gave color to his appeal for Federal funds, but it also produced a momentary awkwardness. How could the scientist sharply criticize the administrative history of the Department and the colleges and, at the same time, urge that the cooperation of the two institutions, if Federally financed for the purpose of establishing college-attached stations, would provide admirably for the needs of scientific research in agriculture? How could he reprove and praise in one breath?

Hilgard's solution was a simple one. He found no fault with the institutions; he criticized only the prevailing administrative policy. Strengthen the institutions, he concluded, but change the policy; let each institution cooperate with the other. Congress could safely grant the all-important subsidy, therefore, and thus promptly provide the corrective action needed to eliminate the critical shortage of experiment stations. Hilgard in this way sought to awaken public interest in obtaining Federal support.

STATION BILL INTRODUCED

The practical winning of a Federal appropriation remained unachieved, however, awaiting the crystallization of a specific plan of station organization and, above all, the insistence of determined spokesmen who could successfully plead before Congressmen the need for Federal aid. In May of 1882, precisely at the time Hilgard's outburst appeared in print, the first station bill made its debut in Congress (4). The new bill rested squarely on the precedent favored by the California director; it proposed that the Federal Government authorize the Department of Agriculture "to establish national experiment stations in connection with the agricultural colleges in the various States" (21, p. 120).

This Carpenter bill, taking its name from Representative Cyrus C. Carpenter of Iowa, traced its heritage to the determined activity of Seaman Asahel Knapp, a former breeder of purebred livestock and currently the professor of agriculture at the Iowa State Agricultural College.

Seaman Knapp, having personally experienced the difficulties of midwestern farming, had been searching 5 years for an opportunity to put science to work for Iowa farmers. Employed in 1877 as the editor of the *Western Stock Farmer and Journal*, Knapp had reported at length in his columns the experience of S. W. Johnson in establishing the Connecticut station. He had then concluded that Iowa should establish a similar station as soon as possible, and other States should do likewise. He understood, of course, that station-founding would take time; therefore he urged that, in the meantime, "until these stations could be set up, and as a supplement to them, let the agricultural college farms, and the Department at Washington do experimental work on the most urgent farm problems" (3, pp. 73-74).

Knapp discovered with keen disappointment, however, that an institution designed to conduct practical research for the Iowa farmer would not soon emerge. He could not induce the Department to direct its attention to the solution of midwestern problems. He could not persuade the Iowa legislature to found a station or to grant more than

43

a trifling sum for research at the college (*3, p. 96*). Finally, after receiving an appointment as the professor of practical and experimental agriculture at the Iowa college early in 1880, he could not, despite his shrewd management of the farm enterprise, administer an effective research program on his tiny budget (*6, pp. 93–94*).

Fully convinced after two seasons of difficulty that Iowa had to have a station, Professor Knapp attended the Teachers' second annual meeting at the Michigan State College in June of 1881. During the following months he collaborated with Professor Charles Edwin Bessey at Iowa State, applied the principle of Federal support to the Teachers' formula for a station; and with Representative Carpenter's help prepared a Federal bill for "national experiment stations" at each college. The Carpenter bill, though primarily a proposal to accomplish local research at Federal expense, intended to channel the research capacity of the Department to the college campus, and there support a research agency specializing in solving farmers' problems, precisely the goals which Knapp had envisioned in 1877.

How did Congressmen react to the proposition that they should substantially increase the budget of the Department in order to establish and maintain stations at college locations? This question came up for discussion when the House, after referring the station bill to its Committee on Agriculture, considered a bill to enlarge the powers of the Department and to create a Secretaryship.

Representative Carpenter, a stalwart advocate of a strengthened Department, forcefully contended that the American farmer, now confronted with the necessity of developing techniques of intensive cultivation, needed as never before the aid of scientific research. A Department properly equipped to supply this service, he observed, "should have experimental stations in every State and Territory, and . . . especially should an experimental station be conducted in connection with every agricultural college in the country."

Representative Grout of Vermont (*10*), also urging an increase in the Departmental scientific work, praised the stations as a means of increasing crop productivity. He favored cabinet status for the Department on the ground that a Secretary would command sufficient influence to initiate a "liberal policy" of Federally supported station research in the States.

Representative Money of Mississippi (*15*) outdid his colleagues by attempting to amend the Department bill. He proposed that "the secretary of the Department of Agriculture is hereby empowered and directed to establish in each State of the Union one or more experimental stations . . . and to appoint the necessary force for conducting them; and at least one [station] . . . shall be connected with the agricultural college. . . ." The House refused to accept the amendment because the motion anticipated the Carpenter bill still in committee. Nevertheless, the persistent outcropping of the station proposition in the debate indicated a favorable sentiment in the House for the principle which Professors Knapp and Hilgard publicized in the spring of 1882.

KNAPP PRESSED HIS PLAN

Knapp pressed ahead with his ambition to win favorable Federal action despite the failure of Congress in the spring session to debate the station bill and to grant to the Department appreciably enlarged facilities for scientific research. Would a display of initiative and mobilized approval from college spokesmen enable the movement for campus stations to capitalize on the receptivity, newly revealed in the House, to the concept of Department-sponsored research in the States?

Fortunately for Knapp's purpose, Commissioner Loring before the year's end decided to hold his second convention in January of 1883. Unfortunately, however, the 2-day agenda for the college delegates, unlike the one for 1882, did not permit the station partisans to focus attention on their project. During the sessions devoted to discussions of agricultural education Knapp found no opportunity to obtain a formal show of convention strength for his station plans. Accordingly Knapp, now the acting president of his college, remained at the convention and attended later sessions having no direct bearing on college problems. He persuaded Theophilus C. Abbot, the longtime President of the Michigan Agricultural College and the presiding officer of the Teachers' meeting held the preceding June, to assist his parliamentary maneuvering. Abbot succeeded, on the third day of the convention, in interrupting the discussions in order to give Knapp the floor; Knapp thereupon moved that the convention endorse the Carpenter bill and further moved that Commissioner Loring appoint five committeemen to support the Carpenter bill before the House Committee on Agriculture. The convention approved the resolutions (6, p. 109–110). This parliamentary play placed Knapp and Abbot plus three other land-grant college presidents on the new committee; it furthermore provided the Carpenter bill with the formal support of the colleges and the Department.

The enterprising Knapp, now chairman of the convention's committee, readied his bill for introduction to the new Congress in December of 1883. The bill requested $15,000 annually from the Federal treasury to pay the salaries of employed personnel and the costs of experimentation at an institution, with a farm, to be "established in connection with each of the agricultural colleges. . . ." It enumerated a broad list of authorized fields of inquiry covering all known types of research. To the college trustees it gave "general control" including the power to employ a faculty professor as the station superintendent. It placed with a triumvirate (the Commissioner of Agriculture, the college president, and the professorial superintendent) the power to determine "the general character of the work and the experiments to be performed at each station." The enactment of this measure, the Knapp phraseology declared, would "enable the Department of Agriculture to fulfill the design and perform the duties for which it was established . . . to-wit, 'to acquire and diffuse among the people of the United States useful information on subjects connected with agriculture' . . ." (21, pp. 121–122).

FEDERAL-STATE ROLE OUTLINED

The Knapp draft proposed an astute combination of features which aimed not only to put science and Federal funds to work for the farmer, but also to obtain for each station the services and the resources of the Department and the land-grant college. That draft seemingly placed each station under the close surveillance of the Department and especially of the college; in fact, however, it permitted each station to remain remarkably free of restrictive control. It entitled each station, for example, to Departmental assistance in planning experiments, but it did not grant the Commissioner a controlling voice in station management or in the expenditure of funds. Although it directed the superintendent to make official reports to the Commissioner, these reports presumably would serve the important purposes of announcing the results of research activity and accelerating the flow of information to a nationwide public. Neither this requirement nor any other made the stations "branch units" of the Department despite the use of the term "national experiment stations."

Knapp's careful phrasing, intentionally giving the impression that an administrative relationship would exist between the Department and the stations, strove to take advantage of the Department's well-established claim to Federal support and thus extend that precedent to cover the station appropriation. Nevertheless, Knapp's bill did not place the stations under the administrative jurisdiction of the Commissioner.

Ostensibly the proposed measure gave jurisdiction to the trustees of the college. Yet the trustees had no authority to select the lines of experimentation or determine the character of the work; likewise the college president had a contributing but not a controlling voice in management. The bill did not establish the station as a collegiate department; on the contrary, it placed the superintendent "in charge of said station" and did not define the administrative relationship between the station force and the college. It did require several duties from the college in behalf of the station, however; the college should receive the Federal appropriation and have some responsibility for audit; and implicit in the bill lay the assumption that the college should supply the physical resources, including land, buildings, and equipment. Placing the station under the "general control" of the trustees incurred a collegiate responsibility to the station but it did not, in turn, require that the station serve the college. The supervisory capacity of the college, like that of the Commissioner, remained nominal.

Thus the Knapp proposal for national experiment stations presented, despite its seeming simplicity, a tangle of peculiarities. It did not appropriate funds to the Commissioner for the purpose of creating Departmental stations in the States; instead it granted funds for State stations having only a tenuous tie to the Department. Nevertheless, it urged Congressmen to regard the appropriation as if made to the Department, in order that the grant might rest on the same precedent as the Departmental type. The bill did appropriate the stipend to the agricultural colleges, but it did not place the Grant on the precedent of the Morrill Act.

The Knapp draft, studiously avoiding a direct reliance on either precedent, kept the stations administratively disengaged from the Department and the colleges. It contrived, in effect, to produce a Federally supported station as nearly independent as financial circumstances would permit. This bill the House of Representatives assigned to its Committee on Agriculture in December of 1883.

ABBOT DIFFERED

Meanwhile the prospect of an independent station increasingly disturbed Michigan's President Abbot, whose philosophy of research differed from Knapp's. Abbot preferred the longstanding Michigan system, which assigned "special experiments to special members of the faculty" and welcomed occasional stipends granted by the State legislature to a selected professor for the purpose of conducting an individual project of research on a part-time basis. Research, in Abbot's scale of values, served its rightful place in an agricultural college when, as an auxiliary to the college's all-important function of teaching students, it provided a necessary tonic to the teacher and, in turn, aroused a "spirit" of inquiry in the college students. The Michigan system of conducting research effectively fulfilled this mission and, in Abbot's judgment, had no need for a "distinct" station. The Michigan president did concede early in 1883, however, that if stations were to be established, they should be located at the agricultural colleges (*6, p. 19*).

The Knapp bill, despite its proposal to establish stations "in connection with" the colleges, troubled Abbot because it accorded farmer-oriented research a separate and equal status with student-centered teaching at the college, and intended to convert into a full-time professional occupation the research activity that Abbot wished to leave on a part-time basis. Furthermore this teacher-administrator perceived that the national stations, if founded as Knapp urged, would adversely affect his college and its system (*1*):

> I would not think it well *for the college*, however it might be with the science of agriculture, to plant here an experiment station to be conducted independently of the various departments of the college and of their separate heads; but if the term [national] means such an enlargement of force and means as would enable our officers greatly to extend their experimental work, I say yes. We have ordinarily done at this college, I believe, more experimenting than any simply experiment station in the United States. It is rather an extension of our work than a superseding of it by a foreign set of workers with new laboratories, that seems to me to be needed. . . .

The sentiment prompted Abbot and like-minded college presidents to contact the House Committee on Agriculture and to urge major revisions in the proposed legislation. Accordingly, the phraseology and content of the revised bill reported from the House Committee by its Chairman, William Cullen, in July of 1884 differed substantially from the Knapp draft. The Cullen bill (*7, pp. 34–35*) clarified several ambiguities contained in its predecessor. It stiffened the role of the college trustees, weakened that of the Commissioner of Agriculture, and eliminated the possibility of an independent station. It specified that each Federally subsidized station must be organized as a "department" of a land-grant college endowed by the Morrill Act of 1862. It placed the station "under the direction and control of the [college] trustees" and empowered the trustees to appoint a director, his assistants and staff, and a treasurer to receive the Federal stipend.

Refusing to compel the college to bear the entire expense of providing facilities, it authorized the expenditure of a fraction of the Federal income for necessary buildings. The power over policy-making in research the Cullen bill tacitly included within the jurisdiction of the trustees, for it eliminated the explicit provision in the Knapp

47

bill that the station superintendent, the college president, and the Commissioner of Agriculture should administer this function.

Moreover, the new bill differentiated the supervisory powers of the trustees from the advisory powers of the Department of Agriculture. It specifically forbade the Commissioner "to control or direct the work or management" of any station; furthermore, it deleted the obligation that each station must send reports to Washington and stipulated, instead, that the Commissioner should receive only a copy of the original report to be submitted to the State governor. The bill did require the Commissioner, nevertheless, "to furnish forms . . . for the tabulation of results of investigation or experiments; to indicate . . . lines of inquiry; and . . . to furnish . . . advice and assistance. . . ." Thus the Cullen bill outspokenly attempted to preclude Federal dictation yet it insistently retained the principle that the Department must help the research efforts of the proposed stations.

The Cullen draft determinedly sought to give to the governing boards of the Morrill Act colleges complete jurisdiction over the station movement and thus provide specific meaning to the historically ambiguous phrase, "in connection with the colleges." Yet the new revisions did not solve—on the contrary they complicated—the problem of constitutional precedents. The careful reduction in the exercise of administrative authority by the Department weakened in like proportion the reliance on the principle of extending Federal appropriations via the Department to agencies in the States. The bill exhibited the troublesome contradiction, which the Knapp bill had tried to mask, that the stations lay beyond the control of the Commissioner, yet were intended "to aid the Department of Agriculture in acquiring and diffusing . . . useful and practical information. . . ." Obviously reluctant to relinquish the tie to the Department, the draftsmen were equally reluctant to place their bill on the precedent of the Morrill Act.

The determination to organize each station as a college department produced an additional headache for the advocates of the Cullen bill. Could the Federal Government grant money directly to a State-chartered college without the approval of the State legislature? Should not the grant go to the legislature, to be placed at its discretion? Should the Federal Government, on the other hand, surrender all claims to its grant and have no power to require expenditures in conformity with Federal standards? Could not the State legislature in any event exercise final control over the spending of moneys given to a department controlled by a State college undeniably under State authority?

The Knapp draft bluntly met this cluster of questions by requiring each State legislature to "pass an act accepting such trust and agreeing to conduct an experiment station in accordance therewith" (*21, p. 122*). The Cullen draft eliminated this forceful language and introduced the softspoken ambiguity that "nothing in this act shall be construed to impair or modify the legal relation existing between any of the said colleges and the government of the States in which they are respectively located." That draft did succinctly specify, however, that the appropriation should go "to each State, to be paid . . . to the treasurer . . . duly appointed by the aforesaid boards of trustees . . ." (*7, p. 35*). This latter provision, so smoothly stated that its simplicity disguised its ingenuity, could supply an administrative opportunity to a subsidy-minded Congress undeterred by a lack of distinct precedents. Yet that provision bypassed the State legislatures; and it did not automatically clear away the constitutional questions obstructing the path of the seekers of Congressional subsidies for State institutions.

The spokesmen for the Cullen bill (22) persuaded the House Committee on Agriculture to report that bill favorably to the House in July of 1884. But their handiwork did not reach the stage of Congressional debate in that year. Henceforth three major tasks confronted the teachers and administrators who had concluded that the station movement, now showing significant strength, must have a positive relationship to the land-grant colleges: first, to win the approval of station-minded men for the proposals in the Cullen bill; second, by personal contact to persuade the chairmen of the agricultural committees in the two Houses to press the bill to favorable action; and third, to present a line of reasoning which would convince Congressmen that the national interest required prompt passage despite the unprecedented nature of the legislation. Good fortune, skill, and perseverance combined to solve this threefold problem during the following 3 years.

COLLEGE DELEGATES CALLED

Fortunately for the station movement in its time of need, Norman Jay Colman was appointed as the Commissioner of Agriculture in April of 1885. He acted promptly to aid the cause of the college station. One month after taking office, Commissioner Colman called a special convention of college delegates to meet at the Department in July 1885 (7).

Convinced even before he took office that experiment stations should be established at the colleges (14, p. 85), Colman placed the station project on the agenda. He delighted the land-grant conventioneers with his earnest pleadings for "a bond of union and sympathy between the Department and the colleges" (7, p. 15). He then demonstrated his sincerity; he openly encouraged the station advocates and accepted the Cullen bill. In Colman the station movement found, precisely at the right time, an influential and sympathetic friend willing to accept without objection the auxiliary position and the advisory function which the Cullen bill assigned to the Department.

The Convention of 1885, composed exclusively of land-grant personnel, unified support behind the Cullen bill and authorized a committee of three college presidents to cooperate with Commissioner Colman in persuading Congressmen to pass the proposed legislation (21, p. 125).

The members of this legislative committee considered carefully the reasoning they advanced to win Congressional sympathy (23). They determined to base their appeal for funds on two forthright propositions: the duty of the Federal Government to aid agriculture, and the duty of the land-grant college to aid the farmer. "No conviction is stronger or more universal among our own people," the first proposition broadly asserted, "than that it is the duty of the Government, by every legitimate means in its power, to aid in preserving and developing the agricultural resources of the country, thereby promot-

49

ing the welfare not only of those who make this branch of industry the business of their lives, but that of every other class of citizens."

Thus the Federal Government would efficiently and effectively execute its public duty by enacting the current bill, so ran the confident prediction, because the stations, already well-tested institutions in the United States and Europe, had positively demonstrated their capacity to teach an improved technology and to fulfill a public need. This reasoning, reminiscent of the Teachers' rationale in 1881, in effect urged Congress to ignore the constitutional unorthodoxy of the station proposal and establish a new precedent in the public interest. This proposition, like the second, the House Committee incorporated in its report of March 3, 1886 recommending the passage of the station bill.

The companion proposition openly contended that the land-grant colleges, acting in response to a public need, had assumed the burden of assisting farmers to solve by experimentation the new problems constantly emerging in a changing farm economy. This assumption of responsibility had placed a heavy handicap on the colleges, however, for those institutions had been compelled to divert their resources, inadequate at best, from their statutory function of teaching.

This line of reasoning, reminiscent of the Gregory thinking in 1871, freely admitted that the colleges had gone beyond the letter of the Morrill law, but it frankly sought to gain Congressional sympathy, not censure, for the public-spirited colleges. Accordingly Congress should act "on the broadest grounds of public policy and of enlightened care for the national well-being." Having subsidized the colleges for teaching students, Congress should subsidize the stations for assisting farmers; it should recognize that the collegiate experience had shown the station movement to be a wise undertaking; and it should understand that collegiate administration would assure sound management.

FEDERAL FUNDS SOUGHT

Thus the second proposition, like the first, urged Congress not to scruple about precedents but, instead, to make a Federal donation as a reward to the colleges for enlarging the field of public education. It revealed, not less significantly, that the committee of college presidents had finally conceded in this cardinal argument for Federal funds that the college via its station research should serve the farmer as well as the college student. Thus the committee of 1885–86 vindicated the conventioneers of 1871.

Meanwhile, in the winter of 1885–86, the committee of presidents assiduously cultivated the Congressional chairmen of the agricultural committees, William H. Hatch in the House and James Z. George in the Senate. Both men thereafter championed the station bill, henceforth known as the Hatch bill. Congressman Hatch successfully guided his measure through the House but Senator George encountered difficulties in the upper chamber. Not until January of 1887 could he get the bill to the floor for discussion.

The fiery debate in January of 1887 revealed, fortunately for the station movement, a widespread Senatorial sympathy with the new concept of Federal subsidies for the conduct of research in State stations. It also revealed, however, a sharp concern for the administrative consequences of an appropriation granted as the Hatch bill stipulated. Had the college draftsmen taken sufficient precautions to maintain local autonomy in stations subsidized by Federal funds and advised by the Commissioner of Agriculture?

Senatorial spokesmen instinctively assumed that Federal dictation would automatically follow the flow of Federal funds. For that reason Senator John J. Ingalls of Kansas, who opened the debate on January 17, bluntly assailed "the interposition of national authority" and opposed "any stipulation as to the methods in which it [the grant] shall be employed outside of its application to the general object of the trust" (*13*). The assignment of duties to the Commissioner aroused Ingalls' apprehensions, despite the explicit limitation on the Commissioner's powers in the Hatch draft, that Federal dictation would nevertheless invade State jurisdictions. Ingalls demanded the insertion of a guaranty that Federal power would assist and cooperate with, but not control "the existing authorities in those States."

Senator George (*9*) did not pacify this sentiment when he declared, "These experimental stations are really but an extension of the Agricultural Department of the General Government; that is all; and they rest and the provisions of this bill and the power to pass it rest upon the same identical power which enabled Congress to establish the Agricultural Department." George's interpretation, which demonstrated that the earlier proposals of Professor Knapp had influential adherents, regarded the colleges as agents employed by the Commissioner in the Federal service. In George's judgment the Hatch bill sufficiently guarded against an overbearing central government; moreover, according to his view, the Senators needed only to decide that the colleges were proper agents and the bill could pass without raising any question of constitutional power.

The George explanation did not silence outspoken dissenters who, mobilizing behind Senator Joseph R. Hawley of Connecticut, demanded that the Hatch bill sever every tie to the Departmental precedent. Hawley proposed a substitute measure which, containing not a single reference to the Department, rested completely on the precedent of the Morrill Act of 1862, made the appropriation to the several State legislatures, and recognized the complete authority of each legislature to assign the stipend as it saw fit (*11*).

In Hawley's view the passage of the committee-supported Hatch bill would produce so significant a reconstruction in the conventional organization and function of the State-chartered colleges that State legislative assent, and control of the placement of funds, would be mandatory. The Hawley bill complied nicely with States-rights' sentiments; it decisively eliminated every possibility of Federal interposition; it catered to the almost unanimous attitude in the Senate that Federal appropriations to the colleges appeared desirable; and at the same time it tacitly enabled a State legislature to hand the Federal stipend to an independent station, a realistic concern confronting the New Haven station in Hawley's own State.

HATCH DRAFT AMENDED

The Senators debated constitutional powers and precedents, yet their contest involved a complex cluster of issues pertaining to the administration of tax-supported scientific research. Should the Senate follow the act of 1862 creating the Commissionership and trust that the exercise of Federal advisory functions, as requested by college spokesmen, would not develop into dictation? Should the Senate follow instead the Morrill Act and deny college personnel, who would administer the system Congressmen selected, the help that experienced scientists in the Department could contribute? Senatorial sentiments inclined toward Hawley's thinking until Senator Preston B. Plumb of Kansas (*19*) pointed out the troublesome weakness of the Hawley plan:

> The [Hawley] amendment . . . gives the money to the colleges without reserving any right of control over its expenditure on the part of the General Government. It would constitute an inducement to combination on the part of the colleges to increase the appropriation from time to time, on the ground that from the local standpoint the existing appropriation was insufficient, while under the language and theory of the original bill the question would be, and continue to be settled from a national standpoint, as it should be . . . .
> I want . . . to give additional resources to the agricultural colleges, but under the substantial direction as to expenditure of the Department of Agriculture located at the national capitol . . . whereby there may be unified and brought together under an intelligent and business supervision and direction all the operations that are to be carried on out of the funds we shall appropriate. . . . [The original] bill would put in the hands of the Secretary [sic] of Agriculture a power which he could wield in connection and cooperation with these agencies of the States heretofore endowed, the agricultural colleges, to great advantage in the promotion of this important interest [agriculture].

Practical values for the future and not precedents of the past, Plumb in effect declared, should guide the Senators' judgment.

Thereupon the Senate refused to substitute Hawley's bill for the Hatch draft. Undeterred, however, the Hawley-led forces successfully added a series of amendments. They made legislative assent a necessary component in the creation of a college station; they enabled the legislature to apply the funds to an independent station; they removed the requirement that a station must operate a farm; they deleted the obligation of the stations to aid the Department of Agriculture; they excised all phrases intimating that the Commissioner had powers beyond those of aiding and assisting the State stations (*24*).

This compromise ended the contest between Senators Hawley and George, ended the long-drawn-out struggle over powers and precedents, and permitted the passage of the amended Hatch bill, which became law on March 2, 1887. The Hatch Act produced the land-grant college stations and, in the process, a new precedent for Federal-State cooperation in agricultural research.

LITERATURE CITED

(1) ABBOT, T. C.
    1884. NATIONAL AGRICULTURAL CONVENTION. Mich. State Bd. Agr. Ann. Rpt. (1882/83) 22: 29–33.
(2) ATHERTON, G. W.
    1900. THE LEGISLATIVE CAREER OF JUSTIN S. MORRILL. Assoc. Amer. Agr. Cols. and Expt. Stas. Proc. 14: 60–72.
(3) BAILEY, J. C.
    1945. SEAMAN A. KNAPP: SCHOOLMASTER OF AMERICAN AGRICULTURE. 307 pp. New York.
(4) CARPENTER, C. C.
    1882. DEPARTMENT OF AGRICULTURE. Cong. Rec., 47th Cong., 1st Sess., pp. 3719–3723.
(5) CONVENTION OF AGRICULTURISTS.
    1882. PROCEEDINGS OF A CONVENTION OF AGRICULTURISTS HELD IN THE DEPARTMENT OF AGRICULTURE, JANUARY 10TH TO 18TH. (First convention.) [U.S.] Dept. Agr. Rpt. 22, 204 pp.

(6) CONVENTION OF AGRICULTURISTS.
      1883. PROCEEDINGS OF A CONVENTION OF AGRICULTURISTS HELD AT THE
             DEPARTMENT OF AGRICULTURE, JANUARY 23, 24, 25, 26, 27, AND 29,
             1883. (Second convention.) [U.S.] Dept. Agr. Misc. Spec. Rpt.
             2, 245 pp.
(7) CONVENTION OF DELEGATES FROM AGRICULTURAL COLLEGES AND EXPERIMENT
     STATIONS.
      1885. PROCEEDINGS OF A CONVENTION OF DELEGATES FROM AGRICULTURAL
             COLLEGES AND EXPERIMENT STATIONS HELD AT THE DEPARTMENT OF
             AGRICULTURE, JULY 8 AND 9, 1885. [U.S.] Dept. Agr. Misc. Spec.
             Rpt. 9, 196 pp.
(8) CONVENTION OF FRIENDS OF AGRICULTURAL EDUCATION.
      1872. DISCUSSION AT MEETING HELD AT CHICAGO, ON THE 24TH AND 25TH
             OF AUGUST, 1871. Ill. Indus. Univ. Ann. Rpt. (1870/71) 4: 215–
             351.
(9) GEORGE, J. Z.
      1887. [DEBATE ON HATCH BILL.] Cong. Rec., 49th Cong., 2d Sess.,
             pp. 729–730.
(10) GROUT, W. W.
      1882. DEPARTMENT OF AGRICULTURE. Cong. Rec., 47th Cong., 1st Sess.,
             pp. 3727–3734.
(11) HAWLEY, J. R.
      1887. [DEBATE ON HATCH BILL.] Cong. Rec., 49th Cong., 2d Sess.,
             pp. 721–729, 1079–1080.
(12) HILGARD, E. W.
      1882. PROGRESS IN AGRICULTURE BY EDUCATION AND GOVERNMENT AID.
             Atlantic Monthly 49: 531–541; 651–661.
(13) INGALLS, J. J.
      1887. [DEBATE ON HATCH BILL.] Cong. Rec., 49th Cong., 2d Sess., pp.
             723–724.
(14) LEMMER, G. F.
      1953. NORMAN J. COLMAN AND COLMAN'S RURAL WORLD: A STUDY IN AGRI-
             CULTURAL LEADERSHIP. Univ. Mo. Studies, v. 25, No. 3, 168 pp.
(15) MONEY, H. D.
      1882. DEPARTMENT OF AGRICULTURE. Cong. Rec., 47th Cong., 1st Sess.,
             pp. 3755–57, 3768.
(16) MORRILL, J. S.
      1858. AGRICULTURAL COLLEGES. Cong. Globe, 35th Cong., 1st Sess.,
             pp. 1692–1697.
(17) NATIONAL AGRICULTURAL CONVENTION.
      1872. PROCEEDINGS OF THE NATIONAL AGRICULTURAL CONVENTION HELD AT
             WASHINGTON, FEBRUARY 15, 16, AND 17, 1872. 84 pp. (U.S. Con-
             gress, 42d, 2d Sess., Senate Misc. Doc. 164.)
(18) OSBORNE, E. A., EDITOR.
      1913. FROM THE LETTER-FILES OF S. W. JOHNSON. . . . 292 pp., illus.
             New Haven.
(19) PLUMB, P. B.
      1887. [DEBATE ON HATCH BILL.] Cong. Rec., 49th Cong., 2d Sess.
             pp. 1081–1082.
(20) TOWNSHEND, N. S.
      1881. AGRICULTURAL MEETING AT LANSING, MICHIGAN. Ohio State Bd.
             Agr. Ann. Rpt. 35: 388–393.
(21) TRUE, A. C.
      1937. A HISTORY OF AGRICULTURAL EXPERIMENTATION AND RESEARCH IN
             THE UNITED STATES, 1607–1925. U.S. Dept. Agr. Misc. Pub. 251,
             321 pp., illus.
(22) UNITED STATES CONGRESS, HOUSE COMMITTEE ON AGRICULTURE.
      1884. [CULLEN BILL.] Report H.R. 2034, to accompany H.R. 7498, on
             agricultural experiment stations. 3 pp. (U.S. Congress, 48th,
             1st Sess.)
(23) ———
      1886. [HATCH BILL.] Report H.R. 848, to accompany H.R. 2933, on agri-
             cultural experiment stations. 9 pp. (U.S. Congress, 49th,
             1st Sess.)
(24) UNITED STATES CONGRESS, SENATE.
      1887. [DEBATE ON HATCH BILL.] Cong. Rec., 49th Cong., 2d Sess. pp.
             1039–1046.

53

Chapter Five—
ASSOCIATION AND THE
ADMINISTRATION OF RESEARCH

Research-minded men at the land-grant colleges attempted, simultaneously with their efforts toward station-founding soon after the ending of the Civil War, to organize an intercollegiate association devoted to promoting efficient experimentation. The movement to establish a permanent organization of college officials made its first significant appearance when the Friends of Agricultural Education convened at Chicago in 1871. The initial proposal to hold that convention originated with Willard Flagg, secretary of the board of trustees at the Illinois Industrial University, and Manly Miles, professor of practical agriculture at the Michigan Agricultural College. The two men, both busily engaged in conducting field tests at their respective colleges, conferred and agreed that a conference of collegiate experimenters would provide timely aid to all who were encountering difficulties in obtaining accurate data.

Flagg and Miles saw clearly that their proposed conference could lead not only to systematizing current procedures but also to holding regular meetings in future to develop and administer an expanded program of intercollegiate experimentation. When the two planners attempted to prepare an invitation list, however, they discovered that they did not know the names of the men who held the professorships of agriculture and the farm superintendencies in many of the land-grant colleges throughout the Nation. Accordingly, the pair decided to communicate with the college presidents, and through those officials extend an invitation to the experimenters on each faculty (*7, p. 312*).[1]

Meanwhile, Willard Flagg, intent on encouraging a station movement, secured the official support of John M. Gregory, president of Flagg's institution, who decided to contact the presidents directly and include them as participants. Consequently, the Gregory call addressed a much broader constituency than that originally anticipated by Secretary Flagg or desired by Professor Miles. President Gregory (*7, p. 215*) invited to the convention the following:

. . . Presidents of Agricultural Colleges, Professors of Agriculture, or other persons in the United States or British Provinces who are engaged or interested in promoting the art or science of Agriculture by experiments in the field or laboratory, for the purpose of organizing, consulting and cooperating in the great work of advancing the cause of Agricultural knowledge and especially by experimentation with similar crops under similar conditions at all the Agricultural Colleges.

This invitation indicated that the discussions would stress subject matter of occupational concern to agricultural experimenters; yet it did not limit attendance to practitioners nor confine the discussion to problems in scientific research. On the contrary, Gregory presented first of all to the college presidents the opportunity for "organizing, consulting and cooperating in the great work of advancing the cause

---

[1] Italic numbers in parentheses refer to Literature Cited, p. 79.

of agricultural knowledge and education." The course of the resulting convention, which included an articulate representation of education-minded presidents as well as a group of experiment-minded professors, soon revealed that politeness alone did not prompt President Gregory to urge presidential participation.

LAND-GRANT ASSOCIATION PROPOSED

Early in the sessions at Chicago, Flagg introduced a proposal to create a formal association (7, p. 221). "Some of us," he remarked, "had a plan under consideration of forming a permanent organization, to meet from year to year, or oftener, for the purpose of continuing consultation, experimentation, and comparison of experimentation, and the continuous laying out of experiments to be performed in common. . . ." An organization concentrating on this single objective, though immediately attractive to the technical experimenter, would obviously have a limited appeal for the presidents. At this point Flagg raised an alternative possibility, one dear to President Gregory's heart. "Perhaps," he added, "the organization ought to go furthery Perhaps it ought to be an organization of the Agricultural Colleges and Technological Schools." This proposition delighted the presidents and the several college trustees present. Nevertheless, it evoked an outspoken division of opinion among the conferees, and it placed Flagg and Miles in opposing camps.

Professor Miles unflinchingly contended that the proposed association ought to deal exclusively with the technical problems implicit in conducting research and, therefore, should limit its membership to the personnel performing the investigations. "It seems to me almost impossible," he announced, "for anyone to discuss this subject of experimentation unless they [sic] are actually engaged in it; they cannot see the force of the arguments; they cannot understand them." Furthermore, Miles disapproved the creation, within a land-grant association of versatile activities, of a section for experimenters and their technical concerns; such a section "would . . . be subject, to a certain extent, to that wider organization. . . ." Having listened to the presidents, as one by one they pleaded for a permanent association enabling college educator-administrators to discuss problems not pertaining to research, Miles recommended, "Make the larger organization an independent one; and then arrange to have the meetings [of the experimenters] at the same time and place" (7, p. 309).

Thus Miles sensed from the outset that an incompatibility of interest between the professional researchers and the professional educators would mark the career of a comprehensive association of land-grant college officials. Lest the presidents accuse him of harboring a narrow-minded antagonism against them, Miles hastened to welcome the college leaders. "We would like to have the Presidents here every time," he declared. Nevertheless, he unrelentingly maintained his position that the association should single-mindedly serve "those who are engaged in experimenting" (7, p. 312).

Flagg disagreed, however, with the Miles analysis. He did not detect any immediate disadvantage in extending membership to all persons interested in land-grant education and especially in the welfare of the Morrill Act colleges. Just as Gregory supported Flagg's sponsorship of the station movement so Flagg sympathized with

Gregory's wish for a formalized association wherein college presidents could deal with the problems of institutional management. Flagg recognized that the presidents needed an association fully as much as did the professorial experimenters. He, unlike Miles, saw no serious separateness of interest between college administration and agricultural research; he saw both activities as vital and complementary efforts "in the general interests of agriculture" (7, p. 313). All workers for agricultural improvement, he observed, shared a "community of sentiment and community of interest" in the land-grant college enterprise (7, p. 299).

Yet Flagg reserved final judgment. The study of agriculture had thus far attracted so few professional devotees, he believed, that a sense of unity should bind them together. "There are not so many of them, as yet," he reminded the convention, "that they would stand in one another's way." Further developments, however, could change the course of association. "The time may come," he conceded, "when it will be necessary to go either into separate sections in the same convention, or else to form a separate convention of experimenters" (7, p. 307).

The professors at the Chicago convention found themselves torn between the divergent viewpoints. They could not easily deny that presidential jurisdiction did properly apply to the research activities of the staff members who, not acting independently of the colleges, used college facilities in their investigations (7, p. 309). Similarly, did not the responsibilities of the presidential office, alike to the trustees and to the public, require each incumbent to understand the trends of research inquiry and to have a voice in making research policy?

The presidents at the convention did not divide ranks; steadily they pressed their advantage and discouraged the convention from forming an organization which would favor the Miles position and thus eliminate them from practical participation. "I don't want any one question," President Adonijah S. Welch of Iowa Agricultural College pronounced in positive tones as he strove to prevent the research specialists from organizing an exclusive body, "or any one specific individual purpose, however important, to absorb the energies of the association, but I want it to gather within all the important topics that must occupy the attention of men who have these institutions in their charge" (7, p. 303).

President Gregory, chairman of the Chicago meeting, encouraged a candid discussion of this divisive issue in order to aid the convention's Executive Committee, which he headed, in the framing of a constitution for the projected association. Chiefly responsible, therefore, for carrying out the convention's directive to draft the organic document, Gregory needed to learn the sentiment of the conventioneers regarding objects and membership (7, p. 297). Gregory guided the group by describing the European experience, as follows:

I know that the experimental stations in Europe have an annual meeting of all the experimenters and chemists—those interested, and the rest of the institution is not represented, nor are its interests represented. They meet in the annual Convention to report upon their experiments, and to discuss conditions of experimentation, and to arrange for experiments; and they meet for that purpose alone, and it is a matter which fully occupies their time and attention. The difficulty in an organization which should embrace all the interests that are represented in an industrial institution, would be this: that we would be as we are now, crowded for time. . . .

Now it remains with this Convention, it seems to me, to determine whether the organization that is proposed to be made, should be an organization like that of the European, for discussion for experiments, reporting experiments, and arranging experiments; or whether it shall be a Convention of educators in these schools who will meet to discuss the general management of schools, experiments included.

The convention did not, despite the specific delineation in the Gregory instruction, make a decision on the controversial theme of constitutional organization. It left the difficult decision as a task for the convention officers after adjournment. Yet those officials did not produce a plan of organization; the Gregory committee presumably found the problem of constitution-making to be equally as difficult in 1871 as that of station-founding. An association did not, therefore, come into existence in the seventies, the decade of discouragements for the college-connected stations.

MOVEMENT REVIVED

The revival of the movement to establish an association coincided with the effort of the Teachers of Agriculture to establish State-sponsored stations. The professors who gathered at Michigan State College in 1881, having already declared station-founding to be an urgent need in every State, sought an administrative arrangement that would enable each station to keep informed of work done at all other stations. "At least once a year," their committee report recommended (11) "those having charge of the experimental work shall meet and review the work done, consider what is required, then by mutual agreement distribute new work, according to the means at the disposal or the special facilities of each institution." Heartily endorsing, in effect, the Miles proposition announced a decade earlier, the Teachers viewed an association of experimenters as a necessary element in the functioning of intercollegiate experimentation at the proposed stations. The absence of a presidential delegation permitted the conference to avoid the friction that the convention of 1871 had generated. The Teachers thereupon passed the following resolutions:

That the agricultural colleges and State experiment stations here represented, so far as the same may be subject to our advice and control, are hereby united as an association for more systematic and efficient experimental work. That each college or station shall report to the Secretary of this association what experimental work it has already done, and what kind and amount of work it is prepared to do . . . .

That all other agricultural colleges and State experimental stations be cordially invited to join this association and co-operate in its work.

In this way the representatives of eight midwestern colleges created an association, regional in fact but national in theory, which anticipated sending reports of research activity to the Department of Agriculture for nationwide distribution. In practice, however, the new organization did not operate as its overly optimistic sponsors had announced in 1881. Though its members met annually until the passage of the Hatch Act, they did not maintain a primary interest in research; instead they soon veered to an emphasis on the problems of college teaching. Their meetings remained informal and did not become national in appeal or scope. Thus the Teachers relinquished leadership in the emerging movement for the Hatch Act, and also in the activities soon to produce a formal and permanent association.

Samuel W. Johnson, 1830–1909

America's first advocate of agricultural research. His efforts led to the establishment in 1876 of the Connecticut Agricultural Experiment Station—first in the United States.

Wilbur O. Atwater, 1844–1907

First director of the Office of Experiment Stations, and a pioneer in agricultural experiment station work in the United States.

Willard C. Flagg, 1829–1878

Illinois educator who helped establish the scope of agricultural research.

John M. Gregory, 1822–1898

First regent of Illinois Industrial University, now the University of Illinois, and eminent leader in agricultural education.

| **George H. Cook, 1818–1889** | **Eugene W. Hilgard, 1833–1916** |
| First director of the New Jersey Agricultural Experiment Station. | A leader in agricultural research and in the movement to establish agricultural experiment stations in the United States. |

Meeting in Washington of representatives of agricultural colleges and experiment stations, July 8–9, 1885.

Henry P. Armsby, 1853–1921

An outstanding research scientist in animal nutrition work, and president of the Association of American Agricultural Colleges and Experiment Stations, 1898–99.

William A. Henry, 1850–1932

President, Association of American Agricultural Colleges and Experiment Stations, 1892–93, and Dean, College of Agriculture, University of Wisconsin, 1887–1907.

Whitman H. Jordan, 1851–1931

Director of New York Agricultural Experiment Station at Geneva, and champion of the plan to separate research and teaching at land-grant colleges.

George E. Morrow, 1840–1900

Dean of the College of Agriculture, Illinois, and a pioneer in research on the production and rotation of crops.

Eugene Davenport, 1856–1941

Dean, College of Agriculture, University of Illinois, 1895–1922, and president of the Association of American Agricultural Colleges and Experiment Stations, 1917–19.

Alfred C. True, 1853–1929

Distinguished director of the Office of Experiment Stations from 1893 to 1915, and director of the States Relations Service from 1915 to 1923. Dr. True made notable contributions to the development of agricultural education and research in the United States. He was president of the Association of American Agricultural Colleges and Experiment Stations, 1913–14.

Established in 1876, the Morrow Plots on the campus of the University of Illinois are the oldest continuous soil experiment plots in the United States. Each year they are visited by many people from all over the world.

Orange Judd Hall at Wesleyan University, Middletown, Conn., where the Connecticut Agricultural Experiment Station—first in the United States—was situated from 1875 to 1877.

Aerial view of the University of California at Davis.

Main buildings of the Ohio Agricultural Experiment Station, Wooster, at the turn of the century.

Aerial view of the Ohio station campus as it looks today.

One of the first devices for measuring respiratory quotient and body heat losses on large animals was developed before 1900 by the Pennsylvania Experiment Station. Called the Armsby respiration calorimeter, it was named after Dr. Henry P. Armsby, one of the pioneers in scientific nutrition work.

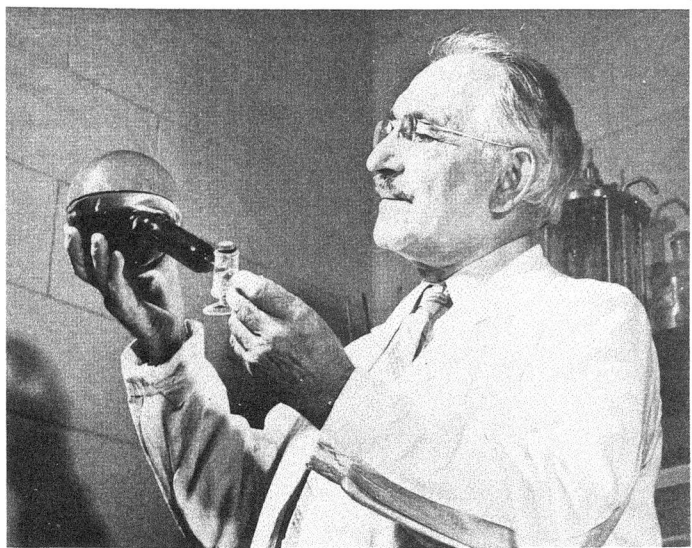

This 1945 photo shows Dr. Selman A. Waksman, New Jersey Agricultural Experiment Station, holding a culture of the organism that produces streptomycin, which he and his associates discovered in 1943, as a result of their work with soil micro-organisms.

Pineapple grown following recommendations of the Agricultural Experiment Station, Puerto Rico, as to control nematodes, insect pests and adequate fertilization.

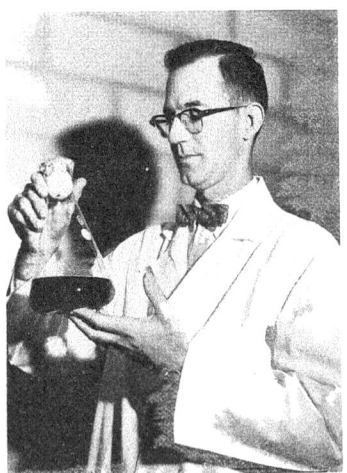

Poultry scientists at the Delaware Agricultural Experiment Station have made much progress in reducing incidence and spread of poultry diseases. Here Dr. William J. Benton examines a solution used in studying avian leucosis.

The national conventions called by Commissioner Loring in 1882 and 1883 opened a new opportunity for land-grant presidents and professors. The sessions enabled the delegates not only to discuss problems in teaching and research but also to perceive the value of meeting regularly for transacting business. No figure at these conventions showed greater skill in winning a position on key committees than President George W. Atherton of the Pennsylvania State College; likewise none worked more determinedly and promptly than he to make land-grant conventions an annual event. Until 1885, however, the power to convene land-grant delegates under Departmental auspices remained in practice with Commissioner Loring, who declined to circulate a call in 1884. The exercise of the convening power passed to land-grant organizers in 1885 when the new Commissioner, Norman Colman, presented unexampled encouragement by inviting delegates from the agricultural colleges and experiment stations to meet in Washington, D.C.

Commissioner Colman granted to the delegates the authority to take action on three pertinent topics: (1) Cooperation between the colleges and the Department; (2) establishment of experiment stations; (3) uniformity in methods of experimenting.

The Colman call did not direct the business of the convention toward college problems, apart from the college and station relationship to the Department and to Congress, except in one incidental passage. "Many other cognate questions," Colman wrote (6), "will suggest themselves." His emphasis on the subject of research did not mean that he did not sympathize with the college educators. On the contrary, as a trustee of the Missouri State College, Colman well knew the exasperating difficulties facing the college presidents in their earnest efforts to popularize the agricultural curricula. Precisely because their difficulties troubled him, Colman offered his help to college officials, and insisted that the convention find ways to institutionalize research activity as effectively as possible. Colman urged, in short, that the colleges make the conduct of research their indelible and identifying characteristic. For this reason he attempted in his welcoming address to fix the attention of the convention on experimentation. "In my judgment," he remarked for the particular benefit of the presidents assembled, "there is nothing which will attract and rivet the attention of the great agricultural public to our agricultural colleges so much as experimental work."

The discussions at the convention did not proceed single-mindedly; nevertheless, on the subject that Colman recommended, namely the administration of research, Professor Seaman A. Knapp, impatient because presidential spokesmen on the first day steered attention away from the problems of research to those of teaching, pinpointed the topic deserving treatment. "How can we practically cooperate," he asked (6, p. 66), "with the Department of Agriculture in carrying on this experimental work?" President Atherton, however, promptly denied Knapp's interpretation of the reason for the Colman call. "We came here," he rejoined (6, p. 67), ". . . not at all with a view to subordinate all others to the one question which . . . [Professor] Knapp suggests."

Atherton wished the convention to devote only a small portion of its time and attention to the administrative functioning of research; instead he urged the convention to effect cooperation between the Department and the colleges in a broad span of issues covering the entire field of agricultural education. In Atherton's view the paramount problem of collegiate attunement to the public involved factors in addition to research alone. Moreover, he sensed that the Colman convention, if skillfully encouraged, could serve as a launching site for a permanent land-grant association holding similar conventions in future.

The divergence in objectives between Atherton and Knapp revealed that the divisive issue of 1871 persisted. President Atherton, like his predecessors in 1871 and his presidential colleagues in 1885, challenged the bid of the partisans of research to use the Colman convention, in effect a temporary association of land-grant personnel, primarily for their purposes.

The pendulum swung to the Atherton position early in the sessions when Colman as presiding officer appointed to the key committee on resolutions and order of business, in addition to Professor Knapp, and Director Henry Elijah Alvord of the Houghton Farm Experiment Station, a panel of four presidents including Atherton. The Commissioner might have selected his appointees from a number of prominent station directors and professors of long experience present at the convention, such as G. H. Cook, C. A. Goessmann, A. R. Ledoux, W. R. Lazenby, I. P. Roberts, E. L. Sturtevant, N. S. Townshend. Yet Colman favored the presidents, men who soon demonstrated their ability to hold the floor.

An outspoken Missourian, Professor J. W. Sanborn (*6, p. 24*), immediately perceiving the consequences of Colman's policy of selection, informed the Commissioner, "On that committee . . . the experiment stations of the country are not represented. . . ." Sanborn's alertness resulted in the additional appointment of Director Charles W. Dabney of the North Carolina station. The decisions of the president-weighted committee soon revealed that the convention would not proceed on the single premise that the delegates would search only for ways to accelerate the efficiency of the research process, but rather on the basis that the conventioneers would consider only those propositions which would assist the colleges to strengthen themselves as educational institutions.

RESOLUTIONS DRAFTED

The committee on order of business used this latter principle in drafting resolutions which, when accepted by the convention, would implement the three objectives announced in the Colman call. The committee endorsed the Cullen bill, which proposed to establish stations exclusively under collegiate jurisdiction (*6, p. 42*). Having acted in this way on one item of the Colman agenda, the committee then acted on a second; it drafted a plan of cooperation (*6, p. 90*), as follows:

Whereas one principal object is the establishment of closer relations between the Department of Agriculture and all institutions systematically engaged in active labors for agricultural progress; therefore,

Resolved, That in the opinion of this convention the first practical measure to secure cooperation is the creation of a bureau or division in the Department of Agriculture, supplied with the necessary clerical force, which shall be the special medium of intercommunication and exchange between the institutions intended

to be represented by this convention and the central office in charge of the details of this general plan of cooperation.

Resolved, That this convention respectfully recommends to the Commissioner, as one of the most important functions of the proposed bureau, the compilation and publication of a periodical bulletin of agricultural progress. . . . This bulletin should contain, in a popular form, ready for the use of the people and the press, the latest experience and results in the progress of agricultural education, investigation. and experimentation, in this and in all other countries.

Thus the committee studiously avoided the position that the "special medium of intercommunication and exchange" in the Department should deal only with research matters, although the conventions since 1872 had regularly recommended the formation of such an agency for aiding the coordination of experimental activity (*6, pp. 103–104*). Moreover, the committee of 1885 assigned, as the first function of the recommended periodical bulletin, the reporting for popular consumption of "progress in agricultural education;" a responsibility preceding that of "investigation and experimentation." This same committee then arranged the program in such a way that numerous speakers could dwell on college rather than station concerns. President Edwin Willits (*6, p. 67*), the able successor of T. C. Abbot at Michigan, revealed the underlying concern of the college presidents when he remarked, "I would like to have you devise, if you can, any system of instruction that will lead the boys, that shall draw the boys, to the institution. . . ."

This preoccupation of the program committee prevented the research-minded men in the convention from discussing the last of Colman's assignments (and the first of Knapp's hopes), namely, the methodology to be followed in arranging immediate experimentation between college researchers and those in the Department. Research interested the presidents only so far as it might be able, in practice, to popularize the colleges; the projected stations appealed to them for the same reason. The approval by the convention of the committee's major resolutions, the assurance that the forthcoming stations would be tied securely to the colleges, Colman's willingness to cooperate with the colleges in the cause of education, the success in the effort to prevent the researchers from dominating the convention and the purposes of "cooperation"—all these points strengthened the presidential position which Atherton had insistently presented at the opening of the convention.

Colman capped the triumph by appointing President Atherton, Willits, and Stephen D. Lee as a legislative committee to collaborate with the Commissioner in persuading Congressmen to enact the Cullen bill. Atherton, who had already championed the Cullen bill before the House Committee on Agriculture in 1884 (*6, p. 41*), headed this committee on Capitol Hill. His capable lobbying aided the passage of the station legislation, a role which in later conventions gave him the prestige of founding father.

Thus Atherton early emerged as a champion of the station movement. In his attitude toward the stations, however, he contended consistently from the mid-eighties and thereafter that the Cullen and Hatch measures were designed solely to assist the *colleges* and to enable them to do via the stations the educational work which heretofore a lack of college funds prohibited. Atherton had small concern for the technical difficulties confronting the scientist; his interest and sympathy, like those of nearly all the college presidents of his day, lay with the prospect of perfecting the public relations of the college, and only incidentally with providing for research men the administrative aids and opportunities which in their judgment would enable the most efficient conduct of research.

The convention of 1885 brought Atherton into prominence, and before adjournment it gave him a key position in the formulation of a permanent association (*6, p. 138–139*). On the evening of July 9, 1885, Henry Alvord of the resolutions committee moved that the current convention "be perpetuated by the appointment of a general committee to be composed of one from each State and Territory; that the chairman of that committee be now elected, and that he be empowered to name from that committee an executive committee of five."

President Willits in the chair promptly recognized President Lee, who from the floor nominated President Atherton for the chairmanship of the new executive committee. The convention by Alvord's resolution then assigned to this Atherton committee the duty of acting for the convention *ad interim*, and in addition stipulated as follows: ". . . the executive committee shall, cooperating with the Commissioner of Agriculture, determine the time of holding the next convention, provide a well-prepared order of business and programme of exercises, and a plan for permanent organization, and that the programme be issued in connection with the call reassembling this convention."

The decisions reached on the evening of July 9, 1885, guaranteed that the presidents would participate prominently in the membership and management of the emerging permanent association. They disclosed that the men of the Morrill Act colleges instinctively understood that an association could perform a variety of useful services for its members; they further revealed that their cause of tax-supported collegiate education needed, for effective promotion, the integrated skills of dedicated trustees and teachers, presidents and professors, and specialists in public relations as well as experts in the classrooms and laboratories.

Within this broad framework, nevertheless, the sessions of 1885 demonstrated, as the earlier conventions of 1871, 1872, 1882, and 1883 had done, that educators immediately needed the association for one purpose, and researchers needed it for another purpose. The researchers sought to develop a scientific technology for productive experimentation and concurrently to devise techniques for administering an institution for agricultural research. The presidents drew inspiration from the Morrill doctrine of public education which invited able administrators to diversify, practically without limit, their instructional offerings and not necessarily confine the curricula to an agricultural emphasis.

The men of 1885, as they voted to perpetuate their assemblage in an association, faced in a vastly enlarged context the same problem—the role of research in institutions dedicated to teaching—which had troubled Professor Johnston in Scotland 40 years earlier. Yet no man raised his voice to disturb the harmony of the session on that July evening in 1885 by insisting that the prospective association in its objectives delineate between experimentation and dissemination, between research and teaching, between the stations and the colleges.

ASSOCIATION GAINED PROMINENCE

The emerging association did not achieve formal organization, however, until 6 month after passage of the Hatch Act. George Atherton
called delegates to a convention in Washington, D.C. in October 1887.
Of the 35 conventioneers, approximately half held appointments as
college presidents while the remaining figures occupied positions as
college professors or as the directors of a number of stations organized
prior to the Hatch Act (8).

Colman's chairmanship at the opening session speedily enabled the
presidents to gain parliamentary prominence. They secured on all
the committees a representation decisively outnumbering the professors and the directors; in like fashion they dominated the nominating
committee and the panel of officers selected for the following year.
Atherton received the presidency of this formally constituted Association of American Agricultural Colleges and Experiment Stations, a
post he retained for the following 2 years.

Only four men with directorial experience won committee posts
commensurate in influence with those of the presidents; namely,
Henry Alvord, formerly of Houghton Farm but soon to take the
presidency of the Maryland State College; Charles Dabney, currently
of the Tennessee station but forthwith to win the presidential chair
at Knoxville; William A. Henry of Wisconsin, and Charles E. Thorne
of Ohio, both of whom would continue as directors for the remainder
of their careers.

The course of this maiden convention revealed clearly that the
presidents did not intend to surrender their control of the formalized
Association or of station policy in the formative years. At the same
time, however, the college executives exhibited an acute and almost
proprietary interest in the stations. Already favored with a Federal
income surpassing the entire yearly revenue of some of the colleges,
the stations had the capacity to obtain widespread popular approval
for the Morrill Act colleges by placing themselves in the farmers'
service. The new constitution, submitted by the committee on executive organization and adopted by the convention, granted the stations
distinct autonomy within the Association and a role of equality with
the colleges. "The object of this Association" the initial paragraph
of the constitution stated (12, p. 13), "shall be the consideration and
discussion of all questions pertaining to the successful progress and
administration of the colleges and stations included in this
Association."

That constitution also gave one vote, in making decisions on the
business of the Association, to each station as well as to each college.
The Hatch Act, technically considered, assigned to each college-connected station a departmental status and, therefore, not a position of
equality with the college, itself a collection of departments. The
action of the convention in 1887, however, did make the stations
co-equal members of the Association. It tacitly recognized the long
history of the station movement as an institutional force; it further
indicated that in the presidents' judgment the Hatch term "department" meant only that each station must have an organic tie to the
college, but in other respects should have a freedom of action befitting the importance of its research function. So important a role
did the new station play in collegiate planning, moreover, that soon

63

many a college president assumed, in addition to his other duties, the directorship of the Hatch station.

A well-defined relationship had not yet crystallized, however, between the research institutions and the colleges authorized by law to acquire them. The Hatch Act, silent on the administrative details of this connection, provided simply that the station should operate as a department "under direction of the college." That act, unlike the Cullen and Knapp drafts preceding it, nowhere mentioned the word "director" and did not specify the powers, duties, qualifications, and rank of the departmental administrator. Sharp-eyed Director Dabney, determined that the Association should clarify the status of the "department," early in the session moved the appointment of a committee instructed "to report a plan for the organization [and] executive management" of the stations (8).

This show of initiative won for Dabney the committee chairmanship.

The Dabney committee, to which Alvord also won an appointment in company with three presidents, submitted to the convention a set of "advisory propositions." This statement of policy, which Alvord later called a "declaration of principles" (1), the committee reported as its interpretation of the station-college relationship intended in the Hatch legislation. "The department," the Dabney report declared, "should be distinctly organized, with its duties and control clearly defined, and with a recognized official head, whose time shall be chiefly devoted to this department...." The report differentiated the operations of station and college when it carefully enunciated the standards to be observed in the expenditure of the Federal funds, as follows:

... all appropriations ... should be applied in good faith to agricultural research and experiment, and the dissemination of the results thereof among the people and that any diversion of funds to the general uses of the college would be a direct violation of the plain spirit and intent of the law, and an inexcusable disappointment of just public expectations.
... the experiment stations ... should be so far separate and distinct from the colleges that it shall be possible at any moment to show ... that all the funds ... have been expended solely for the purposes of agricultural experimentation according to the intent of the law.

The adoption of the Dabney report set a major precedent for the Association and the stations, for the Association thus began its formal business by deliberating on the welfare of the college-connected stations, a concern which in future would occupy many sessions. The advisory propositions in the Dabney report, though significant for differentiating the work of the station from that of the college, nevertheless did not solve the technical difficulties implicit in operating efficient stations in the numerous colleges having no nucleus of skilled researchers with station experience. The spokesmen of 1887 soon perceived the pertinent issues affecting the management of the Hatch-assisted stations (5, p. 3). How, for example, should station activity be started and efficiently conducted? What equipment did investigators need? What lines of research should be selected? How to make available the scientific data which agricultural scientists, especially the European ones, had been accumulating for a half-century? How and what to teach the farmer? These searching queries drove home the realization that station administration would be no easy matter.

For answers, the convention turned to three of its members, Pro-

fessors Atwater, Johnson, and Cook, whose combined experience in the administration of agricultural research surpassed that of their fellow-conventioneers. The convention, acting earnestly and almost desperately, assigned to this trio the impossible task of preparing a report advising inexperienced administrators how to operate the institutions that the Hatch Act would presently spawn. Each of these scientists, from the youthful Atwater to the aging Cook, had gained their administrative skills by studying at close range through a long period of years the particular problems of their individual States. Each had worked out a personalized solution to the questions posed by the convention. Each could have taught his technique via a teacher-student apprenticeship. Yet none could prescribe on paper a set of precise procedures which men, lacking a rigorous scientific training and a longstanding preoccupation with farmer-oriented research, might immediately apply to produce a system of smoothly functioning administration. The three committeemen saw clearly that each new station, like its pioneering predecessors, had no choice but to make its own way and learn by experience; accordingly they elected "simply to inquire and to suggest."

POLICIES ESTABLISHED

The committee used the 30 pages of its report (5) primarily to record the replies of various station officials to the committee's circular requesting a statement of anticipated experimental work. It took the opportunity, however, to stress several problems unavoidably confronting the station enterprise. Station administrators should recognize at the outset, the report urged, that in the interest of scientific research they must devise "means for making the results of accumulated experience conveniently available to the station and their workers." Essentially this service meant a "compilation of the main results" of foreign research and a translation into English "in forms conveniently suited to the use of the American investigators." It further entailed "the preparation of monographs, which should embody not only the results of investigations but descriptions of apparatus and methods of research." The rapidly enlarging station movement must, in short, operate on "the obvious principle that the first condition of successful research is full knowledge of what has been done."

Finally the committeemen in concluding their report earnestly reminded the governing boards to observe the following policy in determining the "general character" of the station work:

It is essential that they [the stations] recognize the immediate demand for things immediately useful; that they find what questions are of direct practical importance, and give such questions an amount of early attention which under other circumstances might be disproportionate. But it is vitally important that the highest scientific ideal be maintained and every effort be made toward its realization. The future usefulness of the stations will depend upon what they discover of permanent value and this must come largely from the most abstract and profound research; to forget this will be fatal.

The stations must also remember that it is their office not only to experiment, but to teach; that it is their duty to gather information as well from accumulated stores as from the fields in which they are working, and to bring it, not 'down to the farmer,' but home to him. By thus using their most honest and earnest effort to help the farmer they will secure from him and from the public at large the support they need for their highest work.

This valedictory expression of seasoned philosophy set a high standard of performance for the Hatch stations. The appearance of this Report on Station Work, the first publication to be issued at the direction of the infant Association, in like fashion identified that Association with the nurture of meaningful research in its member institutions.

The Atwater-Johnson-Cook Report (5) gave astute advice on policy, but it did not present the procedures immediately needed by station administrators to meet a set of practical problems. The report did not enumerate the ways in which the new stations, in order to accommodate the best interests of the station, the college, the farmer, and scientific research as well, could establish an effective rapport with the farm population. It declined to propose any techniques of intercommunication among the stations, on the ground that such proposals lay by the action of the conventions of 1885 and 1887 within the province of the Commissioner of Agriculture. It therefore did not offer methods whereby the Commissioner could exercise the advisory powers allotted in the Hatch Act and thus assist the stations. It guardedly approved the principle of cooperative experimentation among regional stations interested in similar subjects of investigation, but it preferred to leave this activity solely to the initiative and discretion of the individual stations. Thus here, too, it drew on blueprint for the deliberate encouragement of cooperative effort among the stations. Likewise, the authors of the report completely avoided the problem of the administrative relationship between the station and the college, an abstention befitting men whose experience had been largely confined to the management of independent stations.

The seriousness of the issues confronting the stations plus the lack of ready solutions prompted the new Association to convene its membership in early January of 1889 for the concentrated purpose of discussing and taking action on this set of problems (12, pp. 11, 26). The executive committee under Alvord's leadership assigned to station directors the responsibility for presenting papers and leading discussions on the troublesome subjects which in one form or another beset every Hatch station.

For 3 days the conventioneers at Knoxville deliberated and resolved, yet in the end they did not advance beyond the position taken in the Atwater-Johnson-Cook Report. In their adopted resolutions they specified several activities through which the station personnel could volunteer their help and advertise their services for the farmers; they entrusted to the care of the newly-created Office of Experiment Stations, to whose directorship Commissioner Colman had appointed Dr. Atwater, the selection of devices for Federal assistance to the station enterprise; and they left interstation cooperation on a voluntary basis (12, pp. 81–96). Thus the problems which had prompted the Association to convene remained frustratingly unsolved; that they would be hardy perennials in future meetings, any observer could easily have predicted.

Moreover, the Knoxville convention struck ledge on two controversies which during the next decade repeatedly disturbed the annual meetings and seriously threatened the unity of the Association itself. Symbolic of its primary importance, one controversy appeared at the top of the Knoxville agenda: "The relation of colleges and stations" (12, p. 26). This issue, significantly the only one on which the convention of 1889 avoided taking action (*12, pp. 98, 99*), carried over persistently into later conventions and led almost to a breach between the directors and the presidents. The other controversy had no formal position on the program at Knoxville; voluntarily, it emerged when Henry Prentiss Armsby, the director of the Pennsylvania station, attempted to change the organizational structure of the Association. This movement, which also persisted past the turn of the century before it achieved success, reopened the schismatic debate between the directors of scientific research and the college presidents.

Director Armsby, a product of Johnson–Atwater training, interrupted the Knoxville proceedings in order to submit a lengthy amendment to the constitution of the Association (*12, p. 98*) as follows:

There shall be two permanent sections of the Association, to be known as the "college section" and the "experiment station section."

The object of these sections shall be the discussion of such matters relating to the work of the colleges or stations as from their technical nature are unsuited to the general meetings of the Association. It shall be the duty of the executive committee, in arranging for each meeting of the Association, to provide for separate meetings of these sections, allowing such time therefor as may seem expedient, after consultation with the chairmen of the sections, and to include the programme of such meetings in the general programme. . . .

The . . . chairman, who shall be *ex officio* a member of the executive committee . . . shall also arrange for the meeting of the section in connection with each meeting of the Association, and, in conjunction with the executive committee, prepare the program for the same.

ARMSBY DELINEATED FUNCTIONS

What advantages did Armsby expect to gain by his projected reconstitution of the Association? He drew a sharp and distinct line between "experimental work" and "teaching," the two professional functions of the Association's membership; he contended that the Association should conduct its annual meetings in such fashion that it could properly "provide for the separate interests of the two classes of institutions officially represented" (*12, p. 104*). In his judgment the Association, having by now completed its survey of administrative relationships, should give no more attention to these preliminaries; instead it should proceed forthwith to carry out its main function, the discussion of "technical questions." For station researchers "methods of experimenting" would absorb countless sessions in future, while for the college teachers a different set of problems demanded attention.

Armsby further anticipated that his proposed revision would attract to the appropriate section the teachers or the stations workers, respectively, who were subject-matter specialists. To continue the present organization would, he felt, perpetuate the impression among the "workers," noticeably absent from the conventions, that the business of the Association, thus far exclusively administrative in nature, concerned only the presidents and the directors. Armsby considered it essential for the steady development of station work that the specialists in scientific research should attend in large numbers. "We want to hear the specialists talk," he declared, "and know what topics are uppermost in their minds" (*13, p. 50*).

Why did the Pennsylvania director insist on the participation of the research specialists in the annual conventions? If such men

67

habitually gathered not only to discuss their own specialties but also to consider attentively the prepared papers of their co-workers in other branches of agricultural science, then each scientist would profit by keeping abreast of the investigations and the thinking of his scientific brethren. This comprehensive learning process, Armsby believed, could not fail to advance the cause of research in agriculture, a pursuit not yet beyond a pioneer stage of development.

Yet he had a more urgent reason for wishing the immediate establishment of a section dealing exclusively with station work. His proposal would enable the station directors, who in Armsby's estimate should without exception be research scientists in their own right, to mingle with fellow scientists in their deliberations. Would not this practice promote the skillful direction of research by keeping the directors informed of evolving techniques and new trends in scientific thinking? Could it not assist the astute director to evaluate the work of his own staff, to provide him with the background essential, on occasion, to advise and inspire a perplexed staff member, and to select, in terms of the current capability of up-to-date methods, research projects promising the most enduring results?

Armsby, who yearned to become a "director who inspires" (2), sensed that his hoped-for fraternity of researchers would provide a vital stimulus to the directors. "We want something more than printed results," he declared (13, p. 50). He believed, in short, that the Association, if reorganized to permit the professional researchers the full freedom which his amendment anticipated, would intimately encourage efficiency in the administration of station research.

So important did Armsby consider professional and personal intercommunication among all station personnel that, in his view, the Association would have significant value only if it carefully programmed this activity. For the same reason he flatly opposed a division of the Association into several sections according to subject-matter specialties. The Association should not, he contended, permit the chemists, the botanists, the entomologists, and other classifications of scientists to congregate in exclusive meetings, except for brief periods. The loose federation of specialists which would result from such a policy of isolationism would endanger the cohesiveness of the Association, and also retard the growth of an essential unit of purpose among agricultural researchers. "We [researchers in agricultural science] are all one body," he maintained, "and ought to hang together" (12, p. 50). His version of an ideal structure for the Association would require the scientists to commingle and therefore "to hang together."

To the presidents and professors not primarily occupied with the conduct of research, Armsby gave equal opportunity to gather in their section for the discussion of their professional problems. Would this division into twin sections in any way impair the unity of the currently unsectioned Association? Armsby thought not. His reorganizational plan required "the two separate interests" to attend, in addition to their individual meetings, joint or general sessions dealing with the good of the land-grant charge (13, pp. 62, 63). Only the general sessions, therefore, could take official action in the name of the Association.

CONSTITUTION REVISED

The far-reaching implications of the Armsby amendment induced the delegates at Knoxville to postpone their decision to the following annual convention of the Association. The Washington Convention in November 1889 refused, unfortunately for Armsby's purpose, to divide the Association into twin sections. It revised the constitution in a different manner. The revision adopted in 1889 directed the establishment of permanent committees representing subject-matter specialties. It entitled each college and each station in the Association to membership on each permanent committee; it instructed each committee to hold conferences and to elect a chairman responsible for delivering to the general session "a report of progress in his subject during the preceding year;" and it further stipulated that each year two permanent committees, when designated by the executive committee, should "present in general sessions of the convention a portion of the subjects coming before them" (*13, p. 101*).

The adopted amendment directed the creation of separate committees for agriculture, botany, chemistry, entomology, and horticulture. The convention by resolution then added a sixth committee, a special or provisional one on college management (*13, p. 113*). In 1890 this latter committee achieved permanent status (*14, p. 43*). Also in that year the convention officially substituted the term "section" for "permanent committee" in each of the six instances. Henceforth the Section on College Work, devoted to presidential discussions on college administration, did not deal, as did the other five sections, with the problems of agricultural science.

Thus the Association, contrary to Armsby's plea in 1889, refused in the nineties to distinguish in its organization between the functions of research and teaching. Willing in practice to split into *six* sections, it nevertheless refused to split into Armsby's *two* sections. It permitted the presidents increasing freedom to pursue their objective, historic and unchanging since 1871; yet, subject to the compromise arrangement offered by the sectioning into scientific specialties, the system gave no similar encouragement to the station directors of Armsby's caliber to achieve their goal, namely, unobstructed opportunity for the prosecution of research in agriculture. Not until 1903 did the Association agree to accept the Armsby amendment of 1889 and to reorganize into two sections, one on college work and one on station work.

Why, then, did the Association postpone for 14 years its acceptance of the twin-section plan? Armsby discovered at the Washington meeting in 1889 that many of the conventioneers could not share his fixation on research, if only because their diversified collegiate duties of a nonresearch nature, particularly in the classroom, prevented them from developing a professional preoccupation with research.

The placement of the Hatch station within the college framework essentially meant that the members of the teaching staff would comprise the station force. It further meant that, except in rare instances, each investigator would do station work on a part-time basis, depending on his capacity intermittently to put aside his other collegiate concerns. Would not the division of the Association into teaching and research concentrations compel the faculty member at each convention to choose between the twin specialties, both of which in practice he must deal with on the campus? As rapid technical development occurred in the research section, might it not exclude from practical participation the teacher who did not elect to specialize in advanced research? Did not Armsby intend to hasten a specialization which, however desirable for the professional researcher and for scientific productivity, negated the principle, ingrained in the thinking of many professors and presidents alike, that the Hatch department existed in order to help the professional teacher to do some research?

The long-range implications of the Armsby position disturbed the dual-purpose staff members unwilling and unprepared to accept the view that the conduct of research, for its own sake, required specialization and undivided attention. Such men declared that the proposed reorganization would impair the unity of the Association (*13, pp. 51–53*).

The Armsby amendment evoked disapproval from other sources, as well. C. W. Dabney, who served jointly as a station director and a college president, instantly perceived that the Pennsylvanian's plan would send the presidents into the college section and the directors into the station section. No one at the convention understood more acutely than this director, currently metamorphosing into a president, that the proposal would divide the Association into two associations with divergent aims (*13, pp. 53–54*). Voicing the view of the numerous presidents who had recently added the station directorship to their presidential duties, Dabney labeled as unacceptable any arrangement that did not enable the directors and the presidents to meet together in any given session. This type of administrative dualism, therefore, added its strength to the opposition.

Moreover, presidential sentiment grew apprehensive on a related factor of fundamental significance. If research men gathered as Armsby wished, could they not become so involved in the intricacies of scientific research, and so immersed in the discovery of myopic points interesting solely to scientists, that they would lose sight of the farmer anxiously waiting for the station men to help him with his immediate problems (*13, pp. 58–59*)? Such a result would spell catastrophe for the college administrators seeking the all-important attunement with the farm population. Furthermore, would not a trend of this type, after disappointing college hopes and farm expectations, divorce station research from the many-sided commitments and "spirit" of the Hatch Act? The presidents refused to take that risk. Hence they, too, expressed grave misgivings that the plan of the Pennsylvania director would disrupt the Association.

Analysis o
United Sta
CAT87207.
U.S. Depar
[21] an
Jun 03, 201

UNITY CALLED FOR

The refusal to split into sections on college work and station work did not, however, solve the problem of reconciling the diverse objectives of the discordant groups. Each spokesman sincerely called for unity in the Association; similarly, each foresaw immediate disunity if the Association did not permit freedom of action for his group. What purpose then, should the Association serve in future? Dabney presciently observed, "This Association stands at a crisis in its history. . . . I believe that if something be not done to interest the different classes of men, this Association will almost die" (*13, pp. 53–54*).

The crisis had come in part because the presidential position foresaw the Association as a policy-making body responsible for administering intricate relationships with Federal and State Governments and with the American public as the influence of the land-grant institutions grew more pervasive. The crisis had also come because other figures, engaged in teaching and in research, demanded the discussion of "technical questions." The reorganization of the Association into permanent committees and then into six sections came as the only possible compromise which would prevent the disintegration of the young Association. This compromise lived an uneasy existence in the nineties. Not only did it compel the presidents, beset with a host of issues after the passage of the Morrill Act of 1890, to listen to scientific papers in later conventions; it also discouraged within the Association the development of a national fraternity of researchers in agricultural science.

The crisis of 1889 deeply troubled George Atherton, the chief spokesman for the college presidents and the foremost advocate of unity in the Association which he had labored to lead. Recognizing the power of the Armsby position, Atherton conceded that the conventions should discuss items of interest to scientists; nevertheless, by skillfully using his powers as the president of the Association he checked the growing movement at the Washington convention to convert the Association into a scientific society (*13, pp. 61–62*). The system of permanent committees, which in practice did not permit technical discussions to dominate the annual meetings, marked the extent of Atherton's concession; thus in the end the Association followed his wishes. Yet, despite his successful and nimble maneuvering in the crisis, he understood that the thinking which had produced the Armsby amendment would continue to undermine the Atherton version of an ideal Association.

Moreover, Atherton discerned at the conventions of 1889 a deep-running undercurrent of sentiment that the college presidents, having dealt with the administrative aspects of the stations' relationships to the colleges and to Congress, should with gentlemanly grace retire from the Association. Was it not true, so the feeling spread, that the station movement had produced the Association, which had from its birth concerned itself almost entirely with station problems? Had not the founders intended their Association as an aid for the stations rather than the colleges? Should not the membership admit that the Association could offer no congenial accommodation for the colleges and their administrators? Would not Armsby's amendment, if adopted, eventually exclude the colleges? This sentiment, if left un-

71

checked, would undeniably have produced unity—of the type that Atherton wished to avoid! This attitude needed prompt and forceful correction, in Atherton's judgment, if the Association were to achieve his standard of unity.

Other factors in the attitude spearheaded by the Armsby amendment alarmed Atherton. Did not Armsby's intensity of purpose indicate a fundamental sympathy with the goals of the independent station which, unconnected with a college, had no responsibilities to assist the land-grant colleges in institutionalizing the Morrill doctrine of broad educational service to the public?

Atherton assumed that those research-minded men who would exclude the colleges from the Association had failed to understand the land-grant philosophy of agricultural education. "The function of agricultural education," he had told the Knoxville convention in his presidential address (3), "is to teach the great mass of men that these laws [of nature] are at their feet, are about them, that they pervade and control the world, and that if man is to be wise he must be wise by knowing and obeying these laws and thus compelling them into his service." That the colleges could not, unaided, carry out this educational process, Atherton well knew. To the "research stations" he assigned the vital function of finding "the secret . . . of that great and mysterious force that we call life." Thus the colleges and the stations must bind themselves together inseparably in order to achieve the land-grant objective. Teaching and research, directed and subsidized by the Acts of 1862 and 1887, comprised Atherton's concept of essential unity. How, then, could Armsby speak of "separate interests" when they should be considered identical!

Atherton envisioned, furthermore, an intimate relationship between the land-grant educational process and the function of the Association. "The true aim and genius of this Association," he had reminded the Knoxville meeting, ". . . is not only to gather up past results, but to acquire new ones and use all for the benefit of mankind." To Atherton, the Association should be the voice of land-grant education, "of institutions . . . [and] of men, scattered all over the Union, engaged in this grand mission." Thus the unity which he pictured in his educational philosophy he expected would prevail in the Association representing it. Did not the research men understand, therefore, that they must not raise a discordant cry? In Atherton's scale of values, the good of the land-grant charge must always determine the decisions of the Association affecting the interests of the colleges or of the stations.

TWOFOLD PURPOSE SET

Nevertheless, the disunity which did mark the sessions at Washington prompted Atherton in his presidential address to drive home his view, whether station men liked it or not, that the Hatch Act indissolubly locked the stations to the colleges. Accordingly, the Association must operate on the principle that Congress intended the stations, as departments, to assist their parent colleges. The members of the Association must, therefore, harmoniously develop policies and procedures within that context. Pointedly he reiterated for the benefit of the Armsby group that the interests of the college and the station, fortunately for their joint efforts in the future, were identical, not different.

Atherton looked forward optimistically to the success of the joint enterprise, for he saw reciprocal benefit in what would be the most intimate connection between the station and the college, namely, the use of college teachers as the station staff. This identity of personnel, he predicted, would assure scientific productivity and at the same time build a harmonious interdependency between the two institutions. "Thus may it ever be," he concluded (4). "Let the college investigate that it may teach well, and the station teach that it may investigate, and this two-fold cord shall not easily be broken."

This classic statement of the college-station relationship displayed Atherton's dexterity as a polished parliamentarian. Unquestionably this president of Pennsylvania State College scored a triumph as he sought to move the station enterprise "from a right starting-point and in a right direction" (4). Who could deny the force of his view that departmental status, carefully stipulated by the presidents who had drawn the Hatch Act, placed the stations positively under college jurisdiction, and accordingly allowed to station personnel only the freedom of action which college policy chose to grant? Who, therefore, could deny the colleges a position in the Association, no matter how historic had been the researchers' movement for an exclusive body, if the colleges elected to participate? How could professional men of collegiate learning quarrel with the comprehensive breadth of educational vision? Who could insist that research men deserved greater prominence within the Association, without seeming to embody the qualities to which the Pennsylvanian had adroitly alluded (4) in his "hope that no narrowness of view, no petty jealousies springing merely from a diversity of pursuits which have a common aim . . . will ever come in to prevent the cordial, harmonious, and unselfish cooperation of each with the other?" Who, with propriety, could have disturbed the public dignity of that November evening by qualifying the tenets of that presidential address? Atherton's masterful stroke threw the "station men," as Dabney had earlier described them, completely on the defensive.

The suave phraseology of the Association's president could not disguise, however, the practical consequences of his philosophy on the administration of station research. Atherton persuasively postulated a mutually helpful and interdependent relationship between the college and its station; yet his thinking always gave precedence to the college and its interests, and it blandly ignored the farmer and his needs. The leaders of the historic station movement, on the contrary, had stipulated, as the Atwater-Johnson-Cook Report demonstrated, that the stations should exist for the farmer, not for the college. Moreover, the Atherton attitude forbade the directors to build a station force of full-time, professional investigators having no college duties. The insistence on teacher-investigator dualism doomed that practice, typical of the independent stations and incipient in the Knapp proposal of 1882. Similarly, the Atherton view admonished those directors with a career objective like that of Armsby, who stoutly maintained that a director should be "the autocrat of the station" (15, p. 90). The presidential position did not, in short, accept the axiom that the station directors should have at their disposal every possible convenience for the conduct of research.

73

Thus Atherton stressed the philosophical components of a policy which sought to tie the stations conveniently, yet securely, to a system of collegiate administration. The career-directors, however, while not necessarily disagreeing with that philosophy, thought first of all in terms of procedure. What facilities and freedom of action did the stations need for scientific productivity in agricultural research? Did the college-station relationship which Atherton lauded operate as effectively for station purposes as for college purposes; or did it need substantial revision? The Atherton philosophy assumed that this relationship would produce no problems which the individual college could not adjust satisfactorily with its departmental station. Scientists in directors' posts reached an opposite conclusion, however; and in the nineties, prominent station leaders insistently aired their dissatisfactions in the general sessions of the Association.

STATION DIRECTOR ELECTED PRESIDENT

William Arnon Henry, who had directed the Wisconsin station from its establishment in 1883, was elected president of the Association at its sixth annual convention held in New Orleans, La. in November 1892. The first station director to achieve this distinction, Henry grasped the official opportunity to plead on the rostrum the case for the stations. In sympathetic tones his 1893 presidential address (9) pointed out, as it surveyed the national scene, the serious imperfections in the "combination system" of administration which expected the college president to perform "double duty" as the station director, and which further required the professors, already overworked in the classrooms, to assume research duties as well. With climactic emphasis he inquired, "Should there not be a clearer demarcation between the duties of teacher and investigator . . . and has not our work suffered in the past because of the poor definition which now exists?" For proper management, he maintained, a station demanded the full-time attention of its director. Similarly, effective research could not be accomplished unless the investigator, freed of all but a minimum of classroom teaching, could devote his strength and his primary attention to his experimental work. "No man, however able," Henry asserted with conviction, "is properly prepared to do any considerable amount of class-room work and then conduct investigations of the grade that our experiment stations must call for in the future."

The combination system in widespread use supplied assistants, usually recent graduates, to the department heads on the college faculty. It operated in such fashion that the professors carried the teaching load, and the assistants did the station work. Henry urged a converse procedure. "If we can not have men of first grade in both station and college," he proposed, "let us have them in the station, and turn over our general instruction to the assistants."

Yet Henry would not separate his "investigators of first grade" entirely from the teaching function. "The investigators being the strongest men in the institution, were we to bring a class to them one hour a day for one term in the year, they would impart instruction of the highest possible grade." This kind of teaching, he observed, would add "the final polish" to graduating seniors. Moreover this arrangement would provide, as the combination system did not, the essential reciprocal benefit between the college and the station. "Under this system," he concluded, "we can secure the highest sort of investigation in our stations, while the young men as they leave the college will carry an inspiration and an ideal with them that can be gained in no other way."

Thus, within the context which the Hatch Act had assigned and the college presidents had praised, Henry pinpointed the improvements necessary for the effective operation of the land-grant educational process. No figure in the land-grant movement of the 19th century viewed with greater sympathy than did Dean Henry the junction of college teaching and station research. For that reason the trend of his thinking concerning the role of the station had especial significance. Intent on scientific productivity of the first order, Henry sought the same goal as the founders of the independent stations. Deeply concerned, in addition, with the collegiate teaching mission, Henry sought the same results as the champions of the Morrill Act. He would give to the station the freedom to use time and talent, place faith in the directive capacity of an astute scientist imbued with a deep sense of dedication to his craft, and charge station men with the heavy responsibility of achieving excellence in quality of product. Henry sought, in sum, to provide within the college framework an administrative format enabling the station to equal, in objective and performance and very nearly in procedure, the high standard of operational efficiency first voiced by Johnson and Atwater. In Henry's proposal, diplomatically delivered before the Association in the autumn of 1893, the American station movement found its first articulate synthesis of the Johnson-Atwater format and the Congressional directive in the Hatch Act.

Director Henry optimistically and sympathetically accounted for the serious imperfections in the college-station relationship as "incidents of pioneer effort" which would disappear as soon as their disadvantages became obvious. Nevertheless, changes came very slowly, taking not years but decades. The long-continued heaviness of the investigators' teaching load developed into a most corrosive element in the college-station relationship. On this issue the governing boards of most colleges politely but persistently procrastinated, a policy which meant to sensitive directors a stubborn refusal to grant the autonomy essential for significant achievement in research. This fundamental issue invited searching criticism from sharp-tongued station heads who, by the later nineties, spoke with less restraint than had Dean Henry.

JORDAN CHALLENGED DUAL SYSTEM

In 1897, Whitman Howard Jordan, an Atwater protege with a dozen years of directorial experience, began an attack on the combination system. He exploited the opportunity provided by the constitutional requirement of the Association that a designated section deliver a report to the general session. The chairman of the Section on Agriculture and Chemistry, Jordan used his report (10) to challenge the Atherton philosophy which sanctioned the system of teacher-investigator dualism. Jordan spoke incisively, as follows:

This combination of the teacher and investigator has been supported by the somewhat widespread declaration that a man must be a teacher in order to reach his highest mark as an investigator, a declaration that under the conditions which prevail in our State colleges I regard as an unmitigated, though perhaps comfortable, fallacy. It is, perhaps, true that a specialist may derive benefit from preparing a brief course of lectures relating to his special subjects of investigation, for in this way he is forced to clarify disputed points; but to say that the constant grind of teaching three, two, or even one hour a day, generally in elementary work, as do nearly all American college professors, is a help and inspiration to research, I regard as an absurd proposition. . . .

I raise the question, therefore, whether the interests of agricultural research in this country are not suffering because nearly all the men best equipped to carry it on are burdened with instructional duties?

In Director Jordan of the independent Geneva station, Dean Henry found an able ally. Jordan's report of 1897 pioneered a series of similar-toned speeches delivered at later conventions. For the next quarter century the Association would witness the driving energy of the New York director as he relentlessly pursued his theme. Jordan's fearless eloquence did not permit the Association to take its station members for granted, nor to underestimate the obligations which the conduct of research levied on the Association and the colleges as well as on the stations. "Research of the most severe kind" Jordan postulated in 1897 as the duty of the stations to perform, and the responsibility of the Association to insure (10). In Jordan the station movement discovered a spirited spokesman who, in the tradition of Johnson, Atwater, and Armsby, voiced the research conscience of the Association and its membership. The report of 1897 foretold an emerging position of power for Jordan in the policy-making of the Association.

The Jordan critique, though forcefully direct and penetrating, did not present a rationale sufficiently comprehensive to persuade college administrators that, for the best interests of the college as well as for the American public, the research function needed and deserved greater encouragement and freedom. Jordan's position as the director of an independent station connoted, despite his sincere purpose, a special pleading for research unadjusted to the teaching needs of the college. If Henry had seemed too patient with the demands of the college on the station, Jordan appeared overly antagonistic. Undeniably the station cause needed a reasoned statement which, placed squarely on the land-grant concept of an integrated college and station, astutely explained the historic mission of the stations and convincingly demonstrated the obligation of the colleges to assist the stations in that mission. The march of events fittingly gave that task to Henry Armsby.

ARMSBY TOOK BROAD VIEWPOINT

Director Armsby, having attained the presidency of the Association for the year 1898–99, presented as his presidential address an essay of major significance (2). With skillful brevity he challenged, point by point, every feature of the Atherton philosophy which thus far had operated to the stations' disadvantage.

To Armsby's eyes the course of the station movement both in Europe and in the United States, revealed the maturing development of an educational mission of prime importance. The German experience gave unmistakable proof that the Liebig-like investigators, though admittedly professional teachers, owed their discoveries, first, to their intensive scientific training and, second, to their remarkable freedom to use their time and their skills in research, not in undergraduate teaching duties. Furthermore the German experience showed conclusively that the most noted agricultural scientists, when permitted the greatest freedom to do basic research, produced the discoveries having the most useful and practical application to farming. Therefore, Armsby contended, American college authorities need not fear that American researchers, if given similar latitude, would ignore the farmers' welfare. If American colleges did not adopt the German policy, Armsby warned, they could not produce the type of meaningful research which alone could retain for them, in future years, the popularity currently attained by station efforts. The attunement of the college with its constituency, he informed the Association, could not exceed the effectiveness of the research conducted at the college station.

Did the college administrators fully grasp the basic meaning of the Hatch Act? The framers of that act, he stressed, had unquestionably recognized the station as "an educational institution" when they decided to incorporate with the college an agency long independent and firmly committed to aid the farmer. Obviously, Armsby continued, the college assumed the station's obligated function when it attached the station. Moreover, the Hatch Act broadened the station's role of service to the farmer because that law assigned the station a responsible share in accomplishing the land-grant objective, namely, "to give . . . [the farmer] such a practical knowledge of these natural forces as shall enable him to control them for his own advantage." For this wisdom of the Hatch founders Armsby admitted a deep thankfulness. An unattached station ran the risk of doing nothing more than helping the farmer "to raise more corn to feed more hogs to buy more land to raise more corn to feed more hogs." A college-connected station, however, if established in "an institution of liberal education" such as the leading presidential spokesmen advocated as the ideal envisioned in the Morrill Act, fortunately could receive the protection it needed to avoid this overly narrow function.

Pointedly, Armsby reminded the Association that the college had a duty, if it would be true to its Morrill-Hatch mission, to prevent a lowering of station standards. "The materialism . . . which measures the success of the station in terms of dollars and cents is totally at variance with the spirit of a true college and should find no place in an institution of liberal education." If the station were to reach an efficient and effective level of performance, he concluded, it needed help which only the college could supply; fortunately the college would, by supplying that help, help itself.

Thus Armsby examined more searchingly than Atherton the concept of reciprocal benefits in the college–station relationship. His master flourish came, however, when with a vision and phraseology as broad as Atherton's he integrated station research with the enlarging educational effort of the college, as follows:

I look confidently to the time when the agricultural college as we now know it will be but the capstone of a great system. . . . But what shall all these people, young and old, be taught, and who shall teach it to them? Where shall we find the fountain from which shall fructify and vivify this vast system, and prevent it from becoming simply a teaching machine and our teachers mere peddlers of knowledge? We shall find it precisely where it is found in all systems of education—in that first hand knowledge and familiarity with the subject which is gained by independent, original investigation—that is, we shall find it in the experiment station. It is our agricultural university devoted to the advancement of learning, the promoter of investigation, the source not merely

77

of knowledge but of inspiration for the whole organism. . . . My thesis is, then, that the most important function of the American experiment station is that of an institution for higher education in agriculture, the organic head of our whole system, and that it should be supported and managed in the light of this fact."

Thus, the college–station relationship exhibited an admirable capacity for strengthening the land-grant educational process. Yet, as Armsby specifically pointed out, the officers of both the station and the college must make concessions in order to achieve their joint objectives.

"Many station officers," he candidly commented, "are still inclined to regard the separate station as the ideal and the connection with the college as a concession to circumstances." To these men he offered blunt advice, "Discard this notion and . . . recognize the station unreservedly as an integral part of the agricultural college, with its own distinct . . . functions as an educational institution."

Similarly, for college authorities he defined the station responsibility for "higher education." This term meant a maximum of research plus the training of graduate students, who would become the next generation of teachers. The term also meant a minimum of undergraduate instruction, which remained, as always it had been, a college function. Armsby required a further concession. No longer should the president serve as director; furthermore, the director, if he would be "one who inspires," must be a professional scientist.

If the Association would accept these adjustments, the Pennsylvanian would agree that the station and the college "are not doing two distinct kinds of work, teaching and experimenting, but one, education." Likewise Armsby could then say with conviction, "This Association does not stand for two parallel but distinct sets of interests. . . . Nothing that concerns any aspect of the great problem of industrial education is foreign to its aims, and no single phase of this problem can claim any exclusive rights in its deliberations." Armsby then concluded with an evaluation used in 1889 by the men who had opposed his amendment for twin sections: "There may be diversities of judgment as regards means and methods—there can be no conflict of purpose."

Armsby in this way squarely faced the divisive issue which had troubled "station men" and "college men" for a quarter century. His concessions revealed his broad-minded diplomacy, which accepted the longstanding presidential philosophy. His demands, in turn, complemented his statesmanship, which insisted on a policy granting a practical freedom of action for research. His compromise paid tribute to the strength of the land-grant educational ideal, which now had a policy of station–college cooperation.

The unity which Armsby foresaw, however, had not yet arrived in the Association. In the midnineties presidential insistence mounted in favor of a constitutional revision which would eliminate the technical specialists from the conventions, and would reestablish the system of general sessions, open only to presidents and directors for the discussion of administrative questions. Armsby successfully led the opposition in 1897 and again 1899. This contest persisted stubbornly until 1903, when a compromise resulted.

The constitutional revision of 1903 abolished the system of sections prevailing since 1889. It divided the Association into twin sections, one on college work admitting only the president, and the other on

station work, nominally for the directors but admitting all other station officers as well (*16, pp. 13–15*). This arrangement, for the first time in the life of the Association, permitted "a single gathering of station workers" to deal with all phases of station activity (*16, pp. 193, 194*). The revision also reconstituted the Executive Committee. Henceforth the college section elected three members, and the station section two members, to that committee.

Unity within the Association, the goal of college and station men for a quarter century, for the first time became possible by 1903. Each of the twin sections had gained, after long struggle, its major historic interest, and each now had the reassurance that the other would not eliminate it from the Association. Fortunately for the station cause, the emerging unity came not a moment too soon, for in the several years to follow the station movement would undergo its sternest test.

LITERATURE CITED

(1) ALVORD, H. E.
   1896. ANNUAL ADDRESS BY THE PRESIDENT. Assoc. Amer. Agr. Cols. and Expt. Stas. Proc. (1895) 9 : 26. (U.S. Dept. Agr. Misc. Bul. 30.)
(2) ARMSBY, H. P.
   1900. PRESIDENT'S ADDRESS. Assoc. Amer. Agr. Cols. and Expt. Stas. Proc. (1899) : 13 : 22–28. (U.S. Dept. Agr. Misc. Bul. 76.)
(3) ATHERTON, G. W.
   1889. PRESIDENT'S ADDRESS. Assoc. Amer. Agr. Cols. and Expt. Stas. Proc. 2 : 78–79. (U.S. Dept. Agr. Misc. Bul. 1.)
(4) ——
   1890. PRESIDENT'S ADDRESS. Assoc. Amer. Agr. Cols. and Expt. Stas. Proc. (1889) 3 : 73–76. (U.S. Dept. Agr. Misc. Bul. 2.)
(5) ATWATER, W. O., JOHNSON, S. W., AND COOK, G. H.
   1888. REPORT OF THE COMMITTEE ON STATION WORK. Assoc. Amer. Agr. Cols. and Expt. Stas. (1887), 32 pp. Washington.
(6) CONVENTION OF DELEGATES FROM AGRICULTURAL COLLEGES AND EXPERIMENT STATIONS.
   1885. PROCEEDINGS OF A CONVENTION OF DELEGATES FROM AGRICULTURAL COLLEGES AND EXPERIMENT STATIONS HELD AT THE DEPARTMENT OF AGRICULTURE, JULY 8 AND 9, 1885. [U.S.] Dept. Agr. Misc. Spec. Rpt. 9, 196 pp.
(7) CONVENTION OF FRIENDS OF AGRICULTURAL EDUCATION.
   1872. DISCUSSION AT MEETING HELD AT CHICAGO, ON THE 24TH AND 25TH OF AUGUST 1871. Ill. Indus. Univ. Ann. Rpt. (1870/71) 4 : 215–351.
(8) EXECUTIVE COMMITTEE OF THE ASSOCIATION.
   1941. PROCEEDINGS OF THE FIRST ANNUAL CONVENTION (1887) OF THE ASSOCIATION OF AMERICAN AGRICULTURAL COLLEGES AND EXPERIMENT STATIONS, 6 pp. (Note: No account of this convention was printed originally. However, a manuscript summary by C. E. Thorne, Secretary of the convention, which was filed in the Office of Experiment Stations, was ordered printed by the Executive Committee of the Association on May 5, 1941.)
(9) HENRY, W. A.
   1894. PRESIDENT'S ADDRESS. Assoc. Amer. Agr. Cols. and Expt. Stas. Proc. (1893) 7 : 43–45. (U.S. Dept. Agr., Off. Expt. Sta. Bul. 20.)
(10) JORDAN, W. H.
   1898. REPORT OF THE SECTION ON AGRICULTURE AND CHEMISTRY. Assoc. Amer. Agr. Cols. and Expt. Stas. Proc. (1897) 11 : 24–25. (U.S. Dept. Agr., Off. Expt. Sta. Bul. 49.)
(11) TOWNSHEND, N. S.
   1881. AGRICULTURAL MEETING AT LANSING, MICHIGAN. Ohio State Bd. Agr. Ann. Rpt. 35 : 388–393.

(12)   U.S. OFFICE OF EXPERIMENT STATIONS.
         1889. PROCEEDINGS OF THE SECOND ANNUAL CONVENTION (1889) OF THE ASSOCIATION OF AMERICAN AGRICULTURAL COLLEGES AND EXPERIMENT STATIONS. U.S. Dept. Agr. Misc. Bul. 1, 123 pp.

(13)   ———
         1890. PROCEEDINGS OF THE THIRD ANNUAL CONVENTION OF THE ASSOCIATION OF AMERICAN AGRICULTURAL COLLEGES AND EXPERIMENT STATIONS. U.S. Dept. Agr. Misc. Bul. 2, 142 pp.

(14)   ———
         1891. PROCEEDINGS OF THE FOURTH ANNUAL CONVENTION (1890) OF THE ASSOCIATION OF AMERICAN AGRICULTURAL COLLEGES AND EXPERIMENT STATIONS. U.S. Dept. Agr. Misc. Bul. 3, 156 pp.

(15)   ———
         1892. PROCEEDINGS OF THE FIFTH ANNUAL CONVENTION (1891) OF THE ASSOCIATION OF AMERICAN AGRICULTURAL COLLEGES AND EXPERIMENT STATIONS. U.S. Dept. Agr. Misc. Bul. 7, 113 pp.

(16)   ———
         1904. PROCEEDINGS OF THE SEVENTEENTH ANNUAL CONVENTION (1903) OF THE ASSOCIATION OF AMERICAN AGRICULTURAL COLLEGES AND EXPERIMENT STATIONS. U.S. Dept. Agr., Off. Expt. Stas. Bul. 142, 196 pp.

Chapter Six—

TOWARD BASIC RE- SEARCH: THE ADAMS ACT

The comprehensive phraseology of the Hatch Act of 1887 permitted, as it directed the establishment of tax-supported institutions for research, a broad range of station functions. The preamble marked out the widely spaced limits of authorized activity, from "acquiring and diffusing . . . practical information" to "scientific investigation and experiment respecting the principles and applications of agricultural science." With equally generous phrasing, Section 5 instructed the governing board of each station to use the Hatch funds for "paying the necessary expenses of conducting investigations and experiments and printing and distributing the results." Thus the law, which allowed each station to shape its own definition of research activity, approved both "pure" science and "applied" science; yet it did not prescribe the features which research activity must possess in order to be classified as "scientific" and, therefore, to qualify for Federal support. Moreover, the lack of precision in the statute let the stations specialize, if they chose, in carrying known information to the farmer rather than in discovering new knowledge.

The broad latitude of the Hatch Act became the keystone of its popularity. It won the support of those people who saw in it a means for stimulating scientific effort toward new discovery. It also gained cooperation from an increasing number of people who regarded it not only as an incentive toward new discovery, but also as an immediate and practical method for wide application of the scientific knowledge assembled by the stations to farming.

QUALITY RESEARCH EMPHASIZED

Nevertheless the Hatch Act, despite its latitude in dealing with the manifold phases of tax-supported research, did in Section 2 assign to the stations "the object and duty . . . to conduct original researches or verify experiments . . . bearing directly on the agricultural industry of the United States." This provision, though broadly permissive in its long list of areas eligible for study, clearly indicated that station officers must concentrate on scientific research of the highest quality. Borrowed almost verbatim from the Knapp draft of 1882–83, Section 2 of the Hatch Act accurately expressed the scientist's concept of appropriate station activity. Section 2 did not mention the "acquiring and diffusing . . . of practical information;" the preamble did. It drew its precedent from the measure founding the Department of Agriculture in 1862.

The two terms—"practical information" and "original researches"—weathered the storms of revision and deletion in the career of Congressional legislation. Unfortunately, however, the two posed a persistent problem in administration of the Hatch Act. Was the main emphasis to be placed on "original research"? Or, was the primary goal to spread "practical information" relating to agriculture? Had the Act relied specifically on "original research", some of the State station directors could have moved more rapidly toward the fundamental type of research.

Following passage of the Hatch Act, the first generation of station workers early discovered that the scientist's emphasis on "original researches" suffered sharply in the constant competition with the non-scientist's insistence on "practical information." While the latitude of the Act was discouraging to science-conscious leaders like Atwater and Johnson, the attitude of the "practical-minded" men—those untrained in advanced scientific discipline—was destined to predominate for the rest of the century.

The advocates of "original research" accepted the reality that, under a democratic form of government, administration of publicly appropriated monies should follow the course of that which is most popular. Even so, the agricultural experiment stations did, in their early years, write a remarkable record of accomplishment, one that by 1900 had materially raised the status of the stations as scientific institutions of learning. No discovery did more, in the early years of the experiment station movement, than did development of the Babcock test in 1890, which provided a quick, simple test for butterfat in milk and therewith a practical marketing method for a commodity that is vital in the human diet.

What activity did the act of 1887 "intend" the stations to perform? The search for the answer to this many-sided question led the annual conventions of the Association deep into debate and disagreement in the nineties. Dr. Wilbur Atwater, the first Director of the Office of Experiment Stations, set a high standard of station performance during his 2-year tenure as he sought to explain to the directors of the newly created stations the policies and procedures which, to his mind, would most ably fulfill the expectations implicit in the organic legislation. In mid-November of 1889 Atwater interpreted for the Association the spirit of the Hatch Act. Three principles, he maintained, should guide the station enterprise. "The stations should do well whatever they attempt," he declared (7).[1] "They should not attempt too much; they should endeavor to secure permanent rather than temporary results." He then urged each station to adopt the following operational procedure:

By close contact with the farmers of the State the station should ascertain what are the most pressing and important needs of the agriculture of its section; it should then select from those problems a few which it feels itself most competent to deal with, and plan experiments which shall be thorough and far reaching, and patiently set itself to work with due regard to all the details which will make the experiments complete.

Time enough should be taken in making the plan to have it reasonably sure that the correct principles of experimentation are perceived and adopted, and that everything necessary to success has been provided for. In other words, under the Hatch Act, fairly interpreted, it is the primary duty of the individual station to confine its work to a comparatively limited number of important

[1] Italic numbers in parentheses refer to Literature Cited, p. 107.

problems which it may reasonably hope to solve to the lasting benefit of the agriculture of its State. In this way, by such work as is deservedly denominated *scientific*, whether it be in the field, the stable, or the laboratory, can the stations attain that high measure of success which will be of widespread and permanent benefit to the Agriculture of the United States, and, it may be, of the world.[2]

This classic advice, drawn from Atwater's lengthy experience in scientific research, stated in simple terms the elements essential for the successful and productive direction of station work. Select for study only a few problems; plan for each problem a program of painstaking experiments; persist in each program, complete it, and establish a conclusion; and operate the station as a scientific institution at all times. This formula, predicted Atwater, would assure the most effective combination of quality and quantity in scientific output; therefore it would provide in the long run the most practical approach for station investigators.

To what extent, however, should the station's concern with attunement to the "practical farmers" be permitted to influence the policy-making and the operations of the new institutions? The Atwater formula listed only two stages in the process of discovery and diffusion where the station's constituency should influence the station's activity. First, the agricultural public should keep the station management informed of the difficulties encountered in practical farming; this awareness the governing board must have in order to select properly the limited number of problems which the station could most effectively investigate. Beyond this point the farmer could offer very little assistance to the scientist. Second, the station must publish scientific findings in a form enabling the public to understand and adopt them.

Undeniably the successful application of the station discoveries that continuous and assiduous research produced from time to time, alone could make tax-supported research worthwhile; therefore, the scientist must contribute to the public, in return for the latter's support, the tested results of scientific investigation. The station in Atwater's judgment owed no further obligation to the farmer, nor did it need further assistance from the farmer.

SCIENCE VIEWPOINT URGED

The responsibility for exercising shrewd judgment in selecting lines of research, and also for supplying all necessary facilities for the conduct of research, Atwater placed squarely on the governing board. Similarly, the responsibility for the operational effectiveness of the station force and program he placed entirely on the director. Under these circumstances the process of scientific productivity, so ran Atwater's thinking, would demand the development of the director's keenest talents. Successful station work began, then, with a governing board and a director who jointly insisted, as Atwater had penned in the Report of Station Work in 1888, that "the highest scientific ideal be maintained and every effort be made toward its realization" (*8, p. 32*). Thus the viewpoint of the scientist rather than the viewpoint of the farmer, Atwater contended, must govern the administrative policy of a station earnestly desiring to serve the farmers' welfare and the public interest.

[2] His italics.

83

Many stations could not, however, immediately follow Atwater's instructions. Already the course of station development, as Atwater well knew, inclined in a different direction. "The agricultural public," Director W. W. Cooke of Vermont had remarked at the preceding convention in January of 1889 (9) ". . . is compelling the stations to take up lower problems, if you choose to so call them, or 'practical problems,' as the farmers class them, which require immediate work, and give promise, although often visionary, of immediate results." To his sympathetic brethren he further observed, "You all understand . . . how demands from all sides, compelling us to divide our time among a multitude of different subjects, make it impossible for us to work out any one subject broadly. Thorough work," he added with conviction, "gives the best results, but the farmers all over the United States, knowing that these stations have been organized, are demanding immediate results."

The tax-supported stations, vulnerable to local pressures, found it no less difficult, even as the years passed, to escape from an operational framework dominated by the farmers' prevailing concept of the duties and type of research which the stations should perform. Moreover, in 1890 Director Dabney, deeply disturbed because the reports of station work revealed only a "small amount of original investigation," outspokenly accused many stations of surrendering to nonscientific standards. "We believe," he formally reported for the Association's Committee on Chemistry (10), "that our boards of control or directors are, many of them, too anxious to obtain immediate favor with the public, and are . . . [merely] trying to show the farmer how he can make his business pay a little better." This trend Dabney denounced, for it "was leading many to build their stations without any solid foundation whatever in good work." Thus the station movement encountered in its earliest nationwide experience the same difficulty that had plagued Professor Johnston in Scotland a half-century earlier.[3]

How, then, could the stations maintain a close affiliation with the farm population, secure widespread public approval and, simultaneously, not deviate from the Atwater standard? The search for the answer to this central question absorbed the energy of station spokesmen for the remainder of the 19th century.

Unquestionably the circumstances of origin had placed the stations in a democratic environment dictating that the new institutions must, in order to survive, win the farmers' praise. To earn such praise, the stations had no choice but to minister to the farmer and his immediate cares. Nevertheless, would not the ultimate success and value of the enterprise, when judged by the coming generations, depend more imperatively on the stations' record of scientific productivity instrumental in improving and perhaps revolutionizing agricultural technology? Did not that mission of technological improvement demand, in turn, that the stations without delay create a scientific atmosphere, adhere strictly to the rules of scientific investigation, and concentrate a substantial segment of resources and talents on problems which only the scientist, but not the farmer, would call "practical"?

This reasoning had prompted from Atwater's Committee on Station Work the solemn adjuration that the record of scientific produc-

---

[3] See Chapter 2, p. 10.

tivity would decide the issue of life or death for the station movement
(8). "The future usefulness of the stations," that committee had
observed in 1888, "will depend upon what they discover of permanent
value, and this must come largely from the most abstract and profound research; to forget this," the committee had warned, "will be
fatal."

No scientist perceived more acutely and sympathetically than did
Atwater the nature of the farmers' pressure on station personnel, yet
in his judgment the necessity for scientific attainment applied even
more insistently. He contended, furthermore, that the farmers,
recognizing their own long-range interests, would support the enforcement of his high standard of administration. "The American farmer,"
he reassured the directors in 1889 (7), "is after all most interested
in the solution of certain large problems connected with his profession
and is likely to be more patient with a station which holds itself
rigidly to careful and thorough investigations of relatively few but
important matters than with one which gives him many useful hints
on little details but does not undertake any really serious work in his
behalf."

STANDARDS WERE HIGH

The Atwater standard, though simple in its constituent features,
proved difficult to administer, for few stations could supply in the
early nineties the facilities and highly trained personnel necessary
for its observance. Atwater's standard called for a topnotch scientist
as a full-time director; a staff of scientists highly trained in the latest
techniques of research, substantially freed from undergraduate teaching assignments, and motivated to emulate the professional excellence
of the scientific investigators of the European stations; a system of
organization which established activity and built strength only in those
disciplines promising the greatest aid in specific lines carefully selected
for investigation. The station enterprise, viewed nationally, seriously
lacked these prerequisites.

These deficiencies disturbed Director Henry, who had sought
diligently to remedy them in Wisconsin. He reminded the Association in 1893, as he noted in his presidential address the shortcomings
of American station work (13), that the quality of performance would
not reach a satisfactory level until these prerequisites were instituted.
The newness of the American establishment, he conceded, would for a
limited time condone a lack of significant achievement. How much
additional time, however, would the stations require to secure top-
quality researchers, concentrate their attention on selected problems,
and "grow out of amateur efforts into the true scientific spirit?"
Henry sympathized with the governing boards; nevertheless, in his
words there lay a deep apprehensiveness that those boards were postponing the introduction of the administrative system demanded by
the Atwater standard.

Did the personnel of the land-grant institution have a clear concept
of high-level scientific research, its aims and its methods? Did they
grasp the significance of Atwater's expression, "the most abstract and
profound research?" Several skilled directors in the nineties, after
Atwater had resigned from his Washington post, attempted at the

yearly meetings of the Association to prevent the spread of the complacent attitude that Henry had criticized.

George E. Morrow, a stalwart conventioneer since the first gathering in 1871 and the station helmsman at the University of Illinois, advised in 1894 (21), "I would have more of research and experiment along purely scientific lines, not restricting such work to that which gives large promise of immediate and direct practical application, not stopping it even if good men are unable to see its utility." The concentration on agronomy and corn genetics demonstrated in the following decade that the Illinois station took seriously this advice from the founder of its Morrow Plots.

Samuel W. Johnson, a pioneer in station-founding in earlier years but now an elder statesman nearing retirement, amplified the Morrow theme in his presidential address to the Association in 1896. Director Johnson of the Connecticut State station matter-of-factly described his model project in fundamental research, one which for the preceding 7 years had absorbed the entire time of a research chemist supported by a portion of the Hatch income. This project, planned and conducted in a resolute attempt to discover the composition and properties of the protein substances in numerous feedstuffs, Johnson considered a necessary preparation for determining in later long-range studies the nutritive value of individual vegetable proteins. This study, Johnson and his board of control had agreed, should continue without interruption in the coming years until it yielded the answers sought. This line of research, though Johnson in 1896 could not have predicted its specific outcome, led in later decades to the discovery of the vitamin and to other significant advances in the study of human nutrition.

The opportunity and the necessity to conduct abstract research of this type, Johnson prophesied in 1896, lay in the near future for every station. "For some of us," he declared, "that duty is already knocking at our doors; for all of us the time is short during which we can justifiably neglect to kindle and to tend and direct the searchlights of truth."

The more the public could be brought to understand the station's function of scientific productivity, Johnson believed, the more that public would approve an increasing concentration on basic research. Each station, then, must labor patiently and persistently to persuade its current constituency of farmers to appreciate the scientists view of research, and not permit the farmers' contemporary standard of research perpetually to dominate policy-making at the stations. "Let us hope," he observed with patriarchal mildness (17), "that ere long in this country, as in the Old World, the stations will be empowered to put the capable investigators into positions where they can give their powers unreservedly and exclusively to discovery."

JORDAN—THE NEW SPOKESMAN

Whitman Jordan, the emerging spokesman for the younger generation of directors, seized the torch from Johnson's aging hand. A persistent failure to comprehend the distinctions between "instruction" and "inquiry", Jordan aggressively informed the convention of 1897 (18), characterized the attitude of most land-grant personnel. The mounting emphasis on farm institute work, added to the perennial weight of the combination system,[3] so seriously sapped the energy and time of the investigators that in Jordan's judgment the prevailing system of station administration did not and could not get adequate return from the Hatch expenditures. Moreover, the type of investigation actually attempted did not aim in many instances "to discover new truth, but to illustrate the application of old truths, and," he charged, "is really an instructional effort rather than one of real inquiry and should be so classified."

This confusion in thought accounted for the snail's pace toward significant research. "Let us not confuse our aims or misuse our funds," he warned. "Research of the most severe kind is demanded, and the experiment station fund is a research fund."

Moreover, the American station movement would soon exhaust the treasury of basic scientific data which European scientists had laboriously accumulated during the preceding half century. This imminent shortage of fundamental knowledge deeply disturbed Jordan. "Ignorance of fundamentals is . . . a greater obstacle to progress than the lack of a popular appreciation of known facts," he declared. "Should we not ask the expectant public," he challenged the conventioneers, "to have faith in us and allow us to settle down to hard and continuous study of difficult problems [?]"

The attempt by the Geneva director to sting the convention into a declaration approving the Atwater standard produced a sharp debate but no immediate action. It drew a retort from a veteran director, Isaac P. Roberts of the Cornell station, who typified the widespread attitude which Jordan had criticized. The station should function primarily as a diffuser of improved methods, Roberts asserted, and only secondarily as an investigating agency. It should concentrate on rural instruction until "the farming community," at a time far in the future, had fully exploited the technological capabilities of the information already known in the nineties. Not until that time, Roberts contended, should the stations direct "the main part of . . . [their] effort . . . toward original research." Thus the views of the two New York directors collided head-on.

The partiality shown by the conventioneers for the Roberts' philosophy, which neatly fitted the current needs of the colleges for a program of public relations, indicated that the Association in the late nineties would not bestir itself to urge the "original research" for which Jordan crusaded. Nevertheless, Jordan returned to the attack. A featured speaker at the convention of 1900, he capitalized on the opportunity afforded by the 25th anniversary of the Connecticut State station, the theme commemorated in the exercises of the Association (19). Deftly displaying the scholarly incisiveness which had become his trademark, he pleaded again for the Atwater standard; he rehearsed the changes in administration and attitude necessary to achieve the scientific output demanded by that standard; he appealed for an interpretation of the Hatch Act which would, in effect, refute the Roberts' thesis and establish the "independent individuality" of each station. "When a really important fact is established," he declared, "we need have little concern about its ultimate utilization by farm practice. It is easier to cut a diamond to its setting than it is to find it. We can trust the ingenuity and business ability of our progressive agriculturists to assimilate in time all that is of real benefit

---

[3] See chap. 5, pp. 63–65.

to their calling." Most of all, however, Jordan deplored the insufficient quantity of truly scientific research produced thus far in the careers of most stations. This feature of the station movement alarmed him.

Meanwhile Director Henry, equally convinced that the Association must muster its strength in favor of original research, waited expectantly for the close of Jordan's address. After years of patient but fruitless endurance, Henry had concluded that the scientific ideal would achieve victory only if its champions acted resolutely, step by step, in its behalf. First of all the teaching load of the departmental chairmen must be removed or, at least, reduced to a minimum. At the moment of Jordan's finale, when the sympathy of the conventioneers for that fervent appeal reached a climax, Henry presented his resolution for reducing the teaching schedule. The rules of order, however, prevented the convention from acting on his resolution at that time, and the Executive Committee later refused to report the resolution for action in the sessions of 1900.

Tenacious and undaunted, the Wisconsin director introduced the identical resolution at the next convention in 1901. Boldly and bluntly Henry accused the college presidents and trustees of forcing heavy duties on Hatch-paid investigators whose research thereby suffered. The resolution evoked precisely the same storm of objections which the presidents had used in the milder exchanges of earlier years; that storm subsided only when the convention voted to table the resolution (14). Unable to proceed further on this course, Henry thereupon took a different tack. Already involved in the current movement to revise the constitution of the Association, he secured membership on the committee of revision. He succeeded in winning by 1902 the approval of that committee for the twin-section plan first recommended in 1889 by Director Armsby (15). Not only did the new plan, adopted by the Association in 1903, accentuate the professional differentiation between the directors and the presidents, it also hastened the growth of an *esprit de corps* among the directors; and it enabled the station section to place Whitman Jordan on the Executive Committee in 1903 and to keep him there for more than 15 years.

ASSOCIATION BECAME STRONGER

Thus the spokesmen who had worked most vigorously in the nineties for the constitutional overhaul of the Association, for significant revision in the station–college relationship, and for administrative reorganization within the Hatch stations, unwaveringly centered their attention on one unchanging objective, namely, the improvement of the scientific quality of station research. Their intense interest in original research prompted their demands for change, and it forged a bond among Armsby, Henry, and Jordan, the voices of basic research and the parliamentarians of constitutional and administrative reform. To their number a newer figure added his talents: Eugene Davenport, the director of the Illinois Station since 1895. Davenport (11) in 1902 introduced, and the convention of that year adopted, a resolution requesting the Executive Committee to "urge upon Congress at the earliest practicable date that the appropriation to the several States under the Hatch Act be increased by the sum of $15,000 annually."

The Executive Committee, caught at a disadvantage because it already had pending a number of other proposals for Federal appropriations, postponed action on the Davenport resolution. Midway in 1903, however, it requested Dr. Alfred Charles True, who since 1893 had directed the Office of Experiment Stations, to prepare "an account, founded upon the inspections and examinations made through your office of the present condition and work of the several stations, their capabilities for increased work of value to agriculture, and of the need (if it exists) of additional resources to enable such increased work to be undertaken" (*29*).

This action touched off a train of circumstances which in the following 3 years produced a new Federal law endowing and directing the conduct of the type of research for which Armsby, Henry, and Jordan had campaigned. More immediately, however, the request from the Committee brought into key prominence the diminutive and diplomatic gentleman in the Washington office, A. C. True, whose long-continued efforts in the cause of original research entitled him to membership in the select circle of station statesmen.

Dr. True, a professor of Latin and Greek at Wesleyan University in Connecticut in 1888, had come to the infant Office of Experiment Stations as a member of Atwater's modest retinue of Wesleyan teachers. The diligent classicist was at first employed as an editorial assistant in OES. He won promotion after Atwater resigned the directorship in 1891 and his successor, Dr. Abram W. Harris, had done likewise in 1893. True, unlike his predecessors, retained the directorship for nearly a lifetime. During his regime there occurred a series of significant changes in his official powers and duties.

TRUE SHOULDERED NEW RESPONSIBILITIES

Director True inherited in 1893 an office which Atwater had fashioned into an agency supplying to the stations varied information, especially summaries of pertinent European scientific work and concise accounts of investigations in the American stations. Shortly after True's accession to the directorship, however, a cluster of events beyond his control placed on his shoulders a new responsibility to "ascertain" that the stations did in fact expend their Federal grant funds as the Hatch Act directed. The force of circumstances compelled True to initiate in the midnineties and to administer thereafter a policy of inspections of the stations receiving Hatch moneys. Moreover, the developments of the nineties required Dr. True, a nonscientist holding a position originally designed for a scientist, to determine the intent of the Hatch Act, to decide what constituted scientific research in agriculture, and finally to withhold funds for station activity not eligible for support under that act. The steady accretion of responsibilities in the public interest placed True in a position that invited his participation, after the turn of the century, in the movement for additional Federal funds and enabled him to champion the cause of original research. The first decade of True's directorship produced, in short, an emerging system of Federal administration which, based on the exercise by OES of the power of persuasion inherent in a gently developing plan of fiscal accountability, permitted True increasingly to insist that the stations observe the Atwater standard.

The provisions of the Hatch Act, painstakingly protecting the stations from Federal dictation in any form, did not authorize the Commissioner (after 1889, Secretary) of Agriculture or the Secretary

89

of the Treasury or any other Federal official to direct in any way the expenditure of Federal grant funds. Similarly that act, which in fiscal effect made a donation to each station designated as a beneficiary by the individual State legislatures, permitted the governing board of each station a wide discretion in the use of the Hatch income.

The generosity of that measure evidenced the remarkable faith' placed by the Federal lawmakers in the honesty and good judgment of the college authorities. It also raised some questions. Could not the college trustees, often more zealous for teaching than for research, apply the funds to college instruction at the expense of the station interests envisioned by career directors and scientists? Could not the governing board readily justify, in the absence of precise definition and a restrictive authority, almost any expenditure as falling somewhere, somehow, within the categories of experimentation, investigation, and research—not to mention diffusion?

The Association in 1887, thankful for Congressional confidence and for the opportunities for public service offered by the Hatch funds, probed in committee the problem of internal discipline applicable to Hatch expenditures. The Dabney Report, adopted by that first convention, formulated the decisions. That report in its list of "advisory propositions" forbade the colleges to use the funds for non-station purposes; furthermore it urged a separation in the fiscal accounts of the station and the college so distinct that an inspection would immediately reveal, clearly and completely, the pertinent details of every financial transaction. "The stations . . . should be so far separate and distinct from the colleges," the second proposition resolved, "that it shall be possible at any moment to show to any authorized inspector or investigator that all the funds derived from the United States under the Hatch bill have been expended solely for the purposes of agricultural experimentation, according to the intent of the law" (5).

Director Dabney's sponsorship of the movement to commit the Association to a standard of distinct separation reflected the apprehensiveness of the directors that the stations, classified as departments, might lose their identity as research institutions and, succumbing to a teaching emphasis, become merely additions to the teaching facilities. Implicit in the report, nevertheless, lay the significant corollary that an unnamed authority would, with the approval of the Association, "inspect" or "investigate" the accounts—and then the station work—in order to insure the proper observance of the Hatch Act.

A second corollary emerged from the first one: the inspecting agent must interpret the intent of the act of 1887 and then judge the quality of station performance. Who, then, should exercise this function? The Association, discreetly postponing decision and even formal discussion at its conventions, for a half-dozen years took no further action on this sensitive issue.

Henry E. Alvord did not permit the Association, however, to ignore the "Declaration of Principles," his term for the "advisory propositions" adopted in 1887. Major Alvord, who had figured prominently in the framing of the Dabney Report, fervently believed that the stations needed the benefits of a periodic scrutiny in order to remain faithful to the rigorous task of conducting research. Perennially powerful in the decision-making of the Association to 1895, he con-

The Parma Branch Experiment Station in Idaho serves a highly productive vegetable and fruit area of the West. Here new techniques and better onion varieties have been developed in cooperative Idaho-USDA research.

Basic research on soil genesis conducted by the Hawaii Agricultural Experiment Station revealed that sparse, poorly nutritive vegetation (left) is characteristic of the surface soil of an area with rich bauxite deposits. Following simulated mining of the bauxite ore, legumes, grasses, and other crops can be grown on the reclaimed site (right).

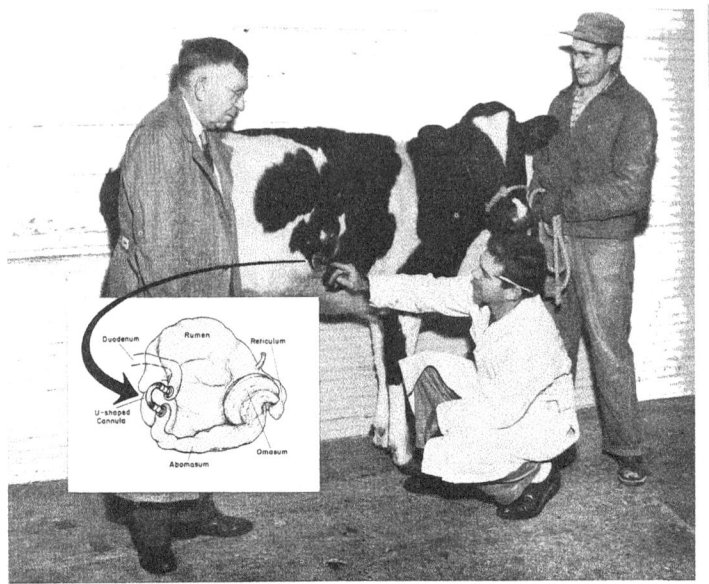

Dr. C. F. Huffman (left), Michigan Agricultural Experiment Station, pioneered in developing the method that permits visual observation of digestion and the milk-producing process in cows. This research led to new and better methods of feeding dairy cattle.

Here's an example of progress in broiler nutrition at the Maryland Agricultural Experiment Station. Both broilers are from the same genetic stock. The bird on the left, fed an experimental ration, weighed 3.02 pounds at 44 days of age; the bird on the right, fed a modified 1912 ration, weighed 1.14 pounds at the same age.

From genetic studies of corn at the Connecticut Agricultural Experiment Station came in 1917 the four-way cross that made hybrid corn practical, and in 1951 the pollen sterile-restorer gene method of producing hybrid corn without detasseling.

In cooperation with USDA, the Nevada Agricultural Experiment Station has developed two new varieties of alfalfa. Lahontan, a winterhardy variety, is resistant to spotted alfalfa aphid, bacterial wilt, and stem nematode. Moapa, a non-winterhardy variety for the warmer areas of the Southwest, is resistant to spotted alfalfa aphid. Aphids killed susceptible Calverde variety.

Dr. Darrell Sullivan of the New Mexico Agricultural Experiment Station inspects a Thompson Seedless grapevine treated with gibberellic acid to increase berry size. Research is being conducted to test grape rootstocks for high production under New Mexico conditions.

The Tennessee Agricultural Experiment Station is working to develop varieties of tobacco resistant to black-shank disease. Resistant varieties Burley 37 (left) and Burley 11–A (right) outproduce susceptible variety Burley 21 (center).

Breeding research at the Wyoming Agricultural Experiment Station has contributed to the development of these fine- and medium-type crossbreeds from Rambouillet foundation sheep, shown here on a ranch in the Red Desert area.

Beef cattle breeding research at the Nebraska Agricultural Experiment Station is aimed at developing economically important traits such as productive efficiency and desirability of product.   (Photo: courtesy Nebraska Farmer.)

The Alabama Agricultural Experiment Station has contributed substantially to growth of the cattle industry in the State through research in forage plant breeding, pasture management, and livestock improvement.

In experiments by the Oklahoma Agricultural Experiment Station and the U.S. Department of Agriculture, scientists are learning much about breeding genetically superior animals. These twin cows have each produced 11 calves. Those dropped by the cow on the left weighed an average of 533 pounds at weaning; those by the cow on the right, 384 pounds.

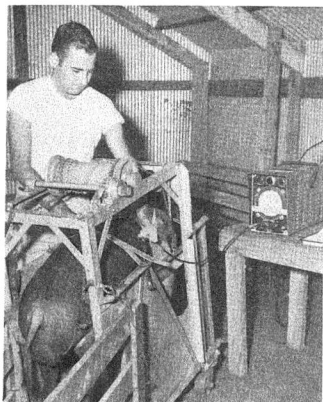

Researchers at the Missouri Agricultural Experiment Station use ultrasonic sound waves to determine meatiness of live animals.

As a part of its research program with forage crops, the Kentucky Agricultural Experiment Station has crossed ryegrass with fescue to produce a pasture grass that combines the high nutrition and palatability of ryegrass with fescue's high vigor and hardiness.

Research at the West Virginia Agricultural Experiment Station is helping to halt the spread of destructive oak wilt disease: A, the causal fungus grows in cavities between bark and wood; B, deep girdling has become the standard method of control in West Virginia; C, the fruiting bodies of different species of the fungus genus Hypoxylon often appear on the trunks of deep-girdled oak wilt trees.

By using techniques developed by the Colorado Agricultural Experiment Station this overgrazed, overcultivated, "blowout" area (above) was restored to production in 5 years (below)—or about 25 years less than required by nature.

tended consistently and forcefully that the members of the Association, duty-bound to keep watch on one another, should report to the Executive Committee any infractions of the principles in the Dabney Report.

The discipline-minded Alvord, who headed the Executive Committee, stood ready to answer the call of duty. He and his committee on several occasions volunteered, after insisting that the director of OES grant permission for their intended action, to investigate rumored delinquencies. These missions they executed to Alvord's proud and lasting satisfaction.

These experiences prompted Alvord to conclude, nevertheless, that the Office of Experiment Stations, rather than the Association, should assume the scrutinizing duty and take appropriate action to require conformity with the principles of the Dabney Report. The advisory powers accorded to the Secretary of Agriculture in the Hatch Act, and delegated in turn to the Director of OES, Alvord considered sufficiently authoritative, if liberally interpreted, to justify a course of resolute intervention.

The reluctance of Dr. True to adopt a disciplinary attitude, however, disappointed and displeased the vigilant major. "There is evidence at times," Alvord reprovingly observed in his presidential address to the Association in 1895, "that the censorial function should be lodged somewhere and fearlessly exercised" (5). Imbedded in the thinking of this duty-conscious custodian of station interests lay his premonitory concern that the Association, once he had retired from the scene, would cast aside his policy of mutual surveillance, and the character of the stations and their work would thereby suffer.

Alvord did not succeed in converting the mild-mannered True to a policy of police action. Nevertheless Alvord's firm management of a related issue—the stations' fiscal accountability to the Federal Government—did in time make the Director of OES responsible for examining annually the performance of each station. During his tenure as the chairman of the Executive Committee in the early career of the Association, Alvord labored to popularize the proposal that the Department of Agriculture should have the power to require from the stations financial reports far more detailed and informative than those heretofore considered sufficient to meet the requirements of the Hatch Act. He urged, in sum, that the Secretary adopt the practice of an annual fiscal review. His committee, satisfied that the Secretary would delegate that power of review to OES, submitted to the appropriate Congressional committees in 1890 and periodically thereafter its drafts of the forms for financial accounting which Congress should direct the Secretary to receive from each station. The Congress did not, however, take action until 1894, a time when the absence of a system of fiscal accountability produced mutual embarrassment for the stations and the Department.

FINANCIAL POLICIES STUDIED

Secretary J. Sterling Morton, who took office in 1893 at the beginning of a severe and prolonged economic depression, studied with care the items in the appropriations bill for his Department. He noted that the Departmental estimates listed the annual Hatch appropriation as an expense of his Department, a budgetary position which

Alvord's Committee had intentionally secured in 1888. When Morton discovered that in practice he had no control over that expenditure, he deleted the station item from his fiscal requests for 1895, submitted to the House early in 1894.

Alvord's committee immediately opened energetic negotiations with the Secretary, who restored the deleted item after accepting the committee's proposal to incorporate in the appropriation bill for 1895 the stipulation that the Secretary "shall prescribe the form of the annual financial statement required by the Hatch Act and . . . shall ascertain whether the expenditures . . . are in accordance with the provisions of the said act, and shall make report thereon to Congress" (12).

Thereupon the committee drafted, and the Secretary adopted, the form for the annual financial statement (4). Secretary Morton, unhappy because his outspoken criticism of the stations' fiscal policy (12) had evaporated his popularity with the Association, conciliatingly explained his action to the convention of 1894 (22). Armsby restored Morton to the good graces of the Association by introducing a resolution, promptly adopted, approving "the measure of supervision" granted by Congress to the Secretary, and welcoming his "closest scrutiny" of station work "either by personal visitation of an agent of the Department, or such other method as the Secretary . . . may deem most efficient."

Secretary Morton, though empowered to decide this delicate issue, preferred that the Association select the "most efficient method" for scrutinizing the station accounts. Major Alvord accordingly presented to the convention of 1894 the alternative courses of action (4). Should the Secretary's agent do no more than examine critically, after the close of a given year, the annual reports of each station for that year; or should he examine, during the course of that year's operations, the work in progress at each station?

Alvord determinedly pressed for "personal visits," a policy which the career-directors approved in 1894 (4). He explained to the convention in 1895 the reasoning which, in his judgment, committed the Association to support a policy of personal visits. "Prescribing forms for reports and examining returns in an office would do very little good," he firmly declared from the presidential rostrum. "The command to 'ascertain' the facts carries with it, necessarily, the power to inspect and investigate. One cannot tell whether the expenditure upon a certain piece of work is right until he sees the work itself, or the results; and judgment of quality as well as quantity is necessary in order to determine the question of value received." Alvord then added pointedly, "As it now stands, the authority of station funds . . . should be actively exercised; and this can be done without in the least interfering with that independence of action as to character, plan, and execution of work which is essential to good results. . . . It must be admitted," he concluded (5), "that this supervisory power is needed."

Axiomatic in the major's thinking lay the conviction that the Office of Experiment Stations must administer, via the delegation of authority from the Secretary of Agriculture, "the supervisory power." Sharply Alvord assailed, for the particular benefit of Dr. True in his audience, the past policy of the Washington office. That office should have taken the initiative, he contended, to exercise more vigorously and broadly the advisory powers accorded to the Department in the Hatch Act. That office, he charged, "has conspicuously failed, in some respects, to meet the expectations of those who first advocated the need of it. . . . And it was certainly expected that the office would act as an expert critic of the work of the experiment stations—a valuable service which has been entirely lacking" (5). That office had too long confined its function to the publishing of reviews and abstracts. It should, while not neglecting that useful service, forthwith concentrate on visiting the stations, advising the station management and providing constructive criticism designed to improve the quality of station work. It should annually assess the performance of each station, point out the imperfections in its quality of product, praise excellence but refuse to condone marked inferiority.

The resolute major must have realized how enormously complex and difficult would be the task which he insistently loaded on the shoulders of the scholarly Dr. True. Nevertheless, Alvord maintained, a central and permanent body must set standards for research activity and, by exercising the skills of a schoolmaster, induce each station to achieve the highest possible level of performance. Thus he saw clearly, as he delivered his valedictory address to the Association, that the station system must subject itself to the discipline of constant self-appraisal and self-improvement, a process which he had sought to establish by elaborating the device of fiscal review into a Federal evaluation of quality of product.

Major Alvord need not have worried that Director True would ignore the earnestness or the wisdom of that presidential critique. Beneath True's quietness and polite reticence there lay a steely intensity of purpose to build, via a policy of patient persuasion, the young stations into permanent scientific institutions devoted to research in agriculture. True accepted without reservation Alvord's operational principle that the Washington office should link together the Hatch grant of advisory powers and the new authority for fiscal review. True explained to the convention of 1895 (24) as quietly he answered Alvord's challenges, the purposes of the "personal visitation" which his office had already instituted:

> These visits . . . are intended to be more than mere inspections regarding expenditures; they are rather in a larger sense to be conferences with station officers to learn the conditions and needs of their work, to get their views on many of the complex problems involved in the management of station work, to ascertain how the funds intrusted to them have been expended, and also how the work of the stations may be made more effective and useful. It is believed that only by taking into account the local environments of the stations and the circumstances under which their work has developed that a just estimate can be formed of what they have accomplished, as well as of the proper limits of their work.
> . . . It is our desire to understand . . . the needs of the stations, what we can do to help them, and how we can improve our lines of work.

ADMINISTRATIVE PROBLEMS GREW

True faced an administrative problem of personal and public relations calling for the most skillful use of tact and diplomacy. Sympathetically he understood that those station officers not wanting unsolicited advice would brand his policy as coercive if he introduced the Alvordian tone of discipline. Hence he studiously avoided giving offense in his emerging professional role as a giver of advice. He elected to counsel, not to reprimand. Philosophically he viewed the task ahead as a career responsibility, one which painstakingly sought to cultivate among the nationwide station force the attitude that the governing boards, the directors, and the researchers collectively were erecting an institutional structure of lasting life and permanent productivity. The station enterprise, if devoted men nurtured it, would bring blessings to coming generations; this True believed. The faith that the men of his day were building permanently for the future gave to Director True the patience in 1895 to believe that men would correct the deficiencies in station organization and administration as soon as "we have consciously adopted the idea that the experiment station is to be a permanent institution having distinct functions." Then, he predicted, the station would "stand out sharply as a distinct entity" (*24*).

Dr. True, while willing to wait patiently and work valiantly for the day when a maturing public attitude would favor "permanency in institutions," nevertheless informed the convention of 1895 that he expected the stations to conform without exception to the standards listed in the Dabney Report of 1887 and currently proclaimed anew in Alvord's presidential address. The stations could not produce significant findings, True contended with quiet conviction, unless their governing boards—whom True held primarily responsible for the quality of work conducted—instituted the type of organization envisioned in the principles of that report. Moreover, he upheld the virtues of the research activity which Atwater had set as the station standard in 1889. "Each station," he declared, "should have a few investigations which it proposes to carry on for a long term of years . . . we must find space and opportunity for permanent work" (*24*). Thus the "idea of permanence" in True's thinking had one all-important objective: the discovery of scientific truth.

Thus in the midnineties, precisely at the time when Armsby, Henry, Morrow, Johnson, and Jordan were stressing the necessity for studying a carefully selected number of long-term projects, A. C. True committed the Office of Experiment Stations to a policy of assisting and persuading the stations to establish an identical program. Concisely he restated his objective in 1897. "The stations should give their attention to original investigations," he told the conventioneers (*25*). "Especially should the Hatch fund be kept as a trust fund given for the special purpose of securing for the farmers of the country the benefits which can only come from thorough and original work along scientific lines in behalf of agriculture." No one could doubt that True had firmly fixed the Atwater standard as the guiding principle in the Washington office.

True had already encountered, however, serious difficulties impeding the successful administration of his program. The governing boards of many stations could not or would not regard the Hatch income as a "trust fund" for original investigations or even for research activity. Refusing to antagonize farm sentiment by insisting that the stations concentrate on research, those boards preferred a program which increasingly emphasized rural education. The demands of the farm electorate for immediately useful information threatened, as Jordan in acid tones had recently observed to the convention of 1897, to convert the "experiment station into a perambulating school" (*18*).

True shared Jordan's worry that the effort, undeniably well-meaning and highly useful, to instruct the farmer would under the existing

94

circumstances sap the vitality and stunt the growth of the research enterprise. "It is in my judgment a great mistake," True declared (25), "to favor or maintain indefinitely a kind of station policy which tends to turn the stations into mere bureaus of information." Against the tide of public sentiment, however, True's objections and his policy of personal visits could not prevail.

Moreover, many State legislatures appeared content to allow the use of the Hatch funds for this rapidly growing movement to which a later decade would give the name "extension." With no conscious grasp of "the idea of permanence" for research, their members begrudged making an appropriation of State tax moneys to support a farmers' program for which, in their view, the Federal Government had already provided funds.

Discouraging experience taught True that the generous inclusion of the word "diffusion" in the Hatch Act placed the interests of research at a serious disadvantage. The States most in need of a concentration on research lacked either the resources to accommodate the extension movement, or the willingness to preserve the Hatch income as a trust fund for research. Furthermore those legislatures which soon did appropriate substantial sums for agricultural programs put their money, as a rule, into college installations and farmers' institutes rather than into the nonspectacular research effort (27). These prospects would have disheartened a less determined man.

True labored to advise and instruct, and to reiterate his view that the Hatch Act obligated the stations to conduct research only of the highest scientific character and quality. Gradually he tightened the administrative interpretation of the expenditures permissible under the act of 1887. "This Department is . . . disposed to more strongly insist on a strict interpretation of this act in this direction," he wrote in his report to Congress in 1900 (26) "and to hold that it is not only in accordance with the obligation, but also to the interest of the States, to devote the Hatch fund to investigations in agriculture, and to supplement the fund as far as may be necessary to promote the interests of agriculture in other lines."

By 1904 he had compressed the intent of the Hatch Act to the point where his office would authorize expenses for "extension" only when the individual station had by its own experimentation ascertained the subject matter (23). Thus Director True pushed to the limit his powers of advice and review.

NEW PROBLEMS DEVELOPED

Nevertheless True's labors, though able and persistent, could not overcome the entrenched obstacles in the path of original research. No station administrator by 1900 could stretch the Hatch grant, once considered lavish, to finance the long-term projects which in 1889 Atwater had proclaimed to be vital. The lack of specific limitations in the law of 1887 permitted even those stations conscientiously striving to observe the Atwater-True standard to use their Federal funds for the expenses of general operation; the Hatch Act did not require the stations to use their Federal subsidy solely for original research.

Nor did the likelihood of funds for such research appear bright even in the States where the well-established stations were eagerly seeking support for fundamental investigations. The legislatures in Illinois,

New York, Wisconsin, New Jersey, and Connecticut inclined toward substantial grants. Yet even these States customarily appropriated funds exclusively for specific investigations and rarely made available unearmarked sums to be expended on the kinds of research which would delight the scientific instincts of the highly-trained professional director.

In the opening years of the 20th century, therefore, a movement for a new Federal endowment authorizing and directing only original research emerged as the necessary solution to the problem which had plagued the station enterprise for a generation.

The Davenport resolution adopted by the convention of 1902 opened the active campaign of station men to secure, in addition to the Hatch appropriation, an annual Federal stipend of $15,000 for each State. Director True carefully prepared in response to the request from the Executive Committee a scholarly statement which declared with incisive finality that the stations could not produce, without an immediate and substantial increase in revenue, the scientific discoveries basic to a steadily improving technology in agriculture. "Under present conditions it is useless to expect that . . . our stations will discover many of the principles on which the permanent improvement of our agriculture must rest," he wrote (27). "But unless the way is opened for them to seriously attack these fundamental problems their future work will necessarily be comparatively fragmentary and inconclusive. They may, as in the past," True conceded, "obtain many results which can be usefully applied in practice, but," he gravely pointed out, "they will not be able to furnish solid foundation for the enlargement of our agricultural industries."

The Executive Committee in October 1903 approached James Wilson, the energetic Secretary of Agriculture and a former director of the Iowa station, who complied with the Committee's request to submit to Congress in the next schedule of estimated expenses for his Department a recommendation, based on the True report, for an increase in Hatch-type funds (29). The published copies of the Wilson recommendation and the True report reached Congress in time for the debates on the appropriations measure early in 1904.

The members of the Executive Committee, as their roundabout activity revealed, did not concertedly and determinedly press the station bill to the attention of the House Committee on Agriculture prior to 1905. Much more intent on urging the passage of a pending proposal for a college subsidy, they gave merely a secondary emphasis to the Davenport resolution. Similarly, the Association in its convention of 1903, willing to accept its committee's view that the college bill should have priority and resigned to the prospect of a time-consuming concentration on that objective, instructed its committee only to continue in 1904 the pattern of activity in 1903 (29). Likewise the station men, absorbed in the parliamentary mechanics of dividing the Association into twin sections, did not produce a bill nor had they yet planned a specific campaign to carry their case to Congress.

The readiness of the Executive Committee to postpone action and the acquiescence of the Association in that decision did not satisfy Director Henry. On the contrary, the procrastination at the convention of 1903 prompted him to take independent action.

Shortly after the adjournment of the sessions held that autumn in Washington, D.C., Henry paid a visit to Capitol Hill. There on

November 20 he contacted a close friend, Henry Cullen Adams, an experienced spokesman for agricultural improvement in Wisconsin and currently a freshman member of the House Committee on Agriculture. Henry explained to his sympathetic listener the "dire poverty of our experiment stations," the importance of conducting fundamental research, and the need for a second Federal donation based on the precedent of the Hatch Act.

Two weeks later Congressman Adams, having sampled in the meantime the attitudes of the men on Capitol Hill, wrote encouragingly to Henry that "a bill, such as outlined in our conversation, can be passed." Thereupon, within a week, A. C. True visited Adams, who asked True "to give the matter of form and details of the bill some thought" (*16*).

ADAMS BILL FORMULATED

True and Adams during the following 2 weeks framed a bill imitating the format of the Hatch Act but incorporating two significant variations. The new bill permitted expenditures solely for original researches; and though it proposed to appropriate a sum not exceeding $15,000 to each State, it stipulated only $5,000 for the first year, with an increment of $2,000 each year thereafter until the payment should reach the maximum. This financial arrangement not only promised to appeal to the Congressional sense of economy at the moment, but it also required each station to grow gradually into a program of complex research. "The enclosed bill," wrote Adams to Henry on Christmas Eve of 1903, "embodies his [True's] idea of what the bill should be." Adams wasted no time; with Henry's approval he introduced this bill in the House early in January 1904.

The success of the Henry-Adams-True triple play caught the attention of the Executive Committee, whose members in mid-January gathered for legislative business in the Nation's Capitol. Their conferences with Adams led the Congressman to request from the director of each station a statement of the reasons demonstrating a new grant to be not only desirable but necessary. Their conferences with Adams also produced several changes in the text of the bill already introduced and prompted Adams to introduce two months later a second and slightly revised bill. The new bill retained intact, however, the purpose and stipend of its predecessor.

The fast-moving Adams lost no opportunity to plead the case for an increased Federal subsidy for the stations. Early in February the House discussed the items in the proposed budget of the Department of Agriculture. When the clerk read that item appropriating to each State the customary Hatch figure of $15,000, Adams sprang to his feet and proposed an amendment that each State henceforth receive an additional sum of $5,000 per year. In a straightforward presentation evincing his expert familiarity with the station movement, Adams described the station labors in a number of States. "I have asked for the passage of this amendment because the stations need the money," he affirmed with spirited candor (*1*). "When in Congress you can do something like this which is definite, which does not take very much money, for Heaven's sake do it, because the American farmer and our agricultural interests deserve it."

The members of the House applauded his address, but they refused to accept his amendment, the adoption of which would have violated the long-standing parliamentary rule that an amendment to an appropriation bill cannot change existing law by increasing that appropriation. The Adams performance did not indicate his ignorance of the rule, still less a wasted effort; it did mean, however, that the Wisconsin Congressman had maneuvered to submit a brisk introductory argument 7 weeks in advance of the calendar position assigned to his bill. Not only did his maneuver give him two opportunities to plead his case; it also enabled him to familiarize his brethren with the figure of $5,000, to emphasize the comparative smallness of that sum, and to prepare them for the forthcoming request in his bill that they immediately appropriate no more than $5,000 (though ultimately $15,000) to each State for the conduct of original research. Most of all it allowed him to gage the House reaction and thus anticipate the strongest criticisms from the opponents of his bill.

Adams profited by his preliminary parliamentary maneuvering, for in March he devoted his major address to subduing the informal objections his February remarks had generated. "I have heard only two arguments against this bill," he announced. "One is that it is paternalistic, and the other is that the States are not doing what they should, and should provide all the funds necessary for the proper development of the experiment station work."

The fact of paternalism Adams freely admitted, but he challenged his hearers to reveal the harm in a "paternalism which benefits special interests to the advantage of all others. If a small appropriation . . . is paternalism," he countered, "then make the most of it. If the actual record of the stations indicates anything, it means that there will come back to the agriculture and the business of the United States hundreds, if not thousands, of dollars for every dollar carried in this appropriation" (2).

Adams answered with equal simplicity the argument that the States should assume complete responsibility for the financial support of the station enterprise: the States, heavily burdened with other expenses, already were contributing to the station cause the maximum maintenance which the legislatures could afford. Thus the relatively few States able to collect large tax revenues were "most generously" financing their research institutions, but the hard-pressed States, far greater in number, simply could not provide the support which the stations needed and merited, and in the public interest should receive.

Adams then spread on 5 pages of the Congressional Record the letters he had received from 23 directors explaining their need for additional funds. The directors' comments, comprising in effect a national survey, left no doubt that the inadequacy of the current station income severely handicapped the station efforts. "The character of the work is constantly becoming more complex and, therefore, more costly," wrote Director Charles E. Thorne of Ohio, a veteran in the business of the Association since 1887 (2). "The problems which were first attacked were the more simple ones, but as the solutions of these are attained we find that beyond them lie others of even greater importance, but whose solution involves an indefinitely greater outlay in the apparatus required for exact research and in the men qualified to conduct such research." Director Hilgard of California, whose pen two decades earlier had aided the Hatch movement, wrote with his customary acuteness (*2*), "We are so beset with local demands that little time or money remains for the direct researches of wider scope, which are considered by many as the main object of the Hatch Act, and which are only indirectly touched by the elaboration of local questions that now mainly occupy our working staff."

The House could not have failed to conclude from Adams' forceful presentation of evidence that the conduct of fundamental investigations, which many directors had declared themselves ready to undertake, depended on the passage of the Wisconsinite's bill. No Congressman could readily have denied that the proposed subsidy would promote a highly useful purpose. Nevertheless Adams could not, despite his resourcefulness, maneuver his bill to the voting stage in 1904.

CONGRESS TOOK ACTION

The House in 1904 did, however, take action which in its repercussions challenged the historic course of the American station movement, prodded the Executive Committee into resolute activity, alerted and unified the entire membership of the Association, and intimately affected the outcome of the Adams proposal. The appropriation bill for the Department of Agriculture contained an unorthodox provision which the House approved without objection or discussion. That provision assigned a new duty to the Secretary; it directed him "to coordinate the work of the several stations, and the work of the stations with the Department of Agriculture, to the end of preventing unnecessary duplication of work, of increasing the efficiency of the stations and the Department of Agriculture, and to unify and systematize agricultural investigation in the United States" (*30*).

With these words the chairman of the Executive Committee, President Henry Clay White of Georgia, informed the conventioneers in the autumn of 1904 that a formidable crisis confronted the station enterprise and the companion colleges as well. His committee, having moved quickly when it learned of the House action, had persuaded the chairmen of the House and Senate agricultural committees to delete the offending provision prior to the final enactment of the appropriation measure. Nevertheless, White warned the Association, the circumstances and the Congressional attitude responsible for the insertion of the unwelcome provision still prevailed. Chairman White (*30*) then explained more fully, as follows:

This incident and the large and careful consideration given during the year to the relations of the experiment stations to the Department of Agriculture, lead your committee to report frankly . . . that, in its judgment, a grave situation has arisen, involving the entire future of agricultural research work in the United States. For many years after the establishment of the State experiment stations these were the main—almost the exclusive—instruments through which research in agriculture in this country was prosecuted. · · · During this period the stations had a right to expect and they did receive much valuable aid from the U.S. Department of Agriculture, particularly through its ability, as a great department of the national government, to give wide circulation to . . . the results obtained by the stations. Within a few years past, however, a number of bureaus of purely scientific research, as related to agriculture, have arisen within the Department of Agriculture, and have been maintained by generous appropriations of money from the National Treasury. The Department has therefore entered upon—or at least been engaged in to a far greater extent than heretofore—a field of endeavor which formerly was occupied almost exclusively by the State stations.

This statement of facts is made by your committee in no spirit of sensitiveness to rivalry. It is freely conceded that the agricultural research work of the Department . . . is of high quality and value. It is as stoutly maintained that the work of the stations is at least equally so. But, with two agents operating in the same field, common prudence and regard for effectiveness dictate that care should be taken that each singly, or the two combined, should operate with maximum economy and for maximum results. . . . The Department is comparatively rich, with a readily approachable and generous Congress at its doors and the resources of the Federal Treasury at its back. The stations are comparatively poor in money, without hope, and perhaps without expectations, in equity, of large aid from their several States, widely scattered and far removed from the ear of Congressional committees. It would not be surprising, therefore, if mere possession of the financial ability to do it might lead the Department to undertake some kinds of research work which the stations are otherwise better qualified to do. There is also danger perhaps that the inability of the stations to compete with the department in the matter of compensation offered qualified and desirable men may lower the standard or impair the enthusiasm of service at the stations in such manner as to disqualify the stations for work which otherwise, by reason of their local conditions, they should be better able to do than a single Department at the National Capital. In fine, it is conceivable that a rich and central agency of research might so overshadow poor and scattered agencies as to seriously impair their standing and efficiency. Your committee, therefore . . . recommends that instruction be given your executive committee to make clear to the proper Congressional committees, if hearings can be secured, the important part taken by the State experiment stations in the agricultural research work of this country, with a view to securing for the stations *some measure of equity in the appropriations* made for this purpose from the National Treasury.[4]

This keen analysis from Henry White, the chemist who had added to his station duties the cares of a presidency, eloquently revealed that the American movement to subsidize and administer scientific research in agriculture had, after a half-century of slow growth, placed the Federal Department in competition with the State stations, a likelihood implicit in the origins of the State and Federal agencies. It demonstrated that the States' legislative policy, characteristically parsimonious, had put the stations in a disadvantageous position, one which in the eighties had compelled the stations to seek Federal funds in order to begin operations, and in the new century forced them to seek additional Federal funds in order to fulfill their scientific function. That policy had not only impelled the stations then to secure Federal funds free from Federal control, but now, in self-defense against competitive activity from a Federal Department, to take the extreme ground that the Federal Government henceforth should finance the State stations, via Hatch-type grants, equally as liberally as its own Department. The stations imperatively needed a larger income whether they elected to follow a course of productive investigation independent of the Departmental programs, or to "cooperate" via contractual agreements with the Department on the Federal projects multiplying in every State.

DECLARATION OF POLICY URGED

These somber concerns made the passage of the Adams bill urgent rather than merely desirable. Yet even that measure, if passed, would quiet the crisis only temporarily. The station movement needed more than a new Federal donation; it needed from Congress a declaration of policy defining the future course of agricultural research subsidized by the Federal Government. Did that Government, with its power

[4] Italics inserted.

The station cause would suffer severely, so ran the tenor of the White report, unless Congress assured parity in appropriations, enabled the stations to cooperate on even terms with the Department, and recognized the historic and continuing distinctions between the stations and the Department as research agencies. Finally, Congressmen should understand that they blurred those distinctions and damaged the station enterprise when they legislatively directed the Secretary of Agriculture "to coordinate the work of the several stations . . . and to unify and systematize agricultural investigation in the United States."

Thus the Executive Committee, when it received authority from the Association to plead the station cause before Congressmen, undertook a delicate mission where success would be difficult to attain and defeat could spell disaster. The Association fortified the Committee by resolving, in response to Jordan's motion, that "the autonomy and paramount position of the stations as institutions of research and experimentation be inviolably maintained within their respective States, in accordance with the terms and spirit of the Hatch Act" (20).

Furthermore, the convention elected to the Executive Committee a panel of officers ready to defend the stations' welfare and permit no other interests of the membership to take precedence. The station section contributed the forensic talents of Director Jordan; the college section, those of President White. The substitution by the college section of Cornell's dean and director, Liberty Hyde Bailey, for George Atherton gave station champions a majority voice on that committee. Director Bailey, the successor of Isaac Roberts at Cornell, added to the group his prestige as a nationally known plant scientist and, in addition, his vocal support for the Adams bill. Chairman White led his Executive Committee in mid-January 1905, to a hearing before the House Committee on Agriculture.

Carefully White chose his words as he introduced his colleagues to the members of the House Committee and then reviewed the salient features of the Federal legislation which, since 1887, had governed the development of the station enterprise. Congress, he explained, had deliberately directed the establishment of a system having noteworthy characteristics; for example, the continuing annual appropriations for the support of station-departments in the land-grant colleges, the advisory function of the Secretary of Agriculture, the financial reports to Congress. Moreover, each of these features, he noted, served an important purpose. The framers of the Hatch Act had, for example, intentionally inserted the stipulation for a specific Federal grant to each State in order to encourage local initiative in research; those founders believed that "more might be expected from experimentation . . . if there was freedom in the several parts of the country to engage in such work." Likewise the legislation founding the Hatch system instructed the Secretary to assist the stations in the preparation of reports which would demonstrate to Congress that the stations were properly using the Federal funds. "It was wise," he observed (*28, p. 3*), "to intrust to the locality the pretty full and free administration of this trust."

White came quickly to the point. Neither accident nor insignificant coincidence but serious and deliberate purpose had produced the Hatch Act and the nationwide network of research institutions in the States. That purpose—local responsibility for initiating and conducting research at public expense—had already demonstrated its soundness in the record of station productivity. To the stations, White continued, should go the credit for accomplishing the major portion of the research already transforming agricultural technology and the "agricultural industries."

Nevertheless, the station delegation had not come to claim credit, nor to beg money, nor to plead for special legislation, but solely to reassure itself that the Congressmen did not misunderstand the intent of the organic legislation nor overlook the continuing and growing usefulness of the State stations. "We are a little fearful," he added gently (*28, p. 4*), "that perhaps there has been unconsciously and unintentionally a misapprehension of the relations of the stations to the Department of Agriculture, for example, and a misunderstanding on the part of the stations as to the views of this committee representing the Congress of the manner in which the stations should administer their affairs."

Having smoothly prepared the House committeemen for the unconventional experience of listening to the station story rather than a plea for funds, White gave way to the waiting Jordan, ready to exploit this first opportunity for a station director to appear before a Congressional committee.

JORDAN TOOK NEW ROLE

Exigency now cast Jordan in a new role. Adept heretofore as a critic of the station's deficiencies in scientific productivity, he now showed his proficiency in praising the strengths of the State institutions. Vigorously Jordan reviewed the station labors. He marshalled his data carefully in order to conclude that the practice of Federal grants had encouraged the States to support their stations so enthusiastically that the total of State contributions currently approximated the total Hatch appropriation. So firmly established in the public esteem had the stations become, in response to public demand, that "the station expert is everywhere." Moreover, the station movement had demonstrated the importance of using as research personnel "specialists whom the people know and trust and who are in close touch with the peculiar conditions and relations existing within the State" (*28, p. 7*). So completely had the stations become in practice "the servants of insistent demands," Jordan concluded, that the station experience proved beyond question the success of the Hatch system founded in 1887 (*28, p. 22*). Accordingly, Congress should encourage, not discourage or impede, a movement firmly approved by popular judgment.

Jordan then ventured boldly into the lions' den. Did not the phenomenal and unprecedented growth of the Federal Department of Agriculture, encouraged by the generous appropriations and comprehensive directives of the Congress, tend strongly to interfere seriously with the Hatch system of research, laboriously built and popularly ratified? Did not the status of the Department, "a powerful and rapidly developing centralized organization," contrast sharply with that of the State stations, "agencies standing close to local sentiment and conditions," and did not the existence of the two systems of administering research raise unavoidable "questions of policy and adjustment"? (28, p. 16). Did not this situation require Congress to appraise the merits of the Hatch system and, in the event Congress wished the State stations to continue as significant institutions, to follow in the public interest a course which would not permit the Federal Department to supplant the stations?

Statistics, Jordan continued, demonstrated the trend and proved the fears of station men not groundless. The Federal Government in the years between 1887 and 1904 had quadrupled that portion of the Departmental budget (excluding the Hatch appropriation) spent for research; the Bureau of Plant Industry, for example, in 1904 operated on a budget larger than the total Hatch appropriation to all the States. Similarly the Departmental scientific staff, composed exclusively of full-time specialists having no college or teaching duties, had grown steadily until in 1904 it substantially outnumbered the nationwide total of station workers.

Therefore, Jordan concluded, in budget and in personnel "the Department has attained a position of supremacy. . . . As a natural and inevitable result the Department with its overwhelming equipment of men and means, is not now, as formerly, confining its research work largely to that which can be done in the laboratories at Washington, but is, of very necessity, as a means of securing opportunities, reaching out into the several States, and . . . is now traversing, to a large extent, the field that had been and still is also traversed by the experiment stations" (28, p. 17).

Jordan soberly posed a piercing question. Did Congress intend not only to perpetuate but also to accentuate the imbalance, already marked, between the Department and the stations; did Congress intend, in short, to reverse the policy established by the Hatch Act? Furthermore the Congressional readiness to increase the Secretary's powers over the stations filled station men with an anxiety that Congress intended "to reduce the stations to a minor and subordinate position." The Geneva director spoke plainly, as follows (28, p. 18):

> Station officials believe that the real question lies farther back even than in the establishment of a system of cooperation between the Department and the stations, although [such cooperation] . . . may be wisely—perhaps necessarily— a means of securing most effective results . . . [The fundamental] question . . . pertains to the policy which shall prevail in the organization and development of agricultural research in this country. Is the movement of the future to be one of centralization with a continued increase of the means and equipment of the Department out of proportion to the enlargement of the stations, or is the 'autonomy and dominant position' of the stations in the several States to be fostered through the enlargement of their means and the maintenance of the original policy established by Congress? The real questioin then is, In the solution of problems of importance in the several States, where should the leadership lie or what instrument may be made most adaptable and efficient in serving the agricultural interests of the several States? That policy now seems to be to enlarge the means of the national Department, partly in order that it may aid the stations. Would it not be wiser, in some fields at least to enable the stations to proceed on an independent basis?

Thus Jordan, the spokesman for the Association, placed squarely on the House Agricultural Committee and on Congress the major

103

responsibility for the future welfare of the State stations. Careful not to violate the theme set by Henry White at the opening of the hearing, Jordan requested neither funds nor legislation; he asked only that the Committee not overlook the station cause in making decisions when at a later time there might appear specific bills or issues dealing with agricultural research. The Committee did not, however, miss the hard point of Jordan's skillful charge. If the station declined in utility and productivity because the Congress financially favored Departmental research at the expense of the State stations, then the coming generations of the American public, so Jordan reasoned, would rightly lay the blame on Capitol Hill.

Jordan did not let slip by, however, an impromptu opportunity to confess a willingness to receive more Federal funds. So ably had he pleaded the station case that at one point a Congressman interrupted him with the query, "Don't you think a fair inference from these figures is that we should give you all the money we have got?" Replied Jordan, "No; you have a great big Department in Washington that needs all the money you can give it. But, on reflection, I would say we will take all the money we can get, and we can use it well" (*28, pp. 14–15*). Moreover, in his quiet conclusion, almost casual in tone, Jordan remarked that a shortage of resources did prevent many stations from investigating problems in original research where the "facts lying deeper down, whose demonstration requires long-continued and expensive effort, must be dug out" (*28, p. 22*).

The intentness of Jordan's lawyer-like pleadings scored decisive points for the station team but it also produced overtones of discomfort for other participants in the hearing, the members of a Departmental delegation led by Secretary James Wilson. Quietly Wilson listened while White and Jordan appraised the assumption of the House Committee that the Secretary could exercise a directive, rather than solely an advisory, power over the stations' experimentation and expenditures. Most attentively Wilson noted the repeated insistence by the station spokesman that any further increase of Departmental control over the stations, regardless of the presumed value of such control, would not only violate the principles of the Hatch Act but also reduce the stations' effectiveness in research productivity.

White and Jordan, acutely aware that necessity forced them into an awkward situation, strove to express no complaints about Wilson's administration of his Department. Nevertheless the House Committee pointedly asked the station men to reveal specific cases of conflict rather than to discuss only future policy; they probed the relationship between the Department and the stations. White and Jordan, apologizing to the Secretary for the unintended and unfortunate reflections on his admittedly competent leadership, declined to answer the Committee's questions. The innuendo reflected adversely on the Department, for it suggested that Wilson's successful efforts to build his Department into a scientific institution should be checked lest they further damage the station cause. Furthermore, the station pleadings intimated that the overly vigorous Wilson, too ready to ignore the stations, had violated the intent of the Hatch Act.

Secretary Wilson waited patiently until the station spokesmen had completed their presentation. Then in self-defense he cross-examined Jordan and White; they readily conceded that the Secretary had not "been meddling with the stations or unduly indicating to them"

(*28, p. 27*). Wilson scored small success, however, when he sought concessions on other points.

The Secretary asked Director Bailey to agree that the Federal Government should not provide "money for local research within the States" and, accordingly, that all research not of that type should legitimately come within the Department's jurisdiction. Bailey neatly parried that thrust by maintaining that "large original problems," supported by Federal grants based on the Hatch principle, would properly lie within the scope of station activity. "So far as possible," Bailey further insisted, "the origination of the scientific work and the research work should lie with the experiment stations in those regions . . ." Thereupon Wilson turned to White and tried to induce him to concede that the stations, in those States where the Department had thus far conducted its work, could not have operated the program more efficiently. That effort failed. White flatly contradicted the Secretary's contention (*28, pp. 32–33*).

Secretary Wilson, unable to win further concessions, then good-humoredly explained the sincere purpose of his intensive efforts to apply science to American agriculture; the goal, already achieved, of building in his Department a corps of full-time specialists, "the greatest scientists in their respective lines today that the world knows of;" the spectacular successes in disease eradication, a duty which Congress had directed his Department to conduct. With complete candor and an infectious warmth Wilson ably defended his Department and gave ample evidence of the enthusiastic ability which had made him an outstanding administrator and his Department an impressive organization. Yet Wilson proved to be the station's most effective advocate. "We are doing a great deal of work which the stations cannot do," he observed, "because the stations have not the means at their disposal to do it. . . . They do not have . . . specialists enough." Forthrightly he then declared, "I believe that the independence of the State experiment stations should be maintained" (*28, p. 35–36*).

No one could have mistaken his sincerity and earnestness in volunteering to cooperate in research with any station, nor have failed to sympathize with his justifiable pride in his corps of specialists. Yet his ready-tongued rebuttal revealed his conviction that his Department, professionally intent on "helping" to solve State problems to the limit of its expanding Federal budget, unquestionably should have the right to multiply the activities which already had prompted apprehensiveness among station men.

CAUSE WAS PLEADED WELL

That display of Wilsonian sincerity, coupled with the repeated affirmation of good will from the station spokesman, assuaged any rancor that the collision of station and Departmental interests could have generated. It also gave Henry White the opportunity to close the 2-hour hearing with a good-natured rejoinder which pointedly reaffirmed the station position. "In the very zeal of the Secretary, it may come to pass that in the minds of the members of Congress there may exist a suspicion that outside the Department of Agriculture nothing is being done. . . . I propose, if it be so, to make evident to you . . . that the experiment stations have done something, too, and they are not asking merely for appropriations of money to help them do more. That, of course, is in your discretion. But we do ask," White went on, "and I think we have a right to ask, that the experiment stations shall be understood; . . . and that you shall know that there are men elsewhere who are doing great work." With gentlemanly grace White bowed to the Committee and smilingly concluded as he praised the Hatch system, "And, as I say, the very zeal of the Secretary emphasizes what we have in mind, namely, that perhaps you gentlemen may not come to know that there are, indeed, others" (*28, p. 37*).

How effectively had White, Jordan, and Bailey—not to mention Wilson—pleaded the station cause? Had the hearing convinced the House Committee that Congressional decisions and Federal policy-making would intimately affect the future course of the station movement? Had the hearing enabled the committeemen to understand the manifold meaning of the Adams bill, scarcely mentioned on that January day but undeniably a current concern of the attentive Adams and his colleagues on that committee?

The proceedings of the hearing did not remain a secret; the committeemen sounded out their legislative brethren; and months slipped by. Congressman Adams, caught in the grip of an incurable illness and visibly weakening, put his last strength into bringing his bill to a vote in the House. He succeeded early in 1906. On February 15, he spoke simply for several minutes prior to the taking of the vote. "I believe that this House is in favor of this bill," he predicted with quiet confidence (*3*), "and I do not see how I could improve the situation by telling them why they are in favor of it."

ACT PASSED IN 1906

Adams accurately gaged the Congressional sentiment. Promptly the House passed his bill; 3 weeks later the Senated concurred. President Theodore Roosevelt affixed his signature on March 16. Thus Henry Adams had the satisfaction, only 4 months before his death, of seeing the station measure written into Federal law; and station men, equally reassured, knew now that the Federal Government solidly approved the reinforcement of the Hatch system.

Meanwhile the movement for the Adams Act prompted the Executive Committee, busily engaged in improving the efficiency of the twin-sectioned Association, to recommend to the convention of 1905 the creation of a permanent committee on experiment station organization and policy (*6, p. 19*). The Association adopted the proposal, and veteran directors received appointments to the six committee seats.

To this committee fell the task of surveying regularly the problems confronting the station enterprise; to it the Association assigned the role of recommending proposals for corrective action. This committee formally inherited the responsibility for appraisal and constructive criticism of the station movement, a function which from the earliest years individual spokesmen had voluntarily and unofficially exercised. Created 4 months before President Roosevelt signed the Adams Act into law, the new Experiment Station Committee on Organization and Policy (ESCOP) began its first major appraisal three weeks after the passage of that act. The chairmanship of ESCOP went with nice propriety to Eugene Davenport, whose initia-

tive at the convention of 1902 had crystallized the determination to secure the Federal grant which now bore Adams' name.

The passage of the Adams Act in 1906 firmly established the principle in American governmental policy that Federal aid shall join with State aid for the purpose of subsidizing scientific research in the State stations. It reaffirmed the public faith in the historic purpose of station statesmen to conduct research of the highest quality and to adhere in administrative policy to the principles of local initiative and Federal assistance. It supplied the opportunity to perform the "original research" for which scientists long had labored. In equal measure, however, it now held the nationwide network of State stations responsible for the conduct of that research. Thus the Federal decision of 1906 compelled station men henceforth to develop to a maximum the research capacity of their stations and to sharpen, in the finest Hatch-Adams spirit, the appraising powers of the Office of Experiment Stations. Finally it necessitated operational harmony between that Office and the new Committee on Organization and Policy, and it accelerated the introduction of new techniques in the administration of station research.

LITERATURE CITED

(1) ADAMS, H. C.
    1904. DEBATE ON APPROPRIATIONS BILL FOR DEPARTMENT OF AGRICULTURE. Cong. Rec. 58th Cong., 2d Sess., pp. 1689–1690.
(2) ——
    1904. [DEBATE ON ADAMS BILL, H.R. 14098.] Cong. Rec. 58th Cong., 2d Sess., pp. 3843–3858.
(3) ——
    1906. REMARKS ON THE ADAMS BILL, H.R. 345. Cong. Rec., 59th Cong., 1st Sess., pp. 2615–2627.
(4) ALVORD, H. E.
    1895. REPORT OF THE EXECUTIVE COMMITTEE. Assoc. Amer. Agr. Cols. and Expt. Stas. Proc. (1894) 8 : 15–18 ; 93–94. (U.S. Dept. Agr., Off. Expt. Stas. Bul. 24.)
(5) ——
    1896. ANNUAL ADDRESS BY THE PRESIDENT. Assoc. Amer. Agr. Cols. and Expt. Stas. Proc. (1895) 9 : 20–31. (U.S. Dept. Agr., Off. Expt. Stas. Bul. 30.)
(6) ASSOCIATION OF AMERICAN AGRICULTURAL COLLEGES AND EXPERIMENT STATIONS.
    1906. STANDING COMMITTEE. Assoc. Amer. Agr. Cols. and Expt. Stas. Proc. (1905) 19 : 19, 50, 66. (U.S. Dept. Agr., Off. Expt. Stas. Bul. 164.)
(7) ATWATER, W. O.
    1890. [THE PRIMARY OBLIGATIONS OF COLLEGES AND STATIONS UNDER THE HATCH ACT:] Assoc. Amer. Agr. Cols. and Expt. Stas. Proc. (1889) 3 : 96–100. (U.S. Dept. Agr., Off. Expt. Stas. Misc. Bul. 2.)
(8) —— JOHNSON, S. W., AND COOK, G. H.
    1888. REPORT OF THE COMMITTEE ON STATION WORK. Assoc. Amer. Agr. Cols. and Expt. Stas. (1887), 32 pp. Washington.
(9) COOKE, W. W.
    1889. HOW CAN THE DEPARTMENT OF AGRICULTURE ASSIST THE STATIONS? Assoc. Amer. Agr. Cols. and Expt. Stas. Proc. 2 : 48–49. (U.S. Dept. Agr., Off. Expt. Stas. Misc. Bul. 1.)
(10) DABNEY, C. W., Jr.
    1891. REPORT OF THE PERMANENT COMMITTEE ON CHEMISTRY. Assoc. Amer. Agr. Cols. and Expt. Stas. Proc. (1890) 4 : 23–29. (U.S. Dept. Agr., Off. Expt. Stas. Misc. Bul. 3.)

(11) DAVENPORT, E.
       1903. INCREASED APPROPRIATION FOR EXPERIMENT STATIONS. Assoc. Amer.
             Agr. Cols. and Expt. Stas. Proc. (1902) 16 : 55. (U.S. Dept.
             Agr., Off. Expt. Stas. Bul. 123.)
(12) HATCH, W. H.
       1894. DISCUSSION ON APPROPRIATION BILL FOR THE DEPARTMENT OF AGRI-
             CULTURE. Cong. Rec., 53d Cong., 2d Sess., pp. 4787, 4891–92.
(13) HENRY, W. A.
       1894. PRESIDENT'S ADDRESS. Assoc. Amer. Agr. Cols. and Expt. Stas.
             Proc. (1893) 7 : 38–45. (U.S. Dept. Agr., Off. Expt. Stas.
             Bul. 20.)
(14) ———
       1902. INVESTIGATION AND INSTRUCTION BY STATION OFFICERS. Assoc.
             Amer. Agr. Cols. and Expt. Stas. Proc. (1901) 15 : 28–33. (U.S.
             Dept. Agr., Off. Expt. Stas. Bul. 115.)
(15) ———
       1903. AMENDMENTS TO THE CONSTITUTION. Assoc. Amer. Agr. Cols. and
             Expt. Stas. Proc. (1902) 16 : 44–45. (U.S. Dept. Agr., Off.
             Expt. Stas. Bul. 123.)
(16) ———
       1907. MEMORIAL TO HENRY CULLEN ADAMS. Assoc. Amer. Agr. Cols. and
             Expt. Stas. Proc. (1906) 20 : 36–39. (U.S. Dept. Agr., Off. Expt.
             Stas. Bul. 184.)
(17) JOHNSON, S. W.
       1897. ANNUAL ADDRESS BY THE PRESIDENT. Assoc. Amer. Agr. Cols. and
             Expt. Stas. Proc. (1896) 10 : 43–46. (U.S. Dept. of Agr., Off.
             Expt. Stas. Bul. 41.)
(18) JORDAN, W. H.
       1898. REPORT OF THE SECTION ON AGRICULTURE AND CHEMISTRY. Assoc.
             Amer. Agr. Cols. and Expt. Stas. Proc. (1897) 11 : 22–25. (U.S.
             Dept. Agr., Off. Expt. Stas. Bul. 49.)
(19) ———
       1901. AMERICAN AGRICULTURAL EXPERIMENT STATIONS. Assoc. Amer. Agr.
             Cols. and Expt. Stas. Proc. (1900) 14 : 42–51. (U.S. Dept. Agr.,
             Off. Expt. Stas. Bul. 49.)
(20) ———
       1905. COOPERATION BETWEEN THE STATIONS AND THE DEPARTMENT OF AGRI-
             CULTURE. Assoc. Amer. Agr. Cols. and Expt. Stas. Proc. (1904)
             18 : 62–63. (U.S. Dept. Agr., Off. Expt. Stas. Bul. 153.)
(21) MORROW, G. E.
       1895. PRESIDENT'S ADDRESS. Assoc. Amer. Agr. Cols. and Expt. Stas.
             Proc. (1894) 8 : 25–33. (U.S. Dept. Agr., Off. Expt. Stas. Bul. 24.)
(22) MORTON, J. S.
       1895. ADDRESS. Assoc. Amer. Agr. Cols. and Expt. Stas. Proc. (1894)
             8 : 47–48. (U.S. Dept. Agr., Off. Expt. Stas. Bul. 24.)
(23) SECTION ON EXPERIMENT STATION WORK.
       1906. HOW MUCH DEMONSTRATION WORK SHOULD THE STATION UNDER-
             TAKE? Assoc. Amer. Agr. Cols. and Expt. Stas. Proc. (1905) 19 :
             170–186. (U.S. Dept. Agr., Off. Expt. Stas. Bul. 164.)
(24) TRUE, A. C.
       1896. SOME ELEMENTS OF PERMANENCY IN EXPERIMENT STATION WORK.
             Assoc. Amer. Agr. Cols. and Expt. Stas. Proc. (1895) 9 : 42–46.
             (U.S. Dept. Agr., Off. Expt. Stas. Bul. 30.)
(25) ———
       1898. ADVERTISING IN EXPERIMENT STATION PUBLICATIONS. Assoc. Amer.
             Agr. Cols. and Expt. Stas. Proc. (1897) 11 : 41–43. (U.S. Dept.
             Agr., Off. Expt. Stas. Bul. 49.)
(26) ———
       1900. REPORT OF THE DIRECTOR OF THE OFFICE OF EXPERIMENT STATIONS
             FOR 1900. U.S. Dept. Agr. Annual Rpt. 1900, 170 pp.
(27) ——— and CROSBY, D. J.
       1904. NEEDS OF THE STATIONS. U.S. Dept. Agr., Off. Expt. Stas. Ann.
             Rpt. 1903 : 27–34.
(28) UNITED STATES CONGRESS, HOUSE COMMITTEE ON AGRICULTURE.
       1905. HEARING ON AGRICULTURAL COLLEGES AND EXPERIMENT STATIONS,
             JANUARY 18, 1905. 37 pp. (U.S. Congress, 58th, 3rd Sess.)

(29) WHITE, H. C.
1904. REPORT OF THE EXECUTIVE COMMITTEE. Assoc. Amer. Agr. Cols.
and Expt. Stas. Proc. (1903) 17: 17–20, 30. (U.S. Dept. Agr.,
Off. Expt. Stas. Bul. 142.)
(30) ——
1905. HEARING ON AGRICULTURAL COLLEGES AND EXPERIMENT STATIONS,
and Expt. Stas. Proc. (1904) 18: 15–19. (U.S. Dept. Agr., Off.
Expt. Stas. Bul. 153.)

Chapter Seven—

THE STATE STATIONS AND THE DEPARTMENT OF AGRICULTURE: Consultation and Cooperation

Born in the same year, the Federal Department of Agriculture and the land-grant colleges also grew up together. Confronted by a mutuality of problems, the colleges and the Department matured into a nationwide system of agricultural research and education. None of the many relationships that were to follow served better to delineate interest differences on the one hand, and, on the other hand, to promote the wholesome spirit of give and take than did the early experiment station movement. In the debates that took place in the early conventions and later in the more convenient section and committee meetings, we find the amalgam of an enduring cooperative Federal and States relations system.

The elements of conflict and compromise came to the surface in the proceedings of the first decade of annual conventions, led principally by the experiment station leaders; subsequently, in the meetings of the Experiment Station Committee on Organization and Policy (ESCOP). These and the intersectional meetings of the Association served as the vehicles through which the station directors sought protection against encroachments on the mission of the experiment stations. Their ideal was the "conception of the experiment station as a research institution—one for discovering, verifying, and establishing the practical bearings of scientific facts and principles in agriculture" (7)[1]. Members of the Federal Department's staff sat in on all these discussions.

The personnel in the Office of Experiment Stations (OES) especially sympathized with the viewpoints of station spokesmen. From the moment it was established in 1888, that Office carefully refrained from taking any action which the members of the Association could consider authoritarian, despite the directive power inherent in the provisions of Federal legislation. Commissioner Colman of the Department and Director Atwater of OES followed the principle that the Association, rather than the Department, should enunciate the advisory role of the Federal Government in the station enterprise. The Association, from the time of its first general session in 1887, (14), and later in its section on experiment station work, undertook the responsibility of formulating "advisory propositions" for ethical patterns of behavior and Federal-grant administration applicable to its member institutions. Within the Association there developed under Alvord's leadership a movement to amend the Hatch Act for the specific purpose of assigning to OES the function of ascertaining that the expenditure of Federal funds conformed to the requirements of the Hatch Act.

Congress acceded to requests from the Association for legislative action; in the departmental appropriation for the fiscal year ending June 30, 1895, Congress directed the Secretary of Agriculture to "prescribe the form of the annual financial statement required by section

---

[1] Italic numbers in parentheses refer to Literature Cited, p. 139.

three of the Hatch Act" and to "ascertain whether the expenditures under the appropriation hereby made are in accordance with the provisions of the said [Hatch] Act and shall make report thereon to Congress." This Congressional stipulation did not initiate a program of Federal dictation, nor did it alter the policy of sympathetic assistance anticipated in the Colman convention of 1885, established in Departmental practice during the Colman commissionership, and administered after 1888 by OES.

The Secretary of Agriculture, made responsible by Congressional fiat for administering Federal funds, delegated responsibility to OES. Thereafter, the Department established policies via the issuance of Secretary's letters and the publication of rules, regulations, reports, and similar documents.[2] Nevertheless, the traditions established in the mideighties held firm. Full and free discussions within the Association always preceded the establishment of Departmental directives applicable to the stations. Moreover, at OES, Director Alfred Charles True, as dedicated a missionary as his mentor, Dr. Atwater, to the cause of freely functioning stations in the States, reaffirmed with quiet conviction in 1896 that the administration of the stations would continue to follow "the principle of local control" (*32, p. 196*). He justified this principle as valid for experiment stations in the following words:

> The principle of local control with a view to meeting the varied needs of the different agricultural regions is in harmony with our governmental and educational system, and in the long run will undoubtedly produce the best results. The responsibility resting upon the State and Territorial authorities to maintain these stations will lead to their development in proportion to the interest taken in them by the people, and when once this interest is sufficiently awakened it will conduce to the building up of strong stations.

True's associate and subsequently his successor, Dr. Edwin West Allen, commented many years later (as quoted by Fletcher (*19*) that "thus there came about in the years that followed a unique example of national administration, in which influence, rather than coercion is the policy."

The principle of local control did lead, as the years passed, to strengthened local support for the stations; yet, conversely, that growth induced the enlarging stations to use Hatch funds for nonresearch purposes. This situation prompted a policy statement from Director True, perennially faithful to his official responsibility and responsive to the appraisals made by ESCOP. Director True on February 25, 1909[3] called the attention of station directors to a growing tendency in the States to use Hatch funds for such nonresearch work as printing, correspondence, administration, and miscellaneous purposes connected with general business operations at the station. He attributed this to various reasons, such as the increase of State appropriations for the stations, which in many cases had taken the form of

---

[2] Major Federal policy statements, including letters issued by the Secretary of Agriculture regarding the successive Federal-grant acts that were to govern Federal administration, are included in the appendix of the main text of this publication. Also in the appendix is a record of Miscellaneous Publication 515 and its predecessors that provided Federal interpretation of the governing laws and use of funds.

[3] Letter to Directors of State Experiment Stations. Mimeographed copies on file in Cooperative State Experiment Station Service, U.S. Department of Agriculture.

appropriations for special investigations, demonstrations, or substations, without provision for printing and general administrative duties of the station. The tendency, he averred, in many cases practically amounted to a diversion of the Hatch fund from the purpose for which it was intended. Director True then issued the following instruction:

Each station shall, as far as may be necessary, change its policy of expenditure of the Hatch fund so as to devote a large share of that fund to definite experimental work, restrict the expenditures for printing as indicated above, and put administrative expenses as far as possible on other funds. . . . Beginning with July 1, 1909, it will be expected that all charges for extension work and printing of compilations will be eliminated from the Hatch fund account. . . . This action is not intended to hinder the development of extension work, the value of which I greatly appreciate. This Office will always be glad to do anything in its power to aid the agricultural colleges in securing funds with which to thoroughly organize and develop extension work along the lines of agriculture and country life.

In reading Dr. True's letter, it should be kept in mind that no Federal authorization for extension work had been enacted and that many institutions considered the liberal use of Hatch moneys for printing and demonstration work a part of the experiment station's responsibility. The Association by this time had a standing committee on extension work out of whose deliberations later came the Smith-Lever Act of 1914. Nevertheless, Director True, who later was to head up agricultural extension work in the Department, stood with ESCOP, which from 1905 on was responsible for the function previously held by temporary committees, volunteer spokesmen, and individual directors. He voiced the tradition of the American experiment station movement, namely that public funds appropriated for research were for scientific investigation and for no other purpose. Only by this interpretation could be satisfied the never-ending quest for new scientific knowledge of permanent and basic benefit to agriculture.

The Joint Committee on Projects and Correlation, established in 1913 (*12*) with three members representing the Association and three members appointed by the Secretary of Agriculture, outlined its functions in a memorandum issued in 1914. Principal among these was consideration of the regulatory, investigational, demonstrational, and other extension work of the U.S. Department of Agriculture and the State Agricultural Colleges and Experiment Stations insofar as such work may bear upon agricultural practice or industries, in distinction from general agricultural education. The Committee announced that it had undertaken a survey of "work done under the various appropriations of Congress to the United States Department of Agriculture and the state agricultural colleges and experiment stations." Requests had been sent to the member institutions "that information regarding their investigational, extension, and regulatory work be furnished" (*25*). The Federal Smith-Lever Act authorizing Cooperative Extension Work had been enacted and approved on May 8, 1914 (*38*, *p. 7*). Commenting on its passage in Congress and concerning its joint sponsorship there by the land-grant colleges and the U.S. Department of Agriculture, Secretary D. F. Houston said during the 1914 Association convention, "We are in reality one family, working in different jurisdictions to serve the same people" (*22*). One outgrowth of the deliberations of the Joint Committee was establishment in the Department of Agriculture of the States Relations Service.

From July 6, 1915, to June 30, 1923, this Service included the Office of Experiment Stations, the Office of Extension Work in the South, the Office of Extension Work in the North and West, and the Office of Home Economics (*36*). Dr. True (*35*), who was to head this Service, said during the 1914 convention:

So far our agricultural experiment stations and Department of Agriculture have been hampered in their research work because of the varied duties imposed on them outside of their research functions and the lack of proper differentiation of lines of work and personnel. The Department is now alive to this deficiency and under the plans for reorganization undertaken by Secretary Houston aims to make a distinct separation between research, extension, and regulatory activities. It will thus be possible to know what funds, equipment, and force the Department actually has for research, to determine definitely what problems it will attempt to solve, and to put a more rigid responsibility on its research workers to formulate good plans and to hold to their work on the chosen projects until something worth while is accomplished. If adequate supervision of the research work of the Department is provided this plan should result in better and more productive research.

At the 1915 convention held in Berkeley, Calif., ESCOP's report dealt at length with the functions of the experiment stations in regulatory activities. ESCOP pointed out that the fundamental idea upon which all our experiment stations are based is that of service to agriculture "in acquiring accurate information, in place of tradition, conjecture, and empirical theory." The report (*7*) continued:

They were a direct response to the need for knowledge resting on a reliable scientific basis, in order to make teaching sound and agriculture a more intelligent art. They represented the introduction of the experimental method in testing experience and theory and securing reliable facts and principles in agriculture. They were to be stations for experiment. . . . Through the years the experiment stations had to take on a good many service activities that were not research. . . . The extension work, which is a direct development of experiment station work and was born of its practical results and the public confidence won through it, has for some time been recognized as illogically grouped under the station and has been split off as a separate division or department. State laws have been modified to permit the new organization. . . . In addition to the three divisions of the agricultural college which we have begun to recognize in research, college teaching, and extension, we now recognize at least one other group which has to do with regulation—the machinery for the enforcement of laws for the protection and promotion of agriculture. . . . The retention of such measures by the agricultural colleges is retarding the formation of strong state departments of agriculture, which it is the interest of the colleges to promote.

The principle that regulatory work should not be a part of the research-teaching-extension activity of the land-grant institutions, as recommended by ESCOP in 1915, was accepted and eventually put into effect by the Federal Department of Agriculture. It was voiced officially in a letter dated February 23, 1923, sent to Governors of all States by Secretary of Agriculture Henr C. Wallace.[4]

In its report, ESCOP reaffirmed that the function of an experiment station is to carry on scientific research for agriculture:

The experiment station has justified research in agriculture. It should be able to justify its own maintenance as a research institution. It is believed that at this time we may propagate to advantage to the whole agricultural system the conception of the experiment station as a research institution—one for discovering, verifying, and establishing the practical bearings of scientific facts and principles in agriculture.

[4] See appendix for USDA policy letters relating to relations with Agricultural Experiment Stations.

114

ESCOP and its closely associated Committee on Projects and Correlation, in their re-evaluation of the experiment stations' job in 1914 and 1915, delineated clearly the responsibilities of two of the three major divisions—research, resident teaching, and extension work—of the land-grant agricultural colleges. And they strengthened a system of Federal-State science-education relations that still is regarded as a most successful model (*39*).

National and world events in the years immediately following were to overshadow consideration of such matters as "project correlation." Nevertheless, from the standpoint of the history of public administration, benchmarks were established. One was the first major effort by the Association and the Department to arrive at mutually acceptable principles and standards relating to the essentials of research project outlines. Some principles and rules were established that set precedents for those now governing cooperative regional research.

SYSTEM TESTED BY FIRST WORLD WAR

With the coming of the First World War, scientific agriculture as organized under the USDA–land-grant college system was to meet its first real test. Emphasis, as later in the Second World War, was on production more than on research. This meant drawing on the reserve of scientific know-how accumulated in previous research.

ESCOP's 1917 report, which dealt primarily with "Publishing the Work of the Experiment Stations," provided further guidelines for station publication policy. The closely cooperative agricultural and home economics extension services of the parent institutions, recognized nationally in the Smith-Lever Act of 1914, authorizing Federal support, had been given the green light for assuming leadership in the production program under the stimulating nationwide slogan, "Food Will Win the War." ESCOP's report (*8*) urged that—

the stations ought frankly to accept the fact that their present field and functions are agricultural investigation and experiment—the discovering and verifying of exact information pertaining to agricultural science and practice, and this view ought to be clearly reflected in their publications. Their success lies in that direction, for they cannot hope to compete with the extension departments now organized in a large way with steadily increasing funds. These on the other hand must rely upon the stations very largely for the matter they attempt to teach and demonstrate, while the stations can secure through their cooperation the desired contact with the public and can effectively place their practical results and recommendations before the farmers. Manifestly, the stations should not be wholly cut off from contact with the agricultural industry, and it is proper and just that to them should be accorded credit for the matter given out through extension channels, so that the public may not lose sight of the practical character of their work and may know the important part they are playing.

The 32d annual meeting which had been planned for the usual time in November 1918, was "postponed on account of the disorganization due to the prevailing influenza." It was held in Baltimore, Md., on January 8–10, 1919. ESCOP's report (*1*) dealt with the relation of agricultural institutions to the changed conditions and the problems arising out of the war. The report is significant in that it laid a sound basis for study of the production and related agricultural problems. If all the thought expressed in this report could have been carried into action, one may question seriously whether such programs might not have proved successful in absorbing for agriculture some of the severe economic shocks of the 1920's and early 1930's.

ESCOP emphasized that "the time has come for us to be more self-reliant as a nation in the development of our science and our thinking." It placed emphasis on "administrative leadership in the stations both competent to guide scientific investigation and with sufficient time for thoughtful study and plans." Registering an early voice for what was later to become legislation under the Purnell Act of 1925, which authorized further funds for station research, ESCOP recognized that "Problems in the field of agricultural economics should be met and solved in the same thorough and scientific way as questions in nutrition and the suppression of disease and soil management." The report pointed to the need for research that would help individuals and segments of agriculture make adjustments as the result of changed conditions.

AGENCIES REGROUPED IN 1923

How long were the experiment stations to enjoy the unique status of participating in a program that was in part nationally financed under the "principle of local control?" At various times this principle had its challengers. As recently as 1921 ESCOP devoted its major consideration to a proposed reorganization of experiment station work. It had been presented the previous year by Dr. J.H. Webber, a former director of the California station (*42*). Briefly, Dr. Webber had urged in terms reminiscent of the Knapp plan of 1882:

> (1) That each experiment station become a State bureau of the United States Department of Agriculture with the director of the station its head; (2) that the experiment station director plan and direct all experimental agricultural work conducted in the State, in consultation with and reporting directly to the Secretary of Agriculture and the dean of the State college of agriculture; (3) that the maintenance for the agricultural investigation in a State be supplied jointly by Federal and State appropriations, analogous to the plan followed in extension work. . . .

A year later, after having given the plan full and free consideration, ESCOP (*9*) reached the following conclusion:

> In the opinion of this committee, if the operation of the proposed plan would in any way tend to lessen the probability of the maintenance of the experiment stations as separate units of the land-grant institutions, it would be a most undesirable step to take. The maintenance of the State stations as distinct entities, with their organization, staffs, and environment favorable to research of the highest type, is an indispensable consideration in all plans for future development of the agricultural research possibilities of the country. The experiment stations which have been established as a result of the operation of the Hatch and Adams Acts constitute one of America's greatest contributions to agricultural organization, agricultural science, and agricultural progress, and their permanency should be carefully safeguarded in any plan for the future development of research in agriculture in the United States. If, however, Dr. Webber's plan contemplates only a closer union of the work of the State stations and that of the United States Department of Agriculture, its purpose is a thoroughly desirable one.

ESCOP then reiterated its faith in the principle of cooperation and coordination between the Federal Department and the stations, but with the administrative autonomy of the research units left intact. It pointed to numerous examples of cooperation and coordination, emphasizing that the principle is each year becoming less of a bugbear and more fully accepted.

The longtime result of this careful review of the Webber plan in 1921 was that it constituted the last time in the initial century of land-grant history that integration of State and Federal research in agriculture was seriously proposed. The immediate result was crystallization of a recommendation which the Association had made repeatedly to the Department of Agriculture, namely that as mentioned previously a director of scientific work be appointed in the Department.

Since the turn of the century the directors of the stations had become increasingly conscious of the need for perfecting and maintaining the stations as truly as scientific institutions for serving agriculture. This objective had brought about passage of the Adams Act in 1905. Since the early 1900's, also, the directors had urged that farm demonstration work, based largely on scientific findings, required a separate staff of demonstrators so that the experiment station scientists could devote more time to research.

In those years the Department's various research activities were organized largely on an independent bureau basis. ESCOP's recommendations for closer coordination of experiment station and bureau research was accepted by the Department. On November 21, 1922, in his address before the general session of the 36th annual convention of the association, Secretary of Agriculure Henry C. Wallace (40) said—

A year ago last July we were authorized by Congress to create the offices of Director of Scientific Work and Director of Regulatory Work. . . . The theory is that not only will the Director of Scientific Work coordinate the scientific work carried on in the Department proper, but that he will gradually . . . endeavor to bring about a more complete cooperation in scientific research work in the Department and the various State experiment stations and colleges.

The proposed reorganization was outlined by Assistant Secretary C. W. Pugsley (27). The Department's activities were divided into three major divisions, namely scientific, extension, and regulatory work. The Office of Experiment Stations was transferred from the States Relations Service, which was discontinued, to the contemplated office of the Director of Scientific Work. The Director of Scientific Work was charged with the responsibility, not only of supervising the scientific work of the Department, but also of "endeavoring to correlate that with the scientific work of the stations, and in every possible way to aid the stations connected with the various colleges to correlate their work, not with a view of imposing any plan of the Department on them, but in a thoroughly sympathetic cooperative spirit" (41).

While the post of Director of Scientific Work had been authorized by Congress in 1921, actual authority for the departmental reorganization did not come until 1923 under the agricultural appropriation act of February 26, 1923 (42 Stat. L., 1289).

In his contemporary monograph, Milton Conover (6, p. 61) wrote as follows:

In the reorganization the States Relations Service as a bureau was abolished, but its component agencies were maintained as separate units. The Office of Home Economics became a separate departmental bureau. The Office of Cooperative Extension Work, also the Office of Exhibits and the Office of Motion Pictures, became a part of the Federal Extension Service administered by a Director of Extension Work. The Office of Experiment Stations was continued as a separate unit in the Office of the Secretary of Agriculture under the direction of a Chief who, also, became Assistant Director of Scientific Work reporting to the Director of Scientific Work.

The primary activities that remained with the Office of Experiment Stations after this reorganization of 1923 were to pass upon and

117

approve the research projects to be carried on under the Adams Act; to make an annual examination of the work being done under the Federal and State funds at each of the stations; to review the expenditures from Hatch and Adams funds; to confer with the local officers regarding matters of policy and administration; to compile annual classified list of projects conducted at each station; to promote coordination and cooperation between the stations and with the Department; to make an annual report to Congress on the progress of the stations; to maintain advisory relations with the stations on a wide variety of matters; and to exert influence on the organization, management, and standards of the stations through editorials in the Experiment Station Record.

ESCOP URGED ACCOUNTING FOR STATE AND FEDERAL FUNDS

Since the fiscal year ending June 30, 1895, annual financial statements had been required by Congress with respect to expenditures of Federal-grant funds by the stations. The annual reports of the Office of Experiment Stations, commencing with the report for 1901, contain statistics concerning State support and expenditures. Yet, in consideration given the matter during the 37th convention in 1923 ESCOP (*31*) reported, as follows:

As the matter stands, it is very difficult to get reliable information of a definite nature regarding the station funds and the use to which they are put. Fully a third of the stations omit from their annual reports a statement of their revenues, or give only those from Federal sources . . . a considerable number of directors are unable to supply more than a rough estimate, sometimes little more than a guess, of the funds devoted to the station, and a far larger number lack information as to the amounts available for research after the routine and service features have been cared for.

Manifestly, before such figures can be published, they must be known; and before they can be known there must be a fairly clear differentiation of the experiment station expense from that of other branches of the college. . . .

The very complexity of the average station is a strong argument for a system of accounting which will enable segregating the expense. If the stations are to carry such a range of duties, it is due to them that the expense of these be charged off or definitely taken account of. Apparently it is our fault if this is not done or at least the basis for it supplied.

To that end it seems desirable for each station to know as definitely as possible: (1) The amount of money it receives in appropriations, allotments, or otherwise, and (2) how much of that amount it employs for its primary function, namely in acquiring and applying scientific information.

After three pages of such reasoning, ESCOP recommended that the Office of Experiment Stations be authorized to request each experiment station to report annually the amounts of its State and other supplementary funds expended for each of the following purposes:

(a) Research and experimentation.

(b) Regulatory work, e.g. inspection and analysis, stallion registration, advance registry tests.

(c) Public service and advisory work, e.g. State entomologists, health and sanitation laboratories, marketing services.

(d) Soil and other surveys.

(e) Management of farms and other commercial enterprises and any other class of activity not embraced in the above.

(f) Capital outlay.

The recommendation was approved in the Section of Agriculture and adopted by the Association (*13*). This was the first time the

Association had authorized the Office of Experiment Stations to request an accounting of State and supplementary as well as Federal funds from the State stations.

STATE-FEDERAL COOPERATIVE POLICIES ESTABLISHED

In other sections and chapters of this volume the reader will find a more detailed report on developments leading to passage of the Purnell Act of 1925, the Bankhead–Jones Act of 1935 and its amendment of 1946, and of the amendment of 1955 to the Hatch Act of 1887, consolidating the previous authorizing acts into a single measure. Reference is made here to underline the fact that they evolved from proposals carefully considered by the experiment station directors. Some of the proposals originated among the experiment station leadership. Others grew through Federal incentive, as, for example, the Bureau of the Budget's requests to consolidate the acts authorizing payments to State experiment stations. Each of the proposals was carefully considered, difference between Departmental and experiment station interests ironed out, and a cooperative approach made to Congressional leaders for support of the proposals.

During the 51st annual convention of the Association of Land-Grant Colleges and Universities in 1937, following passage of the Bankhead-Jones Act which authorized regional USDA laboratories for cooperative research, Dr. R. W. Trullinger, at the time Assistant Chief of the Office of Experiment Stations, traced the historical development of such legislation to the Hatch Act of 1887 (37). He selected a few basic and widely influential policies and procedures involved in the Hatch and subsequent acts and showed how they affected the administration of productive research at the stations. Dr. Trullinger's analysis showed that the Hatch Act was the result of deliberate and purposeful planning for the future stability of agricultural research based upon existing experience and knowledge. The intent of the early agricultural leaders, as emphasized in earlier chapters, was to establish the scientific identity of the agricultural experiment stations and especially to show that the conduct of research in agricultural science was their proper function as distinguished from experimental and demonstration farming. He quoted Dr. Wilbur Atwater as saying that experiment stations were institutions where the rigid tests of scientific experiment were used to gain more certain understanding of the principles that underly the right practice of agriculture. Public funds in support of the stations were to be used in employing competent scientific men to carry on the appropriate work. Agricultural experiment stations would be worthy of the name scientific institution in proportion as they carried on accurate and thorough investigations and experiments in the sciences relating to agriculture.

Along lines of such thinking, Dr. Trullinger pointed out, Commissioner Colman of the Department of Agriculture in 1885 had informed delegates from agricultural colleges and experiment stations that much valuable time and a great deal of money were being lost in desultory and unmethodical experiments. He distinguished between production and demonstration farming and scientific investigation, considering the latter a legitimate experiment station function.

These and other arguments by early agricultural leaders in behalf of scientific research made it clear that, in preparation for the Hatch Act, well-defined ideas as to the organizational structure, type of personnel required, physical equipment needed, and the nature of functions, duties, and responsibilities of an agricultural experiment station had been formulated and agreed upon. Out of these concepts standards had grown which were of such general usage as practically to constitute common law.

The direct or implied provisions of the Hatch and subsequent acts, Dr. Trullinger pointed out, have largely supplied the foundation for the present structure of widely useful policies and procedures which directly influence and largely govern the administration of productive research at the stations. These are—

(1) Provision of a standardized pattern and definition for the agricultural experiment stations based upon long-established and generally accepted procedure.

(2) Establishment of the scientific identity and status of the agricultural experiment stations.

(3) Specification of the purpose, functions, and obligations of the agricultural experiment stations with the systematic manipulation of the natural and social sciences in the prosecution of agricultural research as the keynote and objective.

(4) Justification for the general adoption of the organized specific project as the tangible but flexible basic unit in the administration of research.

(5) Provision for and establishment of the basic principles and practice of cooperation within individual agricultural experiment stations, between agricultural experiment stations, and between the stations and the Department of Agriculture, and for the coordination of their facilities and research.

FEDERAL-STATES RELATIONS DEVELOPED

Mutual efforts of the U.S. Department of Agriculture and the State experiment stations have contributed much to the success of the agricultural industry as a whole and to the success of other industries requiring personnel trained in science. During the 100 years since passage of the acts creating the Department and the land-grant colleges, the number of scientists trained by the land-grant institutions for agricultural research and other scientific enterprises has increased greatly.

A theme of continuity runs through 20th century developments now known as Federal-State relationships. The thread is one of undulating competition between the experiment stations and Federal research activities within the States. Which of the two types of agencies should have priority? During the years of Department lethargy in the 60's, 70's and early 80's, the State stations asserted their independence and in the Hatch Act of 1887 sought and obtained protection against Federal administrative intervention. Likewise, the era of good will under Norman Jay Colman's administration brought precedents that guaranteed Federal assistance without domination. Hence the word "cooperation," as used by the station men in those years, meant administrative cooperation: How could the Department increase its help for the State stations, particularly in assisting the stations to work together?

Analysis of
United Stat
CAT87207
U.S. Depart
[21] an
Jun 03, 2013

This situation changed rapidly, however, by the turn of the century, when the Department became an effective, first class scientific agency under Secretary of Agriculture James Wilson. From that time forward the word "cooperation," used strictly in the administrative sense, meant the arrangements that would result from collision and compromise.

As its research efforts grew, the Department snapped up many promising scientists, poured money into research of different types in the States, and won national prestige and recognition. This friction, however polite the Association spokesmen and the Wilson group may have been to each other, produced the first "crisis" in State-Federal relations. It spurred the framers of the Adams Act to drive for Federal funds to keep the State stations in the race with the Department. It prompted the Association to start a public relations campaign in Congressional hearings to persuade Congressmen that public interest required State stations and further that the stations should not be converted into branches of the Department of Agriculture. The passage of the Adams Act was a major victory on these points as well as on the problem of basic research for the stations. The "blood transfusion" for the stations insured their life, but it made long and rigorous competition with the Department inevitable. At this point "cooperation" took on its modern meaning: The never-ending search for adjustments between the stations and the Department as to the division of responsibility for research in the States. Between 1900 and 1914 agreements, at first informal and voluntary between pairs of individual station and Department administrators, developed into formal contracts with definite procedure.

"Cooperation" in a narrow sense meant agreements between given scientists, State and Federal, for working together. In a larger sense, however, it meant the record of activity of two research systems, each through time trying to settle a jurisdictional dispute in its own favor. The State stations took the position that, first on the ground, they must not permit the Department to undermine the stations, no matter how persuasive the Federal argument or sincere the move. The Department, on the other hand, periodically enlarged through time, discreetly ignored the State position, adjusting to it whenever the Association complained loudly, as in the period 1930–32, or more softly, as in the 1950's, but continually pressing its views.

The time-line of development from 1900 to 1961 shows periodic "crises" or hot spots in this Federal-State relationship, e.g., 1903–1906, 1930–32, 1953–58. Perhaps the term "jurisdictional dispute" connotes too harsh a competition, a pattern of behavior long since outmoded, and therefore, no longer meaningful as a basis for interpretation. It certainly is true, for example, that "land grantism" has tried vocally for 75 years to convince itself and the world that the good fellowship of cooperation has eliminated competitive struggles. Yet sharpness peeks through the phrases of the Report of the Special Committee of 1930–31. We detect a similar phenomenon, more mildy expressed, in the functioning of other similar committees named since that time. This problem can be treated more broadly, however—and perhaps more accurately in the long run—by using the term "improvement in research communications;" i.e., the station position, considered from any point of view, can best be maintained if the station management knows exactly what everybody else is doing.

The foregoing observations still do not help very much with the practical job of recording the specific arrangements which, through time, the administrators of the stations and of the Department of Agriculture have made in order to progress together. These arrangements are, after all, the evidence of practical "cooperation" between the land-grant colleges on the one hand and the Department on the other. Development of this factor seems to have taken form generally in the following stages:

Stage I: *From Commissioner Colman's Convention Through Atwater's Directorship of the Office of Experiment Stations, 1885–1891.*

The establishment of the Office of Experiment Stations and the determination of its functions.

In the beginning, the sole connection between the Department of Agriculture and the stations was through OES and a sincerely interested Commissioner. The Department had one main function, namely, to enable and encourage intercommunication among the stations, and then to publish pertinent information in the public interest. Whatever OES might or could have become—and spokesmen in the early conventions of the Association had a variety of additional duties to recommend—the Association early decided that OES should itself *not* become an experiment station. That is, from the earliest years State station leaders feared that Federally-conducted experimentation could, if started, seriously menace the station position. Not solely the matter of "dictation" from the Department concerning research projects in the stations worried the founders, but also "competition" from a Federal agency which could, because well-financed and free from local pressures, do significant work overshadowing that of the stations.

Stage II: *Expansion of Research Activity in the Department of Agriculture, 1894–1902.*

1. The concentration of Secretary Wilson on Research in Federal Bureaus.

2. The exploratory attempts of OES in the early True years to administer "cooperative" research among college units on a large scale, via special agents. Also, the Atwater nutrition experiments of 1894, irrigation projects undertaken in 1898, and the drainage projects begun in 1902—*despite the feeling of early stations leaders that OES itself should not engage in research.*

Stage III: *Collision and Compromise—A Continuing Process Since 1899.*

Competition in research activities between those carried on in the States by Department agencies, other than OES, and those of the State experiment stations, compelled a settlement of differences between the two systems. Specific guidelines became necessary as to *which* agencies should do *what* and on *what* terms. Compromises based on such consideration in specific cases developed into a firm and realistic basis of State-Federal cooperation.

This basis of administrative cooperation began even before the turn of the century. A. C. True (*33*) was fully aware of the problem and its implications as early as 1899 when he alerted the Association in the following words:

122

I presume that many of you have observed that there is an increasing tendency on the part of Congress to insert provisions in the bill for the support of the Department of Agriculture under which cooperation between the Department and the experiment stations is favored. . . . There is a feeling in Congress that the Department and the stations should work together in the future more than they have in the past, and there is a disposition to give to the Secretary of Agriculture lump sums of money for special investigations, with the understanding that this money shall be used to a considerable extent to promote the investigations of the stations. . . . But as the amount of cooperation increases, and the number of subjects on which there is cooperation increases, it seems desirable that arrangements for cooperation between the stations and the Department should be established on some more formal and comprehensive basis; and therefore the Secretary of Agriculture has, as doubtless many of you know, issued an order under which the officers of the Department desiring cooperation with the stations must first present their plan of cooperation to the Secretary for his approval. When it has received his approval, it must be transmitted to the Office of Experiment Stations, whose duty it then becomes to conduct correspondence with the station with a view to making a contract for such cooperation. . . .

The Congressional position is reflected by the generosity with which Congress gave fiscal support to Secretary Wilson for specific work. Without considering the complex and delicate issue of State vs. Federal conduct of research, Congress directed Wilson to employ the technical know-how of the stations to aid the Department in its research assignment. A. C. True, in his report on the experiment stations for 1899 (*34*), remarked:

. . . This policy of cooperative enterprise has been approved by the action of Congress, which in recent years has in an increasing number of instances authorized or directed cooperation with the stations in the appropriation acts making provision for the maintenance of this Department. These cooperative enterprises have so far increased in extent and variety as to make it desirable to have a more formal plan for arranging for such cooperation than has hitherto been necessary. In recognition of this need, the Secretary of Agriculture made an order under date of February 28, 1899, requiring the offices of this Department to submit their plans for cooperation with the stations for his approval before negotiating with the stations, and designating the Office of Experiment Stations as the representative of the Department in arranging for such cooperation and keeping a record of the cooperative enterprise agreed upon. Under this order the Department and the station each designate the officers who are to have immediate charge of the cooperative work in any given case, and these officers carry out the details of the plan agreed upon.

The Association's action to formalize cooperation came during the evening session of the 13th annual convention when it approved a motion by Director E. A. Bryan of the Washington Agricultural Experiment Station "that a committee of five be appointed to consider the question of cooperative work of the experiment stations with the Department of Agriculture, and report at the next meeting of this Association such recommendations as shall be deemed advisable and desirable in this regard" (*4*). The Committee named included Directors Bryan, H. H. Goodell (Massachusetts), W. A. Henry (Wisconsin), H. J. Waters (Missouri), and L. G. Carpenter (Colorado).

The following year (*5*) the Committee specified five variations of the cooperative approach with examples. It considered the most important type to be cooperation between the Department and the individual stations—"joint experimentation." Excerpts from the Committee's recommendations follow:

1. Both USDA and station may, for its part propose or decline a project.
2. . . . the autonomy of the stations should be preserved, and . . . the stations should in no sense become extensions of the divisions of the Department for the purposes of experimental work.

3. . . . the agreement should take the shape of a formal contract between the station as such and the Department as such . . . Arrangements between individual officers in the two institutions are deemed inadvisable except under such contract.

4. The station and the USDA should jointly pay the cost, each specifying the amount it will spend.

5. Each should have reasonable assurance that the work will continue until completed : reasonable mutual assurance of a fixed policy rather than an absolute guaranty of continuance.

6. Re: publication, agree in the beginning as to who will have priority. Acknowledge the fact of joint experimentation.

7. Re: independent work by USDA within States : . . . desirable that independent work be not undertaken in the several States by the Department without the knowledge of the station or consultation with the station, particularly along lines of investigation in which the State station is engaged.

RESEARCH COMMISSION NAMED

During the 1906 convention, the Association authorized the incoming president, Director Liberty Hyde Bailey of the Cornell station, to appoint a commission of five persons—two representing the "research efforts of the association," one representing the U.S. Department of Agriculture, and "two representative scientific men not connected with official agricultural investigation"—to "inquire into and report to this Association the organization and policy that in the opinion of the commission should prevail in the expenditure of public money provided for scientific experimentation and research in the interests of agriculture, to the end that such funds shall be applied in the most economical, efficient, and worthy manner in the production of results of permanent value" (*11*). Named to the Commission by Bailey were: David Starr Jordan of Leland Stanford University, Carroll D. Wright of Massachusetts, Gifford Pinchot of USDA, H. P. Armsby of Pennsylvania, and W. H. Jordan of New York. The Commission presented its report during the annual convention in 1908 (*23*). It was published in pamphlet form and widely distributed by the Association (*3*). Included was a series of recommendations which, in the opinion of the Commission, "should guide in the promotion, organization, and prosecution of research in agriculture."

The report observed that "the training of investigators is a necessary antecedent to the efficient expenditure of research funds . . . competent investigators are needed more than money. A large investigator and small means do much, but a small investigator and large means will accomplish but little. . . . Scientific truth is a product of the individual mind through the exercise of its judicial capacity in the interpretation of data. . . . Whenever the investigator is for any reason overanxious for popular approval, or is made to consider relation of his conclusions to future support, or in any way is restrained from exercising his unbiased judgment in reaching and in dealing with his results, he is subject to influence dangerous to the integrity of science." Highlights from the recommendations include excerpts as follows:

1. Every effort should be made to promote the training of competent investigators in agriculture both in the agricultural and, so far as practicable, in the nonagricultural colleges and universities, and their training should be as broad and severe as for any other field of research.

2. The progress of agricultural knowledge now demands that agricultural research agencies shall deal as largely as possible with fundamental problems, confining attention to such as can be adequately studied with the means available.

3. The work of research in agriculture should be differentiated as fully as practicable, both in the form of organization and in the relations of the individual investigator, from executive work, routine teaching, promotion and propaganda, and should be under the immediate direction of an executive trained in the methods of science who should not be hampered by other duties of an entirely unlike character.

4. The investigator should be free from all coercion whatever. In reaching his conclusions he should be equally free from the prescription of received opinion and the temptation to exploit his results for the purpose of obtaining future support. To this end, his work should be as far removed from immediate dependence upon legislation as is consistent with due responsibility to the public, and his relations to the public and to the organization of which he is a member should be such as to promote individual initiative and not interfere with freedom of conclusion or utterance on scientific questions.

5. There should be a clearer definition of the relative fields of work of the United States Department of Agriculture and the experiment stations. The dominance of the stations within their respective fields should be preserved and their growth fostered, as agencies for the investigation of local questions and of the more individual scientific problems. The Federal agency, on the other hand, should cultivate the almost limitless field offered by questions having national or interstate relations, and by those broad scientific problems requiring heavy expenditures, elaborate equipment, long continued study, and the correlation of the results of many investigators, which efforts are usually beyond the means of an individual station. On many questions the harmonious cooperation of the two agencies is essential to the highest efficiency of effort.

6. Any research agency charged with a single main line of investigation should be so organized that it may employ within itself all necessary processes in any branch of science. The cooperation of any or all the departments of an experiment station on a single problem, when necessary, should be a fundamental requirement.

7. Research work, both national and state, should be provided for by separate, lump-sum appropriations, to be distributed according to the discretion of the responsible executive head of each agency.

8. Investigation into the business, economic, social, and governmental conditions affecting agriculture should be undertaken and should be maintained on a permanent and effective basis.

9. An advisory board is suggested consisting of members appointed by the Secretary of Agriculture and by the Association of American Agricultural Colleges and Experiment Stations, respectively, which shall confer with the Secretary of Agriculture regarding the mutual interests of the Department and the Stations and shall consider the promotion of agricultural investigation in general.

10. . . . It seems that there should be some central publication in which the results of real investigation should appear after passing through the hands of a competent board of editors. . . . The board of publication, having full authority to criticize and reject or accept contributions, should be one authorized by the Department and Experiment Stations. Such a scheme of centralizing scientific productions obviously should not interfere with, or limit, the present method of distributing information through reports and bulletins.

Concerning the overlapping efforts of the Department and the stations, the Commission remarked:

. . . there is an extensive overlapping of the fields of effort of the United States Department of Agriculture and of the Agricultural Experiment Stations. It is evident that such a situation cannot wisely be allowed to continue. . . . The real question is, how can public funds be distributed to render the greatest possible service in the aggregate, not merely in the promotion of material prosperity but especially in developing the ability of localities and individuals to deal intelligently with their own problems?

This question touches a principle which underlies our Federal system, the observance of which is necessary to preserve the efficiency and method of our democratic institutions. The principle is this "Questions which concern primarily and chiefly the people of the locality are to be left to the determination of the locality. Questions which concern primarily and chiefly the people of the nation are to be left to the determination of the nation."

. . . the policy of developing the State experiment stations should be continued in every possible way. The State should not be encouraged to shirk the duty of developing its own means for agricultural progress and defense.

. . . the States will increasingly care for their local agricultural problems, leaving the appropriations by the national government to be applied to the investigation of questions of general importance.

Thus we see in the first decade of the 20th century the shaping up of a new era. It was that of realistic acceptance of clash and compromise in formulating policies relating to the dual administration of a nationwide State-Federal system of agricultural research.

Frequent collision of interests brought about such benchmarks as enactment of the Adams Act, the establishment of the Experiment Station Committee on Organization and Policy (ESCOP), recognition of the need for demonstration and extension work as separately administered but closely cooperative entities collateral with those of the experiment stations, and practical bases for State and Federal "cooperation" in the administrative sense of that term. All have contributed toward making the State-Federal program of agricultural research an exemplary pattern that is being adopted and adapted in many parts of the world.

Pointing to the friction between Station and USDA interests brought on in the early administration of the Adams Act, E. D. Eddy (*10, pp. 124–129*), in Colleges for Our Land and Time comments: "It was the beginning of frequent disagreement, often friendly but sometimes bitter, between the Department and the Colleges. The complaint was made by the stations that the Department was encroaching upon their exlusive territory. The stations felt that the Deparment should be concerned with national questions, leaving to the States matters of local concern. By the end of the first decade, the Department was conducting a full-scale research program of its own." Eddy then cites Eugene Davenport's criticism, in part as follows:

[The Department] pushes straight ahead in its plan for doing anything anywhere, justifying the procedure by inviting the State institutions to cooperate: In plain terms, it has substituted by main strength its principle of cooperation for the sounder and more acceptable principle of division of labor which has been repeatedly laid down.

VIEWS EXCHANGED ON COOPERATION

Following creation of the Federal States Relations Service in 1915, Dr. Edwin W. Allen, who had been closely associated with Dr. True from 1890 onward, was made Chief of the Office of Experiment Stations. Following the 1923 regrouping, he also became Assistant Director of Scientific Work. He thus had direct relations to the research work of all bureaus in the Department as well as the experiment stations. He continued in this post until his death in 1929. For many years he had been a member of ESCOP and also of the closely related Committee on Projects and Correlation. He wrote the report which was filed by the chairman of the committee in 1929. In the following excerpt from the report (*26*), he expressed his and the committee's basic philosophy on USDA–Experiment Station relations:

. . . Research ought not to be regarded merely from the local standpoint. The experiment stations constitute a national system and they bear an intimate relation to the Federal Department of Agriculture. Correlation of their efforts is essential to economy of effort and efficient progress. After it has been effected, there will still remain sufficient individual opportunity and institutional initiative for self-expression.

The report filed by ESCOP in 1930 gave further guidance to station-USDA cooperation. It was signed by Director J. T. Jardine of the Oregon station as chairman. Director Jardine's research apprenticeship had begun in 1907 under Frederick V. Coville, whose field work in the Cascade Mountains of Oregon started the first sustained national movement toward range management in the West *(30)*. By 1930, Jardine had become nationally recognized for his leadership in developing range forage and had become Director of the Oregon station. ESCOP's report, which he signed as chairman, included the following paragraph:

. . . The station director should have the same responsibility in carefully scrutinizing and approving projects that are to be cooperative between the stations and Federal bureaus or between his station and other stations that exist when the project is limited to the station staff.

A special committee on Federal-States relations in research, composed of Directors M. J. Funchess (Alabama), E. C. Johnson (Washington), and S. W. Fletcher (Pennsylvania), had been named by the Association in 1930. Its full report in the Proceedings for 1931 *(17)* included the following subitems: *Notification of Proposed Research; Memoranda of Agreement; Professional Relations of Workers; Mutual Confidence, the Basis of Cooperation; Origin of Cooperative Projects; Federal Field Stations; Cooperation When No State Funds Are Applied; The Function of the United States Department of Agriculture in Research; What Agencies Should Conduct Fundamental Research; Over-Organization of Research;* and *National Programs in Research.* In closing, the special committee said:

The judgment of the state experiment stations, as evidenced in this survey, is that for the present, at least, the role of the Department in a national system for agricultural research should be that of advisor, contributor, and coordinator, rather than administrator. The Department, with its facilities for travel and observation, and because of its detachment from local influences, could be expected to bring into the cooperation broad and unbiased views of the purposes and relations of research projects. It is in position to coordinate the net results of all local research and to translate them into the broadest and most fundamental meaning.

This report necessarily has considered Federal-state relations in research from the point of view of the state experiment stations only; doubtless much might be said from the point of view of the Department, also. The Committee recommends, therefore, that this report be referred to the Executive Committee of the Association, with the suggestion that a conference be held with representatives of the United States Department of Agriculture to consider the questions here raised, more particularly the following specific suggestions, which appear to be supported by the majority opinion in the state agricultural experiment stations:

1. The United States Department of Agriculture to establish and operate field stations or laboratories in any state only in definite cooperation with the state experiment station, as evidenced by memoranda of agreement, with joint responsibility in planning and conducting the investigations, and joint publication of the results, irrespective of whether the work is maintained with Federal funds only, or with Federal and state funds.

2. The United States Department of Agriculture to advise the director of the state experiment station of any research that it is proposed shall be undertaken within the state, whether this is to be conducted with Federal funds only, or with Federal and state funds jointly; and to furnish an outline of the proposed investigation indicating the objectives and the proposed procedure. The state experiment station to offer suggestions for adapting the project to local conditions and to proffer such facilities for conducting it as may be available. Memoranda of agreement to be necessary only when there is joint leadership and mutual participation in the maintenance of the project.

3. When formulating and conducting projects of wide scope, in which the participation of the state experiment stations would be desirable, the United

127

States Department of Agriculture should recognize the state experiment stations as cooperators, not merely as contributors, and to reserve for them joint responsibility in framing the project, in adapting it to local needs and in the interpretation and publication of the results.

4. The United States Department of Agriculture to consider whether the present somewhat divergent policies of the several bureaus, in their cooperative relations with the state experiment stations, could not to advantage be unified by designating a single office to represent all the bureaus in Federal-state relations in research.

The special committee's recommendation that a conference be held with representatives of the Department to consider these matters was approved by the executive body. Chairman Fletcher, Director of the Pennsylvania Experiment Station, met with representatives of the research agencies of the Department of Agriculture on April 29, 1932. Subsequently, the Department prepared a similar statement presenting the departmental point of view. It was transmitted to the special committee on October 14, 1932, and distributed in November of that year.

The departmental point of view was set forth in mimeographed *Comments on Report of the Committee on Federal-States Relationships in Agricultural Research*. The Department's review committee consisted of Nils Olsen, K. F. Kellerman, H. G. Knight (chairman), and J. M. Jardine, Chief of the Office of Experiment Stations (secretary). The comments were approved by USDA bureau chiefs on October 6, 1932.

With reference to the Federal-State committee's inference that the primary research function of the Department should be to act as a correlating agency in the prosecution of national and regional problems and that its activities should strengthen and supplement rather than duplicate and supplant the activities of the stations, the Department's spokesmen felt further clarification of principle to be necessary. Much of the research of the Department, they maintained, is inextricably connected with the carrying out of nonresearch public service functions. They further emphasized that research activities of the Department cover subjects not assigned in all States to the agricultural experiment stations. Some States specifically assign to other agencies research on problems under investigation by USDA. In other cases the agricultural experiment station is not actively interested in research activities requested of the Department with some insistence by State departments of agriculture, State extension services, agricultural organizations or individuals of the State. Would it not be impractical and unwise for the Department to insist that its research activities in such cases must be with the State agricultural experiment station only and that it merely strengthen and supplement the State research? Until the State organization and cooperation of State agencies are perfected to the point that all State activities and interests in agricultural research are cleared through one authorized agency, the Department averred that it must meet its own national and regional responsibilities and adjust as far as practicable to the individual case variations within a single State and variation in situations as among States.

Mutual understanding and trust, according to the departmental evaluation, could solve the problem of overlapping jurisdictions; these qualities could best be promoted by recognizing that the State stations and the Department together make up a national research agency for agriculture and, accordingly, that effective correlation merits the impartial efforts of all. The Department agreed with the principle that research can be overorganized to the detriment of initiative and productiveness. The Department's statement then offered substitutes for the Station's recommendations, one of which proposed cooperation by written agreements setting forth the arrangements agreed upon and signed by the State station director and the bureau chief concerned.

In its report to the Section on Agriculture during the 46th convention (*18*), the special directors' committee said relative to the departmental statement:

> . . . While not meeting the views of the experiment stations in all respects, it impresses us as a sincere and constructive effort to arrive at a common ground of mutual understanding and agreement. The specific recommendations, particularly as to the conduct of Federal field stations and laboratories, and the respective responsibilities of the Federal and State agencies in various types of cooperative research, seems to us to represent a distinct advance over present procedure. . . .

> These two reports, wherein the respective points of view of the United States Department of Agriculture and the State stations are presented frankly and in a friendly spirit, are a foundation on which it should be possible to build more effective cooperation.

The mutual appraisal of research views revealed the processes involved in the constant development of realistic cooperation. In the administrative competition that was natural between two relatively independent groups of administrators, intelligent study and mutual discussion of their respective responsibilities, vigorously presented and honestly defended, became the amalgam that assured cooperation. In the pattern established a generation ago American agriculture benefited and continues to benefit. Absence of a means for settling the inherent conflicts could well have created an environment under which attainment of the goal of high scientific standards in agricultural research might have been impossible.

The Special Committee on Federal-State Relationships in Agricultural Research was the forerunner of numerous committees that in more recent times have studied similar problems of cooperation, legislation, organization, and joint research planning. Federal–States relations and problems related thereto became a continuing activity in the administration of Federal-grant funds. Exploration for more effective ways of cooperation increased in importance as both the Department and the land-grant institutions sought answers to the agricultural problems brought on by the depression and by World War II.

It would be difficult to interpret relatively recent and current developments in the same way attempted for the earlier historical period. Lengthy minutes of ESCOP meetings, held at least twice annually and sometimes more frequently, reveal a continuing active interest and initiative on the part of State station directors to encourage whatever steps are necessary to retain and improve the position of scientific leadership for their institutions. Of the many areas related to Federal–State cooperation discussed by directors since the beginning of the 1940's, as reported in the official ESCOP minutes, the following may be cited as typical examples.

PROFESSIONAL RELATIONSHIPS IMPROVED

Prior to 1950 there was considerable variation in methods and procedures concerning the employment of professional personnel under State-Federal cooperative agreements. The North Central Directors' Association delegated Associate Director N. J. Volk, subsequently named Director of the Indiana station, to consider with the Agricultural Research Service means for bringing about better understanding and greater uniformity as to precedures employed in cooperative State-Federal projects. Subsequently, Dr. Volk was asked to act in the same capacity for ESCOP.[5] The special study made by Director Volk was the forerunner of the present standing committee on State-Federal Relationships. The study in essence established the present tightened-up system of cooperative agreements under which the Department provides reimbursement for cooperatively planned research carried on with State resources. Previously, there had been considerable complaint because some of the "cooperative agents" had been carrying on their research activities in an administrative no-man's land where neither the Department nor the cooperating experiment station had specific supervisory authority under the agreement.

ESCOP CREATED STANDING SUBCOMMITTEE ON FEDERAL-STATES RELATIONS

The report made by Director Volk met with wholehearted approval by ESCOP, which decided to create a standing Subcommittee on Federal-States Relations and named Dr. Volk as the first chairman. Reorganization of the Department was in progress in 1953, leading Director Volk to postpone the subcommittee's activities until those phases of reorganization affecting USDA–Station activities had become clarified.[6] In the spring of 1954, Director E. V. Smith of the Alabama Experiment Station succeeded Director Volk as chairman of the subcommittee. In addition to meeting with a special ESCOP subcommittee on the USDA reorganization, to be discussed later, the Federal-States Relations Subcommittee began consideration with Agricultural Research Service and Agricultural Marketing Service administrators of a list of variations in cooperative research singled out in the Volk study.

The title of the subcommittee appeared in the minutes of ESCOP as "Federal-States Relations."[7] It was to be composed of four members of ESCOP, appointed by the chairman, one to represent each region, and was to elect its own chairman. Its functions are to review matters pertaining to Federal-States relations and make recommendations concerning these to ESCOP. Whenever the occasion requires, the subcommittee is free to consult with anyone in the Department or at the experiment stations who may be able to assist in solution of the problems presented.

---

[5] Unpublished minutes of ESCOP, Apr. 20–21, 1950; May 22–23, 1952; and Apr. 9–10, 1953.

[6] Unpublished minutes of ESCOP, Nov. 7–11, 1953.

[7] Unpublished minutes of ESCOP, Apr. 27–28, 1955.

On April 24, 1956, the Federal–States Relations Subcommittee of ESCOP and USDA administrators issued a report making agreed-upon recommendations relative to 16 items affecting cooperative research.[8] These ranged from the first item dealing with the need for improved communication between Federal and State administrative agencies and cooperative employees, to remedying the variation in the appointment of cooperative agents as recommended in the Volk study, to extending faculty or staff privileges to professional employees located at each State experiment station. This standing subcommittee continues as an effective agent for fostering good relations.

JOINT COMMITTEE ON COOPERATIVE RESEARCH DESIGNATED

In a talk given before station directors, ARS Administrator B. T. Shaw (29) invited the experiment stations to join ARS in a study that was being made of the problems of agriculture and the extent to which ARS could strengthen its program to meet such problems. ESCOP accepted the invitation and joined with Dr. Shaw in designating a Joint Committee on Cooperative Research. The 11-man group included ARS administrators responsible for the respective ARS research programs and station directors named by ESCOP. ARS Deputy Administrator for Experiment Stations E. C. Elting was named Chairman. The committee was charged with reviewing the existing pattern of cooperation between the Farm Research Divisions of ARS and the several State Agricultural Experiment Stations and asked to make recommendations for strengthening cooperative research with particular reference to ways of developing stronger teamwork and of bringing greater concentration of effort to bear on many problems.

In the three meetings held by this special joint committee, discussions centered on such matters as procedures involved in cooperative research which seemed to have stood the test of time and procedures which in the judgment of the committee should be considered as principles. At its final meeting in November 1960, the committee agreed on a statement of principles, to be distributed to both Federal administrators and Station directors, that would serve as a useful guide in further development of cooperative relationships.[9] The statement of principles follows:

1. That the Agricultural Research Service and the State Agricultural Experiment Stations are individually responsible for accounting for the research results from the moneys appropriated or allocated to them.
2. That the ARS is primarily responsible for research on problems of national and regional concern to agriculture and on those problems involving relationships between the United States Government and the governments of other nations.
3. That the State Agricultural Experiment Stations are primarily responsible for research on problems within the borders of their respective States, and for such regional research as is of importance to the area. Statements 2 and 3 are not intended to be mutually exclusive.

[8] Unpublished report of the Joint ARS–AMS–ECOP Committee on Federal–States Relations, April 24, 1956.
[9] Unpublished mimeographed letter of Jan. 17, 1961, sent by E. C. Elting, Chairman of the Joint Committee, to Administrators and Research Personnel Concerned with Federal-State Cooperation in Agricultural Research, transmitting "Principles Involved in Federal-State Cooperation in Agricultural Research."

4. That basic research is a responsibility both of the ARS and the State Experiment Stations and should be advanced in each institution and in each area so far as feasible.

5. That ARS and the State Agricultural Experiment Stations will cooperate, on a voluntary basis, in research whenever cooperative action will be more effective than separate action (regional research will usually be cooperative).

6. That joint planning should be an essential phase of cooperation.

7. ARS and the State Agricultural Experiment Stations will continue to share facilities to the extent that their respective primary responsibilities permit, and will share the operating costs of such facilities as may be mutually agreed upon.

8. ARS and the State Experiment Stations will examine each of their locations with respect to effective concentration of Federal and State personnel.

9. That, to the fullest extent practicable, necessary adjustments in ARS Farm Research at field locations be fully explored with the Experiment Station Director concerned before such actions are taken.

10. That negotiations on cooperation be conducted between State Experiment Station Directors and Directors of ARS Research Divisions.

11. That locations for regional concentrations will, so far as possible, be mutually agreed upon by the States in the region and ARS.

12. That, so far as budgetary considerations and other limitations permit, there be a full discussion of needs and plans for additional Federal research facilities in the several States.

13. That ARS facilities be located at or adjacent to Land-Grant Colleges or established sub-units thereof unless there are appropriate and compelling reasons for other locations.

14. That the ARS Divisions continue to explore opportunities for their maximum contributions to organized cooperative Regional Research. (While this refers particularly to Regional Research as authorized by Section 3(c)3 of the Amended Hatch Act, it is applicable to all voluntary cooperative regional research.)

15. That ARS, the State Experiment Stations, and other appropriate research organizations, individually and jointly, have responsibility for the evaluation of public programs relating to agriculture with respect to their effectiveness and their consequences.

COOPERATIVE DOCUMENTS

There evolved out of the various joint efforts by the station directors and their counterpart in the Department of Agriculture a series of cooperative arrangements now accepted as standard for the administration of all cooperative research. In 1961 there were nearly 1,300 separate agreements between ARS and State experiment stations, good evidence that the Federal-States relations efforts as described above paid off in the form of productive research.

Definitions of several kinds of documents now in effect, with brief explanations of each, are as follows: [10]

A. *Memorandum of Understanding:* A written plan to cooperate in carrying out a research activity. It is principally distinguished from a Cooperative Agreement in that each party handles and expends its own funds in accordance with its own regulations. It is *not* a fiscal document, that is, there is no payment of funds from one party to the other.

1. *Master Memorandum of Understanding:* Under the general definition given above, this is a document covering cooperative work in its broadest aspects, establishing the mutuality of interest of the parties and setting forth the general principles of the cooperation. This type of document does not carry an identifying number. At the time of the reorganization of the Department, there were a number of Master Memorandums in effect between the State Experiment Stations and the former Bureaus of the Department. It was not practicable to continue using these old Masters indefinitely. Accordingly, there was developed a Master Memorandum of Understanding

---

[10] Mimeographed Memorandum of November 2, 1959, from S. P. Williams, Director, Administrative Services Division, ARS, to E. C. Elting, Deputy Administrator for Experiment Stations, ARS.

on the basis of cooperation between each State Experiment Station and the Agricultural Research Service as a whole. Most of these ARS Masters were signed during 1957. They did *not*, of themselves, replace the former Bureau Masters.

2. *Supplements to Master Memorandums of Understanding:* Again under the general definition given above, these are documents which outline the specific project to be conducted between the Experiment Station and the ARS Program Division in accordance with the general principles stated in the Master. Supplements bear numbers in numerical order, i.e., 1, 2, 3, etc. These numbers are assigned by ARS *after* the supplement has been fully executed and in the order of execution. At the time of the reorganization of the Department, there were in effect a considerable number of supplements to the Master Memorandums of Understanding with the former Bureaus of the Department. As time has permitted these old supplements are being replaced and superseded by supplements under the new ARS Master. When all of the old supplements under any particular Bureau Master have been replaced, the entire document will be cancelled. This arrangement was necessary in order that there would be no gap in the documentation of projects. All new projects will, of course, be documented by supplements under the ARS Master.

3. *Work Plan:* This type of documentation is used primarily by our Farm Economics Research Division. It is a *detailed* procedural outline, is *not* a fiscal document, and is in addition to a Master Memorandum of Understanding and any supplement thereunder. It is not numbered but will refer specifically to the supplement number under the ARS Master to which it pertains. For example, the heading will read, "Work Plan" (or "Renewal of Work Plan") for a Specific Project Under Supplement No. 3 to the Master Memorandum of Understanding between, etc. If no supplement under the ARS Master covering the project has as yet been executed, the Work Plan will refer to the former Bureau agreement, usually Bureau of Agricultural Economics. If for some reason neither the specific supplement under the ARS Master nor the former Bureau of Agricultural Economics is identified, it is safe to assume that the Work Plan is under the former Bureau document.

4. *Individual Memorandum of Understanding:* This is a type of *non-fiscal* document and is used where there is no Master Memorandum of Understanding or where the scope of an existing Master would not cover the situation. An example of this is a multi-party arrangement involving several States. Any supplementation to these will be clearly identified as such in order that they will not be confused with the Master.

B. *Cooperative Agreement:* Like the Memorandum of Understanding, this type of document is a written plan to cooperate in carrying out a research activity. However, entirely unlike the Memorandum of Understanding, it will provide for the Payment of funds from one of the parties to the other. It is, therefore, a fiscal document and must be kept separate and clearly distinguished from the Memorandum of Understanding. Identifying numbers on Cooperative Agreements and other types of fiscal documents are required by the U.S. General Accounting Office and are assigned by ARS *after* the document is fully executed. An example of these numbers is, 12–14–100–2326(34). The number 12 appearing at the beginning denotes the Department of Agriculture (other Departments carry other numbers here). The number 14 denotes the Agricultural Research Service (other agencies of the Department carry different numbers here). The number 100 denotes the location of the office, in this instance, Washington, D.C. The number 2326 denotes the sequence number of the agreement. The number (34) denotes the research division within ARS, in this instance, Crops Research Division. There are, of course, several different types of Cooperative Agreements, depending on how the particular research division and Experiment Station carries out its overall program and the nature of the work itself, but all have one thing in common; they are fiscal documents. We have made every effort to standardize these agreements and believe we have succeeded within the limitations inherent in program procedure and work.

FEDERAL GRANTS LINK TWO GREAT FORCES

Ever since enactment of the Hatch Act of 1887, Federal administration of the grant funds to State experiment stations has served as the medium for linking two great forces for the mutual progress of agriculture. In major legislation such as the Hatch, Adams, Purnell, and Bankhead-Jones Acts, the Secretary of Agriculture issued carefully considered policy letters (reproduced in the appendix of this text), which served as the basic interpretation of Federal requirements in the administration of payments to the stations. As pointed out in the section on publications, the Office of Experiment Stations and its successor during the 1950's, the State Experiment Stations Division, Agricultural Research Service, used these basic interpretations for the preparation of detailed outlines of procedure to help meet the legal requirements. At the time of this writing, the manual governing procedures is Federal Legislation, Rulings, and Regulations Affecting the State Agricultural Experiment Stations, Miscellaneous Publication No. 515, revised in January 1959.

The record of the rules and regulations issued by the Department of Agriculture concerning grant fund administration attests to the cooperative approach followed by the Department over the years. In the face of basic legislation that provides ample authority, Federal administrators of the grant funds have adhered rigorously to the doctrine that their part in the agricultural experiment station program is one of participation rather than that of direction. Although the Department is charged with responsibility for seeing that funds are spent as intended by the Congress, this function is largely carried on in the form of advice and assistance to the Directors of the individual stations, the legally responsible authorities within the framework of their own State governments. The Department's cooperative relationships to the experiment station enterprise are enhanced through frequent contact between ESCOP and the Federal-grant administrators and through annual reviews made by technical leaders of the work at the stations, through comprehensive reviews of Federal-grant research, and through participation in planning of regional research. But the Department's role in administering station research funds of Federal origin always has been and continues to be interpreted primarily as one of service.

The tie that has bound the stations and the Department into cooperative relationship is that of Federal appropriations. Moneys for Federal-grant payments to the States have always been a part of the Department budget. In his talk, given in 1928 before the 42d annual convention of the Association, Dean and Director J. J. Hills of the College of Agriculture, University of Vermont (20), credited Henry E. Alvord, at one time President of the University of Maryland, with the "successful attempt to secure passage of the first Hatch Act *appropriation;*" with being instrumental "in *securing the Hatch appropriation item* with the House Committee on Agriculture *thus making it automatically an item in the annual budget of the Department of Agriculture, a precedent which has carried with all subsequent appropriations; with securing for the first time quarterly advance payments of Federal funds,* now a common practice;" and with helping "loosen up the Post Office franking regulations in respect to station publications."

In the late 1920's, at the request of the Association, Congress provided the U.S. Bureau of Education with a grant to make a 2-year survey of the activities of the land-grant institutions. When Dr. Arthur J. Klein, in overall charge of the survey, unveiled a manuscript copy of the survey before the annual association convention in 1930 (24), he commented concerning agricultural research:

. . . We have collected and presented in easily intelligible form, typical examples of the actual money value of research in the agricultural field, and presented this information in such fashion that I am sure it can be used by you and the experiment stations in a most effective manner in securing better understanding of what research means to the States and to your institutions themselves. I do not believe that anywhere or ever there has been collected and presented in such clear form such a demonstration of the actual values of research in the agricultural field . . .

The 72-year partnership between State Agricultural Experiment Stations and the U.S. Department of Agriculture has indeed been one of family growth. At a seminar of Land-Grant College and University administrators held at Fort Collins, Colorado, on June 26, 1961, Assistant Secretary of Agriculture Frank J. Welch said: [11]

In no area may we claim a closer and more continuous relationship between the Land-Grant Colleges and Universities and USDA than in agricultural research. Since the very beginning the Federal and State systems have been united in a common quest of scientific knowledge for "agricultural improvement." . . . The fact that science in the United States has now become the major influence in our way of life is attributable in no small degree to the early development of Federal-State agricultural research.

Adherence by USDA leaders to a policy of conscientious "participation without control" of experiment station research has stimulated quality research in the Department as well as in the States. The original architect of that policy was Dr. Alfred C. True, from 1889 on the right-hand man of Dr. Atwater, the first Director of the Office of Experiment Stations, and from 1893 to 1914 its Director and subsequent Chief. Closely associated with True, who was by profession an educator rather than a scientist, was Dr. Edwin W. Allen, a graduate in agricultural chemistry at Massachusetts Agricultural College and at Göttingen, Germany. Both had taken part in most of the conventions of the Association of Land-Grant Colleges since it was founded in 1887, following passage of the Hatch Act.

The final chapter of their personal influence and leadership in directing the growth of agricultural research is written dramatically in two memorial tributes that appear in the Proceedings of the 43d Annual Convention (2, 21). Dr. True had died in March of that year, 1929. Dr. Allen had come to the convention prepared to read a memorial tribute to Dr. True. But on the evening prior to opening of the convention, he died unexpectedly.

As they passed from the scene, the esteem of their colleagues was fittingly expressed in Dr. Allen's tribute to Dr. True, read by Director J. L. Hills, and in Dr. Hill's tribute to Dr. Allen.

Also, these tributes provide those seeking to understand present-day policies of Federal-State relationships in research with a background of two men who had much to do with bringing about these policies.

Following the death of Dr. E. W. Allen, Chief of the Office of Experiment Stations in 1929, leadership in the Office was on an acting basis. On September 16, 1931, Director James T. Jardine of the Oregon Experiment Station was named Chief. He combined the qualities of able scientist with a broad background of successful experiment-station administration. He had served for a number of years on

[11] Meeting the Nation's Science and Educational Goals—A Challenge to the USDA–Land-Grant College System, mimeographed statement by Frank J. Welch, Assistant Secretary of Agriculture, U.S. Department of Agriculture, before the Seminar on Implications of Agricultural Adjustments for Land-Grant College Administrators, Colorado State University, Fort Collins, Colorado, June 26, 1961.

135

ESCOP along with the late Chief, Dr. Allen, and had much to do with development of the Project Outline.

Considering the many demands for action programs during the 1930's, the competition for research support, and the need for maintaining the sound principles that had made scientific research in agriculture so productive for nearly 50 years, the agricultural experiment stations were fortunate in the appointment of Dr. Jardine. While Director of the Oregon Experiment Station, Jardine had been active in the Association of Land-Grant Colleges and Universities and served as chairman of the Experiment Station Committee on Organization and Policy from 1927 to 1931. Upon becoming Chief, Jardine worked to bring about closer cooperative relationships between the research agencies of the Department and the States. Following passage of the Bankhead-Jones Act of 1935, he initiated the organization under which nine (originally eight) regional laboratories are administered by different research branches of the Department in close cooperation with State experiment stations.

"The nine regional Bankhead-Jones laboratories," Dr. R. W. Trullinger, who succeeded Jardine as Chief of the Office in 1946, said at the time of the latter's death in 1954, "stand as lasting monuments to the spirit of close State and Federal relationships in scientific agricultural research and development, a spirit that was nurtured and encouraged throughout his lifetime by James T. Jardine." [12]

Trullinger, who had joined USDA's OES staff in 1912 and for many years engaged in the organization, planning, and conduct of research on soils, drainage, fertilizers, and agricultural engineering, was named Jardine's successor in 1946. In 1947, he was appointed to serve also as Assistant Research Administrator of the Agricultural Research Administration. At the time of his retirement, May 27, 1955, Administrator Byron T. Shaw, USDA's Agricultural Research Administrator, paid this tribute to Trullinger: [13]

A leading advocate of close cooperation between the States and the Federal Government in agricultural research, and between research and extension work for the improvement of the Nation's agriculture, Dr. Trullinger has had a distinguished career of 43 years' service in the Department. He is widely known at State land-grant colleges and universities throughout the country, both for his work with experiment stations and for his leadership in establishing agricultural engineering as a profession.

Dr. E. C. Elting, who had joined the OES staff in 1936 as experiment station administrator in the area of dairy science, succeeded Trullinger as ARS Assistant Administrator for Experiment Stations when the latter retired in 1955. Concurrently with Elting's appointment, the position was changed to that of Deputy Administrator for Experiment Stations. Before becoming a member of OES, Elting had become recognized for outstanding dairy research at the Missouri and South Carolina Experiment Stations. He had been named Assistant Chief of OES in 1946 and Associate Chief in 1948. Under Trullinger he served for a year as ARS Deputy Assistant Administrator for Experiment Stations. Dr. H. C. Knoblauch, who had joined the

---

[12] James T. Jardine, 1881-1954, a mimeographed memorial statement issued at the time of Dr. Jardine's death, October 24, 1954, by R. W. Trullinger, Chief, Office of Experiment Stations.

[13] USDA Press Release 1348-55, May 27, 1955.

Analysis of
United Stat
CAT87207A
U.S. Depart
[21] ana
Jun 03, 2013

office technical staff as a soil scientist in 1940, became Director of the newly-established Division of ARS in 1954.

When he was named Chief of the Office of Experiment Stations in 1931, James T. Jardine reported to the Director of Scientific Work. In addition to continuing as Chief of the Office, Jardine in 1936 was made Director of Research for USDA, which position he held until December 1941. As Director of Research he had reported to the Secretary of Agriculture. This arrangement continued until 1942 when the Secretary of Agriculture established the Agricultural Research Administration. After 1942, the Chief of the Office reported to the Administrator of the Agricultural Research Administration, the name of which was changed to Agricultural Research Service by Secretary's Memorandum No. 1320, Supplement 4, November 2, 1953.

REORGANIZATION BROUGHT CHANGES

Following the reorganization of 1953, the Department's research activities followed somewhat the recommendations of the Task Force Report on Agriculture Activities of the Commission on Organization of the Executive Branch of the Government (28). Those recommendations placed all USDA research under a research administrator, with two assistant administrators, one of whom would be responsible for State relations. The Chairman of the Task Force was Dean and Director H. P. Rusk of Illinois, at the time also a member of ESCOP. The Vice Chairman was Dean and Director William H. Martin of New Jersey, at the time Chairman of ESCOP.

Neither the majority of ESCOP nor its parent association accepted the reorganization of 1953 with complete satisfaction. During the spring meeting of 1951, ESCOP had already named a special Subcommittee on Reorganization of the U.S. Department of Agriculture.[14] With authorization of the Executive Committee, this special subcommittee commended the historic effectiveness of the Office of Experiment Stations and strongly recommended the continuation of the organizational processes developed by that Office. In 1954, the Senate of the Association (15) adopted a resolution prepared by the special committee which set forth that "the agency designated by the Secretary to administer Federal-grant funds for research should be in a position to deal directly with the Secretary, the agencies under his administration, other departments of the Government, and the State agricultural experiment stations."

The resolution, later approved and accepted by the Senate of the Association, concluded:

NOW, THEREFORE, IT IS RECOMMENDED to the Secretary of Agriculture that (1) the Office of Experiment Stations be designated as the responsible agency within the Department of Agriculture to administer Federal-grant funds for research to the States; (2) the principal officer be designated as the Administrator, Office of Experiment Stations; and (3) the Administrator of the Office of Experiment Stations report directly to the Assistant Secretary of Agriculture for Federal-States Relations.

The special committee and members of ESCOP continued to confer with Department officials, reiterating the position previously presented. During the 1955 convention, Dean H. Macy of the Institute of Agriculture, University of Minnesota, presented for the Associa-

---

[14] Unpublished minutes of ESCOP, May 8–9, 1951.

tion's Division of Agriculture a lengthy report on development (*16*). Dean Macy reported visits and contacts with departmental officials during 1955. Letters of the Under Secretary and of the Assistant Secretary for Federal-States Relations were cited, indicating the Department's belief in the then current organization. The report included reference to a meeting which had been held in Assistant Secretary Ervin L. Peterson's office in April, and a letter sent by him to Director A. D. Weber of Kansas, Chairman of ESCOP. In that letter Peterson, while defending the reorganization, said:

I want to make it perfectly clear that on all matters of broad policy the experiment station directors either individually or collectively have had, and now have, full access to the Secretary's office to discuss any policy matters which may be of interest or concern to them.

Dean Macy's report also cited action taken on November 2, 1955, by Administrator B. T. Shaw of ARS, creating the position of Deputy Administrator for Experiment Stations in ARS, and setting up an organizational chart for the Office of the Director, State Experiment Stations Division. The report, however, resulted in the following action of the Association:

In view of the action taken by the Department of Agriculture during the past year, we reaffirm for the record of the Association our stand of a year ago.

Those who are familiar with the historical position taken by the experiment station directors since founding of the stations will recognize the consummation of a persistent effort on their part on reading Memorandum No. 1462, issued by Secretary of Agriculture Orville L. Freeman on July 19, 1961. It announced the intention to establish a Cooperative State Experiment Station Service.[15] The first paragraph of item 2 reads as follows:

It is believed that the administration of these functions by a separate service in the Department will give these programs their rightful place in the Department structure and will place the administration of the Act in its proper perspective in relation to the other research of the Department and cooperative relationship between the land-grant colleges and the United States Department of Agriculture. Such reorganization will strengthen and improve the total agricultural research program carried on in the States.

In a press release issued on September 1, 1961,[16] announcing the order establishing the new Service, Secretary Freeman said:

The Department of Agriculture and the Land-Grant Colleges and Universities have had a long and historic relationship in scientific research. This action should be an incentive toward meeting agriculture's scientific needs.

The release pointed out that establishment of the new Service places the research program of the State experiment stations on a basis equal to other research programs of the Department, with the Administrator of the Service reporting directly to the Assistant Secretary for Federal-State Relations. The Service is subject to the coordination of research activities which are assigned to the Administrator of the Agricultural Research Service. The release announced that Dr. George A. Selke, after an extended educational career, including service as staff member of the Minnesota Department of Education and the University of Minnesota, President of St. Cloud College, Chancellor of the University of Montana, and Chief of the Division

---

[15] Secretary's Memorandum No. 1462, U.S. Department of Agriculture, Office of the Secretary, Washington 25, D.C., Issued July 19, 1961.
[16] USDA Press Release 2837, Sept. 1, 1961.

of Cultural Affairs of the U.S. High Commissioner for Germany, would serve as Acting Administrator of the Cooperative State Experiment Station Service. Dr. H. C. Knoblauch was named Deputy Administrator. Dr. E. C. Elting continued in the Agricultural Research Service as Deputy Administrator for Research Planning and Coordination.

The close administrative working relationships between the directors and USDA has served as the keystone of the arch of effective, whole-hearted cooperation. Although the name of the Office of Experiment Stations was changed, following departmental reorganization in 1953, to that of State Experiment Stations Division, Agricultural Research Service, and again in September 1961 to that of Cooperative State Experiment Station Service, the pattern and spirit of realistic cooperation endures.

The above objective review of the administrative relationships and formal and informal cooperation between the stations and the Department of Agriculture leaves no doubt that the cooperative mechanisms that have evolved have been a major force in stimulating productive research that has served the country well.

LITERATURE CITED

(1) ALLEN, E. W. [Secretary].
    1919. REPORT OF COMMITTEE ON EXPERIMENT STATION ORGANIZATION AND POLICY. Assoc. Amer. Agr. Cols. and Expt. Stas. Proc. 32: 114–120.
(2) ———
    1930. MEMORIAL TO DR. A. C. TRUE. Assoc. Land-Grant Cols. Proc. (1929) 43: 41–45.
(3) ASSOCIATION OF AMERICAN LAND-GRANT COLLEGES AND EXPERIMENT STATIONS.
    1908. REPORT OF COMMISSION ON AGRICULTURAL RESEARCH. 23 pp.
(4) BRYAN, E. A.
    1900. [MOTION TO APPOINT A COMMITTEE ON COOPERATIVE WORK BETWEEN U.S. DEPARTMENT OF AGRICULTURE AND EXPERIMENT STATIONS.] Assoc. Amer. Agr. Cols. and Expt. Stas. Proc. (1889) 13: 55.
(5) ———
    1901. REPORT OF COMMITTEE ON COOPERATIVE WORK BETWEEN THE DEPARTMENT OF AGRICULTURE AND EXPERIMENT STATIONS. Assoc. Amer. Agr. Cols. and Expt. Stas. Proc. (1900) 14: 58–59.
(6) CONOVER, MILTON.
    1924. THE OFFICE OF EXPERIMENT STATIONS; ITS HISTORY, ACTIVITIES AND ORGANIZATION. 178 pp. The Johns Hopkins Press, Baltimore. (Inst. Govt. Research, Serv. Monog., U.S. Govt. 32.)
(7) DAVENPORT, E., Chairman.
    1915. REPORT OF COMMITTEE ON EXPERIMENT STATION ORGANIZATION AND POLICY. Assoc. Amer. Agr. Cols. and Expt. Stas. Proc. 29: 123–125.
(8) ———
    1918. REPORT OF THE COMMITTEE ON EXPERIMENT STATION ORGANIZATION AND POLICY. Assoc. Amer. Agr. Cols. and Expt. Stas. Proc. (1917) 31: 37–43.
(9) ———
    1922. REPORT OF COMMITTEE ON STATION ORGANIZATION AND POLICY. Assoc. Land-Grant Cols. Proc. (1921) 35: 178–184.
(10) EDDY, E. D. Jr.
    1956. COLLEGES FOR OUR LAND AND TIME. 328 pp. Harper & Bros., New York.
(11) EXECUTIVE COMMITTEE OF THE ASSOCIATION.
    1907. SCIENTIFIC INVESTIGATION UNDER GOVERNMENT AUSPICES. (Appointment of Committee and Discussion.) Assoc. Amer. Agr. Cols. and Expt. Stas. Proc. (1906) 20: 61–68.

(12) EXECUTIVE COMMITTEE OF THE ASSOCIATION.
    1914. RECOMMENDATION (AND ADOPTION BY CONVENTION) FOR APPOINT-
    MENT OF COMMITTEE ON RELATIONS, COMMITTEE ON PROJECTS, AND
    COMMITTEE ON PUBLICATIONS. Assoc. Amer. Agr. Cols. and Expt.
    Stas. Proc. (1913) 27: 115.

(13) ———
    1924. RECOMMENDATION AND ADOPTION BY THE CONVENTION OF REPORT OF
    COMMITTEE ON EXPERIMENT STATION ORGANIZATION AND POLICY.
    Assoc. Land-Grant Cols. (1923) Proc. 37: 483–484.

(14) ———
    1941. PROCEEDINGS OF THE FIRST ANNUAL CONVENTION (1887) OF THE
    ASSOCIATION OF AMERICAN AGRICULTURAL COLLEGES AND EXPERIMENT
    STATIONS, 6 PP. (Note: No account of this convention was printed
    originally. However, a manuscript summary by C. E. Thorne,
    Secretary of the Convention, which was filed in the Office of
    Experiment Stations, was ordered printed by the Executive
    Committee of the Association on May 5, 1951.)

(15) ———
    1954. POSITION OF THE ASSOCIATION ON STATUS OF THE OFFICE OF EXPERI-
    MENT STATIONS, U.S. DEPARTMENT OF AGRICULTURE. Assoc. Land-
    Grant Cols. and Univs. Proc. 68: 116–117.

(16) ———
    1955. STATUS OF OFFICE OF EXPERIMENT STATIONS, U. S. DEPARTMENT OF
    AGRICULTURE. Amer. Assoc. Land-Grant Cols. and State Univs.
    Proc. 69: 130–131.

(17) FLETCHER, S. W., Chairman.
    1932. REPORT OF THE COMMITTEE ON FEDERAL-STATE RELATIONS IN [AGRI-
    CULTURAL RESEARCH. Assoc. Land-Grant Cols. Proc. (1931) 45:
    266, 514–522.

(18) ———
    1933. REPORT OF COMMITTEE ON FEDERAL-STATE RELATIONS IN AGRICUL-
    TURAL RESEARCH. Assoc. Land-Grant Col., Proc. (1932) 46:
    279–280.

(19) FLETCHER, S. W.
    1937. THE MAJOR RESEARCH ACHIEVEMENTS MADE POSSIBLE THROUGH
    GRANTS UNDER THE HATCH ACT. Assoc. Land-Grant Cols. and
    Univs. Proc. 51: 136–144.

(20) HILLS, J. L.
    1929. THE BUILDERS OF THE ASSOCIATION (PRESIDENTIAL ADDRESS). Assoc.
    Land-Grant Cols. Proc. (1928) 42: 24–33.

(21) ———
    1930. MINUTE CONCERNING THE LATE DR. EDWIN WEST ALLEN. Assoc.
    Land-Grant Cols. Proc. (1929) 43: 45–47.

(22) HOUSTON, D. F.
    1915. ADDRESS OF WELCOME. Assoc. Amer. Agr. Cols. and Expt. Stas.
    Proc. (1914) 28: 20–23.

(23) JORDAN, D. S., Chairman.
    1909. REPORT OF THE COMMISSION ON AGRICULTURAL RESEARCH. Assoc.
    Amer. Agr. Cols, and Expt. Stas. Proc. (1908) 22: 38.

(24) KLEIN, A. J.
    1931. REPORT ON SURVEY OF LAND-GRANT INSTITUTIONS. Assoc. Land-
    Grant Cols. Proc. (1930) 44: 72–79.

(25) MUMFORD, F. B.
    1915. REPORT OF JOINT COMMITTEE ON PROJECTS AND CORRELATIONS. Assoc.
    Amer. Agr. Cols. and Expt. Stas. Proc. (1914) 28: 109–115.

(26) MUMFORD, F. B., Chairman.
    1930. REPORT OF THE JOINT COMMITTEE ON PROJECTS AND CORRELATION OF
    RESEARCH. Assoc. Land-Grant Cols. Proc. (1929) 43: 202–205.

(27) PUGSLEY, C. W.
    1923. ADDRESS OF THE ASSISTANT SECRETARY OF AGRICULTURE. Assoc.
    Land-Grant Cols. Proc. (1922) 36: 209–218.

(28) RUSK, H. B., Chairman.
    1949. TASK FORCE REPORT ON AGRICULTURAL ACTIVITIES FOR THE COM-
    MISSION ON ORGANIZATION OF THE EXECUTIVE BRANCH OF THE GOV-
    ERNMENT. Appendix M: 7–11.

Analysis of
United Stat
CAT87207...
U.S. Depart...
[21] ana
Jun 03, 2013

(29) SHAW, B. T.
1958. DEVELOPMENT OF RESEARCH FACILITIES AND THE ROLE OF REGIONAL LABORATORIES IN STATE AND FEDERAL PROGRAMS. (Abstract.) Amer. Assoc. Land-Grant Cols. and State Univs. Proc. 72: 166–167.

(30) TALBOTT, M. W., AND CRONEMILLER, F. P.
1961. SOME BEGINNINGS IN RANGE MANAGEMENT. Jour. Range Management 14(2): 95–101.

(31) THATCHER, R. W., Chairman.
1924. PUBLISHING THE FINANCIAL RESOURCES OF THE STATION. (*In* Report of Committee on Organization and Policy.) Assoc. Land-Grant Cols. Proc. (1923) 37: 225–228.

(32) TRUE, A. C.
1896. REPORT OF THE DIRECTOR OF THE OFFICE OF EXPERIMENT STATIONS FOR 1896 TO HON. STERLING MORTON, SECRETARY. U.S. Dept. Agr., Off. Expt. Sta. Ann. Rpt., 143 pp.

(33) ———
1900. STATEMENT REGARDING COOPERATION BETWEEN THE STATIONS AND THE U.S. DEPARTMENT OF AGRICULTURE. Assoc. Amer. Agr. Cols., and Expt. Stas. Proc. (1889) 13: 52–53.

(34) ———
1900. A REPORT ON THE WORK AND EXPENDITURES OF THE AGRICULTURAL EXPERIMENT STATIONS FOR THE YEAR ENDED JUNE 30, 1889. U.S. Dept. Agr., Off. Expt. Sta. Bul. 83: 7.

(35) TRUE, A. C.
1915. PRESIDENTIAL ADDRESS. Assoc. Amer. Agr. Cols. and Expt. Stas. Proc. (1914) 28: 92–93.

(36) ———
1937. A HISTORY OF AGRICULTURAL EXPERIMENTATION AND RESEARCH IN THE UNITED STATES, 1607–1925. U.S. Dept. Agr., Misc. Pub. 261: 216, 251.

(37) TRULLINGER, R. W.
1937. THE POLICIES AND PROCEDURE INVOLVED IN THE HATCH ACT FROM THE STANDPOINT OF EFFICIENCY IN ADMINISTERING PRODUCTIVE RESEARCH. Assoc. Land-Grant Cols. Proc. 51: 144–147.

(38) U.S. DEPARTMENT OF AGRICULTURE.
1946. FEDERAL LEGISLATION, REGULATIONS, AND RULINGS AFFECTING COOPERATIVE EXTENSION WORK IN AGRICULTURE AND HOME ECONOMICS. U.S. Dept. Agr., Misc. Pub. 285, 61 pp.

(39) WALKER, E. A.
1960. REORGANIZATION FOR PROGRESS. Amer. Assoc. Land-Grant Cols. and State Univs. Proc. 74: 41–48.

(40) WALLACE, H. C.
1923. ADDRESS OF THE SECRETARY OF AGRICULTURE. Assoc. Land-Grant Cols. Proc (1922) 36: 20–26.

(41) ———
1924. THE DEPARTMENT AND THE COLLEGES (ADDRESS BEFORE THE CONVENTION. Assoc. Land-Grant Cols. Proc 37: 43–49.

(42) WEBBER, H. J.
1921. PROBLEMS OF AGRICULTURAL INVESTIGATION. Assoc. Land-Grant Cols. Proc. 34: 149–158.

141

hapter Eight—
UBLISHING RESULTS OF RESEARCH:
Information, Communications, and Public Relations

Founders of the agricultural experiment stations recognized from
ιe beginning that informational processes played a vital part in the
dministration of scientific research. Publications were regarded as
ιe lifeblood of effective coordination. The theory under which the
ιrly directors launched their stations was that the needs of agricul-
ιre required application of those principles basic to the pursuit of all
ιience, namely, the ascertainment of fact, the grouping of facts to
ιow the laws under which they operate, and verification. In addi-
on the directors knew, as Johnson and Atwater had learned in the
:hool of practical experience, that dissemination of facts, as these
nerged from research and proved practical, was highly important if
ιe stations were to serve as continuing instruments of farm improve-
ιent.

No subject was more frequently discussed by the early experiment
.ation leaders than publications. Nor has there been any other sub-
:ct in which cooperation between the stations and the Department be-
an earlier or proved more enduring. Publications and communica-
ons were prominent in the proceedings of that first Convention of
)elegates from Agricultural Colleges and Experiment Stations, called
y Commissioner Colman in 1885 (*6, pp. 90–104*).[1] The Convention
rged creation of a bureau of public information and exchanges in the
)epartment. "The subject of publications," said ESCOP's report in
)17, devoted entirely to publications (*4*), "their kind and character,
: as old as the experiment stations."

Publication matters early divided themselves into two principal
roblems. As institutions that could not survive without public sup-
ort, communication with the main supporting group of the general
ublic, the farmers, was essential. To communicate with scientists
t the various stations, and with other members of the scientific com-
ιunity, there soon emerged also a need for the precise, carefully docu-
ιented kind of publication later to be known as the technical bulletin.
he philosophy of the earliest directors regarding the popular type
f publication was expressed in the following words by E. Lewis
turtevant, pioneer director of the New York Agricultural Experi-
ιent Station (Geneva) (*26*) in his first annual report of 1883:

The province of an agricultural experiment station is not so much the dis-
)very of new facts as it is the testing of applications and the theory of relations.
:s ultimate object is to give expression to values which shall assist the farmer in
ιe largest sense in meeting and overcoming the various obstacles which arise
ι the practice of his pursuit . . . . The duties of an agricultural experiment

---

[1] Italic numbers in parentheses refer to Literature Cited, p. 155.

station comprise dissemination as well as investigation. To bring its experiments before the public, not alone through its annual report, but as well in other ways, is a duty that could not be neglected.

Questions of what should be published, in what form, and the important problems of communication and contact with farmers, between the stations, with the Federal Department of Agriculture, and with other scientific institutions at home and abroad, were important items on the agenda of the early conventions of the Association of Land-Grant Colleges. Their analysis in convention led to enduring policies on publication and information, written and spoken by men of great vision—by men like Atwater, Henry, and Cooke. As these men looked to the future, they saw as the result of harnessing science to serve agriculture "the most remarkable period of scientific development the world has yet seen" (*19*).

EARLY CONVENTIONS EMPHASIZED PUBLICATIONS

The first annual convention of the Association of American Agricultural Colleges and Experiment Stations, held in October 1887 following passage of the Hatch Act in 1887, emphasized publications (*12*). Next to Association matters, its agenda dealt with advisory recommendations for initiating the program. There were four major recommendations, the fourth outlining the following policy on publications:

That the publications of the stations should be entirely separate from those of the college. The quarterly or more frequent bulletins should give their readers the results of experiments as fast as completed, and only as completed, or as distinct chapters are completed. These bulletins should enlarge on those practical points, such as the improvement or restoration of soils, the development of plants and the breeding stock, when suggested by work done, even to the extent of repeating well-known principles and facts when these need to be taught.

Out of the discussions in the executive body of the conventions, later in the section on experiment stations and in the committees, grew publications such as the first Farmers' Bulletin, "The What and Why of Agricultural Experiment Stations," issued in June 1889 (*31*). Out of them grew "The Agricultural Experiment Stations in the United States," a 636-page documented volume prepared to accompany the Experiment Station Exhibit to the 1900 Paris Exposition (*28*). Out of them grew recognition of the need for what was known then as Farmers' Institutes and what later became cooperative extension work in agriculture and home economics.

The Third Annual Convention of the Association of Land-Grant Colleges in 1889 called attention to the need for providing translation and editing of abstracts of European stations. Director Atwater of the Office of Experiment Stations stated that a beginning had been made for this work, that the only impediment had been lack of funds and the necessity for giving priority to the reports of our own stations for which a beginning had been made (*1*). In September of that year the Office had issued Volume 1, Number 1 of the Experiment Station Record. The design and concept of this publication, which was to have a useful life for 57 years, was largely Director Atwater's and that of his first assistant editor, Dr. A. C. True. The introduction appearing in the first issue (*32*) outlines this concept clearly:

In pursuance of the plan announced in the introduction to Part 1 of the Digest of Annual Reports of the Agricultural Experiment Stations in the United States for 1888 (Experiment Station Bulletin No. 2), the publication of abstracts of station bulletins of the current year is here begun.

The Digest of Reports for 1888 is intended to include such outlines and details of the station work as will be most useful for permanent record and convenient reference. . . . It is hoped that serious omissions may be supplied in a more detailed digest of station work for 1889. It may be added, however, that without regard to the perplexities imposed on this office, as here indicated, it seems not improbable that the stations will be gradually forced, by circumstances peculiar to themselves, to distinguish between the small and numerous bulletins, issued in large editions for the information of practical farmers, and those full and accurate reports of experiments, with which alone the demands of the scientist can be satisfied, and which are to be stored in libraries as the permanent evidence of the industry and success of the investigators.

Besides the abstracts of station literature, it is proposed to include in the Experiment Station Record brief accounts of the publications and work of this Department and such information for station workers and others interested in agricultural science as may from time to time be deemed advisable. In this number will be found a list of the publications of the Department from January 1 to August 15, 1889, as well as a list of station bulletins received at this office during the same period.

The Experiment Station Record will, if the present plan is carried out, be issued in numbers to be paged continuously and form a volume of six or more numbers for each year. Indexes of names and subjects will be published for each volume.

Publication of the Experiment Station Record was begun in 1889. In that year, also, an Office of Experiment Stations Library was organized. In August 1891, Dr. Atwater resigned his directorship and was succeeded by A. W. Harris, formerly assistant editor, and Dr. A. C. True, formerly first assistant editor, became assistant director (33). In 1893, Director Harris resigned to become President of Maine State College. Dr. A. C. True became Director of the Office of Experiment Stations. He announced that the editorial force was being reorganized in the direction of greater specialization of work and that arrangements were being made to give more attention to the bibliography of science (34).

The problems in abstracting scientific reports, indexing them, and making them available for rapid reference by scientists, at the various experiment stations had grown as the experiment stations began issuing individual bulletins and reports on their work. On the evening of November 16, 1892, during the Association's sixth convention, Director Henry of the Wisconsin station called attention to a matter that had been brought before the executive committee. Could not station publications follow a more uniform rule as to numbers?

Director Harris of the Office of Experiment Stations presented a resolution expressing it to be the sense of the convention that publications of the colleges and stations should be named, numbered, and dated according to a uniform method; also that a committee be appointed to devise a uniform system to be made available to member institutions. In the discussions that followed, Director Samuel Johnson of the Connecticut station called attention to the importance, not only of numbering, but of indexing, summarizing, and otherwise facilitating systematic use of publications by other scientists.

Protagonist of the concept that an experiment station was not only a fact-gathering institution but one that by hypothesis and experiment sought to establish new principles that existed in nature, Johnson recognized the significance of documentation in all scientific endeavor. In Johnson's day the principal means of communication in the scientific world was the printed word. Thus was born the idea of the technical agricultural bulletin and the pioneer instrument of American agricultural documentation in the form of the Experiment Station Record. Johnson's philosophy concerning the abstracting and indexing of these for systematic reference becomes even more meaningful today when the number of research projects and their resulting publications have multiplied thousandfold (*35*) :

The stations ought to furnish every facility, so that the student can readily master the contents of publications. There should be an index on the front page, so that he may see at once what is of the most importance to him. . . . The amount of matter published in this country and in foreign countries is so immense that without every facility placed at the disposal of the student it becomes simply impossible to keep track of them. It is of the utmost importance that every single paper have a special table of contents, unless matter of simple sort, for without that it is difficult to take advantage of the information, however valuable, which is published.

The convention adopted Director Harris' resolution and appointed him to represent the Department of Agriculture on the Committee on Uniformity of Station Publications. Other members appointed were Directors Johnson (Connecticut), Johnson (Wyoming), Henry (Wisconsin), and Redding (Georgia). The Association also, for the first time, named among its officers a Bibliographer—Director Samuel Johnson of Connecticut. The recommendations of this committee were presented before the Association in Chicago the following year (*19*). They made recommendations regarding format of annual reports, bulletins, and circulars, the latter to be used "for inquiries or the publication of matter not requiring permanent record, and should never be made the sole repositories of matter of scientific or permanent value. *Newspaper bulletins* should never be made the sole repositories of any information of permanent value." The recommendation also called "special attention to the remarks of Prof. S. W. Johnson on the preparation of bulletins and reports." The resolution adopted at the Knoxville convention in 1889 regarding the size of bulletins, annual reports, and format was reaffirmed.

Following acceptance of the recommendations by the Association and referral to the Executive Committee for distribution to member institutions, Dr. A. C. True (*19*) discussed the nature and purpose of the Experiment Station Record, also of the card index system of experiment station work, for the distribution of which to the stations Congress had authorized funds :

We take the reports of the investigations of the different stations and work them up in a condensed form for the use of other station workers; or we put certain portions of these reports into popular form for general distribution, so that people throughout the country may get information as to what is being done in the different States. Thus far the Office has expanded its energies very largely in publishing documents which are primarily of interest to station workers and others engaged in investigation in agricultural science. Our principal publication, as most of you know, is the Experiment Station Record, which is issued monthly, and contains abstracts of station publications and of publications issued by similar institutions in foreign countries.

In another way we have tried to sum up the work of the stations and put them into the brief form of a card index. This enterprise is in some respects of a kind that has never before been undertaken, and we have met with unexpected difficulties, especially in the way of publication of this work. The classification of the subjects with which agricultural science deals has never been undertaken in the thorough way in which the office has undertaken it. . . . We hope that this index, which in manuscript form now covers all the past work of American stations, will be issued more rapidly, and that soon at least one copy will be found in every college and station library throughout the country, so that those who are interested in such studies may readily find the information they desire. . . .

During the eighth annual convention, President H. H. Goodell of Massachusetts Agricultural College delivered a scholarly talk, "What Is the Mission of the Bulletin?" (16). Should an experiment station bulletin be technical, popular, or techno-popular? He concluded that he was fast "coming to the opinion that there should be two sets of bulletins." The ninth annual convention approved a resolution "that a committee of three be appointed to confer with the Department of Agriculture with reference to the preparation and publication of a catalogue of literature for the use of teachers and students of agriculture. . . ." (17). This Committee on Indexing Agricultural Literature, which included A. C. True of the Office of Experiment Stations, in 1898 presented a suggested scheme of Classification of Agriculture by W. P. Cutter, Librarian of the U.S. Department of Agriculture. The scheme was designed to cover agriculture only and to be used with the Dewey system of classification, which had been adopted in the majority of libraries in which classification existed. It was destined to become the system followed by generations of agricultural college students (7), with the Committee on Indexing making refinements reported at subsequent conventions through 1904 (5).

During the ninth annual convention, Director A. C. True succeeded Samuel Johnson as bibliographer of the Association (36). He was thus listed annually in the Proceedings with the officers of the Association through the post-World War I, 32d Convention held in Baltimore, Md., early in January 1919 (10). In that year the Association drew up a new constitution and dropped "and Experiment Stations" from its name and "bibliographer" from its list of officers (11). In the early interest and emphasis on publication and documentation to aid scientists, one can measure, in retrospect, the great influence of the directors on the progress and success of the agricultural experiment stations.

In addition to the Experiment Station Record, issued from 1889 to 1946, the Office published 256 Experiment Station Bulletins, from 1889 to 1913; 118 circulars, 1889–1913; and annual reports on the State Agricultural Experiment Stations, 1896–1960. It also published other related items, including legislation, rules, and regulations pertaining to the Hatch Act and related authorizations. A list of Workers in Subjects Pertaining to Agriculture in the Land-Grant Colleges and Experiment Stations, commenced in 1889, is still published annually.

Numerous changes were to come in the new 20th century. Prominent influences bringing these changes were to be the Adams Act, the Smith-Lever Act, the Purnell Act, the Bankhead-Jones Act, and its later Amendment, all discussed elsewhere in this publication. But primary emphasis on publication and documentation, as conceived by the early leaders like Samuel Johnson and Alfred Charles True, was to dominate the principal activities of the Office of Experiment Stations as a service to the stations for years to come.

Participants in the constructive debates on publications that took place over the years in the Association's conventions included numerous station directors, deans of agricultural colleges, college presidents. Among them were young men who later acquired world renown in the scientific world, for example, Liberty Hyde Bailey, Dean and Director of the Agricultural Experiment Station, Cornell University, 1903–13. During the 16th annual convention in 1902, Dr. Bailey presented a scholarly paper on "The Editing of Experiment Station Publications" (2).

Administrative changes during the historic period of the first decade of the 20th century are recorded in other sections and chapters of this publication. As reported in Chapter Five, this was the period when the collective decision was reached that the land-grant institutions required national affiliation in the form of an Association. During this period the research-minded directors helped frame legislation for the Adams Act, putting greater emphasis on original research. With passage of the Adams Act, they created a standing Committee on Experiment Station Organization and Policy. During this period they also recognized clearly the need for demonstration work and the emerging extension services on many land-grant campuses. The station directors were among the original and most dedicated sponsors of cooperative extension work as an arm of the land-grant institution, coordinate with that of the agricultural experiment stations. They pressed vigorously for passage of what became the Smith-Lever Act of 1914. The administrative history of the experiment stations in the early 1900's demonstrates in different ways the dedication of the station leaders to the research ideal; for example, the campaign to prevent the research programs of the Federal Department of Agriculture from eliminating the influence of State stations within their respective jurisdictions; the movement to reduce teaching loads and extension assignments in order to free investigators for research; the periodic movements to win additional Federal funds for research in the State stations, on terms suitable to station spokesmen.

In addition to all these administrative discussions leading to policy decisions, the directors were faced with new publication problems brought on by their own administrative decisions. In the frank debates and recommendations dealing with changes in publication policies, we find mirrored the station group's earnest search for an improved administrative technology, viewed by them as the primary and never-ending vital interest of station personnel. As protagonists of the concept that the land-grant institutions should nurture scientific research in station form, they consistently fought any influences they felt might encroach on the effectiveness of the stations as scientific institutions. Thereby they sought and continue to seek to guard the future role of the experiment stations.

Before the advent of the Smith-Lever Act, as early as the 23d annual convention of 1909, Dr. A. C. True defined the confusion resulting from too much emphasis on the popular type of station bulletins in these words (27):

At present we have this condition of things: Our station publications as a whole are of such a miscellaneous character that they fully satisfy nobody. Most of them are written with the primary purpose of reaching a large and popular audience, and whether they embody scientific work or not, the effort is made to present the material in such a way as will be acceptable and instructive to the layman, especially the farmer. At the same time the scientific workers naturally want to present the matter so that it will be acceptable to scientific men. Thus they have in mind as they write these publications the necessities of the scientific presentation of the subject. The result is that they do neither one thing nor the other, and the material is not put in scientific form or in good popular form.

Such reasoning brought approval of ESCOP's recommendation for a JOURNAL OF AGRICULTURAL RESEARCH. The JOURNAL was to be prepared in the Department of Agriculture under the general management of an editorial board jointly named by the Association and the Secretary of Agriculture (8). The Committee on Publication of Research was appointed for the first time in 1913, later to be known as the Joint Committee on Publication of Research (9). The function and operation of this committee were outlined in the Proceedings of 1914 (22). Vol. 1, No. 1 of the JOURNAL OF AGRICULTURAL RESEARCH made its appearance in October 1913 (29). The cover of each issue of the journal carried the imprint, "Issued by Authority of the Secretary of Agriculture with the Co-operation of the Association of Land-Grant Colleges." The Joint Committee on Publication of Research each year filed a report which appears in the annual proceedings of the conventions. The June 15, 1949, issue of the Journal (30) carried this terse message printed on the cover: "A Shortage of Operating Funds Has Forced the Discontinuance of this Journal. This Is the Final Number."

The last listing of the Joint Committee on Publications appeared in the Proceedings of the 63d Annual Convention held in 1949 (13). Thus was terminated the JOURNAL OF AGRICULTURAL RESEARCH which, since 1913, had sought to chronicle discoveries of fundamental research developments of obvious significance to agriculture. The end of this USDA-Experiment Station editorial partnership was not unlike that of the EXPERIMENT STATION RECORD, a few years earlier, the final index number of which appeared in December 1946 (37). In each case it was a matter of lack of funds. Other phases of administering research in agriculture were considered more essential in accordance with strict interpretation of the law. Discussion relative to termination of both publications took place in repeated ESCOP meetings from 1946 to 1949.[2]

STATION PUBLICATIONS EMPHASIZED

Following discontinuation of the Experiment Station Record and the Journal of Agricultural Research, an even greater emphasis was placed on experiment station publication and on publication of scientific findings in technical journals. Publication data submitted by the individual stations for the fiscal year ending June 30, 1961, reported totals of 398 popular, 530 technical printed reports, bulletins, and circulars; 1,132 popular and 5,968 technical articles in journals; 267 popular and 357 periodicals; 515 popular and 83 technical pamphlets or leaflets. For the same period the stations reported 793 popular and 1,810 technical mimeographed or otherwise processed reports, bulletins, and circulars.

A frequently quoted talk on the philosophy of research publication, as this evolved out of the experiment station leaders' discussion in the annual Association meetings, was "The Publication of Research," by Dr. E. W. Allen, Chief, Office of Experiment Stations, Feb. 11, 1925. Significance of the scientific publications was summarized by him as follows:[3]

[2] These discussions are recorded in the unpublished minutes of ESCOP meetings held Dec. 13–18, 1946; Feb. 6, 1947; Nov. 8, 1947; Nov. 6, 1948; May 3–5, 1949; and Oct. 22, 1949.
[3] Dr. Allen's lecture was delivered before the USDA Graduate School, Department of Agriculture, Feb. 11, 1925. It was considered so interesting, stimulating, and helpful to scientists that M. C. Merrill, at the time Assistant Director of

Publication is a serious matter because of the permanence of the Record.
. . . the obligation to publish the results of investigation in suitable form is no less heavy than that of making the work itself exact in method and deduction. The manner in which this is done will reflect not only upon the individual worker but upon his organization and the Department as a whole.
. . . The purpose of writing is not only to *express* ideas, but to communicate them to others. Science is not inherently dull, heavy, and hard to comprehend; it is essentially fascinating, understandable, and full of charm. It is simple, after it has been worked out, and is capable of being stated in concise terms easily understood. But to succeed in conveying ideas correctly and in a readable way requires considerable effort on the part of most of us. It calls for time to do it well. . . .
The aim in publishing research, as well as in carrying it on, is to leave the *field clearer than you found it*. If that cannot be done it is doubtful whether a scientific paper is justified. There cannot be clear writing without clear thinking, and when one learns to write clearly, he will in the process learn to think clearly. Indeed it may be doubted whether thought and its expression can be separated. Vagueness or turbidity of language usually indicates similar qualities in the thinking. The attempt to express a matter clearly in writing thus helps in the process of clear thinking. Bacon wrote that "Reading maketh a full man, conference a ready man, and writing an exact man."

The directors gave frequent consideration to the cost and format of station publications. Steady increases in cost of printing and paper made the bills for this purpose an increasingly important administrative problem. Many of the presentations were chiefly made on the basis of administrative judgment. In 1940, however, Director Fred Griffee of the Maine Agricultural Experiment Station undertook for ESCOP a nationwide survey of experiment station publications (18). The following suggestions were summarized from replies received from 51 stations:

1. That encouragement be given for the standardization of station publications and that fewer types be published. The list suggested is (a) Annual Report, (b) Bulletin, (c) Technical Bulletin, (d) Special Reports, (e) Regulatory Bulletin, (f) Miscellaneous Bulletin, (g) Journal type, and (h) Periodical type.
2. That the number of copies printed of each bulletin be sufficient to supply the needs of the people who can be served from the standpoint of the best interest of agriculture.
3. That the station mailing list should include the name of every farmer in the state who desires his name included; or, some other means be devised to make it possible for any farmer to obtain any bulletin he can use to advantage.
4. That bulletins be sent only on request, except to college and station libraries, public libraries, county agents, agricultural teachers in high schools, foreign libraries, and such individuals and agencies as is required by Federal Acts.
5. That a charge can logically be made for "bulk lot" bulletins sent to commercial agencies, high schools, and individuals.
6. That a news story accompany bulletins sent to newspapers.
7. The inclusion of United States Department of Agriculture publications in Station lists should be a matter for the two agencies to work out cooperatively.
8. Joint publications of the experiment station and extension service can be an asset to both agencies.

In 1950 a committee of experiment station editors, made up of one editor from each region, was asked by ESCOP to study the matter of annual reports. The committee sent a questionnaire to all station directors. It presented its recommendations under the title "Report on Experiment Station Annual Reports by the Editors' Subcommittee to the Experiment Station Committee on Organization

Publication, had it mimeographed. Copies are available from the Cooperative State Experiment Station Service, U.S. Department of Agriculture.

and Policy." A principal suggestion was that annual reports be modified to serve mainly as a report on fiscal matters to the Governors and other officials, and that research developments be reported in periodicals. The number of States publishing such periodicals rose from 18 in 1950 to 40 in 1960. The subject of station publications was given further consideration by a committee of experiment station editors meeting at the invitation of the Office of Experiment Stations and with authorization of their directors in 1949, 1950, 1951, and 1955. The State Experiment Stations Division, ARS, accepted station project proposals in agricultural communications as early as 1955. In 1959, directors were advised that scientific research in various phases relating to agricultural communications had been given project status.[4] Thus research in the many phases of agricultural communications, such as publication needs, cost, and distribution now offers directors and those responsible for policies relative to publications the ability to reach decisions on the basis of scientific findings (24).

FOREIGN DISTRIBUTION STUDIED

At a meeting of the experiment station subsection of the Section on Agriculture at the 45th Convention in 1931, Vice-Director Andrew Boss of the Minnesota Experiment Station presented a statement embodying the report of a special committee of the Minnesota Experiment Station captioned: "The Inadequate Distribution of State Agricultural Experiment Station Bulletins to Foreign Countries." The report (23) stated: "It is generally recognized that the character of the work of the state agricultural experiment stations has undergone a gradual change during the past 25 or 30 years. In recent years a much larger proportion of the bulletins published are technical in nature. Many of them constitute distinct contributions to science and are of interest to agricultural workers throughout the world." The statement ended, "It is the opinion of the writers that some central agency, by proper cooperation with all of the various state agricultural experiment stations, could render a distinct service to agricultural science in bringing about more efficient exchange of research publications." The recommendation was signed by Drs. J. G. Leach, H. Macy, and C. H. Bailey. At the conclusion of the meeting of the Experiment Station Subsection, a committee consisting of Directors Boss of Minnesota, S. B. Doten of Nevada, B. E. Gilbert of Rhode Island, and Dr. J. T. Jardine was named to study the problem of scientific literature exchange with foreign institutions.

Exchange of publications with many foreign countries was disrupted during World War II. In 1947, Director H. Macy of Minnesota was appointed chairman of a new committee on distribution which obtained cooperation from the U.S. Department of Agriculture, the Department of State, and the International Cooperation Administration in the development of an Exchange Desk in the Department of Agriculture Library through which experiment station publications could be exchanged with approved institutions in foreign countries. With support from ICA and his University, Director Macy (Minne-

---

[4] State Experiment Station—Station Letter—2207(a), transmitting to Directors two amendments to the Research Projects Classification Index, SES–OD–1110 listing areas of research submitted in accordance with the customary procedure under the Federal-grant payments to States.

sota) made survey visits to South American countries in 1952, return-
ing with the recommendation of 53 primary repositories in the
countries visited. Similarly, Director I.B. Johnson (South Dakota)
visited Central American countries in 1954. Director L.A. Henke
(Hawaii) surveyed Near East countries in 1955, and Associate Director Noble Clark (Wisconsin) surveyed countries in the Far East in
1956.

ESCOP, during its 1955 annual meeting held on November 15,
1955, in East Lansing, combined the Committee on Distribution of
Agricultural Publications Abroad into an ESCOP Publications Subcommittee. Subsequently, Associate Director Noble Clark was named
chairman of the Subcommittee. During the 1957 Association meeting
the experiment station and extension directors agreed to enlarge the
committee into a Joint ESCOP-ECOP Committee on Agricultural
and Home Economics Publications. The committee took leadership in
studying and recommending remedies for a series of interrelated publication problems involving the State stations, the State extension
services, agricultural libraries, and USDA. Its wide representation
proved cumbersome, however, so that on its own recommendation the
Joint ESCOP-ECOP Subcommittee was dissolved in 1960 with the
recommendation to both groups of Directors that a similar committee
be reconstituted as a standing Committee on Agricultural and Home
Economics Publications, responsible to the Division of Agriculture
of the Association of Land-Grant Colleges.[5]

PUBLIC SUPPORT SOUGHT

The founders of the experiment station movement insisted on popular publications in part because those leaders accepted the reality that
the stations required public support. The role of "public relations,"
i.e., the interplay between direction of tax-supported institutions and
the tax-paying public in influencing the selection and guidance of
research activities, is a subject that requires separate study and treatment. It is pertinent, however, to touch briefly on the significance of
public relations in the continuous and successful pursuit of scientific
research at an agricultural experiment station.

In the 19th century the founders and managers of the stations found
it essential to cultivate favorable public sentiment, to keep farmers
and legislators friendly to station efforts, and to satisfy the taxpayers'
definition of a useful scientific service or product.

The astute director had to consider carefully the need for diligent
and honest salesmanship; the director who did not cater to the taste of
the station's constituency courted trouble. For example, The Connecticut Agricultural Experiment Station at New Haven, in its early
years, had difficulty staying alive because it could not convince a
Grange-aroused sentiment that its program of research aided the
countrymen as ably as a new "farmers' station" at Storrs would aid
them. This Yale-Storrs controversy of the 1880's made necessary a
re-orientation of New Haven's policy and prompted Edward Hopkins
Jenkins, Samuel Johnson's assistant and alter ego to 1900, to develop

---

[5] Mimeographed Minutes of the Final Meeting of the Joint ESCOP-ECOP
Committee on Agricultural and Home Economics Publications, Washington,
D.C., Nov. 13, 1960, State Experiment Stations Division, ARS, U.S. Department
of Agriculture, Washington 25, D.C.

a lifetime skill in building, as he put it, "a close connection between the station work and the practical farmer." The tax-support basis of a scientific laboratory not only made Jenkins a servant to the farmers in his public relations, it also made him an expert in the culture of corn, a Connecticut staple, and induced him, as Director (1900–23), to initiate basic research in corn genetics in 1905. Hybrid corn emerged by 1917.

The history of the Atwater directorship at Storrs demonstrates more dramatically the necessity for an attunement between a director and his public. Atwater, initially popular at Storrs, encountered adversity because he prematurely concentrated his station's energy on problems in human diet, nutrition, and metabolism; mistakenly he assumed that his rural constituency would approve the trend of research and wait patiently for useful discoveries. In 1902 he paid the price for ignoring a changing public attitude. An antagonized farm opinion repudiated his directorship, secured his resignation, and compelled the Storrs station to emphasize dairy and poultry husbandry in a new program of "practical research" useful to market-conscious farmers. Thereafter continuity in research policy suffered because the directorship changed hands repeatedly for a decade. In 1912, however, Storrs persuaded Jenkins to assume its directorship in addition to his duties at New Haven. Jenkins retained his popularity at Storrs and successfully directed genetic research in vegetables and in poultry.

What role has articulate public opinion played in the administration of scientific research? It eliminated the Atwater program; it agitated Storrs until 1912; it badgered New Haven for a time. Yet Jenkins learned to handle it at New Haven by 1900 and triumphed over it at Storrs after 1912; more significantly, he converted antagonistic sentiment into staunch approval by searching constantly for means to connect the station work with the station public. Most important of all, his success at adjustment paralleled and accompanied scientific achievement at both stations.[6]

With the organizational growth of the land-grant agricultural colleges into a generally accepted pattern of three principal departments—research, teaching, and extension work—a development the station directors did much to promote in the early 1900's, public relations discussions increased. The Proceedings of the 34th Annual Convention, held in Springfield, Mass., in October 1920, reflect a growing concern among directors with respect to research support.

Under the Association's new constitution of 1920, policy matters relating to agriculture, research, and extension were discussed in the Section of Agriculture. The Proceedings show that considerable thought and time were devoted to papers and discussions on the great need for additional funds for the stations. There were papers on: "Efforts of the War on Research in Agriculture," "The Needs of the Experiment Stations for Increased Federal Support," "What Should Be the Character of Further Federal Legislation in Providing Funds for Agricultural Research," and "Some Practices Which Help the Popularization of Experiment Stations and Their Work." The latter was a paper by Director F. D. Farrell, Kansas. He presented a point

---

[6] Law, E. M. The Agricultural Experiment Station Movement in Connecticut, 1840–1900. 255 pp. Unpublished doctoral dissertation, Yale University Library, 1951.

of view worth considering even now in matters of station public relations. ESCOP devoted its report to "Distributing the Results of Experiment Station Work." The report stated that "In order to place the results of station work effectively before the public and to keep it advised of what is being done, it is believed that more definite provision for publicity might often be made with advantage" (*15*).

Pointing to varying degrees of popular support of agricultural experiment stations in the respective States, Director Farrell listed some facts that had a bearing on the question of popularizing experiment stations. His conclusions were:

> However irksome it may be to station people to take the pains consciously to popularize experiment station work, the necessity of doing it seems inescapable. To secure the desired popularization requires the devotion of time, effort, and money to activities which are in no sense experimentation or research. If these activities are neglected we cannot be sanguine about the future of our experiment stations. We are confronted by facts which may be distasteful to many of us, but our duty as servants of American agriculture is perfectly clear.
> It is doubtful whether the American people ever make a better investment than they make when they appropriate funds to support agricultural experiment stations. But this fact is unknown to most of the people for whom and by whom the stations are maintained. We need to take advantage of every opportunity to impress the public with the facts. This probably cannot be done by any single method. . . . The public can be relied upon to support an institution which it is convinced it wants.

Recognizing the coutinuing problems of public relations for agriculture, the Association's Division of Agriculture devoted an afternoon session to a panel discussion on the subject. Dean and Director L. L. Rummell of Ohio (*25*), in a talk captioned "Communications in Public Relations" said:

> Surveys among farm families have shown that they do not fully appreciate agricultural research and what institutions do it. Urban residents still look upon research as another farm subsidy. They do not appreciate the fact that research is an investment that pays rural America, it is true, but at the same time all citizens benefit by abundant, economical food and fiber.
> . . . there are more communication tools today [as compared with the days when the Morrill and Hatch Acts were signed] to tell the story of agricultural education and research to the public. Surveys among farm families indicate the farm publications, state and national, are the principal sources of information to change farm practices. Extension agents, experiment station publications, field days and demonstrations have likewise been important. Newspapers, radio and television are newer media and likewise helpful, although to a lesser degree.
> Agricultural colleges and experiment stations may well take frequent self-appraisal, to "see ourselves as others see us." We do not hit the target as often as we dream. This in-bound flow of communication is as important on this two-way public relations street as what we send out to the public.

A recommendation made in 1959 by the chairman of the Division of Agriculture's Intersectional Committee on Public Relations, Dean of Agriculture E. L. Butz, Purdue University, resulted in an ESCOP-approved study of experiment station public relations activities in 1960 (*3*). A summary of the replies from all 53 State stations (*21*) indicated that in light of the very rapid social and economic changes taking place in rural and urban areas, the general public needs a better understanding of the role of agriculture in our total economy. Answers to the questions indicated full recognition among station directors of the need for creating greater public awareness of agricultural experiment stations, but programs, methods, and efforts undertaken by the stations to meet the need varied considerably. Differences between and among regions were apparent but not marked. Total research allotments appeared to be only mildly related to the effort put

U.S. Public Health Service's Aniak house, built for Alaskans with local lumber and insulating materials, uses principles developed and tested by the research program of the Alaska Agricultural Experiment Station.

The Texas A. & M. Aircraft Research Center, at College Station, Texas, in cooperation with the U.S. Department of Agriculture, the Civil Aeronautics Administration, and the National Flying Farmers Association, developed the first experimental airplane designed especially for distributing agricultural chemicals.

This tobacco harvester developed in 1961 by the North Carolina Experiment Station has proved practical in farm tests and will be available commercially in 1963. It will greatly reduce labor costs in the production of tobacco.

Clemson Agricultural College, in cooperation with USDA, has developed a new and more efficient method of handling seed cotton, which employs light-weight 1-bale containers.

Purdue University's farm cardiac project is providing information on
symptoms of heart disease and on
precautions that farmer cardiac
patients can use. (J. C. Allen photo.)

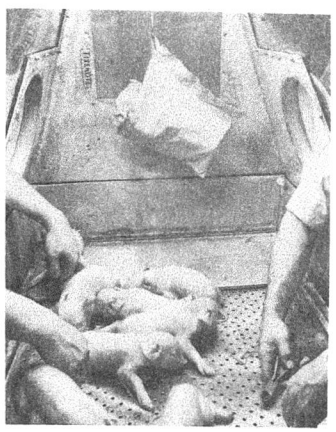

The Ohio Agricultural Experiment Station is doing pioneer work with
specific pathogen-free pigs. This
newly arrived litter is being weighed
and ear-notched.

At the Utah Argicultural Experiment
Station, pioneers in irrigation research are studying the relation of
irrigation to soils, plants, precipita-
tion, and streamflow.

The Kansas Agricultural Experiment
Station has shown that use of mucin
can reduce bloat-producing foam in
cattle fed alfalfa forage. Untreated
alfalfa fed to identical twin (upper)
produced bloat.

In this building near Madrid, Iowa, researchers at Iowa Agricultural Experiment Station measure the genetic effects of X-rays on swine to gain a better understanding of the effects that irradiation may have on the heredity of humans.

Scientists at the Virginia Polytechnic Institute have devised equipment for more exact control of conditions in studying the effects of potassium fertilizer or orchardgrass and legume mixtures.

The Massachusetts Agricultural Experiment Station has pioneered in developing methods for analyzing the complex nature of compounds that make up food aroma. The techniques are capable of detecting concentrations as low as fractional parts per billion.

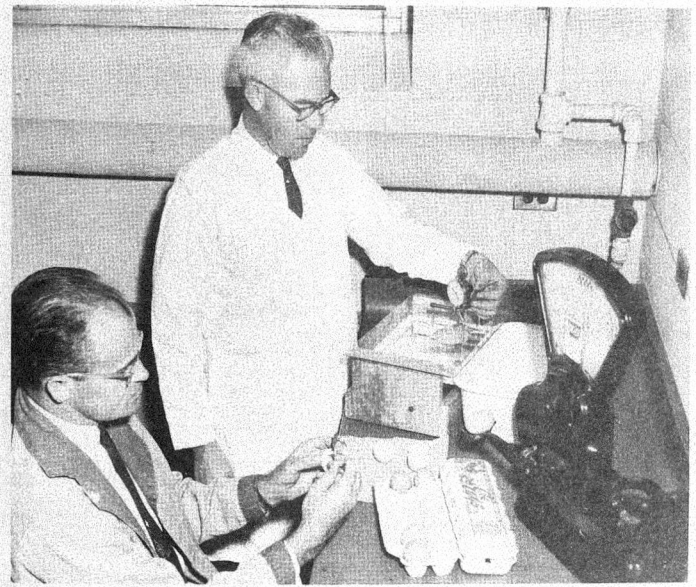

Poultry scientists are checking eggs for interior and exterior quality as part of a breeding project at the Rhode Island Experiment Station.

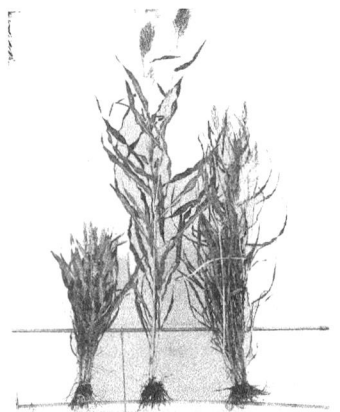

The South Dakota Agricultural Experiment Station has used colchicine to change plant cells and produce true-breeding mutants. Crossing a true-breeding mutant (right) back to the original variety (left) resulted in plants with extreme hybrid vigor (center).

Breeding for rust resistance is one phase of North Dakota Agricultural Experiment Station's long-time research program with wheat. Other research is directed toward improving quality, yield, and processing characteristics.

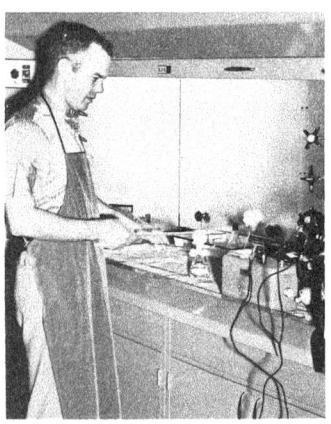

Plant pathologists at the Arkansas Agricultural Experiment Station use radioisotopes to trace the progress of a fungus parasite within its plant host.

Pioneer work in radiation treatment of flowers at the Connecticut (Storrs) Agricultural Experiment Station has resulted in many new and unusual colors in commercial flowers. The experiments also hold promise of new insight into the effects of radiation on the living cell.

Analysis of
United States
CAT872074
U.S. Departm
[21] ana
Jun 03, 2013

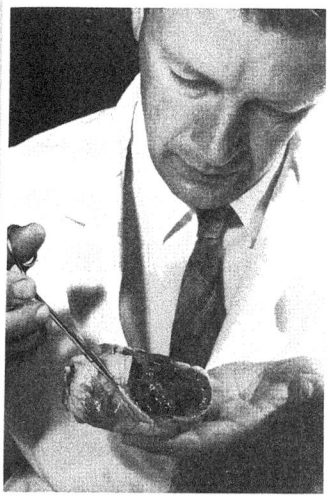

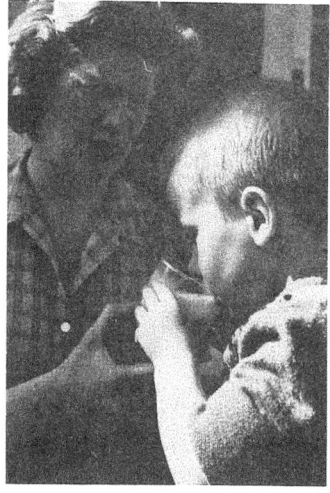

Research workers at Oregon Agricultural Experiment Station have found that white muscle disease in lambs can be prevented by feeding or injecting minute amounts of selenium into pregnant ewes. Results of this work may have application in the study of certain human disorders, such as muscular dystrophy.

Dairy scientists at the Wisconsin Agricultural Experiment Station have developed a new-type concentrated whole milk. Even after prolonged storage, this milk has a rich, fresh flavor—just like good whole milk.

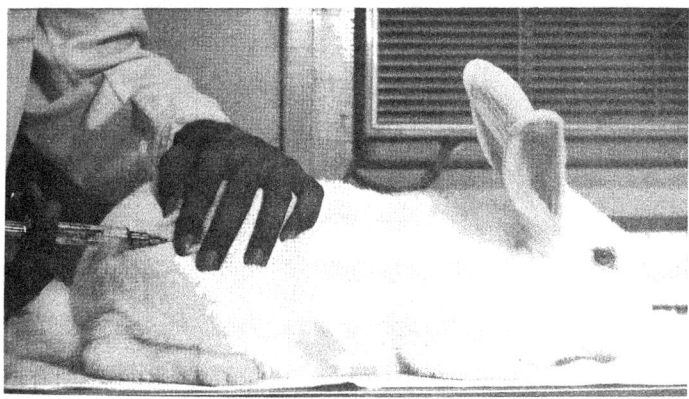

Rabbits are helping Arizona Experiment Station workers in their quest to develop a method of supplying citrus growers with virus-free budding materials. Similar detection of infested mother tree stock by other methods takes from 12 to 20 years.

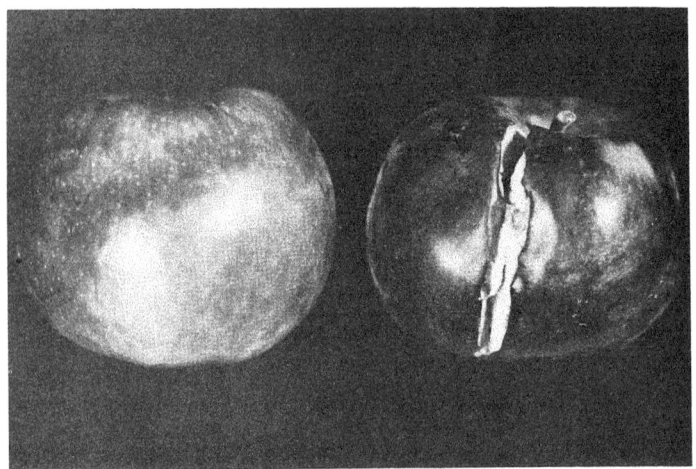

The McIntosh apple (left) was kept in controlled atmospheric storage for 7 months; the other one in ordinary cold storage. The method, developed by the Agricultural Experiment Station of Cornell University, relies on complete atmospheric control, including temperature, humidity, oxygen, and carbon dioxide.

Natural applejuice is processed in this new pilot plant of the Food Research Laboratory at the New York (Geneva) Agricultural Experiment Station. Developed at this station, natural applejuice is appetizing, nutritious, and natural in color.

Analysis of
United Stat
CAT87207A
U.S. Depart
[21] ana
Jun 03, 2013

Researchers at the Maine Agricultural Experiment Station developed this hemispherical dome and air intake tower to study the physiological effects of selected fungicides on apple trees. (Photo: courtesy Philbrick Evening Journal, Lewiston, Maine.)

The Louisiana Agricultural Experiment Station achieved a technical breakthrough when it developed a method by which live pollen can be preserved for long periods under natural environment and shipped in a small container by ordinary mail to any part of the world for plant breeding.

Whey is pumped from a cheese plant in Cabot, Vt., to this pasture. Rates of applying this unwanted byproduct of cheese as fertilizer were developed at the Vermont Agricultural Experiment Station.

Throughout the Cotton Belt, plant breeders are in constant search for desirable traits that can be bred into superior cotton. Sources of some breeding materials are plants like these, which have reached tree height after years of growth in a Mississippi Experiment Station greenhouse.

Dr. N. S. Golding, Professor Emeritus, Washington State University, is shown here running his new solids-not-fat test on milk samples. With this test, milk may now be marketed on a solids-not-fat basis rather than on a butterfat basis.

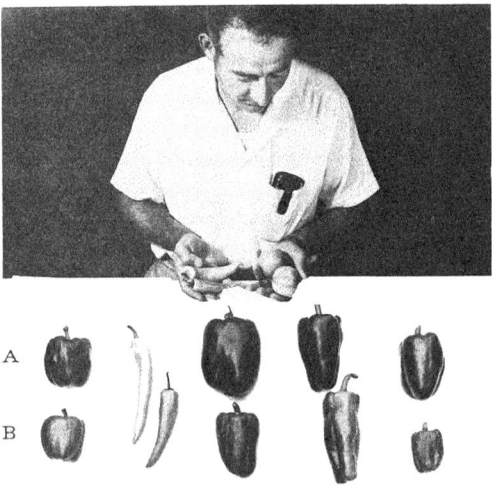

Some common viruses may be responsible for more than a single disease of plants, research at the Pennsylvania Agricultural Experiment Station shows. Plants must be exposed at a certain stage of maturity to contract the disease. Properly timed inoculation with tobacco mosaic virus caused the diseases of peppers shown in this picture: *A*, Healthy fruit; *B*, affected fruit.

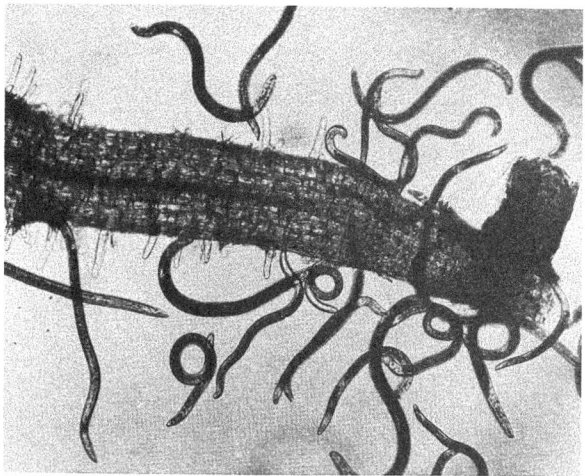

Damage by nematodes is becoming a serious problem in the production of certain agricultural crops. A method of studying this damage under laboratory conditions has been developed by the New Hampshire Agricultural Experiment Station.

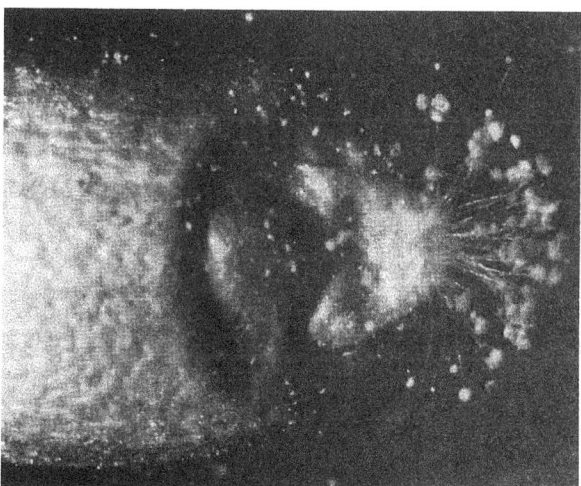

This wheat kernel, showing storage fungus growing from germ or embryo, was typical of grain that was stored in a commercial bin and which, in storage, developed "sick" wheat or germ damage. Minnesota Experiment Station research on this problem over the past decade enables scientists to tell the practical grain men how to avoid this sort of loss.

A view of the Georgia Agricultural Experiment Station located at Experiment, Georgia—one of three main stations coordinated by the University of Georgia. Empire, a cotton variety with high wilt resistance adapted throughout the cottonbelt, was developed here in cooperation with USDA.

The Florida Citrus Experiment Station, Lake Alfred, conducts the largest research program of its kind in the world on all phases of citrus growing.

forth. Other factors appeared to play significant roles. Enough ideas and procedures were suggested in the responses to question that if properly and more widely implemented they could contribute to many improvements in public understanding of agricultural experiment station activities. Less than one-third of all farmers and a still smaller percentage of the nonfarm population had a good understanding of station activities. Only 14 percent of the station releases had been written for the urban population and less than one-third of the stations' public relations efforts had emphasized problems needing attention. The 1960 study demonstrated a need for careful reevaluation of station public relations policies. It showed that greater emphasis on public relations as an essential function of experiment station administration is warranted.

The importance of publications and communications, including intercommunication and mass communications, was recognized by directors of experiment stations when they joined with those of the extension services in endorsing the 7-year National Project in Agricultural Communications undertaken by the American Association of Agricultural College Editors with support from the Kellogg Foundation. A final report on this project is contained in the proceedings for the 72d annual convention of the Association (14). It included recommendations made by the project Board of Control whose chairman was Director M. H. Campbell of the Rhode Island Experiment Station. It was adopted with minor modifications by the Association. Of particular significance was Recommendation II:

> That communications research activities be carried on through agricultural experiment stations as a part of inter-regional or regional research projects. The committee emphasizes the inter-regional approach, recommends that appropriate steps be taken to secure approval by the Regional Directors and the Committee of Nine to develop a project, and that the project include provisions for consulting services.

While research in agricultural communications has in the past been handicapped by lack of sufficiently trained personnel, a number of land-grant institutions are conducting quality research in this area, accompanied by training of an increasing number of graduate students. That this research and training is vital in a day when communications represent one of the most rapidly forward-moving technologies is generally recognized. That it has begun to improve communications phases of research administration is evidenced by the emphasis given to more systematic distribution of publications and improved quality of research reporting. Today there is widespread public interest in wanting to know more about science. However, the word is likely to conjure up images of missiles soaring into the sky, of human beings whirling around the globe, rather than recognizing those at work in less spectacular projects but equally important in helping man reach the ultimate goal of science. Thus the job of telling the story of agricultural science has reached a new crossroad as we enter the 1960's.

LITERATURE CITED

(1) ATWATER, W. O.
    1890. STATEMENT ON NEED FOR FUNDS FOR PRINTING. Assoc. Amer. Agr.
    Cols. and Expt. Stas. Proc. (1889) 3: 103, 112. (U.S. Dept.
    Agr., Off. Expt. Stas. Misc. Bul. 2.)

155

(2) BAILEY, L. H.
    1903. THE EDITING OF EXPERIMENT STATION PUBLICATIONS. Assoc. Amer. Agr. Cols. and Expt. Stas. Proc. (1902) 16: 112–113.

(3) BUTZ, E. L., CHAIRMAN.
    1959. REPORT OF THE INTERSECTIONAL COMMITTEE ON PUBLIC RELATIONS. Amer. Assoc. Land-Grant Cols. and State Univs. Proc. 73: 128–129.

(4) COMMITTEE ON EXPERIMENT STATION ORGANIZATION AND POLICY.
    1918. PUBLISHING THE WORK ON THE EXPERIMENT STATIONS. Assoc. Amer. Agr. Cols. and Expt. Stas. Proc. (1917) 31: 37–43.

(5) COMMITTEE ON INDEXING.
    1905. INDEXING AGRICULTURAL LITERATURE. Assoc. Amer. Agr. Cols. and Expt. Stas. Proc. (1904) 18: 32–33. (U.S. Dept. Agr., Off. Expt. Stas. Bul. 153.)

(6) CONVENTION OF DELEGATES FROM AGRICULTURAL COLLEGES AND EXPERIMENT STATIONS.
    1885. PROCEEDINGS OF A CONVENTION OF DELEGATES FROM AGRICULTURAL COLLEGES AND EXPERIMENT STATIONS HELD AT THE DEPARTMENT OF AGRICULTURE, JULY 8 AND 9, 1885. U.S. Dept. Agr. Misc. Spec. Rpt. 9, 196 pp.

(7) CUTTER, W. P.
    1889. SUGGESTED CLASSIFICATION OF AGRICULTURE. Assoc. Amer. Agr. Cols. and Expt. Stas. Proc. (1898) 12: 50–53. (U.S. Dept. Agr., Off. Expt. Stas. Bul. 65.)

(8) EXECUTIVE COMMITTEE OF THE ASSOCIATION.
    1911. MINUTES OF THE GENERAL SESSION. CONCERNING PROPOSED RESEARCH JOURNAL. Assoc. Amer. Agr. Cols. and Expt. Stas. Proc. (1910) 24: 115–118.

(9) ——
    1914. COMMITTEE ON PUBLICATION AND RESEARCH. Assoc. Amer. Agr. Cols. and Expt. Stas. Proc. (1913) 27: 145

(10) ——
    1919. OFFICERS AND COMMITTEES OF THE ASSOCIATION. Assoc. Amer. Agr. Cols. and Expt. Stas. Proc. (1918) 32: 5.

(11) ——
    1920. CONSTITUTION; AMENDMENT OF THE CONSTITUTION. Assoc. Amer. Agr. Cols. and Expt. Stas. Proc. (1919) 33: 15–17; 66–68.

(12) ——
    1941. PROCEEDINGS OF THE FIRST ANNUAL CONVENTION (1887) OF THE ASSOCIATION OF AMERICAN AGRICULTURAL COLLEGES AND EXPERIMENT STATIONS. 6 pp. (Note: No account of this convention was printed originally. However, a manuscript summary by C. E. Thorne, Secretary of the convention, which was filed in the Office of Experiment Stations, was ordered printed by the Executive Committee of the Association on May 5, 1941.)

(13) ——
    1949. JOINT COMMITTEE ON PUBLICATION OF RESEARCH. Assoc. Land-Grant Cols. and Univs. Proc. 63: 6.

(14) ——
    1958. NATIONAL PROJECT IN AGRICULTURAL COMMUNICATIONS. Amer. Assoc. Land-Grant Cols. and State Univs. Proc. 72: 124–126.

(15) FARRELL, F. D.
    1921. SOME PRACTICES WHICH HELP TO POPULARIZE EXPERIMENT STATIONS AND THEIR WORK. Assoc. Amer. Agr. Cols. and Expt. Stas. Proc. (1920) 34: 105–111.

(16) GOODELL, H. H.
    1895. WHAT IS THE MISSION OF THE BULLETIN? Assoc. Amer. Agr. Cols. and Expt. Stas. Proc. (1894) 8: 69–71. (U.S. Dept. Agr., Off. Expt. Stas. Bul. 24.)

(17) ——
    1896. RESOLUTION CONCERNING INDEXING OF AGRICULTURAL LITERATURE. Assoc. Amer. Agr. Cols. and Expt. Stas. Proc. (1895) 9: 75. (U.S. Dept. Agr., Off. Expt. Stas. Bul. 30.)

(18) GRIFFEE, FRED.
    1940. EXPERIMENT STATION PUBLICATIONS AND MAILING LISTS. (Abstract.) Assoc. Land-Grant Cols. and Univs. Proc. 54: 142–143.

HARRIS, A. W., CHAIRMAN.
1894. REPORT OF THE COMMITTEE ON UNIFORMITY OF STATION PUBLICA-
TIONS * * * AND DISCUSSION. Assoc. Amer. Agr. Cols. and Expt.
Stas. Proc. (1893) 7: 30–33. (U.S. Dept. Agr., Off. Expt. Stas.
Bul. 20.)
HENRY, W. A.
1889. DISCUSSION: [HOW CAN THE DEPARTMENT ASSIST THE STATIONS?]
Assoc. Amer. Agr. Cols. and Expt. Stas. Proc. 2: 45–48. (U.S.
Dept. Agr., Off. Expt. Stas. Bul. 1.)
JEHLIK, P. J., and MEYER, W. P.
1960. PUBLIC RELATIONS ACTIVITIES AT STATE AGRICULTURAL EXPERIMENT
STATIONS. (Abstract.) Amer. Assoc. Land-Grant Cols. and State
Univs. Proc. 74: 135–137.
KELLERMAN, K. F., CHAIRMAN.
1915. REPORT OF THE EDITORIAL COMMITTEE OF THE JOURNAL OF AGRICUL-
TURAL RESEARCH. Assoc. Amer. Agr. Cols. and Expt. Stas. Proc.
(1914) 28: 130–131.
LEACH, J. G., MACY, H., and BAILEY, C. H.
1932. THE INADEQUATE DISTRIBUTION OF STATE AGRICULTURAL EXPERIMENT
STATION BULLETINS TO FOREIGN COUNTRIES. Assoc. Land-Grant
Cols. and Univs. Proc. (1931) 45: 263–264.
MEYER, W. P.
1961. LAW AUTHORIZES STATION FUNDS FOR COMMUNICATIONS RESEARCH.
ACE (official publication of the American Association of Agri-
cultural College Editors). April 1961 issue, 8 pp. East Lansing,
Mich.
RUMMELL, L. L.
1958. COMMUNICATIONS IN PUBLIC RELATIONS. (Abstract.) Amer.
Assoc. Land-Grant Cols. and State Univs. Proc. 72: 175–176.
STURTEVANT, E. L.
1883. FIRST ANNUAL REPORT OF THE BOARD OF CONTROL OF THE NEW YORK
STATE EXPERIMENT STATION FOR THE YEAR 1882 [REPORT OF THE
DIRECTOR]: 10–11.
TRUE, A. C.
1910. RESEARCH JOURNAL FOR EXPERIMENT STATIONS. Assoc. Amer.
Agr. Cols. and Expt. Stas. Proc. (1909) 23: 110. (U.S. Dept.
Agr., Off. Expt. Stas. Bul. 228.)
——— and CLARK, V. A.
1900. AGRICULTURAL EXPERIMENT STATIONS IN THE UNITED STATES. U.S.
Dept. Agr., Off. Expt. Stas. Bul. 80, 636 pp., illus.
U.S. DEPARTMENT OF AGRICULTURE.
1913–14. JOURNAL OF AGRICULTURAL RESEARCH. v. 1. 533 pp.

1949. JOURNAL OF AGRICULTURAL RESEARCH. v. 78, 741 pp.
U.S. OFFICE OF EXPERIMENT STATIONS.
1889. THE WHAT AND WHY OF AGRICULTURAL EXPERIMENT STATIONS.
U.S. Dept. Agr. Farmers' Bul. 1, 16 pp.

1890. INTRODUCTION. Expt. Sta. Rec., v. 1 (1889–90): 1–2.

1891. EDITORIAL NOTES. Expt. Sta. Rec. 3(1): 1.

1893. [EDITORIAL NOTES.] Expt. Sta. Rec. 5(1): 1.

1893. DISCUSSION ON UNIFORM NUMBERING OF EXPERIMENT STATION PUB-
LICATIONS. Assoc. Amer. Agr. Cols. and Expt. Stas. Proc. (1892)
6: 80–87, 109. (U.S. Dept. Agr., Off. Expt. Stas. Bul. 16.)

1896. OFFICERS OF THE ASSOCIATION. Assoc. Amer. Agr. Cols. and Expt.
Stas. Proc. (1895) 9: 4. (U.S. Dept. Agr., Off. Expt. Stas. Bul.
30.)

1946. TERMINATION OF PRINTING NOTICE. Expt. Sta. Rec. 95: Index
(cover.)

157

Chapter Nine—

ORGANIZED SELF-APPRAISAL:
The Project System, Improved Procedures, and Consolidated Legislation

The Adams Act of 1906, primarily the product of A. C. True's careful draftsmanship, deliberately gave substantial authority to the Secretary of Agriculture to administer the "original research" financed by Federal grant funds in the State experiment stations. It was Dean Henry's personal relationship with his friend of long standing, Congressman Adams of Wisconsin, which facilitated having the Adams Bill drawn in such manner as to incorporate the improvements that meant so much to Dr. True. Dean Henry wanted more and better research—and wanted the new Act to help bring this about. Thus, mutual professional interests of Henry and True, and the personal friendship between Henry and his former neighbor, served to strengthen the concept of research advocated by Atwater in 1899 when he said that "in studying the food of animals we have no right to neglect the food of man." Out of the Adams Act were to come a number of fundamental studies leading to the discovery of vitamins and modern nutritional standards. Within a few years after passage of the legislation there came discoveries that not only had enormous significance to farmers, but to the entire world of science.

The Act redefined and recapitulated the Secretary's jurisdiction, which had developed guardedly since 1887 under the watchful care of the Association and the Office of Experiment Stations. The Adams Act directed the Secretary to "prescribe" the schedules on which each station must submit a detailed statement of its disbursements of the new fund. It further directed him to "ascertain" that the stations did in fact expend the Federal appropriation exclusively for the conduct of "original researches or experiments bearing directly on the agricultural industry of the United States." Thus the Adams Act specifically incorporated the features of fiscal review which, never a part of the Hatch Act, had become an integral characteristic of the evolving Hatch system.

Moreover, the Adams Act openly gave to the Secretary a new power and a noteworthy duty: it required him to "certify to the Secretary of the Treasury as to each State and Territory whether it is complying with the provisions of this act and is entitled to receive its share of the annual appropriation." This provision for annual certification empowered the Secretary to withhold payment of the Adams fund to any station failing to demonstrate that its expenditures under that fund did conform to the stipulation for original research. The act of 1906 also assigned to the Secretary additional powers not mentioned in the act of 1887 nor thus far administratively practiced. It instructed him to report annually to Congress "on the receipts and expenditures and work" of the stations, to inform both the President and the Congress in the event of withholding certification, and to insure "the proper administration of this law."

The heavy weight of the Departmental power in the Adams Act contrasted sharply with the powerless position accorded the Secretary in the Hatch Act. The authority assigned to the Secretary in 1906 would have evoked from the station movement in earlier years the most heated protests that the exercise of such Federal functions would spell dictation.

In 1906, however, the prospect of possible dictation arising from the award of powers to the Secretary alarmed no one. The station spokesmen, as the crisis of 1904–05 had conclusively demonstrated, regarded James Wilson with deep respect for his scientific competence and his administrative integrity; they did not regard the Secretary as nursing designs for domination. Similarly the traditions of independence in the station movement, not susceptible to quick dislodgment, impressed Wilson with equal force. Station spokesmen understood, furthermore, that the determination to increase the Federal supervisory strength did not originate with Wilson, nor with Congress, but with their own Director True, earnestly intent on serving the interests of station statesmen and scientific research.

The Federal authority to certify, withhold, and report did not signify, in short, that the Department of Agriculture or the Federal Government would dominate or absorb the State stations; it did signify, however, that once again the station enterprise would subject itself to a self-imposed and self-administered discipline in order to improve the quality of station productivity. The station movement took the calculated risk, when it substantially increased the Federal powers in the Adams Act, that Secretary Wilson would delegate to the Office of Experiment Stations the entire responsibility for administering the Adams fund and thus permit the station enterprise to govern itself.

OES ROLE OUTLINED

The Secretary of Agriculture completely justified the faith that Director True placed in Wilson's capacity to respond to the spirit and purpose of the Adams Act. The Secretary acted promptly. Only 4 days after President Theodore Roosevelt had approved that measure, Wilson issued a reassuring notification to all station directors. "The Director of the Office of Experiment Stations is hereby designated my representative in all matters relating to the business of this Department in connection with the administration of this law," he announced, "and the Office of Experiment Stations will aid in promoting effective work under this Act in the same general way as it has heretofore in relation to the Hatch Act." With these words Secretary Wilson formally commended the decade of effort that True had devoted to the policy of station inspection; and he forthwith encouraged the True policy of fiscal review. "It will be necessary," he continued, "that a separate account of the Adams fund shall be kept at each station, which should be open at all times to the inspection of the Director of the Office of Experiment Stations, or his accredited representative" (8).[1]

Wilson then endorsed the theme which 2 years earlier True had built into the Adams bill, namely that the new appropriation could be used only for original research; this "guiding principle" would govern the administrative procedures followed by Director True "in the interpretation of this Act and the examination of the work and ex-

---

[1] Italic numbers in parentheses refer to Literature Cited, p. 173.

penditures of the stations under it." Had True himself composed the Secretary's instruction he could not have phrased more explicitly or sympathetically a statement that more fully supported True's position and the announcements soon to come from True's office.

The Wilsonian instruction, though it did not define "original research," specifically listed a long series of station expenses and activities lying beyond the pale of support by the Adams fund. Moreover, in a revealing preview of True's forthcoming policy it recommended that "each station should outline a definite programme of experimental work to which it will devote this fund . . . . The work contemplated by this Act will, as a rule, necessarily cover more than one year, and changes in the programme once adopted should not be made until the problems under investigation have been solved, or their solution definitely shown to be impracticable." With a perceptiveness that honored the Atwater standard of 1889, the Secretary then added, "It is much to be desired that this fund shall be a strong incentive to the careful choice of problems to be investigated, thorough and exhaustive work in their solution, and the securing of permanent and far-reaching results . . ." (8). Thus Wilson, precisely as the terms and spirit of the Adams Act directed, placed the prestige and authority of his Department behind True's persistent campaign to increase the scientific productivity of the State stations.

Director True, fortified by Wilson's *carte blanche* of March 20, 1906, proceeded with the intricate task of removing, one by one, the impediments to the steady growth of an atmosphere of scientific inquiry at the stations. Promptly he contacted Chairman Davenport of the Experiment Stations Committee on Organization and Policy and arranged for a meeting of the new committee. Director True and his energetic lieutenant, Assistant Director Allen of the Washington office, attended the ESCOP session in Chicago on April 7. The conferees discussed the necessity for achieving continuity in research effort and for establishing attractive tenure for research scientists. Thereupon they issued a statement setting forth the general principles which should govern the administrative attitude at all stations, as follows (13):

It is evidently the intention of the Adams Act to provide the means for carrying on investigations of a relatively high order with a view to the discovering of principles and the solution of the more difficult and fundamental problems of agriculture. To this end it is very desirable that careful attention shall be given to the choice of definite problems to be studied and the methods by which the solution of these problems is to be sought. . . . In selecting the lines of work due reference should be given to the special needs of the State in which the station is located, but the lines of work adopted should be only such as have a reasonable expectation of leading to the establishment of principles of broad application. These lines of work need not be new lines. Indeed strengthening lines of investigation now in progress may be fully as important as the establishment of new lines. . . . Only a few lines can be advantageously undertaken at a time. What [they] . . . shall be must be determined by the equipment of the station in men and facilities.

The man is the most important factor. . . . [He] and his line of work must be suitable to each other. . . .

After suitable lines of work are decided upon, all payments for salary and labor and purchase of apparatus, tools, books, and other material necessary to carry out this problem are allowable.

Director True, having secured early in April the concurrence of ESCOP in his projected plans for intensifying the participation of his Office in the administration of station research, amplified the

Chicago statement in a circular letter addressed 3 weeks later to all station directors. His advisory letter of April 30, so gently phrased that it could not have antagonized even the most sensitive director or governing board, set forth the procedure to be followed as each station prepared to initiate and conduct the "original research" authorized and financed by the Adams Act. Each station should, first of all, outline a clearcut prospectus of its intended research activity, demonstrate therein its crystallized purpose to seek essential information in a well-defined area, and announce concisely the specific objective of its entire program. Furthermore, each station should incorporate in its prospectus a series of component problems which, selected or devised with discriminating acuteness, would examine the key points of the anticipated program and, when solved, would supply significant data and achieve the central objective of the extended investigations. With equal care each station should draft, as an essential feature of its prospectus, an itemized statement of the estimated expenses to be charged to the Adams fund.

True then added a polite yet pointed proviso to his procedural recommendations. "In order to promote a clear understanding upon the kind of work which may be regarded as appropriate, and the expense involved, it is suggested that a copy of the programme of each station be sent to this Office for inspection. . . . Obviously it will not be our intention to determine what lines of work it will be advisable to undertake," he wrote, ". . . but only to reach such an agreement as to the character of work to be undertaken . . . as will facilitate the passing of intelligent judgment on the legitimacy of expenditures of the Adams fund" (8). With this phrasing Dr. True introduced the policy, soon translated into practice, of requiring all stations to secure from the Office of Experiment Stations approval in advance for all investigations supported by the Act of 1906.

The mildness of this April declaration did not, however, disguise the simple fact that Dr. True, empowered to deny support to station activities not qualifying as original research, intended a conscientious exercise of his collection of powers and a thorough appraisal of the proposals submitted by each station to his staff. The new policy of advance approval, viewed simply, merely extended the preceding practice of fiscal review. Yet this new practice gave to True a directive influence far more effective than any his Office had thus far exerted. Moreover, it entailed a heavy responsibility, for it compelled True to formulate standards for determining whether a given plan of research did or did not merit eligibility for Federal support. Simultaneously the policy of advance approval provided True with the opportunity to require that every station introduce and develop the project system, an approach to research already in force among many nonagricultural scientists and implicit in True's recommendations in the April declaration.

True capitalized on his long record of sympathetic service to the stations as he persevered in administering the new project system. In November 1906, he personally explained to the directors his major concern. "I want to encourage in every possible way the fullest, frankest confidence by correspondence and otherwise, in order that we may get a proper insight into the propositions made. . . . What we want to find out," he told the Station section of the Association, "is the nature of the work you have undertaken—what it actually is that you want to do" (*9*). The Washington director thus reiterated his view that his office, intent on maintaining its historic policy of helpfulness unstained by officious interference, would use the device of appraisal of project proposals solely to assist the stations in improving the quality of their research. Jordan of Geneva reflected the responsiveness of the section when he noted the nature of the decision-making confronting the members of True's staff. "They are in a difficult and delicate position," he remarked, "but we have a great deal of satisfaction in knowing that we can trust them. They are as intensely interested in the proper administration of the Adams fund as any of us can be, and they have at heart the highest interests of all concerned" (*7*).

This solid support from the Station section reinforced True's determination to adhere, when appraising the submitted projects, to the principles announced earlier in the Chicago statement and the April declaration. "Research," True concisely repeated after a year's experience with the new policy, "presupposes a definite aim and a definite problem to be solved, a specific end to be attained rather than a mere accumulation of data. In the matter of projects the Office has insisted that this definite aim should be apparent, and that the work should be directed toward some problem or phase of a problem which would result in a contribution to our knowledge, making it less empirical and more definite" (*8*).

True in this way required each station to select topics and plan investigations, to prepare and submit outlines, and to redraft those proposals not satisfying the project system, the administrative method which would compel all stations to comply with scientific standards. Beyond this point, however, True deliberately refused to carry the weight of Federal influence. Carefully he distinguished between centralized and localized responsibility in the administration of station research as he delimited the exercise of his Federal authority. "In passing upon these projects the Office has undertaken to determine only their suitability and appropriateness under the terms of the act," he reported in 1907. His office on occasion did contribute suggestions for redefining the outlines but it studiously refrained from originating projects. "It has left to the individual initiative of the station workers," he pointed out, "the planning of the investigations and the selection of the topics most important to their localities." This local responsibility underlay the proper operation of the Hatch system which, as Henry White had explained to the House Committee on Agriculture in 1905, enabled and expected the State stations to generate their own research activity.

Thus True's staff could assist the process of research but would not and could not direct it. "The Office," True explained, "has insisted only that the projects as outlined should be such as to characterize them as scientific investigations, embracing some original features. It has not presumed to pass, except in an advisory way, upon the feasibility of the investigations, the method of procedure, or the probability of the work leading to conclusive results." He pointed once more to his guiding star. "Every effort has been made," he earnestly emphasized, "to lead by suggestion, to inspire the spirit of investigation, and to preserve the individuality and initiative of the investigator" (*8*). The administrator of research activity, True wholeheartedly believed, must not violate this principle. Throughout his career, the

Washington director did not deviate from his "True standard," namely, an insistence on the project system tempered by a constant concern for the well-being of the individual researcher.

The True standard, dedicated to the achievement of never-ending scientific proficiency via personalized administration, expected a high level of station performance as it initiated a strict interpretation of the Adams Act. Not easily administered, it demanded a major collective effort from all personnel associated with the station movement. In particular it required, for permanent application, that the directors conscientiously institute and enforce the project approach as a routine procedure. Moreover, the project system could not operate effectively unless the administrators of the college or university sympathetically encouraged the directors, defended the new program in public if necessary, and shielded it from the traditional criticism that research corresponding to the scientist's ideal would not satisfy the current needs of the farmer. Had the directors, the staffs, the trustees, and the vocal constituencies of the nationwide station enterprise reached by 1906 the stage of readiness to concentrate on "original researches"? Could the True standard, in other words, withstand the popular pressures which in earlier years had demanded "practical" rather than "scientific" productivity? Dr. True knew, as ESCOP knew, that the answer to this question would decide the issue of success or failure for the projected administrative system, currently undergoing trial during the critical fiscal year, 1906–07.

PROJECT SYSTEM ACCEPTED

True sensed success in 1907. Fully confident that the directors would strive for the project system, he stoutly maintained what he openly termed his "rigid interpretation." That rigidity gave needed strength to the directors in their campaigns to win local support for the project approach (1). The decisive victory occurred when the governing boards, with few exceptions, gave to the directors and their staffs the full freedom to formulate the new projects. True noted with satisfaction, as he surveyed the initial year of operations, that no station had objected to the regulations set by the Office. In tones of marked relief, mixed with pardonable pride, he further noted that in no case had the withholding of certification proved necessary. "The system . . . of having projects outlined by the stations and passed upon by the Office in advance of beginning work," he concluded in his official report to Congress in 1908, ". . . has worked out very satisfactorily" (10). Rightly could he be proud of the station movement, which had now demonstrated its determination to penetrate more deeply into the intricacies of agricultural research.

Dr. True realized, nevertheless, that numerous imperfections remained in the evolving Hatch-Adams system. These impeded the efficient productivity of the research process. The widespread unfamiliarity with the technique of outlining projects, for example, led inevitably to crudeness in selecting and shaping the research proposals. Many of the station men in those days did not have advanced training. Foremost was the innate complexity of agricultural research, which thus far had in many cases defied the investigators' attempts to achieve penetration in depth. Even those who did had to overcome the difficulties implicit in project selection.

In True's judgment, the overall record of agricultural research revealed that American investigation, admittedly lacking in depth, had not yet produced a systematized science of sufficient breadth. Similarly the characteristic complexity of research, coupled with what appeared in retrospect to be amateurish and superficial experimentation on the part of a scattered host of station men, had led to the publication of a voluminous mass of research activity having uncertain direct usefulness or value as a basis for future studies. True shared ESCOP's view that much prior station work, considered from the standpoint of the project approach, appeared "inconclusive . . . unsystematic . . . fragmentary" (13). Thus the sheer bulk of available literature, on the one hand, and the inconclusiveness of much of its contents, on the other hand, produced an acute problem for the project-planners at the stations and the project-processors in Washington. "It is difficult," True admitted to the troubled directors in the autumn of 1906, "to get together the full body of knowledge which we have acquired in any particular branch of agriculture and determine in a concrete way what has been done already and what remains to be done" (9).

How, then, could True and the directors ascertain the originality in research stipulated by the Adams Act and the True Standard? How could they decide with reasonable certainty that someone, somewhere at some time had not already dealt with a given problem? Did not the prospect of duplication or partial repetition of previous work severely handicap the project system and imperil the theory of operation at the outset? These considerations did not, however, seriously disturb Dr. True. They did prompt him to require only "some original features" in the project outline rather than a demonstration of comprehensive originality. Nevertheless Dr. True, more intent on measuring station projects for their scientific caliber than for their academic uniqueness, relied on the certainty that a scientific investigation, planned and conducted in conformity with the project system, would achieve prior to its termination a significant penetration in depth. Thus "originality" in accomplishment, gained by an assault against the unknown, would unfailingly emerge. Of greater significance for society, the steady and persistent accumulation of new findings would lay the basis for a more efficient and productive agricultural technology.

Dr. True did not assume, however, that the project system would operate automatically as a producer of significant research activity. He confidently expected that the initial crudeness evident in the preparation of the proposals would largely disappear as soon as the station investigators gained experience under the new system. Nevertheless, he knew that the quality of formulated projects would in the future directly reveal the quality and training of the station personnel initiating the projects. The efficient and productive operation of the project system depended, in short, on the prime and continuing necessity that the stations recruit and retain the most highly skilled research talent. True's office could assist the expression of the research desires of the various station staffs, but at no time could it do more than encourage the research potential inherent in the well-trained and highly motivated investigator. The project system relied in the end, as the Hatch system had relied from the beginning, on the trained competence and the ingenuity of the individual scientist. No administrative techniques could supply a substitute for those essential resources.

Thus Dr. True placed a heavy responsibility on the station scientists. They should take professional pride in devising significant projects, in certifying the pertinent originality of their projects, and in prosecuting those projects to a decisive conclusion. In recognition of their exercise of responsibility, moreover, the station researchers must be assured the greatest possible freedom from interference in their concentration on their duties of investigation. "It is clear," True advised the directors in 1908, "that an efficient station worker must have practically all his time, or at least a large definite portion of his time, for the work of investigation and the preparation of reports thereon. This should be his primary business, and everything else that he does should be arranged so as not to interfere with his duties as an investigator." Selecting for special emphasis the teacher-investigator relationship, True pointedly reaffirmed the position which in earlier years Directors Armsby, Henry, and Jordan had stoutly maintained. "The teaching which the station worker should do should be very limited in extent," he declared, "and confined as far as possible to teaching advanced students along the line in which the investigator is working" (2).

The essence of administration, in True's view, lay in providing and maintaining at each station an atmosphere of inquiry wherein the skilled researcher could best devote his energy to the demands of the research process. Not only must Federal administration respect the investigator's freedom and function but, in addition, the various interest groups within each State must not be permitted to ignore this principle or to divert the researcher from his primary task.

No one understood more clearly than True, however, that his Federal office, which from its inception had respected and championed the autonomy of the land-grant institutions, remained substantially powerless to set rules for station operation. The determination to achieve improvement in the State stations could stem vigorously only from State, not Federal, roots. Thus the responsibility for the significant and productive administration of the project system and the True standard lay henceforth not with True and the Washington office but with the station and college personnel. Ultimate success would depend on the proficiency with which the numerous stations could institute and maintain strict scientific discipline, acquire the staff and facilities for research, and collaborate with each other. Immediately, however, the goal of steady improvement required that the directors as a group support a program defining the stations' mission. True accordingly relied on ESCOP to articulate the principles and objectives of station administration which would most fully implement the purposes of the Adams Act.

The Committee on Organization and Policy completely sympathized with True's ambitions for the stations. It understood that the successful administration of research, steadily growing more complex as time passed, depended far less on project-processing and station-inspecting by the Washington office than on the standards of operation set by the stations themselves. Resolutely it shouldered the obligation of formulating recommendations designed to strengthen the stations as institutions for research and to improve their operational efficiency. Energetic from the time of its organizational meeting in April 1906, ESCOP during the following 5 years conducted in annual stages a major appraisal of the station enterprise.

The panel of veteran directors, using a directness of approach that no Federal official could have attempted, conducted its review with a most serious purpose. Did the stations, ESCOP inquired, exhibit a comprehensive readiness to conduct the research stipulated by the Adams Act, expected by the project system, and urged by ESCOP itself? The tone of ESCOP's conclusion revealed that the new committee detected a need for substantial improvement. "It must be said," ESCOP reported after its preliminary survey in 1906, "that there are indications of a certain unreadiness for research of the true type. The difficulty is in a sense a fundamental one, but grows to a considerable extent out of a habit of mind. Many of our station workers see only the immediate duty of the station to the local farmers of today. They forget," ESCOP declared with the firmness that would characterize its later evaluations submitted to the Association, "that the station has a duty to all phases of agriculture in a broad sense, in order that its labors may lead to much more permanent and widespread benefit" (13).

STATION ROLE ESTABLISHED

The Committee determinedly pressed ahead with its appraising function. In 1908 it defined the role of the stations in the 20th century; it announced a set of administrative principles which buttressed and elaborated the True standard; and it re-emphasized the continuing significance of the cardinal theme in the lengthening experience of the State stations, namely, the encouragement of the scientific initiative of the individual investigator. The Committee after careful deliberation concluded that the goal of continuous scientific productivity required the nationwide station establishment to observe faithfully the following tenets of administration (14, pp. 2, 3):

1. The station exists primarily for research in the interest of the public service. If, however, this research is to be made effective there must be administration as well as investigation. . . .

2. The unit of work is the individual, and nothing should come between him and his research. That organization is best, therefore, which most accurately defines the field of each station worker, protects him in his investigations within that field, insures funds and equipment for the pursuit of research, and in the end secures results that are useful to the public that pays the bills.

3. . . . [The] function [of administration] is correlation as between internal interests on the one hand and as between these and the external or public interests upon the other. In theory all administration means delay and some necessary interference with individual initiative. . . . In the interests of [scientific] work, therefore, the less administration the better, if only the proper ends are attained, but workers must recognize the necessity of something like organization, which means administration.

4. The chief function of administration in respect to a piece of investigation may be enumerated as follows:

    (a) To help to determine in advance whether the proposed research is profitable and altogether advisable from the standpoint of the public, whose representative for the time being the administrative officer must be.

    (b) To assist in determining what lines of experimentation are calculated to throw profitable light upon the problem.

(c) To help to determine whether the work is best carried on by one individual representing a single line of inquiry, or by two or more working in conjunction. . . .

(d) The experiment once decided upon, however, and funds provided, administration is over until results are due, when it begins again and does not cease till reports are published and circulated. The less administration during the progress of the work the better for all interests. . . .

Thus the ESCOP appraisal of 1908 candidly and concisely considered a dilemmalike problem confronting all station personnel as the scale of operations deepened and widened in the post-Adams years. Scientific productivity in the public interest required, on the one hand, the stimulation of individual initiative and, therefore, the preservation of the greatest possible freedom of action for the individual researcher. The successful and efficient management of the stations required no less urgently, on the other hand, a more detailed structure of administration. How, then, to develop and maintain a well-disciplined institution which, not suffering from the ills of "too much administration," conducted consistently the kinds of research simultaneously fulfilling public needs and meeting the approval of the men of science? This never-ending problem with its manifold issues continued to preoccupy ESCOP in the following years and decades as successive panels of committeemen sought never-ending improvement.

The Committee in 1908 announced its formula for achieving the continuity of effort which underlay scientific productivity. Each station should provide "suitable facilities for work"; each should "retain experienced and well-trained men . . . completely freed from all responsibility with routine classroom teaching"; each should concentrate on "a few lines of research"; each should adhere closely to thoroughly considered, definite, and well-planned projects" (*14, pp. 7-10*). A station which astutely observed these fundamentals could, in ESCOP's judgment, attain the "two ideals of administrative efficiency and sympathetic helpfulness without interference" (*14, p. 3*). The measure of success in maintaining this balance would, moreover, be evident at all times in the *esprit de corps* of the station staff.

This restatement of the practical ideals of the station movement demonstrated conclusively that ESCOP, representing influential sentiment in the States, concurred with the views of Dr. True, representing the Federal Government, concerning the subsequent course of station organization and policy. This fundamental agreement gave to the station establishment a vital cohesiveness; it assured the success of the project system; and it set substantial precedents for the harmonious collaboration which to the present, has characterized the close relationship between ESCOP and the Washington office.

The Committee on Organization and Policy in later years firmly exercised its established function of evaluating the effectiveness of the research process at the State institutions. The Committee in 1927 re-emphasized, for the benefit of a new generation of station men, the unchanging duty of each station to initiate new research, to plan it thoroughly, and to execute it efficiently and economically. The project leaders and the administrative officers shared the responsibility, ESCOP declared, to draft with the greatest care their new proposals for research and to ascertain that each project concentrated on "a concrete phase of a problem looking to [specific] conclusions. . . ." In particular, ESCOP cautioned, the director and the research leaders at each station must guard against initiating projects so broad in scope that the investigators could not within reasonable time reach decisive findings. Not only must the research leader bear full responsibility for competent handling of the project from beginning to end, but he must formulate, as a necessary step in securing approval of the station management, a statement "which pictures for administrative officers, other investigators, and co-workers the merits of the project, its objective, procedures, in proposed investigation as to technique and methods, the probable period of time and its reasonableness, and the funds required and their adequacy for the proposed work" (3).

This insistent reminder, prompted by the rapid broadening of station activity into the new areas of investigation authorized by the Purnell Act of 1925, reasserted the validity of the administrative standards fashioned from the earlier experience of the station movement. Continued success in scientific productivity required, in short, that the researchers and the administrators faithfully carry out the exacting fundamentals of the project system. The demonstrated merit of the project system, and ESCOP's unflagging interest through the years in maintaining that approach to the conduct of research, have combined to keep the project system functioning vigorously to the present.

The perennial problem of maintaining and improving the stations' scientific productivity encountered a serious obstacle in the thirties, the decade of prolonged economic depression. Budgetary retrenchment threatened to inflict severe damage on the nonspectacular research effort, which operated at a disadvantage in the incessant competition with other types of tax-supported activity. The long-continued skimpiness of funds demonstrated conclusively that station men must establish procedures for presenting their financial needs directly to the appropriate Federal authorities. Accordingly, ESCOP sought the solution to this major difficulty. Opportunity appeared in 1940.

The Federal Bureau of the Budget, engaged in the late thirties in a broad program of revising its methods for handling the annual budget requests, assigned to its Agricultural Section the duty of studying the pattern of activity, supported at Federal expense, conducted under the auspices of the land-grant colleges and the Department of Agriculture. The Bureau, aware of its own lack of contact with the institutions spending the Congressional appropriations, wished to send a panel of its agents to a typical station; there the visitors intended to gain a firsthand familiarity with that station's operational features and its use of Federal funds. Director Robert E. Buchanan of Iowa, the alert chairman of ESCOP, volunteered his station for the appraisal desired by the Bureau.

AMES CONFERENCE HELD

"We went into much detail concerning the organization and significance of research projects," Director Buchanan later recounted when he described the Ames conference. "The Bureau men were particularly interested in knowing how these projects originated. We pointed out that in many cases they came or were developed as a result of inquiries sent to our Extension Service concerning problems demanding immediate study. In other cases they involved careful studies in fundamental science. . . . We outlined, for example, our relationship with certain advisory committees from various agricultural groups." The outspoken responsiveness of the station men led the Bureau appraisers to explore other aspects of station work. "We discussed the problems that arose in the Station due to differences in wording of the several laws authorizing grants-in-aid, such as the Hatch Act, the Purnell Act, the Adams Act, etc.," Dr. Buchanan explained. "We outlined the relationship of the . . . Station and its staff to the Experiment Station Section of the Land-Grant College Association and to the Office of Experiment Stations." Reminding his visitors of a persistent theme in the station movement, Buchanan "stressed the need for much autonomy on the part of the Office of Experiment Stations." With a conviction reminiscent of W. H. Jordan's presentation to the House Committee in 1905, the Iowa director asserted, "We vigorously and I believe successfully combated the concept that Congressional Grants-in-aid made the State Stations arms of the Federal Government."

Dr. Buchanan then capitalized on the opening which the frank exchanges offered. "We discussed the techniques of requesting appropriations from the Congress and the techniques of appearance before Congressional Committees, etc. One of the important results of the conference," he concluded, "was a quite informal agreement that there was no reason why [ESCOP] . . . should not, on occasion, have direct access to the men in the Bureau of the Budget (Agricultural Section) for discussion of some of their special problems." [2] Thereupon ESCOP deftly exploited, under Buchanan's chairmanship, the opportunity afforded by the Ames conference. The Committee at the convention of 1940 requested, and the executive body of the Association granted to it, the authority "to present the point of view of the Stations to the Budget Bureau with reference to agricultural appropriations" and, when directed by the Executive Committee of the Association, "to make such appearances as may be necessary at hearings before the Senate and House" (4).

The difficulties of assuring sufficient financial support did not disappear despite the easing of the long-continued depression. The sharpening of the war crisis in 1941, followed by the years of crucial involvement in World War II, compelled a maximum of governmental expenditure on the defense effort and diverted Congressional attention from the necessity of maintaining, without diminution, the tax-supported program of agricultural research. The Congressional insistence on domestic budgetary cutbacks imperiled important programs at numerous stations. "Wholly without precedent in the history of the Stations," declared Director C. E. F. Guterman of Cornell in 1942, "the Congress in the past two years has failed to appropriate the final increment for research authorized by the Bankhead-Jones Act, and in addition," he observed with alarm, "attempts have been made to reduce the funds from the present level" (6). Thus the stringency of wartime conditions negated the benefits which ESCOP had hoped to gain by its policy-making in 1940.

Meanwhile the Budget Bureau, intent on simplifying fiscal procedures, urged in 1941 that ESCOP draft a bill consolidating the

[2] Letter of Jan. 11, 1960, from Director Emeritus R. E. Buchanan, Iowa State University, to Director H. C. Knoblauch, State Experiment Stations Division, U.S. Department of Agriculture, Washington, D.C.

several statutes that since 1887 had authorized the Federal grant payments to the station system. The Committee, equally as intent as the Budget Bureau in streamlining fiscal procedures, prepared such a measure. Nevertheless, ESCOP acutely sensed the dangers implicit in substituting an act of consolidation for the historic practice of separate grants. Would not a single, lump-sum appropriation invite a practice of Federal budget-cutting which, if followed in the postwar years, would prove detrimental not only to the station enterprise but also to the public interest? Would not a new bill, no matter how carefully drawn to preserve the values of the station system, run the additional risks of amendment and alteration during the course of its Congressional career? Might not such a measure, if changed by Congress for any reason, weaken the capacity of the station movement to accomplish the mission that station men had championed for nearly a century? These basic considerations prompted ESCOP in the early forties to disapprove the proposal for a consolidated act. ESCOP and the Station Section successfully urged the Association to defer action during the war years, and secured the Association's approval of the following recommendations (5):

(a) That an informal discussion or hearing with appropriate members of the Bureau of the Budget be requested, at which hearing there should be presented a clear picture of the approach of the Land-Grant Colleges in making as objective an analysis as possible of the proposal to consolidate the Federal Acts, and that there be a careful review of the advantages and disadvantages of such consolidation.

(b) That the Bureau of the Budget be informed that in the opinion of the Land-Grant College Association the disadvantages of consolidation sufficiently outweigh the advantages to make the consolidation even under the most favorable conditions inexpedient and inadvisable.

(c) That if the Bureau of the Budget concludes that, notwithstanding the objections on the part of the Land-Grant Colleges, the advantages outweigh the disadvantages and that a Bill is to be introduced into Congress effectuating the consolidation, the Land-Grant College Association should assist actively in the preparation of a Bill retaining the essentials of appropriate legislation as these have been determined. Further, the Association should retain complete freedom of action, and oppose vigorously any amendment or change of the bill in any manner regarded as disadvantageous.

The question of consolidated legislation re-emerged in 1945. The Director of the Budget Bureau in July of that year requested that the Secretary of Agriculture support the proposal for consolidation. Nevertheless the Station Committee, unwilling to jeopardize station interests, reasserted in 1946 its policy of indefinite postponement. This position suspended for several years the movement for statutory codification.

Early in 1949, however, the Station Committee, having taken in the meantime the precaution of exploring Congressional sentiment, considered at length the advantages of consolidation. ESCOP reviewed in detail the matter of budget justification for Section 9 as well as Section 10 and Title II of Research and Marketing Act funds. Under the existing administrative and budget arrangement, Section 9 funds for the State experiment stations were considered as a separate item by appropriations subcommittees, which required that justification be presented for all projects to be supported with these funds. This justification was in addition to that presented for funds under all the other Federal acts. Problems of separate justification again raised the question of the need for consolidation of funds to the State stations so that a single justification could be made. ESCOP knew, moreover, that the Subcommittee of the House Committee on Appropriations favored a consolidated act, and that the Department of Agriculture currently was studying the proposition.[3] The Department's draft of a "Consolidation Act" soon appeared, and circulated among the directors for review and comment. ESCOP in October of 1949 approved the proposed bill with minor modifications.[4] Thereupon the Legislative Subcommittee of ESCOP considered the proposed bill with legal representatives of the Department of Agriculture.

The movement for consolidated legislation did not, however, gather significant momentum prior to 1954. ESCOP in November of that year received from its Legislative Subcommittee a draft of the favored form for a consolidated bill.[5] Early in 1955, two bills. H.R. 5562 and H.R. 6851, were introduced in the House of Representatives and S. 1759 was introduced in the Senate. Each bore an identical title: "A Bill to Consolidate the Hatch Act of 1887 and laws supplementary thereto relating to the appropriation of Hatch funds for the support of agricultural experiment stations in the States, Alaska, Hawaii, and Puerto Rico."

OBJECTIVES OF CONSOLIDATED LEGISLATION

The Station Committee in April 1955, studied the features of the several bills submitted for Congressional action. ESCOP noted with satisfaction the many merits of the proposed legislation, and it approved the following objectives of the intended measure:[6]

1. To reduce the number of different operating funds and thereby the number of "sets" of accounting from six to two.
2. To preserve all requirements on existing fund equivalent.
3. To retain the existing pattern of distribution among the several States.
4. To remove restrictions as now imposed by the Adams fund which prohibit use for printing and distribution of results of research; limits purchase or rent of land, erection and repair of buildings to 5 percent of the fund.
5. To place all Federal-grant funds for the State Experiment Stations under uniform rules and requirements of administration and authorization as to use.
6. To introduce no new provision not now contained in the Federal-grant authorizations.
7. To preserve the "open-end" feature of the Research and Marketing Act.
8. To remove the 20-percent marketing requirement on increases above the equivalent of fiscal 1955 appropriation. This is believed desirable since—
    (a) very substantial expansion in marketing research has been made in the States since 1946;
    (b) much of the further increase in this field can best be done by USDA directly, or by contact with the States; and
    (c) further continuation of the requirement (20 percent) against future increases would lead to imbalance of research in the States.
    (d) Title II.

The proposed legislation, highly satisfactory to station men, moved without mishap through Congress.[7] The House Committee introduced

---

[3] Minutes of Experiment Station Committee on Organization and Policy, Washington, D.C., May 3, 4, and 5, 1949.
[4] Minutes of meeting of Experiment Station Committee on Organization and Policy, Kansas City, Mo., Oct. 22, 1949.
[5] Minutes of meeting of Experiment Station Committee on Organization and Policy, Washington, D.C., Nov. 13–17, 1954.
[6] Minutes of Experiment Station Committee on Organization and Policy, Washington, D.C., April 27–28, 1955.
[7] A detailed analysis of existing legislation and changes to accomplish consolidated legislation is presented in House of Representatives Report No. 1298, 84th Congress, 1st Session (10) and Senate Calendar No. 568, Report No. 563.

only one amendment to the final consolidation bill. The Committee (*12*) explained its action as follows:

The only amendment to the bill made by the committee is the insertion on page 5 of a paragraph which will require that experiment stations continue to use 20 percent of their available appropriations for marketing research. Under the provisions of the bill as it passed the Senate, the present requirement of law that 20 percent of each State's allotment be used for marketing research would have applied only up to the level of appropriations for the fiscal year 1955. Appropriations beyond that level would not have been subject to this requirement. The committee is aware of the position of some of the State officials with respect to this requirement and has been informed that in the past some experiment stations have apparently found difficulty in developing sufficient marketing research projects to utilize 20 percent of their allotted funds. Notwithstanding, the committee believes that the present agricultural situation, with surpluses plaguing the producers of many commodities, is a clear indication of the need for continued emphasis on marketing of agricultural products and the research connected therewith.

The Senate accepted the House amendment, and on August 11, 1955, approved Public Law 352, known as The Hatch Act (*11*). This act resulted from 15 years of activity on the part of the Bureau of the Budget, Department of Agriculture, the State Experiment Stations, and Committees of Congress. This lengthy legislative process demonstrated once again that station spokesmen, firmly insistent on the continuing values of their system, may rely on the understanding support of their Federal Government. This democratic process proved once more the necessity for leadership and constructive cooperation between Federal and State officials in improving the fiscal practices fundamental in the attainment of the goal of scientific research.

LITERATURE CITED

(1) CARPENTER, L. G.
    1907. [REMARKS ON KIND AND CHARACTER OF WORK UNDER THE ADAMS ACT.] Assoc. Amer. Agr. Cols. and Expt. Stas. Proc. (1906) 20: 106–107. (U.S. Dept. Agr., Off. Expt. Sta. Bul. 184.)
(2) DODSON, W. R.
    1909. [RELATION OF THE STATION TO INSTRUCTION.] Assoc. Amer. Agr. Cols. and Expt. Stas. Proc. (1908) 22: 106–112.
(3) EXECUTIVE COMMITTEE OF THE ASSOCIATION.
    1928. REPORT OF COMMITTEE ON EXPERIMENT STATION ORGANIZATION AND POLICY. Assoc. Land-Grant Cols. and Univs. Proc. (1927) 41: 196–199.
(4) ———
    1940. REPORT OF COMMITTEE ON EXPERIMENT STATION ORGANIZATION AND POLICY. Assoc. Land-Grant Cols. and Univs. Proc. 54: 281–282.
(5) ———
    1941. CONSOLIDATION OF FEDERAL RESEARCH LEGISLATION. (*In* Report of Committee on Experiment Station Organization and Policy.) Assoc. Land-Grant Cols. and Univs. Proc. 55: 287–288.
(6) GUTERMAN, C. E. F.
    1942. FEDERAL GRANTS TO THE STATE AGRICULTRAL EXPERIMENT STATIONS. (Abstract.) Assoc. Land-Grant Cols. and Univs. Proc. 56: 127– 128.

84th Congress, 1st Session (11). Hearings before the House of Representatives Subcommittee on Research and Extension of the Committee on Agriculture, on July 8, 1955, published in Miscellaneous Hearings of the Committee on Agriculture of the House of Representatives, 84th Congress, Serial DD, pages 25–67 (12) gives a comprehensive record of the objectives and needs for consolidated legislation. See also the comments (pp. 63–67) of Congressman H. A. Dixon of a , a former Land-Grant College president, who actively supported the legislItiồn.

(7) JORDAN, W. H.
    1907. [REMARKS ON KIND AND CHARACTER OF WORK UNDER THE ADAMS
        ACT.] Assoc. Amer. Agr. Cols. and Expt. Stas. Proc. (1906)
        20: 109–110. (U.S. Dept. Agr., Off. Expt. Sta. Bul. 184.)
(8) TRUE, A. C.
    1907. ADMINISTRATION OF THE ADAMS ACT. U.S. Dept. Agr., Off. Expt.
        Stas. Ann. Rpt. 1906: 66–67.
(9) ———
    1907. REMARKS ON KIND AND CHARACTER OF WORK UNDER THE ADAMS ACT.
        Assoc. Amer. Agr. Cols. and Expt. Stas. Proc. (1906) 20: 103–105,
        110–111. (U.S. Dept. Agr., Off., Expt. Stas. Bul. 184.)
(10) ———
    1908. WORK UNDER THE ADAMS ACT. U.S. Dept. Agr., Off., Expt. Stas.
        Ann. Rpt. 1907: 62–63
(11) UNITED STATES CONGRESS
    1955. PUBLIC LAW 352. AN ACT TO CONSOLIDATE THE HATCH ACT OF
        1887 AND LAWS SUPPLEMENTARY THERETO RELATING TO THE AP-
        PROPRIATION OF FEDERAL FUNDS FOR THE SUPPORT OF AGRICULTURAL
        EXPERIMENT STATIONS IN THE STATES, HAWAII, AND PUERTO RICO.
        5 pp. (U.S. Congress, 84th, 1st Sess., Ch. 790, S. 1759.)
(12) UNITED STATES CONGRESS, HOUSE.
    1955. THE CONSOLIDATION OF AGRICULTURAL EXPERIMENT STATIONS AP-
        PROPRIATIONS. Report No. 1298, 44 pp. (U.S. Congress, 84th,
        1st Sess.)
(13) U.S. OFFICE OF EXPERIMENT STATIONS.
    1907. REPORT OF COMMITTEE ON EXPERIMENT STATION ORGANIZATION AND
        POLICY. Assoc. Amer. Agr. Cols. and Expt. Stas. Proc. (1906)
        20: 74–78.
(14) ———
    1908. REPORT OF COMMITTEE ON STATION ORGANIZATION AND POLICY. U.S.
        Dept. Agr. Off. Expt. Stas. Circ. 82, 10 pp.

Chapter Ten—
FEDERAL-GRANT PROGRAMS IN MARKETING RESEARCH, 1940–60

The purpose of this chapter is to relate the history of marketing research at the agricultural experiment stations during the period 1940–60 and to note the policies and activities of the experiment station directors and their committees. The story of the stations in these two decades cannot be told, however, without considering the economic conditions of agriculture; the scope, content, and objectives of marketing research; and the origin, provisions, and purposes of the legislation supporting that research. Accordingly, this treatment attempts the following four objectives: (1) To relate the main events and the currents of interest producing the legislation enacted in 1946 to provide increased support for research, especially marketing research, in both the State agricultural experiment stations and the Department of Agriculture; (2) to outline some of the main purposes and provisions of the legislation of 1946; (3) to indicate the nature of the cooperative administration of the marketing program financed in whole or in part by Federal-grant funds at the experiment stations; and (4) to discuss briefly the nature, content, and trends of research programs currently conducted at the stations.

Farmers, their organizations, their representatives in Congress, and the public agencies serving them have shown keen interest in marketing and its related problems from the time a public policy for agriculture first emerged. The concern with market outlets, market efficiency, and prices and incomes of farmers assumed new dimensions, however, in the 1920's when agriculture failed to recover fully from the post-World War I collapse in prices. This period saw the establishment of the Bureau of Agricultural Economics in the U.S. Department of Agriculture, the formation or strengthening of the Departments of Agricultural Economics in the land-grant colleges and experiment stations, and the passage of the Purnell Act by Congress in 1925 (5).[1] This legislation, providing for the more complete endowment of research at the agricultural experiment stations, stressed the importance of undertaking more studies in the economic problems of agriculture, including marketing and prices.

MORE EFFICIENT MARKETING NEEDED

The great depression and the virtual prostration of much of agriculture during the 1930's dramatized the dilemma of overabundant production and low farm prices in a world where millions were hungry and poorly clothed. Policymakers and analysts sought a better understanding of agricultural-industrial interrelationships; of the differential behavior of farm prices and industrial prices during prosperity and depression; and of demand, supply, and price interrelationships

---

[1] Italic numbers in parentheses refer to Literature Cited, p. 189.

for farm products in order to devise policies which would extend specific aids to agriculture and revive the economy.

By the end of the decade, both agriculture and the general economy had shown some improvement. Nevertheless, new technology had increased the farmers' ability to produce a larger output which could only be disposed of at prices resulting in incomes markedly lower than those received by persons of comparable skill in other sectors of the economy. Governmental price-support programs, although expensive to taxpayers, afforded only limited relief to farmers, and consumers complained of high food costs at the retail level. The belief grew that a special research effort might be both necessary and justified to provide the basis for more efficient marketing practices.

In the early 1940's Congressional action reflected the strongly felt need that public agencies should give more attention to marketing problems. The lawmakers in March 1941 held hearings on the Cooley bill (H.R. 1382) which, having already passed the Senate, authorized annual appropriations of $5 million for apportionment among the various State departments of agriculture.

The Experiment Stations Committee on Policy (ESCOP) at its Chicago meeting in November 1940 strongly opposed the Cooley bill on the ground that it would encourage duplication of functions already exercised by the agricultural experiment stations and extension services. ESCOP further recommended that the legislation ought to provide for a clear differentiation among the three agencies and allocate Federal funds only when the agencies agreed to a coordinated plan in which all would participate (*1, pp. 63–64*). This position, with which the Extension Committee on Policy (ECOP) agreed, reiterated the decision made at an earlier joint meeting in Roanoke of the station and extension committees on policy.

The House Committee thereupon refused to report the Cooley bill. ESCOP, ECOP, and the Land-Grant College Association accordingly formulated a substitute proposal. The Land-Grant college proposal provided for allotments by the Secretary of Agriculture to the State departments of agriculture, State extension services, State agricultural experiment stations, and State colleges of agriculture (teaching).[2]

COOPERATIVE WORK PLANNED

Certain provisions merit special mention. Total appropriations to all four lines of activity were to be apportioned among the States on a formula basis, taking into account farm population, total population, and gross farm income. All Federal funds above $10,000 were to be matched, and provision was made for regional research. The early draft of the bill provided, as ESCOP had urged, that the State departments of agriculture, agricultural experiment stations, and extension services must, in order to qualify for an allotment of funds, prepare a plan for cooperative work. When approved by the

---

[2] Mr. Edward A. O'Neal, president of the American Farm Bureau Federation, had an equivalent bill inserted into the Record in the course of the hearings on the Cooley bill. In his testimony he supported the station position, outlined the activities of the experiment stations and extension services in the marketing field, and emphasized that only a lack of funds had prevented further action (*1, 50–64c.*)

Secretary of Agriculture, this plan would constitute an agreement between the Secretary and the State agencies (*1, pp. 58–59*).

A later version of the proposed legislation, however, eliminated the requirement of a work plan; instead it stipulated that the Secretary should appoint a coordinating committee to meet at least once each fiscal year to review all programs financed under the Act and advise the Secretary concerning programs for the succeeding year. This committee would include representatives of the U.S. Department of Agriculture, the land-grant colleges, State commissioners of agriculture, the major national farm organizations, and one representative at large (*2, p. 53*).

The attack on Pearl Harbor and the subsequent involvement in all-out war compelled the temporary abandonment of efforts to pass new legislation despite the sharp and persistent interest of the experiment stations and other State agencies in the marketing problems of agriculture. Farm production soon expanded during the war, notwithstanding the withdrawal of manpower by industry and the Armed Forces and shortages of machinery, fertilizer, and transportation.

During the war crisis, the Nation and its farmers, adopting techniques which permitted substantial increases in output relative to input, reaped the benefits from the many years of patient research by scientists, most of whom were in the U.S. Department of Agriculture and the State experiment stations. Agricultural leaders recognized, however, that this growth in productivity, so necessary to winning the war, could create a serious problem of oversupply in the postwar period. They did not forget, furthermore, that the efforts to control production during the 1930's had attained only limited success, nor could they overlook the strong preference in Congress and among farm organizations for attacking the problem of surpluses via better marketing and distribution rather than by restraints on the freedom of individuals to operate their farm businesses.

Meanwhile the House of Representatives in May 1943 unanimously passed a resolution introduced by Chairman Hampton P. Fulmer of its Committee on Agriculture. House Resolution 38 authorized and directed the committee "to make a study and investigation of the present system of marketing, transportation, and distribution of farm products from rural areas through the various marketing agencies to the ultimate consumer as it affects farmers, the various types of middlemen, wholesalers, retailers, and consumers" (*3*). The pressure of wartime activities, however, prevented the committee from completing its study during the life of the 78th Congress.

Early in the first session of the 79th Congress, Congressman John W. Flannagan, who had become chairman of the House Committee following the death of Mr. Fulmer, introduced House Resolution 54, providing for a similar but somewhat broader survey than that anticipated by Resolution 38. During the same period a Republican Food Study Committee held numerous hearings in various parts of the country and undertook a thorough study of all matters connected with the production, marketing, and distribution of food.

PROPOSALS INTRODUCED

Both the latter group and those conducting marketing studies under House Resolution 54 concluded that the subject was so important, so complex, and so continuing in nature as to lie beyond the jurisdiction of any Congressional Committee. They further decided that only a program of research, comparable to that which had been carried out successfully in the field of production, could competently deal with the problems of marketing. Accordingly, Congressman Clifford R. Hope introduced in the House on March 28, 1946, H.R. 5925. This he later described as the direct ancestor of Title II of Public Law 733, commonly referred to as the Research and Marketing Act (3). The title of this proposal read: "To improve nutritional standards, reduce the cost of food distribution, provide a broader outlet for American farm products, and promote scientific development of food processing, distribution and marketing, by establishing a National Food Research Institute."

This bill aroused a great deal of interest but a successor, H.R. 6692, was introduced on June 6, 1946. The latter, containing suggestions for improvement made by those who had studied H.R. 5925, was dedicated to the same broad purposes of improving marketing efficiency and market outlets. It proposed to bring together all Governmental agencies concerned with the pricing, distribution, and marketing of food, and to create within the Department of Agriculture a new agency to be known as the Agricultural Marketing Administration (3).

Meanwhile a movement emerged to strengthen the research, both in the States and in the Department, along lines similar to those provided in the land-grant proposals of 1940 and 1941. Congress, under pressure to meet the research and related needs of special groups, heard proposals to provide additional support for research in nutrition, housing, cotton, and forestry. The members of ESCOP, meeting in Washington in April 1946, discussed the requirements of overall legislation that would broaden the Bankhead-Jones Act by including nutrition, housing, and cotton research. There came from these discussions a proposed amendment to the Bankhead-Jones Act. Director Leonard A. Baver of North Carolina, a member of ESCOP and the chairman of its subcommittee on legislation, collaborated with other members of ESCOP in a determined effort to obtain Congressional support.

This bill Chairman Flannagan introduced as H.R. 6548. Thereafter it vied with the Hope bill, H.R. 6692, for Congressional approval. Because both measures dealt with research, and because most of the spokesmen interested in one bill were also interested in the other, and for other reasons, the Committee on Agriculture held a joint hearing to consider the two pieces of proposed legislation. Both bills received the support of the leaders of the farm organizations, representatives of the U.S. Department of Agriculture, State commissioners of agriculture, and representatives of land-grant colleges. Director Baver, Associate Director Noble Clark of Wisconsin, and Director W. B. Kemp of Maryland testified on behalf of the agricultural experiment stations in support of both H.R. 6548 and H.R. 6692.

In the course of the hearings, the committee decided to combine the two bills, H.R. 6548 becoming Title I and H.R. 6692 becoming Title II. It then added a third title providing for the appointment of advisory committees (6). The measure unanimously passed both houses of the 79th Congress and received the signature of President Truman on August 14, 1946, becoming Public Law 733. Unofficially, it frequently has been referred to as the Flannagan-Hope Bill. Although Title II is officially designated as the Research and Marketing Act of 1946, this name frequently is attached to the bill in its entirety.

As finally passed, the legislation contained the ideas of state experi-ment stations, the U.S. Department of Agriculture, farm organiza-tions, farmers, industrialists, State departments of agriculture, and others and was an amalgam of numerous ideas and proposals originally contained in a number of bills initiated as separate pieces of legislation.

PUBLIC LAW 733 PROVIDED FOR MARKETING RESEARCH

Title I specifically mentions the development of new and improved methods of production, marketing, distribution, pricing, and utiliza-tion of plant and animal commodities through all the stages from the original producer to the ultimate consumer; human nutrition; re-search relating to the development of present, new, and extended uses and markets for agricultural commodities and byproducts as food, or in commerce, manufacture, or trade, both at home and abroad, with particular reference to products for which capacity to produce ex-ceeds, or may exceed, economic demand.

Especially significant is the first part of Section 11 which reads as follows: "Notwithstanding any other provision of this title, (1) not less than 20 per centum of the funds authorized to be appropriated under section 9(a) shall be used by State agricultural experiment stations for conducting marketing research projects approved by the Department of Agriculture . . ." (6). This provision had not ap-peared in the original amendment to the Bankhead-Jones Act, pro-posed as H.R. 6548, but was inserted in the course of the conferences which brought about the merger of H.R. 6548 and H.R. 6692. Its inclusion reflected the strong feeling that more marketing research should be undertaken, that the experiment stations as well as the De-partment of Agriculture should participate, and that the stations had not fully complied with the Congressional wish that funds provided under the Purnell Act be used primarily to support research in economics and marketing.

The directives and authorizations of Title II apply to the Secretary of Agriculture and, hence, primarily to the work of the Department. However, the expression of the intent of Congress with respect to marketing work, the objectives of increased activity in the field, the breadth and content of the programs indicated, and the references to cooperative work with State agencies make the provisions of Title II of vital importance to marketing research at the State agricultural experiment stations.

Section 202 stresses the necessity for the United States to achieve and maintain a sound, efficient, and privately operated system for distributing and marketing agricultural products. It firmly an-nounces the determination of Congress to promote a scientific approach to the problems of marketing, transportation, and distribution similar to that used successfully for many years in connection with the produc-tion of agricultural products, and to encourage cooperation among State and Federal agencies, producers, industry, and others in develop-ing programs to reduce distribution costs, improve nutritional stand-ards, and widen market outlets (6).

The direct appropriations under Title II are made entirely to the U.S. Department of Agriculture. Under Section 204(b), however, the Secretary is authorized to make allotments to State agencies to finance cooperative projects to effectuate the purposes of Title II of the Act. Such allotments must be covered by cooperative agreements between the Secretary and the State agency, and the Federal funds assigned to an approved project must be matched by not less than an equal amount of non-Federal funds for such research. Although allotments to the State agricultural experiment stations under Section 204(b) have been relatively small—$500,000 per annum since 1955 and less in earlier years—these funds have had an influence on the entire marketing research program of the stations in the following ways:

(a) They have enabled individual stations having the personnel and other resources to undertake additional work in marketing research without weakening other important programs.

(b) Since the Department has final responsibility for deciding on lines of work to be initiated they have enabled the Department, represented by the State Experiment Stations Division (SESD), in consultation with an advisory committee of experiment station representatives, to activate studies of problem areas which, in the view of SESD and its advisors, have been relatively neglected in the research programs being conducted under other funds.

(c) The authority possessed by the Department for the approval of projects and collaboration between the three committees advising the Department on the use of Section 204(b) funds (research, extension, and State departments of agriculture) has provided a favorable opportunity to encourage and stimulate cooperation among the three agencies at the State level, and between the U.S. Department and these State agencies.

(d) Finally, the administration of the Section 204(b) program has provided the basis for the development of criteria and techniques for administering the marketing requirement of Title I and hence has had an influence extending far beyond the important but relatively small matching-fund research undertaken under Section 204(b).

MARKETING RESEARCH ADVISORY COMMITTEE NAMED

ESCOP appointed a committee on September 14, 1948, to counsel with the Department of Agriculture on problems involved in arranging for State agricultural experiment station participation under Section 204(b) of Title II. This new committee met in Washington on October 10, 1948, and, conferring with representatives of the Office of the Administrator for Research and Marketing and the Office of Experiment Stations, it explored ways and means for facilitating such participation. The conferees agreed that the State experiment stations could make important contributions to the development of an effective national marketing research program under Title II. They further agreed that the marketing research undertaken by the stations under Section 204(b) should not duplicate or overlap, but on the other hand should be integrated and coordinated with Departmental research and also with the marketing work financed by other funds at the stations.

The station committee recommended that ESCOP appoint an Experiment Stations Marketing Research Advisory Committee (ESMRAC) of five members—one representative from each of the four recognized experiment station regions of the United States, and one representative from home economics. It suggested that each

of the four regional organizations of experiment station directors should nominate the regional representative, preferably an individual with training or experience in marketing or related fields. It also suggested that the Home Economics Committee of the Association of Land-Grant Colleges and Universities should select the representative from home economics. It finally proposed that Section 204(b) funds should not be allotted for research on a formula basis but rather that each individual project proposal should be considered on its merits.

Each director-member of ESMRAC was charged with the responsibility for acquainting himself with proposed and active Section 204(b) projects, as well as other marketing projects originating in his region, and also for familiarizing himself with the attitudes and opinions, concerning marketing research, of the directors in his region. Likewise, the members of ESMRAC were expected to be acquainted with the Departmental program of marketing research underway and in process of development. In addition, the Committee received the authority to make recommendations to the National Advisory Committee concerning the overall marketing program of the Department and the experiment stations. The Office of Experiment Stations agreed to provide an executive secretary for the new committee.

The charter members of ESMRAC—M. T. Buchanan, C. M. Hardin, F. F. Lininger, F. J. Welch, and Dorothy Dickins—held their first meeting in Washington in April 1949. Henceforth, until 1957, the Committee met twice a year, in the spring and fall, in response to the call of the State Experiment Stations Division (formerly OES). In recent years ESMRAC has held a single annual meeting in the spring in Washington.

The Committee has worked continuously in close cooperation with the State Experiment Stations Division. Also, it has maintained contacts with representatives of the U.S. Department of Agriculture for the purpose of coordinating project proposals with current and proposed research in the Department and facilitating cooperation between the State stations and the marketing research units within the Department. In cooperation with SESD, it has developed numerous procedures, including a calendar, for submitting and handling research proposals from the States. These procedures have provided the basis for a handbook, brought up to date from time to time, to guide the stations, the Committee, and the Department in handling the Section 204(b) program. The executive secretary of ESMRAC and other staff members of the State Experiment Stations Division also have assumed considerable responsibility for contacts and consultation with the Department.

The current characteristics and functions of ESMRAC, which to some extent have developed in the course of its operations, are as follows:

(1) The Committee, a subcommittee of ESCOP, reports to ESCOP as well as to the Regional Directors' groups.

(2) ESMRAC holds official status as one of the advisory committees under Title III of the Research and Marketing Act. In this capacity the selection of members of ESCOP must meet the approval of the Department (SESD), traveling expenses of members are paid by the Department, and meetings are called by SESD.

(3) The Committee advises SESD concerning the relative importance of marketing problems on which the various stations propose

to undertake research with 204(b) funds, the adequacy of project outlines, the relationship of proposed lines of work to other research underway or contemplated at the stations, the competence of the research personnel in the various institutions, and all other considerations affecting the assignment of priorities to the various project proposals. The exercise of this function is exceedingly important since normally the studies proposed for activation substantially exceed the limited number that can be financed with funds available.

(4) The Committee also advises SESD concerning all phases of its administration of the overall marketing research program at the stations, including the Hatch Act as well as Section 204(b).

(5) Final responsibility for the selection of 204(b) proposals for activation rests with SESD, as does also the responsibility for policy decisions relative to all aspects of the administration of the overall marketing research program for which SESD is given authority under the provisions of supporting legislation. It should be emphasized, however, that decisions by SESD concerning the marketing program, particularly those relating to policy, have always been reached on the basis of the fullest discussions with and the concurrence of ESMRAC. Moreover, the Committee in its advisory capacity has exercised significant influence in two vital areas in the administration of the marketing research program at the State stations, namely, (1) the marketing requirement under Title I of Public Law 733 (since 1955, the Hatch Act as amended) and (2) the integration and coordination of the marketing activities of the State experiment stations, the State extension services, and the State departments of agriculture.

MARKETING RESEARCH INTERPRETED

Section 11 of Title I, as noted above, specified that not less than 20 percent of the funds authorized for appropriation to the States be used by the experiment stations for conducting marketing research projects. This section, however, did not mention any criteria for distinguishing between marketing research and other research, nor did the Hatch Act, as amended in 1955. Once again, therefore, the same necessity which in 1906 had compelled OES to interpret the administrative and fiscal meaning of the term "basic research," after 1946 also compelled SESD to set the standards for deciding whether proposals submitted by the stations in fulfillment of the marketing requirement did, in fact, qualify as marketing research. Furthermore, the Division, historically operating within the spirit of Federal-grant administration—namely, the principle that the experiment stations are State and not Federal institutions—axiomatically understood that the concept of marketing must be liberal. That concept must, in short, permit State initiative the maximum latitude in attacking problems judged to be of highest priority and on which available personnel and other resources may be most effectively employed.

During the first few years in which appropriations were made under Title I, projects submitted by the station in fulfillment of the marketing requirement primarily concerned the economic aspects of marketing. These included proposals dealing with the efficiency of rendering specific marketing services, the efficiency of firms and marketing systems, the economics of transportation, grading, market news, market pricing, and other lines of work within the broad field

of agricultural economics which had always been considered to be a part of agricultural marketing. The project proposals of the States for financing with Section 204(b) funds also fell largely within conventional areas. The substantial increases in Hatch appropriations in the early 1950's, however, enabled and encouraged the stations to attack a wider range of problems. Accordingly, the State Experiment Stations Division and the Directors determined to conduct a searching inquiry into the scope and nature of the marketing field in the light of Congressional intent. ESMRAC and SESD collaborated in this endeavor.

The items on the agenda for each meeting of ESMRAC since 1955 have included an examination of the areas of research eligible for classification as marketing under the Agricultural Marketing Act of 1946 and the Hatch Act as amended. Not only has the Committee devoted many hours of intensive thought and discussion to this subject, but the members have considered the problem at length with ESCOP and members of their respective Directors' groups. In addition, SESD personnel have sought the advice and guidance of individual members of the Committee by means of numerous personal conferences and extensive correspondence. The principles followed in distinguishing between marketing research and other research represent a joint determination by SESD and ESMRAC, and written statements setting forth the relevant distinctions have had the complete concurrence of ESMRAC at the time of their proposal and release to the station (4).

Space limitations do not permit a detailed discussion of the principles developed and the guidelines followed in distinguishing between marketing and other research. In brief, however, ESMRAC and SESD have relied heavily on the specific language and the implication of Title II of the Act of 1946, which begins with the language, "This title may be cited as the 'Agricultural Marketing Act of 1946.'" Since both Title I and Title II were enacted as integral parts of the same piece of legislation, and since the interpretation given the term "marketing" in the two should be consistent, SESD and station personnel have sought guidance in Title II in determining lines of work suitable for classification as marketing under the Hatch Act, as amended.

Section 203 of Title II directs and authorizes the Secretary of Agriculture to carry out research, investigation, and experimentation to determine the best methods of processing, preparing for market, packaging, handling, transporting, storing, distributing, and marketing agricultural products. It specifies that this work shall include studies of marketing costs, with a view to developing more efficient methods, practices, and facilities that, in turn, will bring about more efficient and orderly marketing and reduce price spreads between producers and consumers. It further specifies that the research receiving support shall aim to develop and improve standards of quality, condition, and grade; to find methods for eliminating trade barriers, improving statistical services, and the more orderly marketing of farm products; and in general to facilitate the marketing, distribution, processing, and utilization of agricultural products through commercial channels (6).

The above authorization is exceedingly broad, but the lines of work singled out for special mention and the history of the legislation clearly indicate a distinction between marketing and other research. The personnel of ESMRAC and SESD, utilizing their own background in and understanding of the marketing field and with due regard to the characteristics and interest of the State stations, have singled out three broad areas of research which properly would carry out the purposes intended by Congress in the Act of 1946, as follows:

(1) Projects generally eligible for classification as marketing may deal with a wide range of economic and technological problems occurring in the various stages and functions in the marketing system. Generally these are described by the lines of work mentioned under Section 203 summarized above.

(2) Research projects not eligible for classification as marketing are those dealing with the farm production of agricultural commodities either in their technological or economic aspects.

(3) A third area does not lend itself to a clear-cut delineation. Numerous projects fall in this category, including broad economic studies of a commodity, industry, or geographic area, analyses of the operations and impacts of comprehensive Government programs, projects concerned with farmer and cooperative purchasing, economics of the household, the dissemination of economic information, and studies where marketing objectives are merged with or closely related to production operations on the farm. Projects of this kind, including fundamental or basic scientific studies, receive approval for classification as marketing only when they seek the solution of the marketing aspects of the problem or problems under study. The classification of projects in this third area has often required the exercise of considerable judgment and administrative discretion.

The above policies and principles have left wide latitude for the selection of subject matter suitable for support under the 20 percent requirement of the Hatch Act as amended and Section 204(b) of the Agricultural Marketing Act (Title II). ESMRAC and SESD have steadfastly maintained that all projects classified as marketing must, to be eligible for Federal-grant funds, conform to the requirements of the basic legislation.

MARKETING PROGRAMS COORDINATED

The State extension services and the State departments of markets, as well as the State experiment stations, have important programs underway, the successful operation of which depends in part on steady and reliable results from research. In turn, research agencies rely on Extension and Service agencies to disseminate and apply the findings of marketing research with a view to bringing about actual improvements in the marketing system. Both State extension services and State departments of agriculture receive support under Section 204(b) and from other Federal sources. In 1948, in addition to the Experiment Stations Marketing Research Advisory Committee, there were also established the Extension Services Marketing Advisory Committee and State Departments of Agricultural Marketing Advisory Committee. Like ESMRAC these Committees have functioned continuously since that time. Although originally constituted primarily to advise the Department on programs supported by Section 204(b), like ESMRAC they have been called upon to extend their advisory functions to encompass problems of State, Federal, and interagency marketing programs generally.

The three Committees, early in their history, realized that their

parent agencies must avoid any duplication or overlapping of activities. They recognized, at the same time, that many marketing problems require for their solution the combined and coordinated activities of research, extension, and service. The three Committees and the Department, the latter represented primarily by the respective excutive secretaries, have made a continuous effort to improve and extend desirable interagency working relationships. The Committees at a joint meeting in March 1949 prepared a memorandum, which applied to the working relationships among the agencies at the State level, and recommended it for the use of all Directors of Agricultural Experiment Stations, State Directors of Extension, and State Commissioners of Agriculture. After 5 years' experience under that memorandum, the three advisory Committees held a second joint meeting in October 1954. The conferees of 1954, though they made minor revisions in the memorandum of 1949, reaffirmed the basic concept that primary responsibility for coordination rests with the agencies in each State.

A third meeting held in November 1956 prepared additional recommendations. In a memorandum addressed to the heads of the three agencies in each State and signed by the chairman of the three advisory Committees, the committee members stressed the basic intent of the legislation and the purpose of the matched Federal-State appropriations, namely, the achievement of the closest coordination among State agencies in solving the marketing problems in the various States. Accordingly, the joint Committees recommended, first, that the Department in approving projects under Section 204(b) give priority to those showing an effective and coordinated attack on important marketing problems, and second, that it encourage the administrative heads of the three agencies in each State to meet together to consider marketing problems. By this time the three Committees, much more concerned with the importance of cooperative action than with avoiding duplication and overlapping, advocated the study of marketing problems requiring the exercise of the functions and experience of two or more of the agencies concerned.

The three advisory Committees met jointly again in October 1959. This session endorsed and elaborated the principles and recommendations of the 1956 meeting; it crystallized specific recommendations for coordination and joint action; and it reemphasized the timeliness of cooperative activity. If the State agencies were to meet effectively the needs of agriculture and society during the contemporary period of rapid economic change, and if, furthermore, they were to maintain public approval and support for the scientific study of the marketing system, then they must continue to improve their cooperative working relationships. Moreover, so the Committees noted in their decisions, the State agencies must cooperate at every stage in the process of problem-solving, especially at the initial stage of problem-defining. The conference of 1959 then advocated the following procedures for improving interagency cooperation at the State level:

(1) Top administrative personnel should actively support the principles of cooperation, which apply not only to activities financed under Section 204(b) but to the entire marketing programs of the three agencies.

(2) Each of the three agencies within each State should continue to clarify and define its own function, and also recognize the functions

of its two partners. When, for example, an agency plans a new program or outlines a new project, it should take the initiative in contacting the others. Project outlines submitted to Washington should indicate that the trio of agencies has discussed the proposal. Similarly the reporting of results should explicitly recognize the role of the other agency or agencies.

(3) The three agencies at the State level should meet at least once each year.

(4) The dean of the college of agriculture in each State should be responsible for convening the representatives of the three agencies.

(5) The three advisory Committees at the national level should meet at least once every 2 years, and more frequently if necessary.

(6) The representatives of the three agencies present at the joint meeting should acquaint their colleagues with the proceedings of the meeting and enlist the support of their respective executive committees in implementing the recommendations of the conference.

In their efforts since 1959 to bring their ideas to the attention of leaders in the States, the three advisory Committees have had the complete support of the executive committee representing their respective groups.   ESCOP and other committees representing the directors have given continuous support.

MARKETING RESEARCH EXPANDED

The legislation of 1946, which enabled and required the stations to come to grips with marketing problems, prompted such studies at the stations to expand considerably in number and scope. Expenditures for these purposes (Federal-grant and non-Federal funds combined) increased from a little more than $1 million in 1948 to more than $8½ million in 1960. Nevertheless the stations encountered difficulties in implementing an expanded program of marketing research. The shortage of trained personnel proved particularly serious. The various experiment stations and the Department vied in their efforts to attract each other's employees and the limited number of students completing graduate training. This kind of competition benefited the individual research worker because it tended to raise his salary near the level of other groups with comparable skills and abilities, but in the short run it contributed little to increasing the total supply of available talent. The research institutions had no choice but to spread their personnel excessively thin and make maximum use of graduate students and other partially trained workers. Not until the midfifties did the supply of personnel with advanced training permit the filling of most job vacancies in marketing at the experiment stations.

The newness and the complexity of the subject-matter, moreover, deterred a rapid initiation of research in marketing, for many of the critical problems lay in processing, wholesaling, retailing, and other parts of the industrial and commercial sectors of the economy. Research in these areas required the student to face technical, economic, and institutional situations largely foreign to those whose experience had been primarily with farmers and marketing agencies close to the producer.

Therefore the stations, during the first few years of increased support for marketing research, placed major emphasis on the description of marketing methods, services, charges, and costs. They realized from the beginning, however, that positive improvements in marketing efficiency—using the latter term in its broadest sense—would require not only an acute appraisal of the marketing process but, in addition, the devising of concrete procedures ready for application at key points. Accordingly, in the early 1950's the researchers increased the number of lines of work involving the intensive investigation of alternative methods of performing various functions and services. They compared individual and total inputs and selected the most efficient methods in relation to such variables as overall volume, length of season, location, and relative availability and costs of capital and labor. Frequently optimum means for performing certain functions were integrated and synthesized into plans for model plants. In a number of cases the cooperation between economist and engineer accounted significantly for the successful completion of such research.

Paralleling the shift toward studies of cost and efficiency in firm operations and in the performance of specific marketing services has come a growth in technological studies. This term refers to a wide range of physical and biological research directed toward improving processing methods and maintaining quality of products in storage, transportation, and wholesale and retail channels. Physical and biological scientists on the one hand and economists on the other have worked together to devise new methods and processes and, at the same time, to determine their economic feasibility.

The stations in recent years have paid increasing attention to the organization and structure of markets and the impact of changes in structure, organization, and institutions, on the returns received by farmers. This interest has arisen in turn from important changes that have been occurring in interfirm relationships, in size of individual firms, marketing technology, financing, pricing, and management strategy. Much has been heard of integration in food marketing in the United States, that is, the extension of control by a single firm over two or more stages of production or marketing or both. Integration is not new to industry, but has increased rapidly in the food industries since World War II. Paralleling integration and somewhat interrelated with it is the accelerating movement toward larger firms in food processing and handling. Within the past 25 or 30 years these two developments have proceeded on such a scale as to lead to (1) a marked shrinkage of transactions in markets traditionally regarded as mechanisms for price discovery and (2) substantial disadvantages for small farmers unable to meet the demand of large-scale buyers for continuous supplies of a relatively uniform quality of products. Questions are being raised as to whether elements of monopoly or at least oligopoly are not becoming so widespread as to threaten the elimination of the small firm in both agricultural production and marketing and perhaps pose a serious challenge to public welfare in terms of the ability of marketing agencies to control marketing margins and prices to both producers and consumers.

MARKETING RESEARCH EVALUATED

Despite the increased emphasis placed on marketing research in the past decade, the economic position of agriculture has worsened rather than improved. Does this trend mean that the expanded program of marketing research has had few benefits? This conclusion does not appear warranted, despite the imperfections in the research program of recent years. More clearly evident is the hard fact that forces, much too powerful for marketing improvements to cope with alone, have shaped the structure of income and prices. Undoubtedly marketing research has contributed to increased efficiency in the American marketing system in recent years; nevertheless the downward pressure on farm prices and incomes has exceeded the counteracting power of research activity aimed at lowering marketing costs and expanding outlets.

The forces depressing the level of farm prices include the continued concentration of the population of the United States in large metropolitan areas, a further increase in the proportion of homemakers employed outside the home, continued emphasis by food processors and handlers on the manufacture and promotion of convenience foods, and further specialization of agricultural production in areas distant from the major centers of consumption. These and other developments represent an increased demand for marketing services. Efficiency as measured by output per worker in marketing has risen significantly, but such changes in efficiency have not been sufficient to offset the effect of higher wages and other cost rates.

The rising output of the American farm itself, moreover, has contributed even more significantly to the declining level of farm prices. Aggregate food and fiber output, accompanied by highly inelastic coefficients in both the price and income sense, climbed to a level 23 percent higher in 1959 and 1960 than in the period 1947–49. Production increases of this magnitude have inevitably brought about weakness in farm prices and incomes, notwithstanding rising domestic population, substantial additions to stocks, and various measures designed to dispose of surpluses in foreign markets.

Market researchers still believe that improvements in marketing efficiency are important but are beginning to give increasing attention to other and relatively neglected problem areas heretofore not intensively studied. This trend reflects an increasingly forward-looking attitude in research and an overall maturing of the research program. They believe that scientists should delineate and explore emerging new problems of marketing well in advance of the time when public administrators must make decisions in policy. New directions in research are taking marketing economists farther and farther from the farm and the farmer and leading them into commercial, industrial, and consumer markets where prices are discovered and demand originates. Already scientists are studying price and income policies, searching especially for workable and acceptable mechanisms for adjusting the supply of farm production to demand. Once the causes and the impacts of trends have been discerned, as in the case of integration, economists should be able to develop alternative courses of action to preserve or attain specific situations which society may consider desirable.

The station scientists are beginning to deal more attentively with the problem of finding new or widened markets for products and services traditionally considered to be minor sources of farm income, including forestry and outdoor recreation. If the national timber area, half of which is on farms, is to increase its productivity in line with needs indicated by the Forest Service, then innovations in both

production and marketing, probably assisted by changes in public policy, will be required. Furthermore, outdoor recreation is one of the rapidly increasing industries of recent times. Thus favorably situated farms face the profitable prospect of selling rights to engage in fishing, hunting, camping, and other forms of outdoor recreation. The research required for these purposes often will require the attention of production as well as marketing economists, and in some cases close collaboration between two or more disciplines will be essential.

Finally, economists are increasingly visualizing the problem of national price and income policy, as well as other aspects of policy, from a world-wide perspective. They recognize that the great productive capacity of American agriculture, the pressure to dispose of surpluses abroad, the alleviation of hunger, the promotion of foreign economic development, and the effectuating of overall United States foreign policy must be brought into a more rational harmony.

LITERATURE CITED

(1) EXPERIMENT STATIONS COMMITTEE ON POLICY.[3]
    1940. MINUTES, AGENDA CHICAGO MEETING, NOVEMBER 8. 172 pp.

(2) ———
    1941. MINUTES, AGENDA WASHINGTON, D.C., MEETING, JANUARY 4. 65 pp.

(3) HOPE, CLIFFORD R.
    1951. A VISUALIZED PROGRAM FOR MARKETING. A speech delivered Feb. 12, 1951, under the auspices of the Graduate School of the U.S. Department of Agriculture. 12 pp.

(4) STATE EXPERIMENT STATIONS DIVISION, AGRICULTURAL RESEARCH SERVICE.
    1960. MANUAL OF PROCEDURES FOR STATE AGRICULTURAL EXPERIMENT STATION RESEARCH UNDER THE AGRICULTURAL MARKETING ACT OF 1946. 8 pp. U.S. Dept. Agr.

(5) UNITED STATES CONGRESS.
    1925. [PURNELL ACT.] AN ACT TO AUTHORIZE THE MORE COMPLETE ENDOWMENT OF AGRICULTURAL EXPERIMENT STATIONS, AND FOR OTHER PURPOSES. APPROVED FEBRUARY 24, 1925. (43 Stat. 970.)

(6) ———
    1946. PUBLIC LAW 733. AN ACT TO PROVIDE FOR FURTHER RESEARCH INTO BASIC LAWS AND PRINCIPLES RELATING TO AGRICULTURE AND TO IMPROVE AND FACILITATE THE MARKETING AND DISTRIBUTION OF AGRICULTURAL PRODUCTS. 11 pp. (U.S. Congress, 79th, 2d Sess., Ch. 966, H.R. 6932.)

---

[3] Minutes and agenda of ESCOP meetings referred to in this and other chapters are not generally available in libraries. The archives, however, do contain copies of these documents.

Chapter Eleven—

BROADENING THE SCOPE OF INVESTIGATION:
Regional Approach to Research Problems

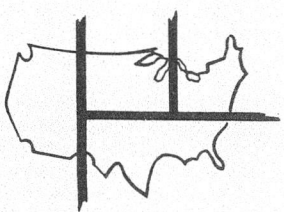

Leaders of the State agricultural experiment stations and of the Department of Agriculture recognized the merits of cooperative research and the regional nature of many research problems in their earliest meetings. As station programs expanded, the need for coordination and correlation among research workers increased. The directors supported regional conferences and cooperative projects for this purpose, but lack of a formal program and of specific funding delayed the growth of regional research. In 1946, the directors framed a special provision for Federal legislation which provided the means for the development of the cooperative regional research program of the State stations (18).[1]

REGIONAL RESEARCH CONCEPTS DEVELOPED

The founders of the State agricultural experiment station system and the first station directors had cooperation and organized effort foremost in mind (13, p. 83). Administrators and research workers readily understood and expressed the potential advantages of cooperation on problems of wide and important concern. Many years elapsed, however, before organized regional effort materialized. There were several principal obstacles to effective regional cooperation: commonwealth restriction of interstate travel, limited funds for research, and the intrinsic reluctance of scientists to participate in group research.

The growth of agriculture in the Nation brought an increase in demands for research on the State stations without proportionate increases in public funds. Research workers of the State stations and the Department agencies organized regional conferences for more effective use of resources and exchange of information. Several pioneering regional research efforts developed out of these conferences. Beginning in 1913, for example, livestock research workers of the Southern States met regularly to discuss their major problems in the production of livestock. They completed plans for cooperative regional research, agreeing among themselves as to what each institution should do, including the precise role to be played by each. In 1922 they established a livestock council which recognized three classes of problems—southwide, regional, and State—and agreed to consider only the first two. A specific problem area, such as soft pork, was selected for regional research. The Department entered into agreement with each cooperating institution (4), specifying: (1) the leaders of the project; (2) objectives of the work; (3) procedures; (4) the cooperative system; (5) physical locations and plans; (6) publication.

---

[1] Italic numbers in parentheses refer to Literature Cited, p. 205.

During the period of general distress in agriculture following World War I, research needs drew increased attention at the regional and national levels. The directors pressed for more Federal-grant support to expand their programs. They also attempted to meet the additional needs by encouraging more cooperative activity. In 1920 they adopted a national policy of payment of travel expenses of workers to regional conferences (7). There was some increase in the number of regional conferences and councils as a result.

During their November 1923 meeting, the directors discussed the regional approach to research in detail (4). Director Dan T. Grey of the Alabama Agricultural Experiment Station outlined the following points of merit in regional attacks upon needed studies:

1. Regional attacks enlarge the scope of most problems, and do this at a saving of money.

2. Regional attacks develop a spirit of greater confidence in us and in our work from the standpoint of the public.

3. Cooperation relieves the State of the necessity of making independent attacks upon all agricultural problems.

4. Cooperation standardizes methods of experimentation.

5. Cooperation prevents individual and departmental workers from losing sight of the final application of the projects.

6. Regional attacks upon research problems give permanency and stability to experimental studies.

Director J. G. Lipman of the New Jersey Experiment Station pointed out that the term "regional" is an elastic one. The boundaries of a region vary with the problem. Regional research helps to differentiate the local from the more general factors. A more clearly defined plan of attack usually results. Common use of standard methods is imperative or the comparison and interpretation of results will be most difficult. Regional conferences acquaint the scientific workers with negative results and conclusions not deemed worthy of publication. Personal acquaintance is one of the major gains. Conversely, personal vanity can be one of the most serious obstacles.

The training of younger men is facilitated whenever a regional problem is attacked by a group of workers located at different points. The regional approach has a tendency to hasten the application of the recommendations made by investigators.

Passage of the Purnell bill on February 24, 1925, brought about a nationwide program of cooperative research and further development of patterns for regional research. The Purnell Act increased the Federal-grants to each State and broadened the field of research the stations were authorized to cover. It was intended to expand economic and sociological investigations. There was no special provision for cooperative regional research, but Federal and State station administrators were determined to expand this aspect of the research programs. Meeting in St. Louis, Mo., on April 20–21, 1925, they formulated plans to promote and develop Federal-State cooperation under six national projects including: (1) distribution and marketing of farm products; (2) the problem of surpluses of farm products; (3) vitamin content of food in relation to human nutrition; (4) rural home management studies; (5) rural social organizations and agencies essential to a permanent and effective agriculture; and (6) factors influencing the production and quality of meats. Special subject-matter committees, each with an advisory administrator, were appointed to for-

mulate project plans. A committee of experiment station directors cleared each plan. Thus for the first time in the history of the State stations, an attempt was made to conduct cooperative research under a formal organization (8).

Experience gained from these early regional and national cooperative projects was to become a foundation for the cooperative regional research program many years later. Director Tom Cooper of Kentucky described from his experiences as administrative adviser to the committee on distribution and marketing of surpluses, the responsibility and problems of the directors serving such committees (2). The development of mechanics for cooperative research could not replace effective leadership or administration. There was also the difficulty of focusing effort on specific regional problems and assigning responsibility to the participating researchers. Projects needed to state definitely the particular phase of research to be performed by each participant. Whether or not executive secretaries or coordinators were used, contacts with the directors had to be maintained to plan the work effectively.

Initial progress was encouraging and the Committee on Experiment Station Organization and Policy (ESCOP) reported that considerable enlargement of the cooperative relations between stations would result (12). Endeavors, however, should be limited to comparatively few, well chosen projects into which the directors could put their best qualified workers and provide sufficient funds to assure useful results. As the years passed, however, the organization set up for cooperative research in 1925 brought about considerably less improvement in regional research between State stations than between USDA and the stations (9). In 1931, the Joint Committee on Projects and Correlations of Research recommended that the special research committees established in 1925 be discontinued (6).

The Christgau bill introduced in Congress on June 30, 1930, provided that there be set up a regional research council in the major agricultural production regions to be composed of the directors of the experiment stations and representatives of the Secretary of Agriculture. The councils were to employ research workers at the various stations working under the administrative direction of the council. The Christgau bill never reached the stage of hearings by the agricultural committees of the House and Senate, nor very serious discussions by the land-grant colleges (19). By 1933, most of the Purnell committees were disbanded and a distinct lull in interstate cooperation occurred. With limited facilities and support, the State stations were faced with unprecedented demands for special emergency research in connection with the economic depression.

The Bankhead-Jones Act of 1935 gave special impetus to cooperative research through the provision for the regional laboratories. It provided additional funds which stimulated the research programs of the State stations and cooperative activity. Increasing interest in the regional approach and in interstate cooperation was marked by the establishment of planning groups, such as the Corn Belt Livestock Marketing Research Committee and the North Central and the Southwestern Land Tenure Research Committees (1). Each was charged with the responsibility for planning a regional project, or projects, within their respective fields. On each project, the unit for collaboration and teamwork on research became the technical committee, with overall guidance provided by an administrative adviser.

In retrospect, the period predating 1940 may be viewed as one of very gradual evolvement of regional research concepts. The growing problems of agriculture and periods of recession directed attention to regional and national levels of research. Federal legislation stimulated the programs of the State stations and cooperation between the States. The main elements of regional research organization developed, including the administrative adviser, the technical committee, and the regional project. The essential requirement still lacking was the specific funding to support a nationwide, stable program.

The continuing difficulty in the use of regional committees was securing the funds for out-of-state travel for State men and women to attend the regional conferences. Many States had stringent laws, and sharply limited funds for such travel. Assistance was provided in some instances by certain private agencies, such as the National Livestock and Meat Board and the Farm Foundation. The Directors became increasingly concerned, however, that the provision of the necessary travel expense should not be left to the chance that some outside agency would defray the costs. They also recognized that with some projects it was highly important that the researchers be completely free from any possibility that they were under even indirect obligations to a donor. In the regional laboratories supported with Bankhead-Jones funds, the Department assumed the travel expenses of the collaborators. The necessity remained, however, of providing funds for coordination on the regional and national levels of a considerable number of important projects and proposals not connected with the regional laboratories.

In a final report summarizing the situation in 1942 (5), the Joint Committee on Projects and Correlation of Research stressed this need:

. . . Beginning in 1920, the Committee on Projects and Correlation of Research has repeatedly emphasized the desirability of regional conferences of scientific workers, and has recommended that funds be provided to defray necessary travel costs. Experience has demonstrated that most States find it difficult, and sometimes impossible, to assume the expense of sending representatives to many of these conferences. With the Department carrying the responsibility for securing the regional and national application of research results secured in individual states, it seems appropriate to look to the Department to pay the necessary travel costs, if the stations will furnish the time of their staff members. . . .

Another factor serving as a catalyst for the origin of Federal support for interstate cooperation was the continual concern of members of the appropriations committees of the Congress over the control of duplication of research. Varying conditions within the States meant that projects of similar objective were not duplication, but more or less replication under different conditions. This explanation, however, did not seem adequate to satisfy the criticism. It was felt that certain specialized problems within a region could be more efficiently solved if efforts were concentrated or pooled at given locations rather than being dispersed. Some formal mechanism was needed to bring about the desired coordination of research.

REGIONAL RESEARCH FUND CREATED

Several legislative proposals involving cooperative research relating to human nutrition, forestry, and marketing were pending in 1941 when the outbreak of war shifted interest to research mobilization for food and fiber production. Continuation of concern toward increasing coordination of research and cooperative effort was evidenced by the renewal of legislative proposals relating to marketing and nutrition and introduction of others, including cotton and rural housing, in postwar planning. Support from the farm organizations became strong in 1946. ESCOP was called upon in April 1946 to decide whether a new bill or an amendment to the Bankhead-Jones Act would be most appropriate from the viewpoint of the State agricultural experiment stations. A proposed amendment was prepared by a subcommittee of ESCOP, including Directors Baver (N.C.), Guterman (N.Y. Cornell), and Dorman (Miss.). It included a provision for the desired regional research and coordination which especially interested the farm organizations and Congress. In recent correspondence,[2] Director Baver states his thinking back of the regional research provision as follows:

> I must confess that I am guilty of suggesting some kind of provision within the act that would make possible the setting up of funds for regional research. This idea stemmed from two facts that were very obvious at that time. The more important from the standpoint of serving as a catalyst for the origin of the regional research funds was the continual harping by members of the Appropriations Committee over the duplication that was existing within the research of the various agricultural experiment stations. . . . The second factor was one that concerned me a great deal. After getting into administrative work at North Carolina I was very disturbed over the fact that various technical workers within a given field in adjacent states were not getting together to discuss mutual problems that would improve the efficiency of research within their respective institutions. . . . Then I had an idea, which, from subsequent experiences, I reckoned must be considered as being in the visionary class. I definitely felt that, in a way, the members of Congress were correct in that there was a certain amount of duplication that could be eliminated. I felt that there were certain specialized problems within a region that could be more efficiently solved if our efforts were concentrated at a given location for the solution rather than being dispersed between a number of scattered institutions. . . . As a result of this thinking, which was concurred with by Directors Guterman and Dorman, we drafted the provision for the Regional Research Fund.

The subcommittee, with the counsel and advice of ESCOP and other directors, worked with representatives of other groups on the Research and Marketing bill and in the process inserted the provision establishing a Regional Research Fund. ESCOP appointed a committee with a representative from each region to make the presentation before the House of Representatives, Committee of Agriculture. This group included Directors P. S. Burgess of Arizona, C. Dorman of Mississippi, C. E. F. Guterman of New York (later replaced by Director W. B. Kemp of Maryland) and Noble Clark of Wisconsin with Director L. D. Baver as overall chairman representing the special legislative committee. These men played stellar roles in 1946 working for House Bill 6548, which became known as the Research and Marketing Act (*14, pp. 37-70*).

As a result of the work of this special Legislative Committee, the Special Committee appearing before the House Committee on Agri-

---

[2] Personal communication from L. D. Baver to M. A. Farrell.

culture, the members of ESCOP and other directors, the Office of Experiment Stations, farm organizations and the Committees of Congress, the statement establishing regional research was developed and became a part of the Research and Marketing Act of 1946. This description of regional research as it appears essentially unchanged in the amended Hatch Act of 1955, Sec. 3(c)3, is shown below:

Not more than 25 per centum shall be allotted to the States for cooperative research in which two or more State agricultural experiment stations are co-operating to solve problems that concern the agriculture of more than one State. The funds available for such purposes, together with funds available pursuant to subsection (b) hereof for like purpose shall be designated as the 'Regional research fund, State agricultural experiment stations,' and shall be used only for such cooperative regional projects as are recommended by a committee of nine persons elected by and representing the directors of the State agricultural experiment stations, and approved by the Secretary of Agriculture. The necessary travel expenses of the committee of nine persons in performance of their duties may be paid from the funds established by this paragraph.

The intent and objectives of regional research *then* as determined from the legislation itself and testimony given at the hearings may be summarized as follows:

1. To stimulate and facilitate inter-State cooperation on research of a regional and national character, both between Agricultural Experiment Stations and with the USDA.

2. To plan and coordinate research so as to avoid unnecessary duplication in research effort.

3. To organize regional technical committees consisting of State and Federal representatives that will plan and coordinate work on regional problems.

In the hearings of June 13–26, 1946, before the House Committee on Agriculture, the Directors emphasized that passage of the bill would bring coordination of research and that expansion of cooperative research was needed on important problems. Although only 25 percent of the total funds to be gained by the States was earmarked for cooperative regional research, the farm organizations and Congress expressed special interest in this provision. Policy or procedure for cooperative regional research was not prescribed. Attention was directed almost entirely to problems of research which needed solution—cotton, nutrition, farm buildings, and marketing. The content of the program was practically set, however comprehensive, whereas organization and procedure for the regional approach were not.

The reason for the 25 percent limitation was not made clear and some Directors felt it was an unnecessary, if not a possibly undesirable limitation, especially considering marketing problems crossing State lines, and because the intent of the individual station would be to deal with local objectives. There was no doubt left after the hearings, however, that Congress intended the legislation overall to support joint effort directed toward the solution of the most pressing problems in agriculture, to provide against duplication, and to earmark emphasis for marketing research.

A special provision (Section 11) proposed by the Directors calling for close coordination between the States and the Department was notably modified in the final legislation. It called for appropriate cooperative agreements to prevent duplication.

The directors were definitely committed to budget a certain portion of the Regional research fund in the fields stressed during the hearings. The Experiment Stations Committee on Organization and Policy proceeded with preliminary planning to outline important

problems in collaboration with the regional associations of directors and USDA administrators. Organization of the Committee of Nine was completed in December 1946, and the Committee, consisting of eight agricultural experiment station administrators and one administrator of home economics research, convened December 16–17, 1946, in Chicago, Ill.[3] The early activities of the Committee were summarized by E. C. Elting;[4] as follows:

. . . Fully cognizant of the responsibilities imposed upon it for recommending to the Secretary of Agriculture the projects to be financed by the Regional research fund, and the allocation of the funds, project by project, and State by State, the newly created committee felt compelled to lay down certain guides for the planning groups to follow. . . .

Fortunately, this original committee of nine included a number of experiment station directors who had been influential in promoting the passage of the Research and Marketing Act, and who were fully familiar with the extensive hearings on the bill, and the fact that the bill was to a large extent a composite of a number of individual bills on specific subjects which had previously been under consideration. These circumstances made it mandatory that certain subject-matter fields have high priority in the developing of the new program if faith was to be maintained with the sponsors of the various research bills which finally had been merged into the Research and Marketing Act.

The first report of this committee . . . strongly recommended that for the first year's program under the Regional research fund, major emphasis be placed upon projects in marketing, rural housing and farm buildings, human nutrition, the introduction and testing of new plants offering promise for industrial and other uses, cotton improvement and mechanization, and such other subjects to be designated by the regional groups of directors as funds might permit. A review of the program finally adopted for fiscal year 1948 will indicate that these recommendations were well heeded.

Confronted at that point with setting up an organization for speedily swinging into action on program planning, it is not surprising that the regional associations of directors turned to the type which was already functioning smoothly in connection with a number of existing regional projects . . . . That organization consisted of an administrative adviser for each major project selected from the directors' group to represent them and to have responsibility for establishing and guiding the project technical planning committee. The technical committee became the mainspring of the organization and upon it falls the major responsibility for a well planned, smoothly operating research project. The operation of such a committee may be varied to suit the needs of the particular problem involved. The plan is sufficiently flexible to deal with narrow line projects or broader types of undertakings, frequently involving a number of distinct phases or subprojects without departing from the basic type of organization. . . .

The regional boundaries of the four associations of experiment station directors were accepted without question as the administrative and physical regions for the cooperative research program. In project planning, however, the need for overlap and interregional participation soon developed, attended by problems of allocating funds.

Since Title I of the Research and Marketing Act of 1946 was an amendment to Title I of the Bankhead-Jones Act of 1935, the rules and regulations prescribed by the Secretary of Agriculture applied equally to both. The Office of Experiment Stations thereby became responsible to act as the Secretary's authorized representative in the approval of the cooperative regional research projects. Coordination in planning research to be supported under the Regional research fund and other USDA-supported cooperative research has been maintained

[3] The proceedings are recorded in the unpublished minutes of the Committee of Nine meeting held on Dec. 16–17, 1946.
[4] Unpublished address, Problems of Planning Regional Research under the Research and Marketing Act, by E. C. Elting to the New England Research Council, Apr. 14, 1949.

by regular meetings of Department administrators with the Committee of Nine and through the Office of Experiment Stations. Coordination also takes place in the meetings of technical representatives planning the research, and by the regional coordinators adopted by a number of the committees.

The Regional research fund was activated at a level of $625,000 by the Agricultural Appropriation Act of July 1947. The first program included allotments for 25 cooperative regional projects distributed 40.99 percent for marketing research, 58.31 percent for other research, and 0.8 percent for Committee of Nine expenses. The paticipating stations more than matched the allotments with funds from other sources. The Office of Experiment Stations issued initial instructions on August 25, 1947, on designation of projects, separation of marketing and nonmarketing research, accounting for expenditures, annual reporting, allotments to specific projects, use of trust funds for travel, use of Title I funds other than Regional research funds for planning regional projects, and the general applicability of rules and regulations governing use of Federal-grants fund to Regional research funds.[5]

PROCEDURES ESTABLISHED

During 1948 the Committee of Nine developed definitions of regions, regional projects, functions of advisers, technical committees, and coordinators, in consultation with the regional associations of directors, and Office of Experiment Stations. The words "cooperating" and "participating" were differentiated, the latter being made specific for State stations receiving allotments of the Regional research fund. It was agreed to set up the projects for ensuing fiscal years within the regions on approximately the same ratio between regions as fiscal year 1949, without precedent or prejudice. Additional projects could be submitted above the allocated regional amounts for consideration by the Committee. The directors were informed that this was best judgment at the moment, but that no policy had been set on a percentage basis. This apportionment of Regional research funds, however, has been followed to date, with the only reservation in 1953 by the Committee of Nine that up to 10 percent of funds above $2,500,000 may be used for interregional proposals.[6]

At each successive meeting of the Committee additional procedures were adopted. The four regional associations of directors likewise developed supplementary policy and procedures as needs arose. By late 1949 there was considerable reaction toward the intricacies of procedure and complex pattern developing in the program. In 1950 a manual of procedures was approved by the Committee of Nine, cleared with ESCOP and the directors, and distributed to OES. The manual was reviewed, revised, amended, and reissued in 1953, 1955, 1956, and 1958 as policy and procedures were expanded or modified (18). The essential considerations in the manual are (1) organization of the directors and researchers for the regional approach, (2) development of

[5] Letter dated Aug. 25, 1947, from the Chief, Office of Experiment Stations to the Directors of the Agricultural Experiment Stations.
[6] As stipulated on p. 9 of the unpublished minutes of the Nov. 6 and 10, 1953, meetings of the Committee of Nine.

the cooperative regional projects, and (3) administration of the Regional research fund.

The organization for the regional approach to research represents a triangle, the vertices of which are the administrative adviser, the technical committee, and the Committee of Nine. It is the interrelation of these three units which determines the development and accomplishment of a regional project. The directors, as a whole, and their committees and the Cooperative State Experiment Stations Service staff operate in the periphery in administration of the Regional research fund.

Cooperative regional projects usually develop at the grass roots as proposals and recommendations to the directors to meet the needs of agriculture. The appointment of an adviser by the regional Association of Directors is followed by organization of a technical committee, which develops a specific plan and assignment of responsibilities. Review and recommendation by the Committee of Nine and approval by CSESS is prescript for funding under the Regional research fund. Preliminary estimates for allotments of Regional research funds to regional projects are developed about a year in advance of the fiscal year.

By 1960 a cumulative total of over $118,000,000 from all sources had been used in cooperative regional research activities.[7] The Regional research fund program had expanded to 198 regional projects, including some 1,750 contributing State and Federal agency projects and involving more than 3,500 personnel in some 220 technical meetings each year. In 1960 the regional research fund contributed $5,878,036, or 34 percent of the total funds expended in the program in 1960. The participating State stations added other Federal-grant funds (27 percent) and non-Federal funds (39 percent). The cooperative regional program is now attracting about 12 percent of the total funds available to the State experiment stations. More than 2,000 technical publications on many phases of biological, economic, social, and physical science are being published annually as a result of this research.[8]

POLICIES AND PROCEDURES EVALUATED

The first major criticism of the intricacies and complex machinery for cooperative regional research came from the State station directors themselves and their administrators during the meetings of the Association of Land-Grant Colleges and State Universities at Kansas City, Mo., in 1949. The program was requiring a seemingly disproportionate amount of administrative attention. The directors decided, however, that it was the most valuable device that they had ever had for supplying ways and means of conducting cooperative research.

In January 1950 the Chairman of the House subcommittee (Agricultural Appropriations), Mr. Whitten of Mississippi, expressed concern that the regional research program had just "gravitated into a

[7] Summation of unpublished data compiled annually since 1948 by the Office of Experiment Stations and the State Experiment Stations Division, USDA, SES–OD–1195, table 2.
[8] Compiled by actual count of publications as reported annually in the regional project progress reports by the technical committees.

mad scramble on the part of the State experiment stations to get a little money out of the various funds set aside for various types of work" (*16, pp. 172–174*). The source of his opinion was not disclosed other than "that is the complaint I hear in some places." Dr. Trullinger, Chief of the Office of Experiment Stations, assured the chairman that this was no longer the case, although "it undoubtedly was a contemplated thing in the beginning because of a confusion as to what the law meant." Mr. Whitten redirected attention to the primary purpose of the Act:

> . . . But we do need to see that the money is wisely spent, and I was particularly interested in this so-called regional approach. The act was passed to permit two or more States to cooperate on a given problem; that sounds mighty good. But then if we find that the way you are handling it is that each State has three or four divisions of it, it is to be wondered if we are handling it as it was contemplated by the act. . . . If we just decide what the problem is that we need to answer or what problem we need to meet, and having made that determination, will allot the money it will take to do it and select the best place to do it, that will meet the objectives I am attempting to outline. . . .

The Committee of Nine annually evaluated progress on each project. This became a formidable task by 1956 and the Committee adopted a system of having the major review conducted by a special review subcommittee, in consultation with the technical staff of the State Experiment Stations Division, ARS. The regional associations of directors, also finding the task of project review and evaluation unwieldy by the whole, turned to a device of using special Regional Research Committees of several directors to perform this function. The burden of machinery still fell heavily on the shoulders of the administrative advisers, however, to such an extent that institutional administrators in 1957 criticized the amount of time being required for the program (*20*). Some steps were taken to streamline administration of the Regional research fund but no major change in organization or procedure was accomplished. The Committee of Nine, in attempting to reduce the time of its members in the administration of the program, cut the number of its meetings from 4 to 3 per year. The directors, the Committee of Nine, and SESD continued to review each new or revised project proposal, and to evaluate progress on continuing work.

The Department of Agriculture participated in the cooperative regional research program from the outset. Initially cooperation consisted of consultation and assistance in project development, coordination of research, and support of State projects of mutual concern with Federal funds. In several cases Federally organized and coordinated regional research that was in progress when the Regional research fund was created, served as the framework for the new regional projects. Direct participation by USDA personnel in technical committee activities increased, and in 1955 formal procedures were developed for determining Department cooperation on regional research projects. In 1957, the Administrator of the Agricultural Research Service (ARS) specified the procedure for documenting the research of participating Department researchers and for its acceptance by the technical committees.[9] By 1961 there were more than 100 recorded contributing line projects.

---

[9] Administrative Memorandum No. 110.3, Policy with Respect to Regional Research Projects, July 22, 1957, superseded September 10, 1959.

In 1958, the Department undertook steps to accelerate efforts in developing regional centers for research and concentrating forces (*10*). At the request of the Research Administrator of ARS, a Joint Committee on Cooperative Research was formed, including ARS and State station administrators. The Committee develops recommendations for carrying out these efforts, including a comparable appraisal of all cooperative regional research (*3*). A set of 15 principles relating to Federal-State cooperation in agricultural research centered on cooperative research to serve as a guide in developing cooperative relationships. Closer coordination of all regional research is a prime objective.

The Directors continued to express concern for the administrative demands of the regional research program and to seek ways to improve it. In November 1958, the retiring Chairman of the Committee of Nine, A. A. Spielman of Connecticut (Storrs) (*11*), expressed the view that the administrative load could be reduced by having fewer regional projects. Efforts should be concentrated on urgent problems amenable to the application of known principles—developmental research. He stressed the need for more extensive use of regional conferences, since such meetings require no administrative supervision or attendance. Regional technical committees, he stated, should be charged with the responsibility of taking an objective look at the overall problem with three questions in mind:

1. Is there a real *definable problem* of regional significance on which two or more States can work cooperatively?

2. Will research results be expedited by making it a regional project?

3. Has sufficient progress been made so that further research on the problem can best be done by individual stations?

In summary, Director Spielman stated:

We have, unwittingly I am sure, developed a complex administrative pattern, the further growth of which fair promises to strangle us with our own red tape. It has been proposed that this administrative dilemma can be solved by further proliferation of regional organization; or by transferring the responsibility, authority, and function legally vested in the directors to additional subcommittees or to some other agency. Simplification of organization and procedures; termination of unproductive projects and those of questionable regional significance appears to me to be the more constructive approach. A comprehensive and constructive study of the basic structure and administrative procedures of regional research is essential if we are to achieve the maximum contribution from the scientists of the state stations and the United States Department of Agriculture. The net result of this study should be the development of a more productive organization for teamwork research with less emphasis on organized research.

The advantages of cooperative research were clearly recognized in 1889 when the Association so wisely adopted resolutions that: (1) groups of States should cooperate in the study of problems of common interest; (2) the Department of Agriculture should aid the stations singly and in groups as circumstances indicate; and (3) the stations should extend similar aid to the Department in the study of mutual problems. Over the past 10 years the outstanding contributions of the Regional Research program have clearly demonstrated the value of the cooperative research.

The following year, the next retiring Chairman of the Committee of Nine, Director D. W. Thorne of Utah,[10] reviewed the status of progress in improving the program for the directors:

---

[10] Unpublished report by Chairman D. W. Thorne of Committee of Nine to section of agriculture-experiment station work, Assoc. Land-Grant Cols. and State Univ., November 14–15, 1960.

Regional Research seems to have become the sacrificial lamb for the complexities and frustrations of Station research programs. Criticisms have been made of the travel involved, the administrative time entailed, the procedures needed for routine business, and of the tendency to orient individual station programs toward regional research projects. There has been considerable discussion and some sharp disagreements concerning the causes and cures for these alleged deficiencies. In many regional meetings and in our national meeting we have resolved that something must be done. But action has been slow. . . .

The quality of regional projects has improved, but most important has been the attitude toward regional planning and the extent of participation in it. Whereas in early years, regional projects were approached in many cases merely as a means to secure funds, now we find research workers asking for regional projects even without regional fund allocations.

The present controversy about Regional Research is healthy. The future is open to make it what we will. The State Experiment Stations Division and the Committee of Nine have solicited suggestions as to how Regional Research administration can be simplified and the program made more effective. During the past year, several significant suggestions have been received and a study of the entire program has been initiated. . . .

The Committee contends that Regional Research has unique values worth preserving, and that regional research meets a distinctive need in our varied system of State, federal, and industrial research in the United States. This is an opportune time to take firm steps, not toward curtailment, but toward improvement.

REGIONAL PROGRAM APPRAISED

During 1960 the State Experiment Stations Division of the Department, with the concurrence of the Committee of Nine and the regional associations of directors, deemed it desirable, after 14 years of experience with cooperative research under the Regional research fund, that the program be appraised, particularly those aspects dealing with operational policies and procedures. Director M. A. Farrell of the Pennsylvania station, a former member of the Committee of Nine, was employed for the purpose. He visited some 25 experiment stations during 1960–61 and conferred with more than 400 administrators and researchers. Recommendations based on this study are being developed.

In April 1961 the House Subcommittee on Agricultural Appropriations examined the Department's request for increased payments to the States and Puerto Rico for fiscal year 1962 (15). The subcommittee once again expressed concern whether duplication of effort was controlled, and how effective effort on particular problems could be with money distributed on a formula basis (17, p. 564). Question was raised if there was any way to meet particular problems through a national fund that might be allocated to meet a particular problem through the State approach, which would not necessarily be committed to the distribution formula (17, pp. 577–581). Dr. Elting, Deputy Administrator for Federal-States Relations, ARS, pointed out:

. . . As you know, the only fund that is not now distributed by formula is the 25 percent set aside as a regional research fund. Here we have some discretion as to where this money is allotted. Dr. Knoblauch and I recently have had serious discussion with the Committee of Nine, which was created by law to recommend the program of research under this regional fund.

We have examined the possibilities there for perhaps creating some reserve or other devices where we might attack some of these emergency problems that arise from time to time. I am sure there is merit in exploring how the reserve fund or the special grant authority might be created that would permit channeling money into the special problems as they arise.

The Committee of Nine and the regional associations of directors
ı their 1961 meetings continued to seek ways to improve and
·rengthen the Regional research fund program. Some feel that
ɔoperative research on many major problems has become entrenched.
Iany additional needs for research are not being met.

There is no question that accomplishments under the Regional
ɜsearch program have been outstanding. A wealth of new knowl-
dge has been compiled. Each year over 2,000 publications emanate
rom researchers in the program. Central facilities and centralized
ffort have been developed for many major problems. Regional
ɔultry breeding facilities now serve the State stations, the Depart-
ıent, and industry needs. Beef, dairy, sheep, and turkey breeding
ɜsearch are regionally and nationally coordinated. The introduction
nd evaluation of new crops and plants has become a closely knit team
ɜsearch effort of the State station and Department scientists. Inter-
ɜgional stations are maintaining and developing potato and fruit
tocks essential for industry and research needs. Progress in cotton
·reeding, basic genetics, and production efficiency through improved
ɪechanization has been greatly accelerated by organized and long term
ɜgional research in these areas.

Many other outstanding examples could be enumerated. Coopera-
ive marketing research has pyramided and produced many fine
ɔractical results which have brought industry into closer relationship
rith State and Federal researchers and increased industry support of
ɜsearch. Basic research has grown steadily in relation to each area
ɪnd regional researchers have made many shifts in emphasis from
ɑrlier applied studies to direct concentration on the search for funda-
ıental knowledge.

Perhaps more significant than the contributions to scientific knowl-
ɪdge, the regional research program has led to more efficient use of
ɜtate and Federal research resources and manpower. Practically
very segment of the research programs of the State stations has been
.ffected. The concepts of the Directors concerning the possible ad-
'antages and benefits of cooperative regional effort, as expressed,
luring the twenties, have been more than verified. The popularity of
he program is one of the main factors creating the administrative and
nanagement problems which the Directors continually seek to alle-
·iate. Accomplishments under the program have been outstanding
ınd a wealth of new knowledge has been compiled.

But many additional problems requiring the regional approach
tand waiting support and the regional research funds are inadequate.
Vays must be found to improve or streamline the administrative ma-
hinery which seems to be overtaxed already. There is uncertainty as
o what the next course of action might be to more effectively meet
he continuing pressures for solutions to the perplexing and shifting
ɔroblems of agriculture. The directors of the State stations, USDA
.dministrators and the Congressional committees stand at a crossroads
leciding whether policy and procedures for use of the Regional
·esearch fund will continue along lines established in 15 years of
ɔperation, or whether some of the recommendations of the Farrell
tudy and other perhaps even more drastic modifications of the
·egional approach to research must be adopted to effectively cope with
he regional and national problems of agriculture. One of the first
teps to be taken must be the clarification and general acceptance of

the philosophy of the regional approach to research under the amended Hatch Act. The following section represents some reflections along this line.

PHILOSOPHY OF REGIONAL RESEARCH DEFINED

The term "regional research" as applied to agricultural research during the past 100 years is broad and elastic, encompassing nearly all of the activities cooperative between the States and most of the Federal-State relations. The limits of the regions depend on the problem or intent of the cooperation. Such cooperative research has included a range of activity from discipline-oriented professional society meetings and research administrators' conferences to intimate joint effort of researchers across State lines and Federally contracted single laboratory studies.

The regional research prescribed by the Directors in developing the program using the Regional research fund is considerably more restricted in scope. While the limits of the regions are still adapted to the intent of the cooperation—or more specifically to the problem at hand—the research is to be joint effort directed toward the solution of defined problems of important concern to agriculture. There are two distinguishing requirements of research conducted under the Regional research fund. First, *the research is to be defined by project plans focused on the solution of specific and important problems of agriculture.* Second, *each research project should represent a concerted effort involving two or more States in a region of concern.*

The Congress expects that Federally supported regional researchers will give first consideration to the most pressing problems of agriculture. By law a portion of the funds are earmarked for marketing research.[11] The Congressional committees have consistently raised questions of progress on lines of work directed to the solution of such problems as farm surpluses, utilization of agricultural products, and new or replacement crops. Under these conditions selection of the most pressing problems must continue. There are categories of problems that can be handled to better advantage by the regional approach. They may cover the entire range from those of basic research which represent bottlenecks to progress, to the application of known principles in developing recommendations for policy decisions. The Regional research fund (RRF) was intended to be a source of support for such a range of problems. It should be flexible enough in assignment and administration to facilitate reasonable shifts of emphasis as the needs demand.

There is a validating test which can be applied to segregate RRF regional research from the universe of cooperative relations in agricultural research. One asks "is the research a team effort primarily centered on the solution of a specific regional problem?" One common criticism of regional research conducted since 1947 is lack of focus or lack of a regional approach to the problem.[12] It means simply that the cooperators fail to demonstrate in plan and procedure sufficient

---

[11] See section 3 (c) 4 of the Hatch Act of 1955, appendix p. 233.
[12] A summary of review comments on regional research projects is contained in the unpublished report, "Summary of Committee of Nine Comments in Review of Regional Research Projects," December 1946–November 1960 (SES–OD–1212).

evidence of effective teamwork. If interest centers on individual projects, the regional approach to the problem is incidental or secondary. Individual effort, creativity, and initiative are essential to the development of regional project plans, procedure, and analysis of results. But a pattern of joint planning and effort must prevail which demonstrates that most effective use of personnel, facilities, funds, and other resources is being made. Attainment of the proper degree of teamwork without adverse effect on individual creativity and the so-called academic freedom of researchers is one of the most difficult problems underlying the regional approach.

Regional research is better planned and conducted than it was a decade ago. The record shows that continued improvement and progress can be anticipated.

LITERATURE CITED

(1) BORJKA, K.
1945. REGIONAL RESEARCH IN AGRICULTURAL MARKETING. Jour. Farm Econ. 17: 121–137.
(2) COOPER, T.
1926. ORGANIZATION FOR AND RELATIONSHIP IN COOPERATIVE RESEARCH. Assoc. Land-Grant Cols. Proc. (1925)) 39: 169–176.
(3) ELTING, E. C.
1959. REPORT OF JOINT COMMITTEE ON COOPERATIVE RESEARCH. Assoc. Land-Grant Cols. and State Univs. Proc. 73: 135–136.
(4) EXECUTIVE COMMITTEE OF THE ASSOCIATION.
1924. REGIONAL CONVENTIONS AND REGIONAL COOPERATION IN PROJECTS OF EXPERIMENT STATION WORKERS. Assoc. Land-Grant Cols. Proc. (1923) 37: 236–249.
(5) JOINT COMMITTEE ON PROJECTS AND CORRELATION OF RESEARCH.
1942. REPORT OF THE COMMITTEE. Assoc. Land-Grant Cols. and Univs. Proc. 56: 206–207.
(6) MANN, A. R., ACTING CHAIRMAN.
1932. REPORT OF THE JOINT COMMITTEE ON PROJECTS AND CORRELATION OF RESEARCH. Assoc. Land-Grant Cols. Proc. (1931) 45: 267–269.
(7) MUMFORD, F. B., CHAIRMAN.
1921. REPORT OF COMMITTEE ON PROJECTS AND CORRELATION OF RESEARCH. Assoc. Land-Grant Cols. Proc. (1920) 34: 128–133.
(8) ——
1926. REPORT OF THE JOINT COMMITTEE ON PROJECTS AND CORRELATION OF RESEARCH.——Assoc. Land-Grant Cols. Proc. (1925) 39: 184–187.
(9) ——
1929. REPORT OF THE JOINT COMMITTEE ON PROJECTS AND CORRELATION OF RESEARCH. Assoc. Land-Grant Cols. Proc. (1928) 42: 205–209.
(10) SHAW, B. T.
1958. DEVELOPMENT OF RESEARCH FACILITIES AND THE ROLE OF THE REGIONAL LABORATORIES IN STATE AND FEDERAL PROGRAMS. (Abstract.) Assoc. Land-Grant Cols. and State Univs. Proc. 72: 166–167.
(11) SPIELMAN, A. A.
1958. REPORT OF THE COMMITTEE OF NINE. Assoc. Land-Grant Cols. and State Univs. Proc. 72: 161–163.
(12) THATCHER, R. W., CHAIRMAN.
1926. REPORT OF COMMITTEE ON EXPERIMENT STATION ORGANIZATION AND POLICY WITH SPECIAL REFERENCE TO THE PURNELL ACT. Assoc. Land-Grant Cols. Proc. (1925) 39: 176–184
(13) TRUE, A. C., and CLARK, V. A.
1900. THE AGRICULTURAL EXPERIMENT STATIONS IN THE UNITED STATES. U.S. Dept. Agr., Off. Expt. Sta. Bul. 80, 636 pp. illus.
(14) UNITED STATES CONGRESS, HOUSE COMMITTEE ON AGRICULTURE.
1946. AGRICULTURAL RESEARCH. (Hearings on H.R. 6548 and H.R. 6692: H.R. 6932 reported.) Serial M, 245 pp. (U.S. Congress, 79th, 2d Sess.)

(15) UNITED STATES CONGRESS, HOUSE OF REPRESENTATIVES.
    1961. DEPARTMENT OF AGRICULTURE AND RELATED AGENCIES APPROPRIATION
          BILL, 1962. Report No. 48, 45 pp. (U.S. Congress, 87th, 1st Sess.)
(16) UNITED STATES CONGRESS, SUBCOMMITTEE OF THE HOUSE COMMITTEE ON
    APPROPRIATIONS.
    1950. DEPARTMENT OF AGRICULTURE APPROPRIATIONS FOR 1951. Hearings,
          Part 1, 370 pp. (U.S. Congress, 81st, 2d Sess.)
(17) ———
    1961. DEPARTMENT OF AGRICULTURE APPROPRIATIONS FOR 1962. Hearings,
          Part 1, 868 pp. (U.S. Congress, 87th, 2d Sess.)
(18) UNITED STATES DEPARTMENT OF AGRICULTURE.
    1958. MANUAL OF PROCEDURES FOR COOPERATIVE REGIONAL RESEARCH.
          25 pp.
(19) WILSON, M. L.
    1936. THE ROLES OF THE UNITED STATES DEPARTMENT OF AGRICULTURE
          AND THE STATE EXPERIMENT STATIONS IN REGIONAL RESEARCH PRO-
          GRAMS. Assoc. Land-Grant Cols. and Univs. Proc. (1935) 49:
          170–177.
(20) YOUNG, HAROLD, Chairman.
    1957. EXPERIMENT STATION MARKETING RESEARCH AND ADVISORY COMMIT-
          TEE (ESMRAC). Assoc. Land-Grant Cols. and State Univs. Proc.
          (1957) 71 : 157–158.

Chapter Twelve—

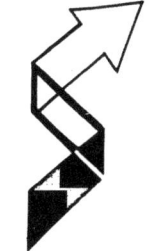

MOVING FORWARD:
The Stations as a Force for Progress

The American system of State Experiment Stations, dedicated to encouraging scientific initiative at research centers dispersed throughout the Nation, provides for the American people an enduring example of significant tax-supported research activity. The station administrators in each generation have successfully maintained the separate identity and the localized control of the station establishment. Moreover, they have repeatedly illustrated the soundness of the principle, first formulated in the Hatch Act of 1887, that local responsibility for research, financed in part by Federal authority but never dominated by that authority, economically and efficiently produces scientific dividends in a democratic society. Plurality and decentralization of organization and support of agricultural research have demonstrated their value and effectiveness, just as has our American system of divided and joint Federal and State responsibilities for so many other governmental activities.

The station movement has perennially prized the individual enterprise of its personnel and the autonomy of its member institutions. Simultaneously, however, it has participated prominently in building, with the collaboration of the Federal Department of Agriculture, a unique system of cooperation which has organized State and Federal funds, personnel, institutions, and resources of all types into the most comprehensive structure in the 20th century world for the continuous conduct of scientific research in agrculture. This pattern of cooperative activity, evolving steadily in a process of administrative adjustment to the needs of research, has sought to insure and to stimulate freedom of expression for scientific initiative and, at the same time, to combine with local individualism and responsibility the benefits of centralized coordination.

The nationwide network of State stations has demonstrated a time-tested capacity not only to serve the local and immediate interests of the people of each State but also to provide, via a continuous and systematic concentration on applied and basic research, scientific discoveries universally vital to human health and nutrition. The stations' record of outstanding accomplishments, which span the years from the discovery of the vitamin a half century ago to the discovery in recent years of streptomycin and dicoumarol, would fill the pages of a fascinating book. The American people would appreciate, could they know the story of the long-continued scientific productivity and the brilliant achievements which the illustrations in the present volume can only suggest, the continuing utility implicit in the station system for administering Federal grants to dispersed institutions. They would realize, furthermore, that research in agriculture via the sta-

207

tion system has contributed in the past—and will contribute in the years to come—benefits so pervasive in the American way of life that the title "Biological Experiment Stations" would aptly designate the preeminent function and mission of these scientific institutions in the 20th century. Similarly they would recognize the merit of a most important feature of station activity; namely, the specialized training of graduate student-apprentices who assist top-notch scientists on station projects in every State.

The American people should not overlook, as they face decision-making in the troubled years ahead, the values perennially present in the station system for administering scientific research, a system developed patiently and managed carefully for decades before tax-supported research in nonagricultural applications achieved spectacular victories in man's endless attempts to solve the mysteries of his physical environment. American legislatures, both State and Federal, have through the years sought to keep the stations securely financed and thus insured the efficient operation of a scientific enterprise which, pioneered in the 19th century and astutely developed for the public benefit in the 20th century, has demonstrated its permanent usefulness. The American public can view with justifiable pride the carefully built capacity of its nationwide system of agricultural research. If adequately administered in future years, this system should yield a broad and steady penetration into the biological sciences.

Does not the station movement reveal in the present day, furthermore, the instructive experience that governmental policy in other scientific areas could and should allocate Federal funds "to a wide number of [university-connected] institutions in a deliberate attempt to develop a geographically diversified research competence"? With these words President Eric A. Walker of the Pennsylvania State University stressed in November 1960 the current and many-faceted problem of the relation between the Federal Government and American universities in the sponsorship of scientific productivity. "In casting around for models on which to base these arrangements," he noted with perceptive concern, "we have almost completely overlooked the oldest active program of this sort in the country. Yet, ironically, it is probably the most successful of them all. I'm speaking here of the Federal support program for agricultural research." [1]

The champions of the experiment station movement, America's first major experience with the nationwide administration of tax-supported scientific research, have consistently contended from the earliest years that the tax-paying public, the Federal and State legislators, and the professional station personnel must assume a collective responsibility for the steady encouragement of research in agriculture. Always, however, the station leadership has insisted that station men themselves accept the prime obligation for directing the development of their numerous institutions in the public interest. This obligation has expected each director to stimulate scientific enterprise in his station and his State. This obligation has also expected, no less firmly, the encouragement of cooperative endeavor and voluntary joint action among station leaders in the various States in order that American station research, guarding itself against too great a dis-

---

[1] Walker, E. A., "Reorganization for Progress," 74th Annual Meeting, American Association of Land-Grant Colleges and State Universities. 8 pp. (Processed.) Washington. November 16, 1960.

persion of its energy, could develop with interstate cohesiveness despite the geographic dispersion of the research institutions.

STATIONS FACE CHALLENGES

The station movement in its century-long history has exhibited the vigor, the resourcefulness, and the independent individuality inherent in its democratic environment. No one in the western world would deny the importance of retaining these indigenous assets. The responsibilities of the coming years, however, require that the station men of the present generation build anew the *esprit de corps* characterizing the earlier years and, in addition, discipline themselves to a greater measure of group and cooperative activity. To achieve a balance between applied and basic research; to attract and recruit the finest talent as a working force; to maintain institutional strength and leadership; to take time, in the midst of daily pressures, to think and to plan: these realistic challenges confront the station directors in the dynamic world of today.

The perceptive wisdom of the Atwater-Johnson-Cook report applies as meaningfully in 1961 as it did in 1887. "The future usefulness of the stations will depend upon what they discover of permanent value," that trio of pioneer directors counseled, "and this must come largely from the most abstract and profound research." [2] This maxim could well stand as the station motto across the land. The administrators and the scientists of today can take pride in the origins of their stations and draw inspiration from the enduring traditions and high standards established by their predecessors in the public service.

As the anniversary year begins, we come to the close of a text that began in modest form in reply to a scientist's question: "How old is ESCOP?" Members of that important policy-making committee themselves couldn't answer. So they took action to gather, assemble, and interpret the facts for the record. Those of us who have been able to observe for some years the integrity and dedication to principle that prevails when ESCOP and the Directors of Experiment Stations meet—differing frequently relative to means, but after careful evaluation and debate always adhering devotedly to decisions reached—have faith in the future of the agricultural experiment stations. We know that great contributions will continue to come from them, as in the past. Even as this chapter ends, ESCOP is actively engaged in evaluating challenges that lie ahead. Progressive and forward looking action was taken during its annual meeting in November 1961. It presages better coordination and planning of cooperative research in the future, and continued close working relations with the Department of Agriculture.

For those youthful scientists embarking on a career in agricultural research and to all others seeking to understand how publicly supported research, under a dual Federal-State system, can be democratically administered in a republic made up of 50 States, the record presented above is worthy of careful study.

The strength of the cooperative State-Federal agricultural research system, built on the framework of free governments as conceived under the Bill of Rights, reflects the brilliance of those who created

---

[2] See Chapter 5, p. 65.

our political institutions. The great contributions contributed by the State Experiment Stations and the Department of Agriculture to scientific advancement and national progress reflect the highest quality of administrative decision making, intellectual democracy at its best.

PAST IS PROLOGUE

"What Is Past Is Prologue" are the words inscribed near the Pennsylvania Avenue entrance of the National Archives Building in Washington, D.C. To those engaged in agricultural research, both at the State experiment stations and in USDA, these words have a practical meaning.

Late in 1961 the Department of Agricultural Graduate School presented a Centennial Lecture Series, featuring five distinguished leaders, nationally recognized and each with some past practical experience in land-grant or USDA administration. The chairman of the series was Assistant Secretary of Agriculture Frank J. Welch, himself the former Dean of Agriculture and Director of the Agricultural Experiment Station, University of Kentucky.

Vernon Carstensen, historian and associate dean of the graduate school, University of Wisconsin, traced the modest beginnings of three items of legislation, recommended by Abraham Lincoln in his first annual message to Congress: [3]

There is nothing in this modest, almost tentative proposal to suggest that during the next year Congress would pass three acts of monumental importance to American agriculture. The Department of Agriculture was created, the Homestead Act was finally adopted, and the Morrill Act was passed providing public lands for the establishment of colleges of agriculture. All were adopted during the second year of the Civil War and, except for the Homestead Act, received very little notice. That was true then. It seems to be almost true today thanks to the ardent and aggressive 'celebration' of the centennial of the Civil War. . . .

Many men of George Washington's generation assumed the perfectability of man and society. Equally important was the companion idea that man not only could improve himself but ought to do so. Although much of the eager innocence of a century and a half ago has been dissipated by bitter experience, one has only to consider the assumptions underlying many of our public acts—our technical aid programs, our enormous expenditures for education and research—to realize that we continue to live in that faith.

Concerning the part of the agricultural experiment stations in subsequent administrative developments, Dr. Carstensen said:

The experiment station development with its close and intimate connection with the Department of Agriculture, represents a unique achievement as a national cooperative research establishment supported by State and Federal funds. It was important for the scientific investigations conducted; it was important for demonstrating the fruitfulness of collaborative research so brilliantly revealed in the cattle fever inquiries; and it was also important, in a much more subtle way, in providing the example of how organized research could be conducted.

---

[3] "Profile of the USDA—First Fifty Years" address by Vernon Carstensen. University of Wisconsin in the Centennial Lecture Series, Graduate School. in Thomas Jefferson Auditorium, USDA, Washington, D.C., October 25, 1961.

N.B.—This lecture and the other four in the series are available in processed form from the USDA Graduate School. They will be combined in a volume to be published by the USDA Graduate School. The remaining footnotes are from addresses given before the 75th Annual Meeting of the American Association of Land-Grant Colleges and Universities. These may be read in processed form and will be published in the Association Proceedings.

Another centennial series lecturer was Jesse W. Tapp, economist and vice president of California's Bank of America. The following are excerpts from what he said: [4]

The Hatch Act in 1887 established an Experiment Station for each Land Grant college and set up funds and guidelines for research designed to make farmers more efficient. In 1914 the Smith-Lever Act established the Federal-State Extension Service, thus completing the three-cornered program of teaching, research and extension by the Land Grant Colleges.

The establishment of the USDA and the Land Grant College system was an attempt to improve the opportunities for rural people. Prior to that time, only the relatively wealthy normally attended universities. The new program meant the opportunity for a college education would be available to just about everyone who wanted it and who was otherwise determined to get it. Furthermore, it elevated the study of agriculture and the mechanical arts to the university level.

Although in actual dollars it doesn't bulk very large, relative to the cost of other factors, the most significant inputs that were made in American agriculture, I believe, are those spent in the establishment of the U.S. Department of Agriculture and the Land Grant College System, and their subsequent programs of research and education. In few, if any, other ventures has the marginal productivity of capital been so great.

In the same series Hon. Henry A. Wallace, Secretary of Agriculture from 1932 to 1940, and subsequently Vice President of the United States said: [5]

We cannot turn our backs on science or on world hunger. When I was Secretary many people suggested that we should greatly curtail or halt altogether our scientific research programs because they contributed to the surplus problem. Since I left the Department in 1940, farm workers have been increasing their efficiency at the rate of 4.6 percent a year. One farm worker today can support 26 people. In 1940 one farm worker could support only 11 people. . . .

We should be proud of our ever expanding agricultural technology. Properly used, our technology and our surpluses represent national strength, not weakness. Only in agriculture is it definitely certain that we shall remain superior to the rest of the world for many years to come. Food and our technological skills properly used can help the crowded hungry lands into a position to help themselves.

From among the Land-Grant College Presidents of 1961, President James H. Hilton of Iowa State University, Ames, Iowa, a former director of the North Carolina Experiment Station, voiced the following challenges: [6]

In a world in which great masses of men are still lacking the bare necessities for existence itself, in a world in which a growing population is pressing ever harder on existing resources, the Land-Grant college must continue to carry on research which will increase the world's capacity to produce more food, more clothing, more shelter, more of the things that make life comfortable.

But our research task can no longer end there. The Land-Grant colleges can no longer see their major research function as solely that of discovering the means for more abundant production of either manufactured or agricultural goods. Nor can we assume that our *only* research task today is to make scientific and technological discoveries which will "put us ahead" in the nuclear and space fields as vital as these needs may be in the times in which we live.

---

[4] "Contributions of Agriculture to Our Economy", address by Jesse W. Tapp, Bank of America, given in the Centennial Lecture Series, Graduate School, Thomas Jefferson Auditorium, USDA, Washington, D.C., October 11, 1961.

[5] "The Department as I Have Known It" address given by Henry A. Wallace in the Centennial Lecture Series, Graduate School, Thomas Jefferson Auditorium, USDA, Washington, D.C., November 1, 1961.

[6] "The Land-Grant College: Past and Present," address by President James H. Hilton, Iowa State University, in the Centennial Lecture Series, USDA Graduate School, given in the Jefferson Auditorium, USDA, Washington, D.C., October 18, 1961.

Today, the Land-Grant colleges, in their programs of research, must *also* deal with the complex problems of economic and social adjustments, which are so important to men's welfare and survival. Increasingly, the orientation of our research must be more around people and their welfare. . . .

One of the first needs in organizing a research program which deals with economic and social problems will be—as it has been in the physical and biological sciences—to find a fruitful balance between basic and applied research. In all of our research areas—both old and new—we must withstand the pressures to put too large a share of our resources into applied research. We all know that our applied research projects which have produced immediate, concrete rewards, have drawn their information from the well of basic research. We all know that if our applied research is to continue to be productive and rewarding, we cannot allow the well of basic research to run dry. Fortunately, so many of the recent great "useful" and "practical" scientific discoveries, such as atomic energy, have been so directly the result of the basic research of so-called impractical "theorists" that today the value of basic research is being more widely recognized and materially supported.

Second, we must recognize the restrictions which limitations in budget, trained personnel, and research facilities place upon the scope and types of research projects undertaken. Although we must work toward building research organizations which will fill all of our new research needs, such a retooling process takes time. In the meantime, we should carefully confine our efforts to only those projects which can be adequately carried through. Our limited research energies should not be dissipated and wasted in diverse and scattered undertakings.

Third, many of the new problems which are troubling Americans today are a combination of socio-political and economic factors. The complex which in real life does not break down neatly into problems which are either scientific, economic, sociological, or political. The difficulties which confront farm and urban families are no respectors of academic disciplines. And their solution will often require the special knowledge and competence of a variety of disciplines. . . .

Fourth, we must recognize that we cannot stop at the State line in our investigations of economic and social problems. Such problems do not recognize state boundaries.

A direct challenge came from Secretary of Agriculture Orville L. Freeman [7] after he had given full credit to the Department and the agricultural experiment stations for their accomplishments, but had also pointed out that all problems confronting agriculture in 1961 must be presented in terms of the scientific and technological revolution that dominates the age. His challenge came in the following excerpts:

The magnitude of the potential effect of this revolution upon our lives and our future is so great that the impact of previous great historical developments, such as the industrial revolution, fade into relative insignificance. . . .

Science has shown us that we can produce more abundantly than we can consume (in both commercial channels and by special programs to provide food where it is needed) but social science has not yet shown us how to engineer this efficient productivity to benefit the producer.

Technological advance has decreed that a constantly dwindling number of farmers, on fewer acres, but with greater investment of such inputs as machinery and fertilizer, can continue to increase total production; but we have not yet determined how to make the best use of those excess acres, nor have we developed programs for maximum benefit of the human beings whose labor is no longer needed by this efficient agriculture.

We can and must fined the answers to these questions—and without delay. We can do it by devoting to these problems the same kind of talent, ability, study and research that we have given to problems of increased production.

I submit that this presents a major challenge to our land grant colleges, to our experiment stations, to our Extension Service, and to the Department of Agriculture. It presents a challenge that some would prefer to avoid because it

---

[7] "Agriculture Today and Tomorrow", address by Orville L. Freeman, Secretary of Agriculture, given on October 4, 1961, in the Centennial Lecture Series, Graduate School in the Thomas Jefferson Auditorium, USDA, Washington, D.C.

involves controversial matters, because it relates to the formulation of public policy, because it deals with matters that cannot be proved or disproved by chemical analysis or controlled experiments.

But I submit that we cannot avoid this challenge. We cannot avoid it, simply because it deals with the welfare of human beings, with the future of our resources and our children, with principles and ideals relating to human dignity, and with values we regard as vitally important.

SECOND CENTURY BEGINS

The historical centennial conference of the American Association of Land-Grant Colleges was held at Kansas City, Mo., November 12 to 16, 1961. In the traditional spirit of the Land-Grant institutions, while full tribute was given to the founders and contributions of the past, the emphasis was on the forward look, the problems, the challenges of the century of land-grantism that lies ahead. A new constitution was adopted and with it a new name, effective January 1, 1962, "Association of State Universities and Land-Grant Colleges."

Probably the most historic contribution of the 75th annual (centennial) convention was the honest soul-searching each division did. A grant from the Carnegie Foundation had enabled some carefully planned self-evaluation as the new century begins—where we are, the problems we face, the direction to be taken in order to advance the basic functions of land-grant leadership—efficacy of learning by the many and advancement of knowledge and search for truth.

The evaluation session in the Division of Agriculture was held under the chairmanship of R. D. Lewis, Director of the Texas Agricultural Experiment Station. The Division of Agriculture heard from its two principal evaluators, J. Earl Coke, Vice President of the Bank of America, a former Assistant Secretary of Agriculture and before that Director of Extension Work in California; and Paul A. Miller, Provost of Michigan State University and President-designate of the University of West Virginia at the time he presented his paper. While they had received assistance from persons all over the United States in the preparation and documentation of their papers, the two evaluators took full responsibility for the conclusions drawn and the recommendations made.

The papers reflected considerable thought and study. They revealed tremendous accomplishments in the century that has passed. They also recognized great challenges that must be faced if the agricultural colleges, experiment stations, and extension services are to continue influencing national progress as in the past. Mr. Coke [8] underlined the fact that the consumer is the long-run beneficiary of agricultural research. He accepted that the change from rural to urban life has taken place and that the "comfortable past" has been blown to bits by the technological revolution. He recommended revisions in college curricula, with greater emphasis on basic understanding of finance, management, and organization in undergraduate studies plus better communications training in all levels of study. Dr. Miller [9] pointed

---

[8] "Evaluation of Agriculture in the Land-Grant Universities." Address by J. Earl Coke, Vice President, Bank of America, before the Division of Agriculture, American Association of Land-Grant Colleges and State Universities, Kansas City, Mo., November 14, 1961.
[9] "The Agricultural Colleges of the United States—Paradoxical Servants of Change." Address by Paul A. Miller, Provost, Michigan State University, before

to the National design of the Land-Grant Colleges in terms of response to a national purpose, the organizational linkage with the people the land-grant institution serves. A problem of first concern seen by Dr. Miller was how to express the technology of agriculture in the organization of the colleges. Although the commodity departments are in the right direction, he reasoned, the colleges may wish to consider two sets of vantage points from which to give leadership, preparation to serve technological needs in agriculture along with preparation to serve society's needs with the fruits of agricultural technology.

Following the two evaluations, each section of the Division—residence instruction, experiment stations, and extension—discussed the evaluations made. Associate Director W. E. Krauss of the Ohio Experiment Station spoke for the Experiment Station Section. Following are excerpts from Dr. Krauss' comments: [10]

Research is the process of critical inquiry or examination in seeking facts or principles. It may be extremely simple, as in a study of existing documents, or extremely complicated as in the case of building an atomic pile based upon complex formulae of mathematics, physics and chemistry. It may be "basic" or "applied" or "developmental", or a combination, as is usually the case; it may be superficial or profound. Agricultural research has all these elements but may be distinctive in that historically some reason for doing it must be apparent. . . .

. . . both depth and breadth of the research effort will vary from year to year and from state to state. We should not be guilty of looking down at applied research, for this must definitely be an important part of a Land-grant institution's research effort if it is to fulfill its obligation to serve the needs of people. Neither do we need to avoid production research that results in greater production efficiency and higher quality in terms of consumer needs and consumer demands. . . .

The flow of research results directly into scientific channels affords a communications problem in itself. The scientific literature has become so voluminous as to defy keeping up to date in one's reading of the literature even in a highly specialized field. Some study is being given to this problem but greater consideration needs to be given to development of improved library services and central storehouses of scientific data from which references and abstracts in any language in any given field may quickly be assembled on request. This is a need of the scientist that will demand the best in communications research to solve. . . .

Successful launching of satellites and the knowledge that this is only the forerunner of an era of almost infinite dimension, practically guarantees support with public funds for research, and development of research personnel, in those areas directly related to defense and war. This is covered under the now familiar phrase "scientists for basic research". While at first emphasis may need to be on those basic sciences and technological developments that make for destruction it is inevitable that other scientific needs will be met and even ultimately benefit from a "crash research program" in missiles and space travel. It must never be forgotten that the secret of life and the secret of manufacture of food nutrients by plants have not been solved and that since all biological activities are related to these two basic processes there is as much need for encouragement of research in life-building and life-preservation as there is in life-destruction even as a defensive mechanism.

The proceedings for the above Centennial session of the Division of Agriculture on November 14, 1961 merit careful reading. The following *Postscript on the Future*, ending Dr. Miller's presentation before the Division of Agriculture, sums up the challenges facing the

the Agricultural Division, American Association of Land-Grant Colleges and State Universities, Kansas City, Mo., November 14, 1961.

[10] "Evaluation of the Division of Agriculture—Experiment Station Point of View"—Remarks by W. E. Krauss, Associate Director, Ohio Agricultural Experiment Station, Wooster, Ohio, November 14, 1961.

agricultural colleges and experiment stations as 1961 comes to a close
and as the Centennial year 1962 is about to begin :

Every land-grant college leader must search his heart and mind today as to
whether or not the agricultural colleges have received the message of great
excitement and adventure which the world community now sends out to them.
And he must be asked if he is confident that the colleges are making their way
between one world that is dead or dying and another which is as yet unborn.
And collectively, are we as sure as we ought to be that the colleges' finest
chapters are ahead and are we stoutly free of cringing at the occasional claim
that these chapters may be behind us? Are we willing to serve faithfully the
states and counties about us but intellectually encircle our hopes with national
and international needs?   And are we as determined as we ought to be that our
choices for the future will be as sufficient as they were in the past?

.

APPENDIX

Basic Legislation Authorizing Establishment of and Federal Grant Payments to Agricultural Experiment Stations

Act of 1862 Donating Lands for Colleges of Agriculture and Mechanic Arts

[First Morrill Act]

AN ACT Donating public lands to the several States and Territories which may provide colleges for the benefit of agriculture and the mechanic arts

Be it enacted by the Senate and House of Representatives of the United States of America in Congress assembled, That there be granted to the several States, for the purposes hereinafter mentioned, an amount of public land, to be apportioned to each State a quantity equal to thirty thousand acres for each Senator and Representative in Congress to which the States are respectively entitled by the apportionment under the census of eighteen hundred and sixty; *Provided,* That no mineral lands shall be selected or purchased under the provisions of this act.

SEC. 2. *And be it further enacted,* That the land aforesaid, after being surveyed, shall be apportioned to the several States in sections or subdivisions of sections, not less than one-quarter of a section; and whenever there are public lands in a State subject to sale at private entry at one dollar and twenty-five cents per acre, the quantity to which said State shall be entitled shall be selected from such lands within the limits of such State, and the Secretary of the Interior is hereby directed to issue to each of the States in which there is not the quantity of public lands subject to sale at private entry at one dollar and twenty-five cents per acre, to which said State may be entitled under the provisions of this act, land scrip to the amount in acres for the deficiency of its distributive share: said scrip to be sold by said States and the proceeds thereof applied to the uses and purposes prescribed in this act, and for no other use or purpose whatsoever: *Provided,* That in no case shall any State to which land scrip may thus be issued be allowed to locate the same within the limits of any other State, or of any Territory of the United States, but their assignees may thus locate said land scrip upon any of the unappropriated lands of the United States subject to sale at private entry at one dollar and twenty-five cents, or less, per acre: *And provided, further,* That not more than one million acres shall be located by such assignees in any one of the States: *And provided, further,* That no such location shall be made before one year from the passage of this act.

SEC. 3. *And be it further enacted,* That all expenses of management, superintendence, and taxes from date of selection of said lands, previous to their sales, and all expenses incurred in the management and disbursement of the moneys which may be received therefrom, shall be paid by the States to which they may belong, out of the treasury of said States, so that the entire proceeds of the sale of said lands shall be applied without any diminution whatever to the purposes hereinafter mentioned.

SEC. 4 [original]. *And be it further enacted,* That all moneys derived from the sale of the lands aforesaid by the States to which the lands are apportioned, and from the sales of land scrip hereinbefore provided for, shall be invested in stocks of the United States, or of the States, or some other safe stocks, yielding not less than five per centum upon the par value of said stocks; and that the moneys so invested shall constitute a perpetual fund, the capital of which shall remain forever undiminished, (except so far as may be provided in section fifth of this act,) and the interest of which shall be inviolably appropriated, by each State which may take and claim the benefit of this act, to the endowment, sup-

217

port, and maintenance of at least one college where the leading object shall be, without excluding other scientific and classical studies, and including military tactics, to teach such branches of learning as are related to agriculture and the mechanic arts, in such manner as the legislatures of the States may respectively prescribe, in order to promote the liberal and practical education of the industrial classes in the several pursuits and professions in life.

SEC. 4 [as amended March 3, 1883]. That all moneys derived from the sale of lands aforesaid by the States to which lands are apportioned, and from the sales of lands scrip hereinbefore provided for, shall be invested in stocks of the United States or of the States, or the same may be invested by the States having no State stocks, in any other manner after the legislatures of such States shall have assented thereto, and engaged that such funds shall yield not less than five per centum upon the amount so invested and that the principal thereof shall forever remain unimpaired: *Provided*, That the moneys so invested or loaned shall constitute a perpetual fund, the capital of which shall remain forever undiminished (except so far as may be provided in section five of this act), and the interest of which shall be inviolably appropriated, by each State which may take and claim the benefit of this act, to the endowment, support, and maintenance of at least one college where the leading objects shall be, without excluding other scientific and classical studies, and including military tactics, to teach such branches of learning as are related to agriculture and the mechanic arts, in such manner as the legislatures of the States may respectively prescribe, in order to promote the liberal and practical education of the industrial classes in the several pursuits and professions in life.

SEC. 4. [as amended April 13, 1926]. That all moneys derived from the sale of lands aforesaid by the States to which lands are apportioned and from the sales of land scrip hereinbefore provided for shall be invested in bonds of the United States or of the States or some other safe bonds; or the same may be invested by the States having no State bonds in any manner after the legislatures of such States shall have assented thereto and engaged that such funds shall yield a fair and reasonable rate of return, to be fixed by the State legislatures, and that the principal thereof shall forever remain unimpaired: *Provided*, That the moneys so invested or loaned shall constitute a perpetual fund, the capital of which shall remain forever undiminished (except so far as may be provided in section 5 of this Act), and the interest of which shall be inviolably appropriated, by each State which may take and claim the benefit of this Act, to the endowment, support, and maintenance of at least one college where the leading object shall be, without excluding other scientific and classical studies and including military tactics, to teach such branches of learning as are related to agriculture and the mechanic arts, in such manner as the legislatures of the States may respectively prescribe, in order to promote the liberal and practical education of the industrial classes in the several pursuits and professions in life.

SEC. 5. *And be it further enacted*, That the grant of land and land scrip hereby authorized shall be made on the following conditions, to which, as well as to the provisions hereinbefore contained, the previous assent of the several States shall be signified by legislative acts:

First. If any portion of the fund invested, as provided by the foregoing section, or any portion of the interest thereon, shall, by any action or contingency, be diminished or lost, it shall be replaced by the State to which it belongs, so that the capital of the fund shall remain forever undiminished; and the annual interest shall be regularly applied without diminution to the purposes mentioned in the fourth section of this act, except that a sum, not exceeding ten per centum upon the amount received by any State under the provisions of this act, may be expended for the purchase of lands for sites or experimental farms, whenever authorized by the respective legislatures of said States.

Second. No portion of said fund, nor the interest thereon, shall be applied, directly or indirectly, under any pretense whatever, to the purchase, erection, preservation, or repair of any building or buildings.

Third. Any State which may take and claim the benefit of the provisions of this act shall provide, within five years, at least not less than one college, as described in the fourth section of this act, or the grant to such State shall cease; and said State shall be bound to pay the United States the amount received of any lands previously sold, and that the title to purchasers under the State shall be valid.

Fourth. An annual report shall be made regarding the progress of each college, recording any improvements and experiments made, with their cost and results, and such other matters, including State industrial and economical statistics, as may be supposed useful; one copy of which shall be transmitted by mail free, by each, to all the other colleges which may be endowed under the provisions of this act, and also one copy to the Secretary of the Interior.

Fifth. When lands shall be selected from those which have been raised to double the minimum price, in consequence of railroad grants, they shall be computed to the States at the maximum price, and the number of acres proportionately diminished.

Sixth. No State while in a condition of rebellion or insurrection against the Government of the United States shall be entitled to the benefit of this act.

Seventh. No State shall be entitled to the benefits of this act unless it shall express its acceptance thereof by its legislature within two years from the date of its approval by the President.

SEC. 6. *And be it further enacted*, That land scrip issued under the provisions of this act shall not be subject to location until after the first day of January, one thousand eight haundred and sixty-three.

SEC. 7. *And be it further enacted*, That the land officers shall receive the same fees for locating land scrip issued under the provisions of this act as is now allowed for the location of military bounty land warrants under existing laws; *Provided*, That their maximum compensation shall not be thereby increased.

SEC. 8. *And be it further enacted*, That the governors of the several States to which scrip shall be issued under this act shall be required to report annually to Congress all sales made of such scrip until the whole shall be disposed of, the amount received for the same, and what appropriation has been made of the proceeds.

Approved July 2, 1862 (12 Stat. 503).

Act of 1887 Establishing Agricultural Experiment Stations

[Hatch Act]

AN ACT To establish agricultural experiment stations in connection with the colleges established in the several States under the provisions of an act approved July second, eighteen hundred and sixty-two, and of the acts supplementary thereto

Be it enacted by the Senate and House of Representatives of the United States of America in Congress assembled, That in order to aid in acquiring and diffusing among the people of the United States useful and practical information on subjects connected with agriculture, and to promote scientific investigation and experiment respecting the principles and applications of agricultural science, there shall be established, under direction of the college or colleges or agricultural department of colleges in each State or Territory established, or which may hereafter be established, in accordance with the provisions of an act approved July second, eighteen hundred and sixty-two, entitled "An act donating public lands to the several States and Territories which may provide colleges for the benefit of agriculture and the mechanic arts," or any of the supplements to said act, a department to be known and designed as an "agricultural experiment station": *Provided*, That in any State or Territory in which two such colleges have been or may be so established the appropriation hereinafter made to such State or Territory shall be equally divided between such colleges, unless the legislature of such State or Territory shall otherwise direct.

SEC. 2. That it shall be the object and duty of said experiment stations to conduct original researches or verify experiments on the physiology of plants and animals; the diseases to which they are severally subject, with the remedies for the same; the chemical composition of useful plants at their different stages of growth; the comparative advantages of rotative cropping as pursued under a varying series of crops; the capacity of new plants or trees for acclimation; the analysis of soils and water; the chemical composition of manures, natural or artificial, with experiments designed to test their comparative effects on crops of different kinds; the adaptation and value of grasses and forage plants; the composition and digestibility of the different kinds of food for domestic animals; the scientific and economic questions involved in the production of butter and cheese; and such other researches or experiments bearing directly on the agricultural industry of the United States as may in each case be deemed advisable, having due regard to the varying conditions and needs of the respective States or Territories.

SEC. 3. That in order to secure, as far as practicable, uniformity of methods and results in the work of said stations, it shall be the duty of the United States Commissioner [now Secretary] of Agriculture to furnish forms, as far as practicable, for the tabulation of results of investigation or experiments; to indicate from time to time such lines of inquiry as to him shall seem most important, and, in general, to furnish such advice and assistance as will best promote the purpose of this act. It shall be the duty of each of said stations annually, on or before the first day of February, to make to the governor of the State or Territory in which it is located a full and detailed report of its operations, including a statement of receipts and expenditures, a copy of which report shal' be sent to each of said stations, to the said Commissioner [now Secretary] ot Agriculture, and to the Secretary of the Treasury of the United States.

SEC. 4. That bulletins or reports of progress shall be published at said stations at least once in three months, one copy of which shall be sent to each newspaper in the States or Territories in which they are respectively located, and to such individuals actually engaged in farming as may request the same, and as far as the means of the station will permit. Such bulletins or reports and the annual reports of said stations shall be transmitted in the mails of the United States free of charge for postage, under such regulations as the Postmater General may from time to time prescribe.

SEC. 5. That for the purpose of paying the necessary expenses of conducting investigations and experiments and printing and distributing the results as hereinbefore prescribed, the sum of fifteen thousand dollars per annum is hereby appropriated to each State, to be specially provided for by Congress in the appropriations from year to year, and to each Territory entitled under the provisions of section eight of this act, out of any money in the Treasury proceeding from the sales of public lands, to be paid in equal quarterly payments on the first day of January, April, July, and October in each year, to the treasurer or other officer duly appointed by the governing boards of said colleges to receive the same, the first payment to be made on the first day of October, eighteen hundred and eighty-seven: *Provided, however*, That of the first annual appropriation so received by any station an amount not exceeding one-fifth may be expended in the erection, enlargement, or repair of a building or buildings necessary for carrying on the work of such station; and thereafter an amount not exceeding five per centum of such annual appropriation may be so expended.

SEC. 6. That whenever it shall appear to the Secretary of the Treasury from the annual statement of receipts and expenditures of any of said stations that a portion of the preceding annual appropriations remains unexpended, such amount shall be deducted from the next succeeding annual appropriation to such station, in order that the amount of money appropriated to any station shall not exceed the amount actually and necessarily required for its maintenance and support.

SEC. 7. That nothing in this act shall be construed to impair or modify the legal relation existing between any of the said colleges and the government of the States or Territories in which they are respectively located.

SEC. 8. That in States having colleges entitled under this section to the benefits of this act and having also agricultural experiment stations established by law separate from said colleges, such States shall be authorized to apply such benefits to experiments at stations so established by such States; and in case any State shall have established under the provisions of said act of July second aforesaid, an agricultural department or experiment station, in connection with any university, college, or institution not distinctively an agricultural college or school, and such State shall have established or shall hereafter establish a separate agricultural college or school, which shall have connected therewith an experimental farm or station, the legislature of such State may apply in whole or in part the appropriation by this act made, to such separate agricultural college, or school, and no legislature shall by contract, express or implied, disable itself from so doing.

SEC. 9. That the grants of moneys authorized by this act are made subject to the legislative assent of the several States and Territories to the purposes of said grants: *Provided*, That payment of such installments of the appropriation herein made as shall become due to any State before the adjournment of the regular session of its legislature meeting next after the passage of this act shall be made upon the assent of the governor thereof duly certified to the Secretary of the Treasury.

SEC. 10. Nothing in this act shall be held or construed as binding the United States to continue any payments from the Treasury to any or all the States or institutions mentioned in this act, but Congress may at any time amend, suspend, or repeal any or all the provisions of this act.

Approved March 2, 1887 (24 Stat. 440).

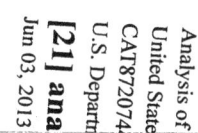
Act of 1906 for the Further Endowment of Agricultural Experiment Stations

[Adams Act]

AN ACT To provide for an increased annual appropriation for agricultural experiment stations and regulating the expenditure thereof

Be it enacted by the Senate and House of Representatives of the United States of America in Congress assembled, That there shall be, and hereby is, annually appropriated, out of any money in the Treasury not otherwise appropriated, to be paid as hereinafter provided, to each State and Territory, for the more complete endowment and maintenance of agricultural experiment stations now established or which may hereafter be established in accordance with the act of Congress approved March second, eighteen hundred and eighty-seven, the sum of five thousand dollars in addition to the sum named in said act for the year ending June thirtieth, nineteen hundred and six, and an annual increase of the amount of such appropriation thereafter for five years by an additional sum of two thousand dollars over the preceding year, and the annual amount to be paid thereafter to each State and Territory shall be thirty thousand dollars, to be applied only to paying the necessary expenses of conducting original researches or experiments bearing directly on the agricultural industry of the United States, having due regard to the varying conditions and needs of the respective States or Territories.

SEC. 2. That the sums hereby appropriated to the States and Territories for the further endowment and support of agricultural experiment stations shall be annually paid in equal quarterly payments on the first day of January, April, July, and October of each year by the Secretary of the Treasury upon the warrant of the Secretary of Agriculture, out of the Treasury of the United States, to the treasurer or other officer duly appointed by the governing boards of said experiment stations to receive the same, and such officers shall be required to report to the Secretary of Agriculture on or before the first day of September of each year a detailed statement of the amount so received and of its disbursements, on schedules prescribed by the Secretary of Agriculture. The grants of money authorized by this act are made subject to legislative assent of the several States and Territories to the purpose of said grants: *Provided,* That payment of such installments of the appropriation herein made as shall become due to any State or Territory before the adjournment of the regular session of legislature meeting next after the passage of this act shall be made upon the assent of the governor thereof, duly certified by the Secretary of the Treasury.

SEC. 3. That if any portion of the moneys received by the designated officer of any State or Territory for the further and more complete endowment, support, and maintenance of agricultural experiment stations as provided in this act shall by any action or contingency be diminished or lost or be misapplied, it shall be replaced by said State or Territory to which it belongs, and until so replaced no subsequent appropriation shall be apportioned or paid to such State or Territory; and no portion of said moneys exceeding five per centum of each annual appropriation shall be applied, directly or indirectly, under any pretense whatever, to the purchase, erection, preservation, or repair of any building or buildings, or to the purchase or rental of land. It shall be the duty of each of said stations annually, on or before the first day of February, to make to the governor of the State or Territory in which it is located a full and detailed report of its operations, including a statement of receipts and expenditures, a copy of which report shall be sent to each of said stations to the Secretary of Agriculture, and to the Secretary of the Treasury of the United States.

SEC. 4. That on or before the first day of July in each year after the passage of this act the Secretary of Agriculture shall ascertain and certify to the Secretary of the Treasury as to each State and Territory whether it is complying with the provisions of this act and is entitled to receive its share of the annual appropriation for agricultural experiment stations under this act and the amount which thereupon each is entitled, respectively, to receive. If the Secretary of Agriculture shall withhold a certificate from any State or Territory of its appropriation, the facts and reasons therefore shall be reported to the President, and the amount involved shall be kept separate in the Treasury until the close of the next Congress, in order that the State or Territory may, if it shall so desire, appeal to Congress from the determination of the Secretary of Agriculture. If the next Congress shall not direct such sum to be paid, it shall be covered into the Treasury; and the Secretary of Agriculture is thereby charged with the proper administration of this law.

SEC. 5. That the Secretary of Agriculture shall make an annual report to Congress on the receipts and expenditures and work of the agricultural experiment stations in all of the States and Territories, and also whether the appropriation of any State or Territory has been withheld; and if so, the reason therefor.

SEC. 6. That Congress may at any time amend, suspend, or repeal any or all of the provisions of this act.

Approved March 16, 1906 (34 Stat. 63).

(Section 1 of the Adams Act was clarified and construed to limit the annual appropriation under the act to $15,000 for each State and Territory in the act making appropriations for the United States Department of Agriculture for the fiscal year ended June 30, 1907 (34 Stat. 669, 696).)

Act of 1925 for the More Complete Endowment of the Agricultural Experiment Stations

[Purnell Act]

AN ACT To authorize the more complete endowment of agricultural experiment stations, and for other purposes

Be it enacted by the Senate and House of Representatives of the United States of America in 'Congress assembled, That for the more complete endowment and maintenance of agricultural experiment stations now established, or which may hereafter be established, in accordance with the act of Congress approved March 2, 1887, there is hereby authorized to be appropriated, in addition to the amounts now received by such agricultural experiment stations, the sum of $20,000 for the fiscal year ending June 30, 1926; $30,000 for the fiscal year ending June 30, 1927; $40,000 for the fiscal year ending June 30, 1928; $50,000 for the fiscal year ending June 30, 1929; $60,000 for the fiscal year ending June 30, 1930; and $60,000 for each fiscal year thereafter, to be paid to each State and Territory; and the Secretary of Agriculture shall include the additional sums above authorized to be appropriated in the annual estimates of the Department of Agriculture, or in a separate estimate, as he may deem best. The funds appropriated pursuant to this act shall be applied only to paying the necessary expenses of conducting investigations or making experiments bearing directly on the production, manufacture, preparation, use, distribution, and marketing of agricultural products and including such scientific researches as have for their purpose the establishment and maintenance of a permanent and efficient agricultural industry, and such economic and sociological investigations as have for their purpose the development and improvement of the rural home and rural life, and for printing and disseminating the results of said researches.

SEC. 2. That the sums hereby authorized to be appropriated to the States and Territories for the further endowment and support of agricultural experiment stations shall be annually paid in equal quarterly payments on the 1st day of January, April, July, and October of each year by the Secretary of the Treasury upon a warrant of the Secretary of Agriculture out of the Treasury of the United States, to the treasurer or other officer duly appointed by the governing boards of such agricultural experiment stations to receive the same and such officers shall be required to report to the Secretary of Agriculture on or before the 1st day of September of each year a detailed statement of the amount so received and of its disbursement on schedules prescribed by the Secretary of Agriculture. The grants of money authorized by this act are made subject to legislative assent of the several States and Territories to the purpose of said grants: *Provided,* That payment of such installments of the appropriation herein authorized to be made as shall become due to any State or Territory before the adjournment of the regular session of the legislature meeting next after the passage of this act shall be made upon the assent of the governor thereof duly certified to the Secretary of the Treasury.

SEC. 3. That if any portion of the moneys received by the designated officer of any State or Territory for the further and more complete endowment, support, and maintenance of agricultural experiment stations as provided in this act shall by any action or contingency be diminished or lost or be misapplied, it shall be replaced by said State or Territory to which it belongs and until so replaced no subsequent appropriation shall be apportioned or paid to such State or Territory, and no portion of said moneys exceeding 10 per centum of each annual appropriation shall be applied directly or indirectly, under any pretense whatever, to the purchase, erection, preservation, or repair of any building or buildings or to the purchase or rental of land. It shall be the duty of each of the said stations annually, on or before the 1st day of February, to make to the governor of the State or Territory in which it is located a full and detailed report of its operations, including a statement of receipts and expenditures for the fiscal year next preceding, a copy of which report shall be sent to each of the said stations and the Secretary of Agriculture and to the Secretary of the Treasury of the United States.

SEC. 4. That on or before the 1st day of July in each year after the passage of this act the Secretary of Agriculture shall ascertain and certify to the Secretary of the Treasury as to each State and Territory whether it is complying with the provisions of this act and is entitled to receive its share of the annual appropriations for agricultural experiment stations under this act and the amount which thereupon each is entitled, respectively, to receive. If the Secretary of Agriculture shall withhold from any State or Territory a certificate of its appropriation, the facts and reasons therefor shall be reported to the President and the amount involved shall be kept separate in the Treasury until the close of the next Congress in order that the State or Territory may, if it shall so desire, appeal to Congress from the determination of the Secretary of Agriculture. If the next Congress shall not direct such sum to be paid, it shall be covered into the Treasury. The Secretary of Agriculture is hereby charged with the proper administration of this law.

SEC. 5. That the Secretary of Agriculture shall make an annual report to Congress on the receipts and expenditures and work of the agricultural experiment stations in all of the States and Territories, and also whether the appropriation of any State or Territory has been withheld; and if so, the reason therefor.

SEC. 6. That Congress may at any time amend, suspend, or repeal any and all of the provisions of this act.

Approved February 24, 1925 (43 Stat. 970).

Act of 1935 Providing for Agricultural Research and More Complete Endowment and Support of Land-Grant Colleges

[Bankhead-Jones Act]

AN ACT ᵀTo provide for research into basic laws and principles relating to agriculture and to provide for the further development of cooperative agricultural extension work and the more complete endowment and support of land-grant colleges

Be it enacted by the Senate and House of Representatives of the United States of America in Congress assembled,

TITLE I

SECTION 1.[1] The Secretary of Agriculture is authorized and directed to conduct research into laws and principles underlying basic problems of agriculture in its broadest aspects; research relating to the improvement of the quality of, and the development of new and improved methods of production of, distribution of, and new and extended uses and markets for, agricultural commodities and byproducts and manufactures thereof; and research relating to the conservation, development, and use of land and water resources for agricultural purposes. Research authorized under this section shall be in addition to research provided for under existing law (but both activities shall be coordinated so far as practicable) and shall be conducted by such agencies of the Department of Agriculture as the Secretary may designate or establish.

SEC. 2. The Secretary is also authorized and directed to encourage research similar to that authorized under section 1 to be conducted by agricultural experiment stations established or which may hereafter be established in pursuance of the act of March 2, 1887, providing for experiment stations, as amended and supplemented, by the allotment and payment as provided in section 5 to Puerto Rico and the States and Territories for the use of such experiment stations of sums appropriated therefor pursuant to this title.

SEC. 3. For the purposes of this title there is authorized to be appropriated, out of any money in the Treasury not otherwise appropriated, the sum of $1,000,000 for the fiscal year beginning after the date of the enactment of this title, and for each of the four fiscal years thereafter $1,000,000 more than the amount authorized for the preceding fiscal year, and $5,000,000 for each fiscal year thereafter. Moneys appropriated in pursuance of this title shall also be available for the purchase and rental of land and the construction of buildings

---

[1] Amended by Act of August 14, 1946.

necessary for conducting research provided for in this title, for the equipment and maintenance of such buildings, and for printing and disseminating the results of research. Sums appropriated in pursuance of this title shall be in addition to, and not in substitution for, appropriations for research or other activities of the Department of Agriculture and sums appropriated or otherwise made available for agricultural experiment stations.

Sec. 4. Forty per centum of the sums appropriated for any fiscal year under section 3 shall be available for the purposes of section 1: *Provided*, That not to exceed 2 per centum of the sums appropriated may be used for the administration of section 5 of this title. The sums available for the purposes of sec₁ion 1 shall be designated as the "Special research fund, Department of Agriculture," and no part of such special fund shall be used for the prosecution of research heretofore instituted or for the prosecution of any new research project except upon approval in writing by the Secretary. One-half of such special research fund shall be used by the Secretary for the establishment and maintenance of research laboratories and facilities in the major agricultural regions at places selected by him and for the prosecution, in accordance with section 1, of research at such laboratories.

Sec. 5.[2] (a) Sixty per centum of the sums appropriated for any fiscal year under section 3 shall be available for the purposes of section 2. The Secretary shall allot, for each fiscal year for which an appropriation is made, to Puerto Rico and each State and Territory an amount which bears the same ratio to the total amount to be allotted as the rural population of Puerto Rico or the State or Territory bears to the rural population of Puerto Rico and all the States and Territories as determined by the last preceding decennial census. No allotment and no payment under any allotment shall be made for any fiscal year in excess of the amount which Puerto Rico or the State or Territory makes available for such fiscal year out of its own funds for research and for the establishment and maintenance of necessary facilities for the prosecution of such research. If Puerto Rico or any State or Territory fails to make available for such purposes for any fiscal year a sum equal to the total amount to which it may be entitled for such year, the remainder of such amount shall be withheld by the Secretary. The total amount so withheld may be allotted by the Secretary of Agriculture to Puerto Rico and the States and Territories which make available for such year an amount equal to that part of the total amount withheld which may be allotted to them by the Secretary of Agriculture, but no such additional allotment to Puerto Rico or any State or Territory shall exceed the original allotment to Puerto Rico or such State or Territory for that year by more than 20 per centum thereof.

(b) The sums authorized to be allotted to Puerto Rico and the States and Territories shall be paid annually in quarterly payments on July 1, October 1, January 1, and April 1. Such sums shall be paid by the Secretary of the Treasury upon warrant of the Secretary of Agriculture in the same manner and subject to the same administrative procedure set forth in the act of March 2, 1887, as amended June 7, 1888.

Sec. 6. As used in this title the term "Territory" means Alaska and Hawaii.

Sec. 7. The Secretary of Agriculture is authorized and directed to prescribe such rules and regulations as may be necessary to carry out this act.

Sec. 8. The right to alter, amend, or repeal this act is hereby expressly reserved.

Sec. 22.[3] In order to provide for the more complete endowment and support of the colleges in the several States and the Territory of Hawaii entitled to the benefits of the act entitled "An act donating public lands to the several States and Territories which may provide colleges for the benefit of agriculture and the mechanic arts," approved July 2, 1862, as amended and supplemented (U.S.C., title 7, secs. 301–328; Supp. VII, sec. 304), there are hereby authorized to be appropriated annually, out of any money in the Treasury not otherwise appropriated, the following amounts:

(a) For the fiscal year beginning after the date of the enactment of this act. and for each fiscal year thereafter, $980,000; and

(b) For the fiscal year following the first fiscal year for which an appropriation is made in pursuance of paragraph (a) $500,000, and for each of the two fiscal years thereafter $500,000 more than the amount authorized to be appropriated for the preceding fiscal year, and for each fiscal year thereafter $1,500,000. The sums appropriated in pursuance of paragraph (a) shall be paid annually

[2] Amended by Act of September 21, 1944.
[3] Amended by Act of June 12, 1952.

224

to the several States and the Territory of Hawaii in equal shares. The sums appropriated in pursuance of paragraph (b) shall be in addition to sums appropriated in pursuance of paragraph (a) and shall be allotted and paid annually to each of the several States and the Territory of Hawaii in the proportion which the total population of each such State and the Territory of Hawaii bears to the total population of all the States and the Territory of Hawaii, as determined by the last preceding decennial census. Sums appropriated in pursuance of this section shall be in addition to sums appropriated or authorized under such act of July 2, 1862, as amended and supplemented, and shall be applied only for the purposes of the colleges defined in such act, as amended and supplemented. The provisions of law applicable to the use and payment of such sums under the act entitled "An act to apply a portion of the proceeds of the public lands to the more complete endowment and support of the colleges for the benefit of agriculture and the mechanic arts established under the provisions of an act of Congress approved July second, eighteen hundred and sixty-two," approved August 30, 1890, as amended and supplemented, shall apply to the use and payment of sums appropriated in pursuance of this section.

Approved June 29, 1935 (49 Stat. 436).

Amendment of the Bankhead-Jones Act and the Agricultural Marketing Act of 1946

AN ACT To provide for further research into basic laws and principles relating to agriculture and to improve and facilitate the marketing and distribution of agricultural products

Be it enacted by the Senate and House of Representatives of the United States of America in Congress assembled,

TITLE I

Title I of the Act entitled "An Act to provide for research into basic laws and principles relating to agriculture and to provide for the further development of cooperative agricultural extension work and the more complete endowment and support of land-grant colleges", approved June 29, 1935 (the Bankhead-Jones Act), is amended as follows:

(1) By substituting for section 1, title I, the following section:

"SECTION 1. It is hereby declared to be the policy of the Congress to promote the efficient production and utilization of products of the soil as essential to the health and welfare of our people and to promote a sound and prosperous agricultural and rural life as indispensable to the maintenance of maximum employment and national prosperity. It is also the intent of Congress to assure agriculture a position in research equal to that of industry which will aid in maintaining an equitable balance between agriculture and other sections of our economy. For the attainment of these objectives, the Secretary of Agriculture is authorized and directed to conduct and to stimulate research into the laws and principles underlying the basic problems of agriculture in its broadest aspects, including but not limited to: Research relating to the improvement of the quality of, and the development of new and improved methods of the production, marketing, distribution, processing, and utilization of plant and animal commodities at all stages from the original producer through to the ultimate consumer ; research into the problems of human nutrition and the nutritive value of agricultural commodities, with particular reference to their content of vitamins, minerals, amino and fatty acids, and all other constituents that may be found necessary for the health of the consumer and to the gains or losses in nutritive value that may take place at any stage in their production, distribution, processing, and preparation for use by the consumer ; research relating to the development of present, new, and extended uses and markets for agricultural commodities and byproducts as food or in commerce, manufacture, or trade, both at home and abroad, with particular reference to those foods and fibers for which our capacity to produce exceeds or may exceed existing economic demand ; research to encourage the discovery, introduction, and breeding of new and useful agricultural crops, plants, and animals, both foreign and native, particularly for those crops and plants which may be adapted to utilization in chemical and manufacturing industries ; research relating to new and more profitable uses for our resources of agricultural manpower, soils, plants, animals, and equipment than those to which they are now, or may hereafter be, devoted ; research relating to the conservation, development, and use of land, forest, and water resources for agricultural purposes ; research relating to the design, development, and the more efficient and satisfactory use of farm buildings, farm homes, farm machinery, including the application of electricity and other forms of power; research relating to the diversification of farm enterprises, both as to the type of commodities produced, and as to the types of operations performed, on the individual farm; research relating to any other laws and principles that may contribute to the establishment and maintenance of a permanent and effective agricultural industry including such investigations as have for their purpose the development and improvement of the rural home and rural life, and the maximum contribution by agriculture to the welfare of the consumer and the maintenance of maximum employment and national prosperity; and such other researches or experiments bearing on the agricultural industry or on rural homes of the United States as may in each case be deemed advisable, having due regard to the varying conditions and needs of Puerto Rico, the respective States, and Territories. In effectuating the purposes of this section, maximum use shall be made of existing research facilities owned or controlled by the Federal Government or by State agricultural experiment stations and of the facilities of the Federal and State extension services. Research authorized under this section shall be in addition to research provided for under existing law (but both activities shall be coordinated so far as practicable)."

(2) By adding at the end thereof the following new sections:

"SEC. 9. (a) In order to carry out further the purposes of section 2 of this title, there is hereby authorized to be appropriated in addition to all other appropriations authorized by this title the following sums:

"(1) $2,500,000 for the fiscal year ending June 30, 1947, and each subsequent fiscal year.

"(2) An additional $2,500,000 for the fiscal year ending June 30, 1948, and each subsequent fiscal year.

"(3) An additional $5,000,000 for the fiscal year ending June 30, 1949, and each subsequent fiscal year.

"(4) An additional $5,000,000 for the fiscal year ending June 30, 1950, and each subsequent fiscal year.

"(5) An additional $5,000,000 for the fiscal year ending June 30, 1951, and each subsequent fiscal year.

"(6) In addition to the foregoing such additional funds beginning with the fiscal year ending June 30, 1952, and thereafter, as the Congress may deem necessary.

"The moneys appropriated in pursuance of this title shall also be available for the purchase and rental of land and the construction or acquisition of buildings necessary for conducting research provided for in this title, for the equipment and maintenance of such buildings, and for printing and disseminating the results of research. Sums appropriated in pursuance of this title shall be in addition to, and not in substitution for, sums appropriated or otherwise made available for agricultural experiment stations. The said agricultural experiment stations are authorized to plan and conduct any research provided for under this title in cooperation with each other and such other appropriate agencies and individuals as may contribute to the solution of these problems and sums appropriated in pursuance of this title shall be available to meet the necessary expenses of such research.

"Unexpended balances of allotments to experiment stations from appropriations made under this section during the first five fiscal years may remain available for expenditure by the same experiment stations at which the unexpended balances occurred for the purposes specified in section 1 and for the following periods: Unexpended balances of the first year's allotments, five years; of the second fiscal year's allotments, four years; of the third fiscal year's allotments, three years; of the fourth fiscal year's allotments, two years; and of the fifth fiscal year's allotments, one year; and any unexpended balances of allotments to any experiment stations from appropriations made under this section of any subsequent fiscal year shall be deducted from the next succeeding annual allotments to such experiment stations.

"(b) Not less than 97 per centum of the sums appropriated for any fiscal year under this section shall be available for the purposes of section 2 to be allotted to Puerto Rico, each State and Territory as follows:

"(1) Twenty per centum of the sums appropriated for any fiscal year under this section shall be allotted equally to Puerto Rico, each State and Territory: *Provided,* That no allotment and no payment under any allotment shall be made for any fiscal year in excess of the amount which Puerto Rico or the State or Territory makes available for such fiscal year out of its own funds, for research and for the establishment and maintenance of necessary facilities for the prosecution of such research. If Puerto Rico or any State or Territory fails to make available for such purposes for any fiscal year a sum equal to the amount to which it may be entitled for such year, the remainder of such amount shall be withheld by the Secretary.

"(2) Not less than 52 per centum of the sums appropriated for any fiscal year under this section shall be allotted to Puerto Rico, each State and Territory as follows: One-half in an amount which bears the same ratio to the total amount to be allotted as the rural population of Puerto Rico or the State or Territory bears to the total rural population of Puerto Rico and all the States and Territories as determined by the last preceding decennial census; and one-half in an amount which bears the same ratio to the total amount to be allotted as the farm population of Puerto Rico or the State or Territory bears to the total farm population of Puerto Rico and all the States and Territories as determined by the last preceding decennial census: *Provided*, That no allotment and no payment under any allotment shall be made for any fiscal year in excess of the amount which Puerto Rico, or the State or Territory makes available for such fiscal year out of its own funds for research and for the establishment and maintenance of necessary facilities for the prosecution of such research. If Puerto Rico or any State or Territory fails to make available for such purposes for any fiscal year a sum equal to the amount to which it may be entitled for such year, the remainder of such amount shall be withheld by the Secretary.

"(3) Not more than 25 per centum of the sums appropriated for any fiscal year under this section shall be allotted to the States for cooperative research in which two or more State agricultural experiment stations are cooperating to solve problems that concern the agriculture of more than one State. The funds available for such purposes shall be designated as the 'Regional research fund, Office of Experiment Stations' and shall be used only for cooperative regional projects recommended by a committee of nine persons elected by and representing the directors of the State agricultural experiment stations and approved by the Secretary of Agriculture or his authorized representative. The necessary travel expense of said committee of nine in performance of their duties may be paid from the regional research fund, Office of Experiment Stations, provided for under this subsection.

"(c) Three per centum of the sums appropriated for any fiscal year under this section shall be available to the Office of Experiment Stations of the United States Department of Agriculture for administration of research under this section, including participation in planning and coordinating the cooperative regional research.

"SEC. 10. (a) In order to carry out further research on utilization and associated problems in connection with the development and application of present, new, and extended uses of agricultural commodities and products thereof authorized by section 1 of this title, and to disseminate information relative thereto, and in addition to all other appropriations authorized by this title, there is hereby authorized to be appropriated the following sums:

"(1) $3,000,000 for the fiscal year ending June 30, 1947, and each subsequent fiscal year.

"(2) An additional $3,000,000 for the fiscal year ending June 30, 1948, and each subsequent fiscal year.

"(3) An additional $3,000,000 for the fiscal year ending June 30, 1949, and each subsequent fiscal year.

"(4) An additional $3,000,000 for the fiscal year ending June 30, 1950, and each subsequent fiscal year.

"(5) An additional $3,000,000 for the fiscal year ending June 30, 1951, and each subsequent fiscal year.

"(6) In addition to the foregoing, such additional funds beginning with the fiscal year ending June 30, 1952, and thereafter, as the Congress may deem necessary.

"The Secretary of Agriculture, in accordance with such regulations as he deems necessary, and when in his judgment the work to be performed will be carried out more effectively, more rapidly, or at less cost than if performed by the Department of Agriculture, may enter into contracts with such public or private organizations or individuals as he may find qualified to carry on work under this section without regard to the provisions of section 3709, Revised Statutes, and with respect to such contracts he may make advance progress or other payments without regard to the provisions of section 3648, Revised Statutes. Contracts hereunder may be made for work to continue not more than four years from the date of any such contract. Notwithstanding the provisions of section 5 of the Act of June 20, 1874, as amended (31 U.S.C. 713), any unexpended balances of appropriations properly obligated by contracting with an organization as provided in this subsection may remain upon the books of the Treasury for not more than five fiscal years before being carried to the surplus fund and covered into the Treasury. Research authorized under this subsection shall be conducted so far as practicable at laboratories of the Department of Agriculture. Projects conducted under contract with public and private agencies shall be supplemental to and coordinated with research of these laboratories. Any contracts made pursuant to this authority shall contain requirements making the results of research and investigations available to the public through dedication, assignment to the Government, or such other means as the Secretary shall determine.

"(b) In order to carry out further the purposes of section 1, other than research on utilization of agricultural commodities and the products thereof, and in addition to all other appropriations authorized by this title, there is hereby authorized to be appropriated for cooperative research with the State agricultural experiment stations and such other appropriate agencies as may be mutually agreeable to the Department of Agriculture and the experiment stations concerned, the following sums:

"(1) $1,500,000 for the fiscal year ending June 30, 1947, and each subsequent fiscal year.

"(2) An additional $1,500,000 for the fiscal year ending June 30, 1948, and each subsequent fiscal year.

"(3) An additional $1,500,000 for the fiscal year ending June 30, 1949, and each subsequent fiscal year.

"(4) An additional $1,500,000 for the fiscal year ending June 30, 1950, and each subsequent fiscal year

"(5) In addition to the foregoing such additional funds beginning with the fiscal year ending June 30, 1951, and thereafter, as the Congress may deem necessary.

"(c) The Secretary may incur necessary administrative expenses not to exceed 3 per centum of the amount appropriated in any fiscal year in carrying out this section, including the specific objects of expense enumerated in section 3 of this title.

"(d) The 'Special research fund, Department of Agriculture', provided by section 4 of this title, shall continue to be available solely for research into laws and principles underlying basic problems of agriculture in its broadest aspects; research relating to the improvement of the quality of, and the development of, new and improved methods of production of, distribution of, and new and extended uses and markets for, agricultural commodities and byproducts and manufactures thereof; and research relating to the conservation. development, and use of land and water resources for agricultural purposes. Such research shall be in addition to research provided for under other law (but both activities shall be coordinated so far as practicable) and shall be conducted by such agencies of the Department of Agriculture as the Secretary of Agriculture may designate or establish.

"SEC. 11.[4] Notwithstanding any other provision of this title, (1) not less than 20 percentum of the funds authorized to be appropriated under section 9(a) shall be used by State agricultural experiment stations for conducting marketing research projects approved by the Department of Agriculture, and (2) cooperative research projects provided for under sections 9(b) (3) and (10)(b) shall be carried out under cooperative agreements between the Secretary of Agriculture and the cooperating agencies and shall include appropriate provisions for preventing duplication or overlapping of work within the State or States cooperating. Should duplication or overlapping occur subsequent to approval of a cooperative research project, the Secretary of Agriculture is authorized and directed to withhold unexpended balances of such projects notwithstanding the prior approval thereof. The Secretary of Agriculture shall include in his annual report to Congress a complete statement of research work being performed under contracts or cooperative agreements under this title, showing the names of the agencies cooperating and the amounts expended thereon, segregated by Federal and non-Federal funds."

TITLE II

This title may be cited as the "Agricultural Marketing Act of 1946".

SEC. 202. The Congress hereby declares that a sound. efficient, and privately operated system for distributing and marketing agricultural products is essen-

---

[4] Amended by Act of July 31, 1947.

tial to a prosperous agriculture and is indispensable to the maintenance of full employment and to the welfare, prosperity, and health of the Nation. It is further declared to be the policy of Congress to promote through research, study, experimentation, and through cooperation among Federal and State agencies, farm organizations, and private industry a scientific approach to the problems of marketing, transportation, and distribution of agricultural products similar to the scientific methods which have been utilized so successfully during the past eighty-four years in connection with the production of agricultural products so that such products capable of being produced in abundance may be marketed in an orderly manner and efficiently distributed. In order to attain these objectives, it is the intent of Congress to provide for (1) continuous research to improve the marketing, handling, storage, processing, transportation, and distribution of agricultural products; (2) cooperation among Federal and State agencies, producers, industry organizations, and others in the development and effectuation of research and marketing programs to improve the distribution processes; (3) an integrated administration of all laws enacted by Congress to aid the distribution of agricultural products through research, market aids and services, and regulatory activities, to the end that marketing methods and facilities may be improved, that distribution costs may be reduced and the price spread between the producer and consumer may be narrowed, that dietary and nutritional standards may be improved, that new and wider markets for American agricultural products may be developed, both in the United States and in other countries, with a view to making it possible for the full production of American farms to be disposed of usefully, economically, profitably, and in an orderly manner. In effectuating the purposes of this title, maximum use shall be made of existing research facilities owned or controlled by the Federal Government or by State agricultural experiment stations and of the facilities of the Federal and State extension services. To the maximum extent practicable marketing research work done hereunder in cooperation with the States shall be done in cooperation with the State agricultural experiment stations; marketing educational and demonstrational work done hereunder in cooperation with the States shall be done in cooperation with the State agricultural extension service; market information, inspection, regulatory work and other marketing service done hereunder in cooperation with the State agencies shall be done in cooperation with the State departments of agriculture, and State bureaus and departments of market.

SEC. 203. The Secretary of Agriculture is directed and authorized:

(a) To conduct, assist, and foster research, investigation, and experimentation to determine the best methods of processing, preparation for market, packaging, handling, transporting, storing, distributing, and marketing agricultural products: *Provided*, That the results of such research shall be made available to the public for the purpose of expanding the use of American agricultural products in such manner as the Secretary of Agriculture may determine.

(b) To determine costs of marketing agricultural products in their various forms and through the various channels and to foster and assist in the development and establishment of more efficient marketing methods (including analyses of methods and proposed methods), practices, and facilities, for the purpose of bringing about more efficient and orderly marketing, and reducing the price spread between the producer and the consumer.

(c) To develop and improve standards of quality, condition, quantity, grade, and packaging, and recommend and demonstrate such standards in order to encourage uniformity and consistency in commercial practices.

(d) To conduct, assist, foster, and direct studies and informational programs designed to eliminate artificial barriers to the free movement of agricultural products.

(e) To foster and assist in the development of new or expanded markets (domestic and foreign) and new and expanded uses and in the moving of larger quantities of agricultural products through the private marketing system to consumers in the United States and abroad.

(f) To conduct and cooperate in consumer education for the more effective utilization and greater consumption of agricultural products: *Provided*, That no money appropriated under the authority of this Act shall be used to pay for newspaper or periodical advertising space or radio time in carrying out the purposes of this section and section 203 (e).

(g) To collect and disseminate marketing information, including adequate outlook information on a market-area basis, for the purpose of anticipating and meeting consumer requirements, aiding in the maintenance of farm income, and bringing about a balance between production and utilization of agricultural products.

(h) To inspect, certify, and identify the class, quality, quantity, and condition of agricultural products when shipped or received in interstate commerce, under such rules and regulations as the Secretary of Agriculture may prescribe, including assessment and collection of such fees as will be reasonable and as nearly as may be to cover the cost of the service rendered, to the end that agricultural products may be marketed to the best advantage, that trading may be facilitated, and that consumers may be able to obtain the quality product which they desire, except that no person shall be required to use the service authorized by this subsection. Any official certificate issued under the authority of this subsection shall be received by all officers and all courts of the United States as prima facie evidence of the truth of the statements therein contained.

(i) To determine the needs and develop or assist in the development of plans for efficient facilities and methods of operating such facilities for the proper assembly, processing, transportation, storage, distribution, and handling of agricultural products.

(j) To assist in improving transportation services and facilities and in obtaining equitable and reasonable transportation rates and services and adequate transportation facilities for agricultural products and farm supplies by making complaint or petition to the Interstate Commerce Commission, the Maritime Commission, the Civil Aeronautics Board, or other Federal or State transportation regulatory body with respect to rates, charges, tariffs, practices, and services, or by working directly with individual carriers or groups of carriers.

(k) To collect, tabulate, and disseminate statistics on marketing agricultural products, including, but not restricted to statistics on market supplies, storage stocks, quantity, quality, and condition of such products in various positions in the marketing channel, utilization of such products, shipments and unloads thereof.

(l) To develop and promulgate, for the use and at the request of any Federal agency or State, procurement standards and specifications for agricultural products, and submit such standards and specifications to such agency or State for use or adoption for procurement purposes.

(m) To conduct, assist, encourage, and promote research, investigation, and experimentation to determine the most efficient and practical means, methods. and processes for the handling, storing, preserving, protecting, processing, and distributing of agricultural commodities to the end that such commodities may be marketed in an orderly manner and to the best interest of the producers thereof.

(n) To conduct such other research and services and to perform such other activities as will facilitate the marketing, distribution, processing, and utilization of agricultural products through commercial channels.

SEC. 204. (a) In order to conduct research and service work in connection with the preparation for market, processing, packaging, handling, storing, transporting, distributing, and marketing of agricultural products as authorized by this title, there is hereby authorized to be appropriated the following sums:

(1) $2,500,000 for the fiscal year ending June 30, 1947, and each subsequent fiscal year.

(2) An additional $2,500,000 for the fiscal year ending June 30, 1948, and each subsequent fiscal year.

(3) An additional $5,000,000 for the fiscal year ending June 30, 1949, and each subsequent fiscal year.

(4) An additional $5,000,000 for the fiscal year ending June 30, 1950, and each subsequent fiscal year.

(5) An additional $5,000,000 for the fiscal year ending June 30, 1951, and each subsequent fiscal year.

(6) In addition to the foregoing, such additional funds beginning with the fiscal year ending June 30, 1952, and thereafter as the Congress may deem necessary.

Such sums appropriated in pursuance of this title shall be in addition to, and not in substitution for, sums appropriated or otherwise made available to the Department of Agriculture.

(b) The Secretary of Agriculture is authorized to make available from such funds such sums as he may deem appropriate for allotment to State departments of agriculture, State bureaus and departments of markets, State agricultural experiment stations, and other appropriate State agencies for cooperative projects in marketing service and in marketing research to effectuate the purposes of title II of this Act: *Provided*, That no such allotment and no payment under any such allotment shall be made for any fiscal year to any State agency in excess of the amount which such State agency makes available out of its own funds for such research. The funds which State agencies are required to make available in order to qualify for such an allotment shall be in addition to any funds now available to such agencies for marketing services and for marketing research. The allotments authorized under this section shall be made to the agency or agencies best equipped and qualified to conduct the specific project to be undertaken. Such allotments shall be covered by cooperative agreements between the Secretary of Agriculture and the cooperating agency and shall include appropriate provisions for preventing duplication or overlapping of work within the State or States cooperating. Should duplication or overlapping occur subsequent to approval of a cooperative project or allotment of funds, the Secretary of Agriculture is authorized and directed to withhold unexpended balances on such projects notwithstanding the prior approval thereof.

SEC. 205. (*a*) In carrying out the provisions of title II of this Act, the Secretary of Agriculture may cooperate with other branches of the Government, State agencies, private research organizations, purchasing and consuming organizations, boards of trade, chambers of commerce, other associations of business or trade organizations, transportation and storage agencies and organizations, or other persons or corporations engaged in the production, transportation, storing, processing, marketing, and distribution of agricultural products whether operating in one or more jurisdictions. The Secretary of Agriculture shall have authority to enter into contracts and agreements under the terms of regulations promulgated by him with States and agencies of States, private firms, institutions, and individuals for the purpose of conducting research and service work, making and compiling reports and surveys, and carrying out other functions relating thereto when in his judgment the services or functions to be performed will be carried out more effectively, more rapidly, or at less cost than if performed by the Department of Agriculture. Contracts hereunder may be made for work to be performed within a period not more than four years from the date of any such contract, and advance, progress, or other payments may be made. The provisions of section 3648 (31 U.S.C., sec. 529) and section 3709 (41 U.S.C., sec. 5) of the Revised Statutes shall not be applicable to contracts or agreements made under the authority of this section. Any unexpended balances of appropriations obligated by contracts as authorized by this section may, notwithstanding the provisions of section 5 of the Act of June 20, 1874, as amended (31 U.S.C., sec. 713) remain upon the books of the Treasury for not more than five fiscal years before being carried to the surplus fund and covered into the Treasury. Any contract made pursuant to this section shall contain requirements making the result of such research and investigations available to the public by such means as the Secretary of Agriculture shall determine.

(*b*) The Secretary of Agriculture shall promulgate such orders, rules, and regulations as he deems necessary to carry out the provisions of this title. In his annual report to Congress, he shall include a complete statement of research work being performed under contracts or cooperative agreements under this title, showing the names of the agencies cooperating and the amounts expended thereon, segregated by Federal and non-Federal funds.

SEC. 206. In order to facilitate administration and to increase the effectiveness of the marketing research, service, and regulatory work of the Department of Agriculture to the fullest extent practicable, the Secretary of Agriculture is authorized, notwithstanding any other provisions of law, to transfer, group, coordinate, and consolidate the functions, powers, duties, and authorities of each and every agency, division, bureau, service, section, or other administrative unit in the Department of Agriculture primarily concerned with research, service, or regulatory activities in connection with the marketing, transportation, storage, processing, distribution of, or service or regulatory activities in connection with, the utilization of, agricultural products, into a single administrative agency. In making such changes as may be necessary to carry out effectively the purposes of this title, the records, property, personnel, and funds of such agencies, divisions, bureaus, services, sections, or other administrative units in the Department of Agriculture affected thereby are authorized to be transferred to and used by such administrative agency to which the transfer may be made, but such unexpended balances of appropriations so transferred shall be used only for the purposes for which such appropriations were made.

SEC. 207. When used in this title, the term "agricultural products" includes agricultural, horticultural, viticultural, and dairy products, livestock and poultry, bees, forest products, fish and shellfish, and any products thereof, including processed and manufactured products, and any and all products raised or produced on farms and any processed or manufactured product thereof.

SEC. 208. The Secretary of Agriculture shall have the power to appoint, remove, and fix, in accordance with existing law, the compensation of such officers and employees, and to make such expenditures as he deems necessary including expenditures for rent outside the District of Columbia, travel, supplies, books, equipment, and such other expenditures as may be necessary to the administration of this title: *Provided*, That the Secretary of Agriculture may appoint and fix the compensation of any technically qualified person, firm, or organization by contract or otherwise on a temporary basis and for a term not to exceed six months in any fiscal year to perform research, inspection, classification, technical, or other special services, without regard to the civil-service laws or the Classification Act of 1923, as amended.

TITLE III

SEC. 301. In order to aid in implementing the research and service work authorized under titles I and II of this Act, and to assist in obtaining the fullest cooperation among Federal and State agencies, producers, farm organizations, and private industry, in the development of and in effectuating such research and service programs, and in order to secure the greatest benefits from the expenditure of funds, the Secretary of Agriculture shall establish a national advisory committee. The functions of such advisory committee shall be to consult with the Secretary of Agriculture and other appropriate officials of the Department of Agriculture, to make recommendations relative to research and service work authorized by this Act, and to assist in obtaining the cooperation of producers, farm organizations, industry groups, and Federal and State agencies in the furtherance of such research and service programs. The chairman of the committee shall be the Secretary of Agriculture or such other official of the Department of Agriculture as he shall designate. The committee shall consist of eleven members, six of whom shall be representatives of producers or their organizations. The committee shall meet at least once each quarter and at such other times as are deemed necessary. Members of the committee may not appoint alternates to serve in their stead. Committee members other than the chairman shall not be deemed to be employees of the United States and are not entitled to compensation, but the Secretary of Agriculture is authorized to allow their traveling and subsistence expenses necessary in connection with their attendance at meetings called by him for the purposes of this section.

SEC. 302. In the furtherance of the research and service work authorized by this Act, the Secretary of Agriculture may, in addition to the national advisory committee, establish appropriate committees, including representatives of producers, industry, government, and science, to assist in effectuating specific research and service programs.

Approved August 14, 1946 (60 Stat. 1082).

Act of 1955 Consolidating the Hatch Act and Laws Supplementary Thereto

An Act to consolidate the Hatch Act of 1887 and laws supplementary thereto relating to the appropriation of Federal funds for the support of agricultural experiment stations in the States, Alaska, Hawaii, and Puerto Rico.

Be it enacted by the Senate and House of Representatives of the United States of America in Congress assembled, That the Hatch Act of March 2, 1887, relating to the appropriation of Federal funds for the support of State agricultural experiment stations, is hereby amended to read as follows:

"SECTION 1. It is the policy of Congress to continue the argricultural research at State agricultural experiment stations which has been encouraged and supported by the Hatch Act of 1887, the Adams Act of 1906, the Purnell Act of 1925, the Bankhead-Jones Act of 1935, and title I, section 9, of that Act as added by the Act of August 14, 1946, and Acts amendatory and supplementary thereto, and to promote the efficiency of such research by a codification and simplification of such laws. As used in this Act, the terms 'State' or 'States' are defined to include the several States, Alaska, Hawaii, and Puerto Rico. As used in this Act, the term 'State agricultural experiment station' means a department which shall have been established, under direction of the college or university or agricultural departments of the college or university in each State in accord-ance with an Act approved July 2, 1862 (12 Stat. 503), entitled 'An Act donating public lands to the several States and Territories which may provide colleges for the benefit of agriculture and the mechanic arts'; or such other substantially equivalent arrangements as any State shall determine.

"Sec. 2. It is further the policy of the Congress to promote the efficient pro-duction, marketing, distribution, and utilization of products of the farm as es-sential to the health and welfare of our peoples and to promote a sound and prosperous agriculture and rural life as indispensable to the maintenance of maximum employment and national prosperity and security. It is also the intent of Congress to assure agriculture a position in research equal to that of industry, which will aid in maintaining an equitable balance between agriculture and other segments of our economy. It shall be the object and duty of the State agricultural experiment stations through the expenditure of the appropriations hereinafter authorized to conduct original and other researches, investigations, and experiments bearing directly on and contributing to the establishment and maintenance of a permanent and effective agricultural industry of the United States, including researches basic to the problems of agriculture in its broadest aspects, and such investigations as have for their purpose the development and improvement of the rural home and rural life and the maximum contribution by agriculture to the welfare of the consumer, as may be deemed advisable, having due regard to the varying conditions and needs of the respective States.

"Sec. 3. (a) There are hereby authorized to be appropriated for the purposes of this Act such sums as Congress may from time to time determine to be necessary.

"(b) Out of such sums each State shall be entitled to receive annually a sum of money equal to and subject to the same requirement as to use for marketing research projects as the sums received from Federal appropriations for State agricultural experiment stations for the fiscal year 1955, except that amounts heretofore made available from the fund known as the 'Regional research fund, Office of Exeperiment Stations' shall continue to be available for the support of cooperative regional projects as defined in subsection 3 (c) (3), and the said fund shall be designated 'Regional research fund, State agricultural experiment stations', and the Secretary of Agriculture shall be entitled to receive annually for the administration of this Act, a sum not less than that available for this purpose for the fiscal year ending June 30, 1955: *Provided*, That if the appro-priations hereunder available for distribution in any fiscal year are less than those for the fiscal year 1955 the allotment to each State and the amounts for Federal administration and the regional research fund shall be reduced in pro-portion to the amount of such reduction.

"(c) Any sums made available by the Congress in addition to those provided for in subsection (b) hereof for State agricultural experiment station work shall be distributed as follows:

"1. Twenty per centum shall be allotted equally to each State:

"2 Not less than 52 per centum of such sums shall be allotted to each State, as follows: One-half in an amount which bears the same ratio to the total amount to be allotted as the rural population of the State bears to the total rural population of all the States as determined by the last preceding decen-nial census current at the time each such additional sum is first appropriated; and one-half in an amount which bears the same ratio to the total amount to be allotted as the farm population of the State bears to the total farm popula-tion of all the States as determined by the last preceding decennial census current at the time such additional sum is first appropriated;

"3. Not more than 25 per centum shall be allotted to the States for cooperative research in which two or more State agricultural experiment stations are co-operating to solve problems that concern the agriculture of more than one State. The funds available for such purposes, together with funds available pursuant to subsection (b) hereof for like purpose shall be designated as the 'Regional research fund, State agricultural experiment stations', and shall be used only for such cooperative regional projects as are recommended by a committee of nine persons elected by and representing the directors of the State agricultural experiment stations, and approved by the Secretary of Agriculture. The necessary travel expenses of the committee of nine persons in performance of their duties may be paid from the fund established by this paragraph.

"4. Not less than 20 per centum of any sums appropriated pursuant to this subsection for distribution to States shall be used by State agricultural experi-ment stations for conducting marketing research projects approved by the De-partment of Agriculture.

233

"5. Three per centum shall be available to the Secretary of Agriculture for administration of this Act.

"(d) Of any amount in excess of $90,000 available under this Act for allotment to any State, exclusive of the regional research fund, State agricultural experiment stations, no allotment and no payments thereof shall be made in excess of the amount which the State makes available out of its own funds for research and for the establishment and maintenance of facilities necessary for the prosecution of such research: *And provided further,* That if any State fails to make available for such research purposes for any fiscal year a sum equal to the amount in excess of $90,000 to which it may be entitled for such year, the remainder of such amount shall be withheld by the Secretary of Agriculture.

"(e) 'Administration' as used in this section shall include participation in planning and coordinating cooperative regional research as defined in subsection 3 (c) 3.

"(f) In making payments to States, the Secretary of Agriculture is authorized to adjust any such payment to the nearest dollar.

"Sec. 4. Moneys appropriated pursuant to this Act shall also be available, in addition to meeting expenses for research and investigations conducted under authority of section 2, for printing and disseminating the results of such research, retirement of employees subject to the provisions of an Act approved March 4, 1940 (54 Stat. 39), administrative planning and direction, and for the purchase and rental of land and the construction, acquisition, alteration, or repair of buildings necessary for conducting research. The State agricultural experiment stations are authorized to plan and conduct any research authorized under section 2 of this Act in cooperation with each other and such other agencies and individuals as may contribute to the solution of the agricultural problems involved, and moneys appropriated pursuant to this Act shall be available for paying the necessary expenses of planning, coordinating, and conducting such cooperative research.

"Sec. 5. Sums available for allotment to the States under the terms of this Act, excluding the regional research fund authorized by subsection 3 (c) 3, shall be paid to each State agricultural experiment station in equal quarterly payments beginning on the first day of July of each fiscal year upon vouchers approved by the Secretary of Agriculture. Each such station authorized to receive allotted funds shall have a chief administrative officer known as a director, and a treasurer or other officer appointed by the governing board of the station. Such treasurer or other officer shall receive and account for all funds allotted to the State under the provisions of this Act and shall report, with the approval of the director, to the Secretary of Agriculture on or before the first day of September of each year a detailed statement of the amount received under provisions of this Act during the preceding fiscal year, and of its disbursement on schedules prescribed by the Secretary of Agriculture. If any portion of the allotted moneys received by the authorized receiving officer of any State agricultural experiment station shall by any action or contingency be diminished, lost, or misapplied, it shall be replaced by the State concerned and until so replaced no subsequent appropriation shall be allotted or paid to such State.

"Sec. 6. Bulletins, reports, periodicals, reprints of articles, and other publications necessary for the dissemination of results of the researches and experiments, including lists of publications available for distribution by the experiment stations, shall be transmitted in the mails of the United States under penalty indicia: *Provided, however,* That each publication shall bear such indicia as are prescribed by the Postmaster General and shall be mailed under such regulations as the Postmaster General may from time to time prescribe. Such publications may be mailed from the principal place of business of the station or from an established subunit of said station.

"Sec. 7. The Secretary of Agriculture is hereby charged with the responsibility for the proper administration of this Act, and is authorized and directed to prescribe such rules and regulations as may be necessary to carry out its provisions. It shall be the duty of the Secretary to furnish such advice and assistance as will best promote the purposes of this Act, including participation in coordination of research initiated under this Act by the State agricultural experiment stations, from time to time to indicate such lines of inquiry as to him seem most important, and to encourage and assist in the establishment and maintenance of cooperation by and between the several State agricultural experiment stations, and between the stations and the United States Department of Agriculture.

"On or before the first day of July in each year after the passage of this Act, the Secretary of Agriculture shall ascertain as to each State whether it is

234

entitled to receive its share of the annual appropriations for agricultural experiment stations under this Act and the amount which thereupon each is entitled, respectively, to receive.

"Whenever it shall appear to the Secretary of Agriculture from the annual statement of receipts and expenditures of funds by any State agricultural experiment station that any portion of the preceding annual appropriation allotted to that station under this Act remains unexpended, such amount shall be deducted from the next succeeding annual allotment to the State concerned.

"If the Secretary of Agriculture shall withhold from any State any portion of the appropriations available for allotment, the facts and reasons therefor shall be reported to the President and the amount involved shall be kept separate in the Treasury until the close of the next Congress. If the next Congress shall not direct such sum to be paid, it shall be carried to surplus.

"The Secretary of Agriculture shall make an annual report to the Congress during the first regular session of each year of the receipts and expenditures and work of the agricultural experiment stations in all the States under the provisions of this Act and also whether any portion of the appropriation available for allotment to any State has been withheld and if so the reasons therefor.

"SEC. 8. Nothing in this Act shall be construed to impair or modify the legal relation existing between any of the colleges or universities under whose direction State agricultural experiment stations have been established and the government of the States in which they are respectively located. States having agricultural experiment stations separate from such colleges or universities and established by law, shall be authorized to apply such benefits to research at stations so established by such States: Provided, That in any State in which more than one such college, university, or agricultural experiment station has been established the appropriations made pursuant to this Act for such State shall be divided between such institutions as the legislature of such State shall direct.

"SEC. 9. The Congress may at any time, amend, suspend, or repeal any or all of the provisions of this Act."

SEC. 2. The following listed sections or parts of sections of the Statutes at Large heretofore covering the provisions consolidated in this Act are hereby repealed: Provided, however, That any rights or liabilities existing under such repealed sections or parts of sections shall not be affected by their repeal:

Bankhead-Jones Act, title I, sections 2 to 8, June 29, 1935 (49 Stat. 436; 7 U.S.C. 427 a-g).

Section 9, and related provisions of section 11 of the Bankhead-Jones Act, title I, as added by title I of the Research and Marketing Act (60 Stat. 1082; 7 U.S.C. 427h, 427j).

Department of Agriculture Organic Act of 1944, title I, section 105, amending the Bankhead-Jones Act, title I, section 5, by adding subsection (c) (58 Stat. 735; 7 U.S.C. 427d).

Act approved June 7, 1888, amending the Hatch Act (25 Stat. 176; 7 U.S.C. 372).

Adams Act approved March 16, 1906 (34 Stat. 63; 7 U.S.C. 369, 371, 373, 366, 374, 375, 361, 376, 380, 382).

Purnell Act approved February 24, 1925 (43 Stat. 970; 7 U.S.C. 370, 371, 373, 374, 375, 376, 366, 361, 380, 382).

The Acts extending the benefits of the foregoing Acts to the Territory of Hawaii, the Territory of Alaska, and Puerto Rico; Hawaii, Act of May 16, 1928 (45 Stat. 571; 7 U.S.C. 386, 386a, 386b); Alaska Act of June 20, 1936 (49 Stat. 1553), as amended by Public Law 739, approved August 29, 1950 (7 U.S.C. 369a); Alaska, Act of February 23, 1929 (45 Stat. 1256; 7 U.S.C. 386c); Puerto Rico, Act of March 4, 1931 (46 Stat. 1520; 7 U.S.C. 386d, e, f).

Such portion of the Department of Agriculture Appropriation Act of 1890, approved March 2, 1889, as related to examination of soils by experimental stations (25 Stat. 841; 7 U.S.C. 364).

That part of the Act of October 1, 1918, relating to the Georgia Agricultural Experiment Station (40 Stat. 998; 7 U.S.C. 383).

Approved August 11, 1955.

USDA Policy Letters Concerning Federal Grant Payments to States Programs

UNITED STATES DEPARTMENT OF AGRICULTURE,
OFFICE OF THE SECRETARY,
Washington, D.C., March 20, 1906.

To the Directors of the Agricultural Experiment Stations:

Congress having passed the Adams Bill, which provides for an increased annual appropriation for agricultural experiment stations, and the measure having been approved by the President, it becomes my duty to undertake the administration of this law.

In order to facilitate the prompt and effective organization of work under this Act, and to provide for a proper accounting for expenditures authorized by said Act, I have prescribed a schedule for the report of such expenditures for the fiscal year ending June 30, 1906, and until further orders, in accordance with section 2 of said Act. Copies of this schedule will be sent later.

The Director of the Office of Experiment Stations is hereby designated my representative in all matters relating to the business of this Department in connection with the administration of this law, and the Office of Experiment Stations will aid in promoting effective work under this Act in the same general way as it has heretofore in relation to the Hatch Act.

Under the terms of the Act, it will be necessary that a separate account of the Adams fund shall be kept at each station, which should be open at all times to the inspection of the Director of the Office of Experiment Stations, or his accredited representative.

In the interpretation of this Act and the examination of the work and expenditures of the stations under it, I have instructed the Director of the Office of Experiment Stations to be guided by the following principles:

The Adams fund is "to be applied only to paying the necessary expenses of conducting original researches or experiments bearing directly on the agricultural industry of the United States." It is for the "more complete endowment and maintenance" of the experiment stations, presupposing the provision of a working plant and administrative officers. Accordingly, expenses for administration, care of buildings and grounds, insurance, office furniture and fittings, general maintenance of the station farm and animals, verification and demostration experiments, compilations, farmers' institute work, traveling, except as is immediately connected with original researches in progress under this Act, and other general expenses for the maintenance of the experiment stations, are not to be charged to this fund. The Act makes no provision for printing or for the distribution of publications, which should be charged to other funds.

In order that there may be no doubt as to the disposal of the Adams fund, each station should outline a definite programme of experimental work to which it will devote this fund, and expenses for other work should not be charged to it. The work contemplated by this Act will, as a rule, necessarily cover more than one year, and changes in the programme once adopted should not be made until the problems under investigations have been solved, or their solution definitely shown to be impracticable. This will give ample opportunity for making plans for winding up any particular piece of work and beginning another with such deliberation as will provide for the suitable and economical expenditure of this fund without resort to doubtful expedients or expenditures. It is much to be desired that this fund shall be a strong incentive to the careful choice of problems to be investigated, thorough and exhaustive work in their solution, and the securing of permanent and far-reaching results on which can be safely based demonstration and verification experiments leading to the general improvement of farm practice in many particulars.

No change will be made in the attitude of this Department toward expenditures under the Hatch Act. The Hatch fund should be as carefully guarded as ever, and be devoted to substantial experimental work and the printing and dissemination of the results of such work.

The increased liberality of the Federal Government in providing for the endowment of research and experimentation in agriculture should be a further incentive to the States and local communities to supplement these funds for the extension of demonstration experiments, farmers' institutes, agricultural colleges, schools, and courses of instruction, and the general education of the rural communities along industrial lines, in order that the masses of our farmers may be so educated from early youth that they will appreciate the benefits of original research and experimentation as applied to agricultural problems, and be able to appropriate in the most effective manner for their own benefit and the general welfare of the Nation whatever practical results are obtained from the work of the agricultural experiment stations.

Very truly yours,

(S) James Wilson, *Secretary.*

United States Department of Agriculture,
Office of Experiment Stations,
Washington, D.C., February 25, 1909.

Dear Sir: The examination of the expenditures from the Hatch fund during the past two years has brought out the fact that there is a growing tendency to use that fund for printing, correspondence, administration and other miscellaneous purposes connected with the general business of the stations, and this has materially reduced the amount used for carrying on definite experimental work. It is believed that this is an unfortunate tendency and in many cases practically amounts to a diversion of the Hatch fund from the purposes for which it is intended.

Reference to Sections 4 and 5 of the Hatch Act will show that the Hatch fund was created to "pay the necessary expenses of conducting investigations and experiments and printing and distributing the results."

Various causes have contributed to the increasing use of the Hatch fund for the general purposes above mentioned. Among these is the increase of State appropriations for the stations, which in many cases have taken the form of appropriations for special investigations, demonstrations, or substations, without provision for printing or the general administrative business of the station. The recent rapid growth of enterprises in agricultural extension has brought much pressure on the stations to aid in this work through issuing popular publications, correspondence, etc.

The existing conditions make it necessary for this Office once more to define its position with reference to the expenditure of the Hatch fund. As is well known, our administration of that fund has been progressive. In the earlier days of the stations, it seemed necessary that there should be considerable liberality exercised in order that the stations might become well established and gain the confidence and support of their constituency. At the outset, however, use of the Hatch fund for inspection service was forbidden. Later on expenditures for substations and the management of the farmers' institutes were disallowed. Now it becomes necessary for us to hold that expenses for extension work should not be charged against the Hatch fund, and that only such printing should be done with that fund as will record the experimental work of the stations established under the Hatch Act. This will rule out compilations, bulletins of substations, and a variety of publications which are useful in extension work, but are not included within the terms of the Hatch Act.

It is urged that each station shall, as far as may be necessary, change its policy of expenditure of the Hatch fund so as to devote a large share of that fund to definite experimental work, restrict the expenditures for printing as indicated above, and put administrative and miscellaneous expenses as far as possible on other funds.

Beginning with July 1, 1909, it will be expected that all charges for extension work and printing of compilations will be eliminated from the Hatch fund account.

This action is not intended to hinder the development of extension work, the value of which I greatly appreciate. This Office will always be glad to do anything in its power to aid the agricultural colleges in securing funds with which to thoroughly organize and develop extension work along the lines of agriculture and country life.

Very truly yours,

(S) A. C. True, *Director.*

United States Department of Agriculture,
Office of the Secretary,
Washington, D.C., May 20, 1925.

Subject: *Administration of the Purnell Act.*
To the Directors of the Agricultural Experiment Stations:

The administration of the Purnell Act, with which the Department of Agriculture is charged, will be guided by the following general principles:

The underlying purpose of the Act is "the more complete endowment and maintenance of agricultural experiment stations," a fact which recognizes the existence of an experiment station in each State as a going concern with an organization, administrative machinery, buildings, lands, and other basic facilities for research. In view of this and since the States are making substantial contributions toward the support of the stations, it would seem that general and overhead expenses such as apply to administration and upkeep, the care of buildings and grounds, maintenance of the farm and livestock, and similar ordinary expenses, might readily be cared for without drawing upon the new fund. It is the expectation, therefore, that the demand on the Purnell Fund for general overhead expenses of the station will be reduced to the minimum.

The new Act is designed to add to and strengthen the work of investigation: it directs that the funds appropriated in accordance with it "shall be applied only to paying the necessary expenses of conducting investigations or making experiments [in lines which are defined] and for printing and disseminating the results of said researches." It is important, therefore, that the fund should represent definite pieces of investigation of substantial character, such as is called for in the present stage of agricultural inquiry.

With this idea in view, it will be expected that expenditures from the Purnell Fund will be limited to those incurred primarily for specific investigations, with such charges for publication and for special buildings and lands as pertain directly thereto. The list need not be wholly restricted to new projects, but may include existing ones which it is desired to strengthen.

This will enable the Purnell Fund to be administered on the same general plan as that followed with the Adams Fund; namely, on the basis of a program of specific projects and a budget for expenditures, these to be submitted annually in advance for consideration and discussion in order that a good understanding may be reached. It is the more important because of the provision for expansion of investigation in several comparatively new fields, and the possibility of applying the fund to existing projects in other lines. All projects supported partly or wholly from the Purnell Fund should therefore be submitted in outline in advance for examination and approval as to their suitability to the new appropriation.

Since an annual financial report on the Purnell Fund is required under the Act, it will not be possible to pool it with other funds, but a separate account upon it will be necessary, and the above plan will facilitate such an accounting. Where the support of projects is shared in by other funds, it should be possible to show quite definitely what the Purnell Fund is being used for. As in the case of the Hatch and Adams Funds, the account should be a current one, and should be supported by a set of vouchers readily available for examination on due notice. The classification will be on the same basis as for other funds, and the financial report will be rendered on the same blank with them.

The Office of Experiment Stations has been designated to represent this Department in matters relating to the details of administration of this law, and will aid in the promotion of activities under this Act in the same general way as it has heretofore in relation to the Hatch and Adams Acts. It will also be represented in negotiations for cooperation between the Department and the experiment stations, and will maintain a file of such cooperative agreements.

Sincerely yours,

(S) **W. M. JARDINE,** *Secretary.*

UNITED STATES DEPARTMENT OF AGRICULTURE,
OFFICE OF THE SECRETARY,
Washington, D.C., September 11, 1935.

Subject: Administration of the Bankhead-Jones Act.
TO THE DIRECTORS OF THE AGRICULTURAL EXPERIMENT STATIONS:

The *Bankhead-Jones Act,* providing for research into basic laws and principles relating to agriculture and to provide for the further development of cooperative agricultural extension work and the more complete endowment and support of land-grant colleges, approved June 29, 1935, places responsibility for administration of the research features of the Act upon the Secretary of Agriculture. Title I of the Act, in so far as it deals with research by the agricultural experiment stations, will be administered by the Office of Experiment Stations, designated to represent the Department of Agriculture in all matters relating to the administrative details in the expenditure of the funds allotted, and to aid in the promotion of research activities under this Act and their coordination with other agricultural research following the same general relationships now followed in the administration of the Hatch, Adams, and Purnell Acts.

The major underlying purpose of Title I of the Act, which deals with research, is to provide more adequately for thoroughgoing coordinated research into laws and principles underlying basic problems of agriculture in its broadest aspects, and research along defined lines into other features of agriculture. While the broader authorization as to lines of work for which the funds may be expended, as set forth in Section 1 of Title I, will be the basis for decision as to eligibility of projects, every effort should be made to formulate and develop a strong coordinated program of research basic to major problems of agriculture.

In this connection attention is directed to provisions of the Act making available a "Special Research Fund" for expenditure by the Department of Agriculture and to the language of Title I, Section 2, which authorizes and directs the Secretary of Agriculture to encourage research by the State stations similar to that authorized for the Department.

The annual appropriation act of the Department of Agriculture also provides that the Secretary of Agriculture shall coordinate the work of the Department of Agriculture with that of the State agricultural colleges and experiment stations. Therefore, the desirability of selecting subjects for study and of organizing research at the experiment stations under the Bankhead-Jones Act, so that the work may be logically and effectively coordinated, so far as practicable, on a regional basis with similar research being conducted or contemplated by the Department of Agriculture seems apparent. The Office of Experiment Stations will be expected to advise and assist the experiment stations in this respect to the fullest extent possible in order that advantage may be taken of the larger organization and more adequate facilities incident to integrated and coordinated attacks of this character within regions on common basic problems of agriculture.

The new Act specifies in Title I, Section 1, that the research authorized to be conducted by the Department of Agriculture shall be in addition to research provided for under existing law, but that both activities shall be coordinated so far as possible. While this limitation appears not to apply as strictly to the experiment stations, at the same time it is felt that the provision is applicable to the extent that research initiated under the new Act might well be directed to a study of those basic laws and principles which must be better understood before there can be permanent solution of practical problems now under study. In this same connection, the Act also specifies in Title I, Section 3, that sums appropriated for agricultural research to be conducted by the experiment stations shall be in addition to and not in substitution for sums appropriated or otherwise made available for agricultural experiment stations.

Considering the present needs of agriculture locally, regionally, and nationally for a greater body of basic facts and principles upon which to build sound agricultural practices, these would appear to be wise provisions. Following the maturity of the Adams Act in 1911, there was an increasing recognition of the need for making greater use of results of scientific research in the service of agriculture and rural life. The efforts by the stations to accomplish this without lowering scientific standards or interfering with unbiased search for fundamental facts have been noteworthy but not wholly encouraging in many instances. Even in some of the better financed experiment stations this situation has been acute, owing to the frequent practice of earmarking State appropriations, thereby confining their use largely to practical adaptation and service application of the results of research. In the light of the more rigid modern needs of agriculture based upon regional and national concepts of efficient and economical production, research is necessarily being forced into consideration of causes of observed phenomena and the principles governing their manipulation and integration into useful practices. Accordingly modern research cannot be content with empirical observations and results, either in the production or in the economic fields. The new Act, and especially the provisions noted above, would seem to encourage this fundamental consideration by specifying that the funds authorized are available for basic research and also by prohibiting their substitution for the appropriations already provided for the support of research. In this respect, the Act appears to offer special encouragement and support for the type of research into problems of agriculture which many of the stations have heretofore felt unable to undertake with the limitations and restrictions placed upon their resources.

For example, the field of pasture development is revealing aspects of both regional and national importance. It is bristling with widely applicable funda-

239

mental problems of plant breeding and genetics, soil fertility, animal nutrition, economics, and the like, most of which have necessarily remained practically untouched in their broad aspects. Similarly, the fields of animal production and animal diseases include many uncharted areas of fundamental character which have served as barriers to most effective production and control or cure of disorders of considerable economic importance, both regionally and nationally. Other important fields of research might be mentioned where, of necessity, major effort in the past 25 years has been devoted to empirical testing and experimentation and in which permanent progress has been retarded by the lack of adequate attack on the fundamental aspects.

The new Act appears to open the way to acquire some of this important foundation knowledge which is now lacking! The wisdom of careful analysis of experiment station programs, locally and by regions, to identify the more important basic problems of agriculture is obvious. A high degree of coordinated research effort within stations and between stations in regions seems essential to the best use of the new fund, especially in view of its present rather limited amount and the manner of its distribution. For these reasons, also, coordination with similar work, which the Department of Agriculture may undertake under the new Act or under its current appropriation, would seem to be a worthwhile objective, not only from the standpoint of the provision of more adequate facilities and a broader and more mature point of view, but also with the prospect that effective results from the new work may thereby be made available more quickly than through the necessarily more limited efforts of individual institutions.

Section 5(a) of Title I provides that no allotment and no payment under any allotment shall be made for any fiscal year in excess of the amount which the State or Territory makes available for such fiscal year out of its own funds for research and for the establishment and maintenance of necessary facilities for the prosecution of such research. There is further provision that any sums withheld by the Secretary through failure of any State or Territory to provide the necessary offset under the above provision may be allotted by the Secretary, with certain limitations, to other States or Territories which have provided funds from State sources in excess of the amount of the Federal allotment under the Act for the fiscal year in question. To administer these provisions wisely and effectively will require a high degree of cooperation. Each State and Territory should file adequate information with the Office of Experiment Stations far enough in advance of June 30 each year to enable the Secretary of Agriculture properly to ascertain and certify to the Secretary of the Treasury on or before July 1 the amount that each is entitled to receive the succeeding fiscal year, beginning July 1, under the Bankhead-Jones Act. Such statements may provide only estimates as to offset funds in case the respective legislatures have not acted upon appropriations for the experiment station by the time adequate information must be filed with the Office of Experiment Stations. However, inasmuch as payments to the States are to be in accordance with the general provisions of the Hatch Act, which authorizes deductions from the succeeding fiscal year to cover disallowances during the closing year, certification to receive the Federal allotments can be made on the basis of acceptable estimates of offset funds subject to adjustment through quarterly payments within the year and final adjustment, if necessary, in the first quarterly payment of the succeeding year.

Section 3 of Title I provides that "sums appropriated in pursuance of this title shall be in addition to, and not in substitution for, appropriations for research or other activities of the Department of Agriculture and sums appropriated or otherwise made available for agricultural experiment stations." It seems obvious that Congress, in thus specifying that sums mentioned in the new Act, when appropriated, must be in addition to, and not in substitution for, sums appropriated or otherwise made available for agricultural experiment stations, meant that it would be using the Bankhead-Jones funds "in substitution" if a State should fail to provide funds for a phase of research work formerly financed by funds available from any or all State sources and the Bankhead-Jones funds were used for such research. Here again a high degree of cooperation will be imperative in carrying out this provision of the Act. The representatives of the Office of Experiment Stations necessarily will be expected to ascertain, with care, that funds from State sources have not been reduced and funds from this new Act substituted therefore in a manner contrary to the provisions of the Act. Funds from State sources, as indicated in the provision quoted, will include, in addition to State appropriations for research, sales funds derived from research activities and properly belonging to the experiment stations, fees, gifts, cooperative contributions, allotments of institutional funds, and funds from any other source for research by the agricultural experiment station. The wording of the above provision is such that similar care necessarily will be exercised to avoid substitution of the Bankhead-Jones funds for other Federal-grant funds of the Hatch, Adams, and Purnell Acts and the use of the released funds in any way which might be interpreted as substitution resulting in a reduction in the financial support for research. Should evidence develop that the Bankhead-Jones Act funds have been used "in substitution," the Secretary of Agriculture will be obliged to consider action appropriate to the individual case in certification as to the amount of subsequent allotment to which the State is entitled.

The Act provides that the moneys appropriated for agricultural research shall be available also for the purchase and rental of land and the construction of buildings necessary for conducting the research provided for in the Act, for the equipment and maintenance of such buildings, and for printing and disseminating the results of research. The language of the Act is such that expenditures for these purposes are limited to those necessary for conducting the research financed under the Bankhead-Jones Act funds. *While the authorization for printing and disseminating the results of research might seem to apply in a broader sense than results of research financed by the Bankhead-Jones Act, such a broader interpretation obviously is not the intent and purpose of the Act. The publication of results of research is regarded as the completion of the research.* The Bankhead-Jones Act provides specifically that the new funds made available are in addition to, and not in substitution for, funds otherwise made available for agricultural experiment stations. Individual cases will arise where results of research are the joint product of work under Bankhead-Jones funds and work under other funds. Use of the Bankhead-Jones funds for publication in such cases may be warranted. The use of Bankhead-Jones funds for publication of results clearly the product of research on other funds will necessarily be considered in the nature of a substitution of funds and not in accordance with the provisions of the Act.

With the foregoing statements relative to interpretation, intent, and purpose of the Act, the following more specific points, supplementing the general regulations set forth in U.S.D.A. Miscellaneous Publication No. 202, "Federal Legislation, Rulings, and Regulations Affecting the State Agricultural Experiment Stations", will be a guide in the payment, administration, and use of the Bankhead-Jones funds:

(1) Payments of the allotments of funds authorized in Title I, Section 5, of the Act, will be made only to the treasurer or other officer of the experiment station duly appointed by the governing board of the college to receive the same, whose duty it will be to receive and bank the funds, account for them to the director, and account for the interest accrued on them annually. The director of the experiment station, in relation to these funds is expected to have full authority and responsibility for their budgeting, expenditure, and accounting, and for determining the details of the research program conducted with them, similarly as with the Hatch, Adams, and Purnell funds. Also, the director will be expected to assume full responsibility for the manner in which the Bankhead-Jones funds will be offset, as required by the Act, and for determining the research for which such offset funds are to be made available. The Office of Experiment Stations will deal with the director in regard to all such matters.

(2) Since the Act specifies the purpose for which the funds authorized may be expended, it is expected that the program of research so financed will represent definite pieces of investigation of substantial character relating to the lines specified in Title I, Section 1. Conforming to this principle, these funds will be administered on the same general plan as that followed with the Adams and Purnell funds, namely on the basis of a program of specific projects and budget for expenditures, to be submitted annually in advance to the Office of Experiment Stations for consideration and discussion on or before June 15 of each year, in order that a full understanding and agreement may be reached. All projects supported partly or wholly from the Bankhead-Jones funds, therefore, should be submitted in outline in advance for examination and approval as to their suitability to the new appropriation.

(3) It will be expected that expenditures from the Bankhead-Jones fund will be limited to those considered necessary for specific investigations along the lines provided for in the Act, with such charges for special buildings and land as are necessary and pertain directly to research conducted under the provisions of this Act, and for publishing results of research resulting in whole or in substantial part from expenditures under this Act.

241

(4) An annual financial report on the manner in which each State and Territory has expended its allotment of the Bankhead-Jones fund and the offset funds thereto specified by the Act will be required, this to be of the same character as that required for the Hatch, Adams, and Purnell funds and rendered on the same blanks with them. Therefore. the Bankhead-Jones funds cannot be pooled with other funds. A separate account of the fund must be kept. This account, as in the case of Hatch, Adams, and Purnell funds, should be a current one, supported by a set of vouchers, similiar to Adams and Purnell vouchers, and corresponding claims with evidence of their payment, readily available on due notice for examination by the Chief of the Office of Experiment Stations or his accredited representative. All vouchers and claims should bear the approval of the Station Director or his authorized representative. The classification of expenditures from the Bankhead-Jones fund will be on the same basis as for the Hatch, Adams, and Purnell funds.

(5) Where the support of projects initiated under the Bankhead-Jones Act is shared in by other funds, it should be possible to show quite definitely what the Bankhead-Jones fund is being used for.

(6) The Act not only authorizes the provision of additional funds for specific lines of research, but also authorizes substantial contributions of funds for the support of extension work and the teaching activities of the land-grant colleges. It also authorizes the expenditure of the research funds by the State agricultural experiment stations established in pursuance of the Hatch Act. Thus it recognizes the existence in each State of an experiment station with an effective organization, established administrative procedure, buildings, lands and other basic facilities already available for research. Under the circumstances, therefore, there would appear to be no justification for encroachment by the land-grant colleges upon the time and energies of research staffs, research facilities, or research equipment of the experiment stations. It is expected, therefore, that general and overhead expenses, such as apply to administration and upkeep and the care of buildings and grounds, and of college teaching and extension work will be cared for without drawing upon the Bankhead-Jones fund. Similarly, expenditures for the maintenance of experimental farms and livestock and other ordinary expenses for the maintenance of facilities for research should not be made from the Bankhead-Jones fund, except in so far as they specifically apply to the support of research projects approved under this Act. Accordingly, the Office of Experiment Stations, in its administrative relationships with the experiment stations, will be expected to scrutinize closely all salaries and parts of salaries paid from the Hatch, Adams, Purnell, and Bankhead-Jones funds, particularly those salaries paid jointly by the station and the college, to insure that the station work receives a full measure of the time and energy of specialists assigned to it with due regard to the character, scope, and productiveness of the work itself as projected. Expenditures from these funds for research supplies, equipment, and other facilities, including especially buildings, land, livestock, and the maintenance thereof, likewise will be scrutinized carefully to insure that such expenditures are limited to the legitimate needs of the research programs of the stations.

(7) Title I of this Act states that the sums appropriated shall be in addition to, and not in substitution for, sums appropriated or *otherwise* made available for agricultural experiment stations. There is no provision for relieving the States or Territories during any fiscal year of the responsibility of supporting research already in operation and which is being financed for that fiscal year from funds of non-Federal origin. This applies to all funds of non-Federal origin used by the station in support of its research, including gifts, grants, endowments, fees, and sales income. It is therefore not permissible to transfer research projects already supported from funds of non-Federal or other origin to the Bankhead-Jones fund with the idea of reducing the State support to the research program of the station for any fiscal year.

(8) It will be necessary for each station to submit evidence satisfactory to the Department as to the amount of offset funds which will be made available for research from other than Federal sources for each fiscal year. Such evidence must be submitted by each experiment station, on forms which will be provided by the Office of Experiment Stations, not later than June 15 of each year, in order that certification of the station to the Treasury to receive the allotment of funds provided for in the Act may be made in due time. At the time of the annual official examination of the work and expenditures of each experiment station by the Office of Experiment Stations for any fiscal year, it will be expected that evidence of the expenditure for agricultural research of an amount

242

of funds from other than Federal sources, equal to the amount of Bankhead-Jones funds expended during the year, will be submitted for verification in detail.

Sincerely yours,

(S) HENRY A. WALLACE, *Secretary.*

USDA Policy Statements Concerning Departmental Organization Affecting Relations With Experiment Stations

LETTER FROM THE SECRETARY OF AGRICULTURE TO GOVERNORS OF THE STATES OUT-LINING POLICY OF USDA–STATES RELATIONS IN RESEARCH, EXTENSION, AND REGULATORY WORK

WASHINGTON, *February 23, 1923.*

DEAR GOVERNOR: In view of the cooperative relations which this department is forming from time to time with various agencies, I am venturing to bring to your attention the policy which we observe in our cooperative relations with the State public agencies.

In all regulatory work and matters of law enforcement, we cooperate with the State department of agriculture, or such law enforcement agencies as the State may have created.

Our research work, if done in cooperation with the States, is carried on with experiment stations of the land-grant colleges.

Our extension work in agriculture and home economics is carried on with the extension divisions of the agricultural colleges. This cooperation is made mandatory in the Federal Smith-Lever Law itself, the provisions of which have been accepted by the State legislatures. We also have an agreement with the State agricultural colleges to the effect that any Federal funds which may come to this department direct from Congress for extension work with the various States will be expended for work carried on in cooperation with the extension divisions of the State agricultural colleges.

I am informed that the National Association of Commissioners, Secretaries, and Departments of Agriculture and the Association of Land-Grant Colleges have endorsed and recommended this general plan of administration, and that it is spreading rapidly. General development along this line, it appears, will enable the Federal government to cooperate with the different State agencies without confusion of functions.

The above, in brief, states the principles which guide us in our cooperative relations with the States and which, I trust, may be in accord with your general views.

Sincerely yours,

(S) HENRY WALLACE, *Secretary.*

ESTABLISHMENT OF AGRICULTURAL RESEARCH ADMINISTRATION

UNITED STATES DEPARTMENT OF AGRICULTURE,
OFFICE OF THE SECRETARY,
Washington, D.C., December 13, 1941.

MEMORANDUM NO. 960

ORGANIZATION OF DEPARTMENT FOR WAR EFFORT

Part III—Agricultural Research Administrator

11. The Bureau of Animal Industry, the Bureau of Dairy Industry, the Bureau of Plant Industry, the Bureau of Agricultural Chemistry and Engineering, the Bureau of Entomology and Plant Quarantine, the Bureau of Home Economics, the Office of Experiment Stations, and the Beltsville Research Center are hereby placed under the direction and supervision of an Agricultural Research Administrator. The Administrator, or, in his absence or inability to act, an Assistant Administrator, shall, as personal representative of and under the general direction and supervision of the Secretary, be responsible for the activities carried out by these agencies.

12. In the exercise of the authority vested in him by paragraph 11 of this memorandum, and in accordance with the applicable laws and regulations, the Administrator, or the Acting Administrator, shall, among other things, with respect to the agencies placed under his direction,

    a. direct and supervise their activities;

    b. direct and supervise the work of their officers and employees;

    c. delegate, in his discretion, his authority to their officers and employees;

    d. utilize their personnel, funds, property, and services; and

    e. consolidate or integrate their administrative, technical, staff, and other services.

13. Mr. E. C. Auchter is hereby detailed from his post as Chief of the Bureau of Plant Industry and designated as the Agricultural Research Administrator.

(S)   CLAUDE R. WICKARD, Secretary.

UNITED STATES DEPARTMENT OF AGRICULTURE,
OFFICE OF THE SECRETARY,
Washington 25, D.C., March 19, 1947.

MEMORANDUM NO. 1187

Coordination of Research Activities of the Department

The Agricultural Research Administrator, in addition to authorities heretofore conferred upon him, is hereby authorized and directed to coordinate all research activities (other than economic research) of the various agencies of the Department of Agriculture and, in carrying out this responsibility, shall (1) examine all current and contemplated research activities of such agencies, (2) review and approve all research proposals or projects prior to their initiation, (3) advise and consult with the heads of the agencies concerning the planning of research projects and programs, and (4) make reports and recommendations to the Secretary of Agriculture regarding the research activities of the various agencies of the Department. The heads of agencies shall submit to the Agricultural Research Administrator such proposals, reports, and other information as he may request.

All previous memoranda or orders, or parts thereof, which are inconsistent with the provisions of this memorandum are superseded.

(S)   CLINTON P. ANDERSON, Secretary.

UNITED STATES DEPARTMENT OF AGRICULTURE,
OFFICE OF THE SECRETARY,
Washington 25, D.C., July 1, 1947.

MEMORANDUM NO. 1197

Designation of Agencies to Administer Functions Transferred to the Secretary of Agriculture under Section 301 of Part III of Reorganization Plan No. 1 of 1947

Pursuant to the authority vested in me by Section 301 of Part III of Reorganization Plan No. 1 of 1947, effective July 1, 1947, under the Reorganization Act of 1945 (Public Law 263—79th Congress), the functions transferred therein to the Secretary of Agriculture are vested in an Agricultural Research Administration which is hereby established, and shall be administered, through the following bureaus and offices, under the direction and supervision of an Administrator: The Bureau of Animal Industry, the Bureau of Dairy Industry, the Bureau of Plant Industry, Soils and Agricultural Engineering, the Bureau of Entomology and Plant Quarantine, the Bureau of Agricultural and Industrial Chemistry, the Bureau of Human Nutrition and Home Economics, the Office of Experiment Stations, the Agricultural Research Center, and the Office of Agricultural Research Administrator.

The Agricultural Research Administration created hereunder shall have the same organization, personnel and functions and shall exercise the same authorizations and delegations as the Agricultural Research Administration established in accordance with Part III of Secretary's Memorandum 960 of December 13, 1941, as amended and supplemented, and Executive Order 9069, February 23, 1942 (7 F. R. 1409).

The provisions of this order shall become effective July 1, 1947.

(S)   CLINTON P. ANDERSON, Secretary.

Analysis of
United State
CAT872074
U.S. Departn

[21] ana

Jun 03, 2013

MEMORANDUM NO. 1237

Administration of the Research and Marketing Act

The Agricultural Research Administrator, in addition to authorities heretofore conferred upon him (1 AR 120), is authorized and directed, effective July 30, 1949, to administer the Research and Marketing Act, and to take such action as may be necessary or appropriate to the carrying out of this responsibility.

As of such effective date, all funds, records, facilities, and personnel of the Office of the Administrator, Research and Marketing Act, shall be transferred to the Research Administrator.

The heads of agencies shall submit to the Agricultural Research Administrator such proposals, reports, and other information as he may request.

Secretary's Memorandum No. 1199, issued July 18, 1947, is superseded effective July 30, 1949; however, regulations, procedures, delegations of authority, and similar instruments heretofore issued or approved by the Administrator of the Research and Marketing Act shall continue in full force and effect unless and until withdrawn or superseded by action of the Agricultural Research Administrator.

(S)   CHARLES F. BRANNAN, *Secretary.*

UNITED STATES DEPARTMENT OF AGRICULTURE,
OFFICE OF THE SECRETARY,
Washington 25, D.C., November 2, 1953.

MEMORANDUM NO. 1320, SUPPLEMENT 4 [5]

Reorganization of the Department of Agriculture

Pursuant to the authority vested in the Secretary of Agriculture by Sec. 161, Revised Statues (5 U.S.C. 22), and Reorganization Plan No. 2 of 1953, as well as all other statutes and prior Reorganization Plans vesting authority in the Secretary of Agriculture, the following assignments and reassignments of functions, and related delegations of authority are made. Announcement of intention to reorganize the Department of Agriculture was made on October 13, 1953.

All service agencies of the Department are grouped as follows: (1) Federal-States Relations, (2) Marketing and Foreign Agriculture, (3) Agricultural Stabilization, and (4) Agricultural Credit.

FEDERAL-STATES RELATIONS

Agricultural Research Service

This Service will conduct all of the production and utilization research of the Department (except forestry research) and the inspection, disease and pest control and eradication work closely associated with this research. The Administrator of this Service is also responsible for the coordination of all research of the Department.

Except as otherwise provided herein, all the research, inspection, disease and pest control work now in the Agricultural Research Administration are hereby assigned to this Service.

UNITED STATES DEPARTMENT OF AGRICULTURE,
OFFICE OF THE SECRETARY,
Washington 25, D.C., July 19, 1961.

SECRETARY'S MEMORANDUM NO. 1462

Establishment of Cooperative State Experiment Station Service

1. *Statutory Functions Involved.* The Agricultural Experiment Station Act. of August 11, 1955, the "Hatch Act of 1887" as amended, provides for the support by the Federal Government of a comprehensive program of research in agriculture carried on by the States through their State agricultural experiment

---

[5] Except from memorandum signed by Secretary Ezra T. Benson, other parts of which do not apply.

stations. This work is provided for by grants of Federal funds in support of research work conducted by State stations. Such research encompasses the fields of research of the several agencies of the Department conducting agricultural and forestry research. The Act directs the Secretary to furnish such advice and assistance as will best promote the purposes of the Act, including participation in coordination of research initiated under the Act by the State agricultural experiment stations, from time to time to indicate such lines of inquiry as to him seem most important, and to encourage and assist in the establishment and maintenance of cooperation by and between the several agricultural experiment stations, and between the stations and the United States Department of Agriculture. Functions under this Act have previously been carried out by the Agricultural Research Service.

The Agricultural Research Service has also been assigned responsibilities under Section 204(b) of the Agricultural Marketing Act of 1946 (7 U.S.C. 1623) authorizing the Secretary to make grants to State agricultural experiment stations for marketing research.

2. *Cooperative State Experiment Station Service.* It is believed that the administration of these functions by a separate service in the Department will give these programs their rightful place in the Department structure and will place the administration of the Act in its proper perspective in relation to the other research of the Department and the cooperative relationship between the land-grant colleges and the United States Department of Agriculture. Such reorganization will strengthen and improve the total agricultural research program carried on in the States.

Accordingly, there will be established in the Department a separate Service designated as the "Cooperative State Experiment Station Service." This agency will be headed by an Administrator and will be subject to the coordination of research activities presently assigned to the Administrator of the Agricultural Research Service.

3. *FUNCTIONS TRANSFERRED.* Under the general direction and supervision of the Assistant Secretary, Federal-State Relations, the Cooperative State Experiment Station Service will administer the statutory functions described in section 1 of this memorandum. The Assistant Secretary, Federal-State Relations, is assigned responsibility for arrangements incident to the transfer of the administration of these functions from the Agricultural Research Service to the new Service.

4. *TRANSFER OF PERSONNEL, PROPERTY AND FUNDS.* The administrators of the Cooperative State Experiment Station Service and the Agricultural Research Service shall jointly and in consultation with the appropriate Departmental staff offices develop recommendations for the transfer of personnel, property, and funds relating to the functions to be re-assigned for submission to and approval by the Assistant Secretary, Federal-State Relations and the Administrative Assistant Secretary.

5. *PUBLIC NOTICE.* In accordance with Reorganization Plan No. 2 of 1953, which became effective June 4, 1953, under terms of the Reorganization Act of 1949 as amended (5 U.S.C. 133z), the Department is hereby giving advance public notice of delegations of functions proposed to be made and will afford interested persons and groups opportunity to place before the Department their views with respect to the organization adjustments to be made. Consideration of comments received will require that submission be made by August 18, 1961.

(S) ORVILLE L. FREEMAN, *Secretary.*

UNITED STATES DEPARTMENT OF AGRICULTURE,
OFFICE OF THE SECRETARY,
Washington 25, D.C., August 30, 1961.

SECRETARY'S MEMORANDUM NO. 1462, SUPPLEMENT 1

Establishment of Cooperative State Experiment Station Service

1. *Reorganization Made Effective.* Pursuant to Reorganization Plan No. 2 of 1953 under terms of the Reorganization Act of 1949 as amended (5 U.S.C. 133z) intention to transfer certain functions within the Department incident to reorganization plans was announced in Secretary's Memorandum No. 1462, dated July 19, 1961. This Memorandum will carry out the reorganization contemplated

in Secretary's Memorandum 1462 and provide for interim procedures essential to an orderly transfer of responsibilities between the Services involved. The assignment of functions made herein is effective September 1, 1961.

2. *Cooperative State Experiment Station Service.* There is hereby established the Cooperative State Experiment Station Service, headed by an Administrator authorized to exercise the general delegations provided in 9 AR 116 of the Department's Administrative Regulations. George Selke is designated Acting Administrator, Cooperative State Experiment Station Service.

3. *Functions Assigned.* Under the general direction and supervision of the Assistant Secretary, Federal-States Relations, the Cooperative State Experiment Station Service will administer, subject to the coordination of research activities by the Administrator, Agricultural Research Service, the following functions heretofore carried out by the State Experiment Stations Division of the Agricultural Research Service:

a. The Administration of the Agricultural Experiment Stations Act of August 11, 1955 (Hatch Act or 1887, as amended—7 U.S.C. 361a–361i).

b. Payments under Section 204(b) of the Agricultural Marketing Act of 1946 (7 U.S.C 1623) to State agricultural experiment stations.

4. *Research Coordination.* The Department's responsibility for research requires analysis and evaluation of projects carried on by all agencies of the Department and, also those conducted by the State agricultural experiment stations under Federal-grant funds. It is by this means that effective use of resources and essential integration of the planning and conduct of research is achieved. Responsibility for research coordination is assigned to the Administrator, Agricultural Research Service (9 AR 200a). Review and evaluation of State and Federal research proposals as a means of achieving coordination between Department and State research has been carried on by the State Experiment Stations Division within Agricultural Research Service. This function will be performed by the Cooperative State Experiment Station Service under the supervision of the Administrator of the Agricultural Research Service pending further studies and review.

5. *Incidental Transfers.* The Administrative Assistant Secretary will approve such transfer of funds, records, property and personnel as are involved in the organizational assignments made in this Memorandum. Pending the actual transfer of the personnel involved, they shall be considered on detail to the Cooperative State Experiment Station Service. Administrative support functions will continue to be performed in the Agricultural Research Service with appropriate reimbursement or payment of costs involved pending further studies and review.

6. *Views of Interested Persons and Group Acknowledged.* Decisions made in connection with these transfers of functions have involved careful consideration of views expressed by interested persons and groups in response to advance public notice given on July 19, 1961. Thorough study and evaluation of comments received from the public provide assurance that the organizational changes approved will strengthen the Department's service to the agricultural economy and the Nation.

(S) ORVILLE L. FREEMAN, *Secretary.*

Some Major Policy Recommendations Made by Directors of Agricultural Experiment Stations

REPORT OF THE JOINT STANDING COMMITTEE ON PROJECTS AND CORRELATION OF RESEARCH [*]

The Joint Standing Committee on Projects and Correlation of Research was appointed for the purpose of studying the research projects now active in the Federal Department of Agriculture and in the State Experiment Stations. It seeks:

1. To determine if there now exists any wasteful, unnecessary or perhaps harmful duplication of effort within these agencies.

[*] Proceedings of the Thirtieth Annual Convention of the Associaion of American Agricultural Colleges and Experiment Stations, Washington, D.C., Nov. 15–17, 1916, p. 133.

2. To recommend general principles which may be applied at this time, to the end that public funds may be more efficiently and economically utilized.

3. To suggest definite opportunities for the correlation of investigative projects, planned with a view of solving the same or similar problems.

4. To determine the facts, to interpret the results, and to make recommendations, in order that greater efficiency may be obtained; in some cases by hastening the completion of important work and in others by securing the advantages which may be derived by a combined attack on the same problem at the same time at several locations.

The committee has undertaken to make as careful and complete a survey as may be made of existing research projects in the State stations and the Federal Department. This survey has not been completed. Every station director has been asked to file a list of the projects now active in his station, and two-thirds of them have supplied this information. The printed program of work published by the Federal Department indicates the nature and scope of its research projects. The committee now has on file a list of about 1,200 investigative projects located in the stations and about 750 in the Federal Department. No final generalizations as to the extent of duplication can now be made. However, the information already available justifies the statement that the duplication is frequent and that in part it may be avoided by voluntary cooperation through conference of investigators.

The committee believes that if the information now on hand touching station projects were made available in some such way as is done by the Federal Department in connection with its published program of work, a most valuable means would be afforded of bringing about cooperation of effort and greater efficiency and economy would be secured. It hopes to present at the next convention of this Association a reasonably complete list of the active research projects of the several stations similar to the previously mentioned departmental list.

W. A. TAYLOR.
J. G. MOHLER.
MILTON WHITNEY.
W. R. DODSON.
JACOB G. LIPMAN.
F. B. MUMFORD.

On motion, the report of the joint committee on projects and correlation of research was received.

RECOMMENDATIONS MADE BY THE EXPERIMENT STATION COMMITTEE ON ORGANIZATION AND POLICY WITH REFERENCE TO GENERAL PRINCIPLES TO BE ADOPTED BY THE ASSOCIATION OF LAND-GRANT COLLEGES ON THE BASIS OF POLICY IN THE ADMINISTRATION OF THE PURNELL ACT AND APPROVED SUBSEQUENTLY BY THE ASSOCIATION AT ITS THIRTY-NINTH ANNUAL CONVENTION, NOVEMBER 19, 1925

"In order to provide for definite action, the committee recommends that the following general principles be adopted by the association as the basis of policy in the administration of the Purnell Act.

"(1) This act is supplementary to the two previous ones for experiment stations. It is to build upon what already has been provided. It is for a going concern, and it is not designed to relieve the states of their financial obligations. It is for new investigation or putting new force into work already under way.

"(2) As it is supplementary and for increasing investigation, general overhead charges, except such as relate to the support of definite projects, are not considered to be warranted. The purpose which the fund is to serve will stand out more clearly if its admixture with other funds in the support of projects is held down to the minimum. To scatter it unduly and in small amounts over projects supported mainly from other funds will increase the task of administration and may suggest that it is being dissipated.

"(3) The Purnell Act is designed to promote sound investigation in accordance with modern conceptions of that term and the present status of knowledge. Progress at this stage calls for clear-cut, concrete proposals. This implies analysis of complex problems and the study of individual features by the most adequate means that research has disclosed, with the constant aim of strengthening methods and making inquiry more penetrating.

"(4) Only a relatively small field in the several branches of a station can be covered at a given time. Hence the plan of concentrating on a few topics in

248

each field and making the work comprehensive, thorough, and conclusive is highly important. A few things should be done well rather than many things indifferently.

"(5) A systematic, well-rounded research program promises more at this stage than a fortuitous, disconnected set of projects. It enables a more adequate attack on the selected topics and a better related whole.

"(6) The problem is the natural unit in the organization of research on many-sided subjects. A relationship will thus be established between the research in production and that in economics, sociology, and the home, as a basis for 'the establishment and maintenance of a permanent and efficient agricultural industry.'

"(7) The importance of cooperation and coordination within the stations, between stations, and with other agencies is now so definitely indicated as to make it a leading principle of administration. It is emphasized by the new fields of economics and rural life into which the stations are expanding. The breadth of many problems and their similarity in different sections favors joint effort in place of unrelated action. It is logical that the United States Department of Agriculture and the experiment stations should work in close cooperation, and every effort should be directed to that end.

"(8) Effective research requires trained workers, with a sound background in science quite as much as in their specialties. The need for investigators with vision, initiative, and keen perception is imperative at the present stage. The securing of such qualifications will require the maintaining of a high standard of requirements and the making of positions sufficiently attractive to warrant the necessary preparation.

"(9) The experiment station is one of the primary features of the college. Responsibility for discharging its functions does not cease with its administrative officers, but is reflected on the parent institution. Sympathetic recognition and support of the essentials for research, the type of workers required, and the adjustment of their duties are fundamental to the meeting of just expectations under the new act.

"(10) The administration of an experiment station has become a large and exacting matter. It has assumed an importance it has never had before. It calls for breadth of understanding and critical judgment in research, coupled with organizing ability and a familiarity with the leading problems of agriculture. With rapid growth in prospect, effective direction will call for time to study the whole situation—the needs of the state, the proposals submitted, the organization of joint efforts, and the maintenance of contacts with the progress of the work. Upon wise administration will depend in the first instance the effective use of the large new appropriations for agricultural research.

E. W. Allen,
F. D. Farrell,
J. T. Jardine,
H. G. Knight,
R. W. Thatcher,
Committee."

A Recommendation by the Committee on Experiment Station Organization and Policy, on Outlining Projects [7]

More Critical Scrutiny Still Needed in Outlining New Research Projects

The importance of improving or maintaining standards of experimental station research and to this end the need for careful study of project plans for new projects were discussed by the Committee on Experimental Station Organization and Policy in 1925 and again in 1926. Yet, so far as your committee is able to judge from individual experience and information available as to general practice, there is still opportunity for improvement, and there is still need for more careful scrutiny on the part of project leaders and administrative officers in outlining new research projects so as to insure "concrete investigations of such limited range as to make them feasible of accomplishment" within reasonable time.

The authorization of new projects is an important administrative matter, and merits the most careful consideration and cooperation of the research leader .

---

[7] Proceedings of the 41st Annual Convention of the Association of Land-Grant Colleges and Universities, Chicago, Illinois, November 15–17, 1927.

and his co-workers with the responsible administrative officers in narrowing the proposed investigation to a concrete phase of a problem looking to conclusions with minimum qualifications.

Practices and policies followed at different experiment stations in initiating a new piece of research or in drawing up and adopting a research project differ widely. The plan followed depends in part at least upon the size of the station staff and upon the way in which the different directors are accustomed to handle administrative business. The methods in vogue may be roughly classified as follows:

(1) The director takes full responsibility in passing upon projects.

(2) The director appoints a standing committee to act in an advisory capacity and to make a careful study of all projects submitted.

(3) The director calls into conference members of the station staff who are in a position to contribute to the study or the drafting of the project.

Whatever the method of procedure the leader of the proposed project should assume responsibility for knowledge and analysis of previous investigation, or investigations under way, which may have a bearing on the research proposed by him. In like manner, he should be prepared to support his proposed methods of investigation as adequate for accomplishment in the research proposed, and feasible of being carried out with the facilities and equipment which may be made available.

After thorough consideration of these matters, the next important task is to formulate a project statement which pictures for adminisrative officers, other investigators, and co-workers the merits of the project, its objective, procedure in the proposed investigation as to technique and methods, the probable period of time and its reasonableness, and the funds required and their adequacy for the proposed work.

Your committee recommends as a policy to research workers and responsible administrative officers more careful scrutiny of new projects, keeping in mind:

The Title. This should characterize the concrete limited unit of work to be undertaken and not cover the entire field to which the project is related.

The Objective. It should be clear cut and specific, and not involved with statements of procedure.

The Outlook. The project should be constructive in character. It should take account of the status of the question, attack points which need further study, supplement other work, exhibit vision and ingenuity, and give prospect of success.

What, specifically, is it proposed to add to the sum of knowledge of the subject? Such a contribution may deal with some new point, or those still in doubt, or determine applications to the conditions in the region.

The Procedure. It should be up-to-date, representing the progress and current views on methods and technique. It should give data that will stand statistical analysis and be comparable with other similar accepted data. Does it cover the requirements of the subject, or is it one sided or inadequate in some respects?

Thoroughness. The project should be designed to undertake thoroughly and with reasonable completeness the investigation of the subject and should not be fragmentary and superficial.

Probable Duration. Is the time element a reasonable one? Does the project commit the station to a course it may not be desirable to carry through?

The Funds Required. Is the estimate ample for the proposed investigation? Are the expenses and other essentials within the means of the station budget?

COOPERATIVE RESEARCH WITH COMMERCIAL ENTERPRISES AND INTERESTS [8]

The establishment of the agricultural experiment station as a publicly supported research institution was based upon the premise that the results accruing from research in the field of agriculture benefited all society. That this premise was correct has been amply demonstrated by the broad application that has been made of the results of such research. Since research in this field benefits all society, it should be supported not by a single class or by a few groups of especially interested classes, but by society as a whole. Commercial agencies, therefore, that have a particular interest in such work because of its close relation to their own activities can usually best serve their own interests, those of the

---

[8] Policy Recommended by the Committee on Experiment Station Organization and Policy, November 21, 1928.

stations, and of the general public by using their influence to secure for the station adequate financial support from public funds.

When public funds are not available for the conduct of research of a special character for which there is urgent and immediate need, private grants from commercial agencies may make possible the securing of prompt results and thus serve both these interests and those of the public.

There is ample evidence that experiment stations and the farmers whom the stations serve have profited materially by contacts and cooperation with commercial enterprises and interests. The committee feels, therefore, that under certain definite limitations and conditions it is proper for the experiment stations to accept grants for agricultural research from such agencies. The following general conditions are laid down as the basis for a broad policy:

1. The research supported in this way should be of general public importance and in the field of the agricultural experiment station.

2. All such researches should be institutional and not cooperative with individual departments or staff members, and salaries and other expenditures should be handled through regular institutional channels.

3. Carefully worded project agreements should be drawn, setting forth the nature and purpose of the project, and the conditions under which the grant is accepted and is to be used. In this the interest of the station and of the public should be safeguarded in the same way as research under other station funds and the right to patent any discovery be reserved to the institution.

4. Results should first be made public through the regular station channels, whether favorable or unfavorable to the cooperating agency.

Outside Work and Relationships of Station Staff

The question of part-time employment or acceptance of fees for extra service rendered to outside agencies is one that needs to be considered from time to time by practically all staff members and administrative officers. Your Committee has given serious consideration to this matter and realizes the difficulty of setting up definite policies that would be applicable under all conditions. There are certain general policies, however, which we feel might aid in guiding both staff members and directors.

1. As a general rule it seems inadvisable for station employees to accept fees or to engage in any regular work for compensation while they are employed as full-time research workers on an experiment station staff.

2. Where outside work of any nature is permitted a definite understanding should be had as to the nature of the service, time required, and compensation.

3. It is realized that there are so many different aspects to the question of accepting compensation for writing that is is difficult to set up a definite policy which would always apply. This, however, should be a matter of administrative control, and should exclude articles promoting the sale of particular agricultural commodities. Articles using unpublished research material of the station or committing the institution to any practices or policy should have the approval of the regular authorized agency of the institution.

> H. W. BARRE,
> L. E. CALL,
> J. C. KENDALL,
> C. A. MOOERS,
> E. W. ALLEN,
> J. T. JARDINE, *Chairman,*
> Committee.

UNITED STATES DEPARTMENT OF AGRICULTURE

COOPERATIVE STATE EXPERIMENT STATION SERVICE

ESSENTIALS OF AN EXPERIMENT STATION PROJECT OUTLINE [9]

Title. A brief, clear, specific designation of the subject of the research. The title, used by itself, should give a good indication of what the project is about.

---

[9] As revised May 3, 1955, and in effect at the time of this printing.

Justification. Should present (1) the importance of the problem to the agriculture and rural life of the State or region; (2) reasons for doing the work such as the needs the project will fill and the importance of doing the work now; and (3) ways in which public welfare or scientific knowledge will be advanced.

Previous Work and Present Outlook. A brief summary covering pertinent previous research on the problem (citing the more important and recent publications from other stations, as well as your own station); the status of current research; and the additional information needed, to which the project is expected to contribute. (Literature citations may be listed at the end of the project outline.)

Objectives. A clear, complete, and logically arranged statement of the specific objectives of the project.

Procedure. A statement of the essential working plans and methods to be used in attaining each of the stated objectives. The procedures should correspond to the objectives and follow the same order. Phases of the work to be undertaken currently should be designated. The location of the work and the facilities and equipment needed and available should be indicated. Wherever appropriate, the procedure should provide data suitable for statistical analysis. The statement on procedure should indicate that the research has been carefully planned and should provide for changes when they are necessary to improve the work.

Probable Duration. An estimate of the maximum time likely to be required to complete the research originally planned and publish the results. Whenever any material change in the objectives of a project is advisable, a new or revised project outline should be prepared. A major change in procedure might also necessitate a revision of the project outline.

Financial Support. Estimated annual allotments (by funds) to (1) salaries, (2) maintenance, based on analysis of requirements for labor, equipment, supplies, travel, and other operating expenses.

Personnel. The leader or leaders and other technical workers assigned.

Institutional Units Involved. Each subject matter unit in the agricultural experiment station and any other units of the institution contributing essential services or facilities. The responsibilities of each should be indicated. If there is an advisory, coordinating, or directing committee for the project, this should be shown.

Cooperation. A statement as to cooperation with the U.S. Department of Agriculture or any other stations, institutions, or other agencies cooperating formally or informally on the project. List Regional project if project is contributing.

252

SUBJECT INDEX

Act of 1862 (May 15) Establishing the USDA, 3
Act of 1862 (July 2) Donating Lands for Colleges of Agriculture and Mechanic
  Arts (Morrill Act)
    establishment of land-grant colleges, 3, 29
    impetus to station movement, 32–34
    provisions for research and teaching, 3, 19, 29–34, 72, 77
    signing, Abraham Lincoln, IV
    text, 217–219
Act of 1887 Establishing Agricultural Experiment Stations (Hatch Act)
    historical background, IV, 19, 29–52
    initiation of conjoint experimentation, 33, 34, 38
    passage, 52
    provisions for station research, 52, 63, 64, 90
    station-college relationship, 63, 64, 72, 73
    text, 219–220
Act of 1906 For the Further Endowment of Agricultural Experiment Stations
  (Adams Act)
    federal-state research cooperation, 126, 159
    passage, 106
    provisions for expanding research, 107, 117, 159–164
    text, 221, 222
    USDA administrative policy letter, 236, 237
Act of 1914, Smith-Lever Agricultural Extension
    provision for cooperative extension services, 113, 115
Act of 1925 for the More Complete Endowment of the Agricultural Experiment
  Stations (Purnell Act)
    administration, 237, 238, 248, 249
    provisions, 116' 175
    support of cooperative regional research, 192, 193
    text, 222, 223
    use of funds, 134, 179
Act of 1935 Providing for Agricultural Research and More Complete Endow-
  ment and Support of Land-Grant Colleges (Bankhead-Jones Act)
    administration, 119, 238–243
    amendment, ESCOP recommendation, 178
    amendment (1946), provisions, 179
    amendment (1946), text, 225–228
    provisions, 193, 194
    text, 223–225
    use of funds, 134
Act of 1946, Agricultural Marketing
    administration, 179–187
    passage, 178, 195
    provisions, 179–183, 186
    text, 225–232
Act of 1947 (July), Agricultural Appropriation
    first program, 198
Act of 1955 Consolidating the Hatch Act and Laws Supplementary Thereto
    consolidating federal payments to stations, 170–173
    provision for regional research, 196
    text, 232–235
Adams Act
    See Act of 1906 for the Further Endowment of Agricultural Experiment
      Stations.
Adams bill
    See under Bills of Congress.

Agricultural Appropriation Act of July 1947
  See Act of 1947 (July), Agricultural Appropriation.
Agricultural Chemistry Association of Scotland, 8–11
Agricultural colleges
  See Colleges, agricultural and under individual names and states.
Agricultural economics
  establishment of BAE, 175
  Purnell Act provisions for economic research, 116, 175–179
  See also Marketing research.
Agricultural education
  emergence in United States, 11–14
  See also Agricultural training and Colleges, agricultural.
Agricultural Marketing Act of 1946
  See Act of 1946, Agricultural Marketing.
Agricultural research
  accomplishments, 153, 203, 207
  conjoint college-station experimentation, 31–34
  definition of regional research, 204
  duplication of efforts, 125, 194, 202
  economics. *See* Agricultural economics.
  extent of cooperative regional work, 19, 207, 210
  federal-state relations, 120, 121, 126–128
  government-university sponsorship, 208
  historical background, 1, 2, 5–11, 15–17, 19–24
  impact of chemistry, 5–13, 16, 17
  introduction of project system, 162–167
  marketing. *See* Marketing research.
  plurality and decentralization, 207
  practical problems vs. scientific inquiry, 84–89, 164
  procedures for cooperative regional, 196, 198, 199
  public relations, 153
  regional, under Purnell Act, 192
  role of colleges and universities, 23, 24, 30, 31, 59, 62
  scope under Adams Act, 106, 107, 159–164
  scope under Hatch Act, 81, 82
  strengthening basic, 81, 82, 107, 124, 159, 161, 212, 214
Agricultural Research Administration, 137, 243, 244
  See also Agricultural Research Service.
Agricultural Research Service
  administration of cooperative research, 132
  establishment, 137
  inclusion of Office of Experiment Stations, 139
  Joint Committee on Cooperative Research, 131
  See also under specific divisions.
Agricultural science
  emergence, 1–4, 21
  Liebig's treatise, 16
  impact of chemistry, 5–13, 16, 17
  movements towards subsidy, 17, 22, 23
  See also Agricultural research.
Agricultural societies
  See Societies, agricultural and under specific names.
Agricultural training
  aid of cooperative research program, 192
  emphasis of Morrill Act on instruction, 27, 28
  federal-state relations in science education, 115
  utilization of college faculty in experiment stations, 30, 31
Agriculture
  Civil War, 30, 55, 210
  depression of the 1930's, 175
  factors affecting farm prices, 187–189
  historical highlights, 1–3, 19–28
  legislation. *See* Legislation.
  public relations, 121, 152, 154
  technological growth, IV–VI, 188, 191, 211
  World War I, 115, 175, 192
  World War II, 129, 170, 177, 187

Agriculture, Department of
    cabinet rank, elevation to, proposed, 25, 26, 44
    conduct of own research, 122, 126, 148
    cooperation in regional research, 200, 201
    early conventions convened by Commissioners, 35, 40, 41, 49, 59, 62, 112
    early research policy, 27, 28
    establishment, IV, 19, 27
    federal-state cooperation at college stations, 45-52, 122, 123, 127, 128
    Graduate School, 210
    history, 1, 2, 25-27
    policies and activities under different Commissioners, 35, 40, 41, 45, 49, 122
    policy letters concerning federal payments to state programs, 236-243
    policy statements concerning departmental organization affecting relations
      with experiment stations, 243-247
    publications. See Publications.
    relations with agricultural colleges, V, 122
    relations with stations, V, VI, 89, 99, 100-107, 113, 120, 126-129
    reorganization of 1923, 117
    reorganization of 1947, 136, 244
    reorganization of 1953, 137, 139
    responsibilities under Adams Act, 126, 159, 160
    USDA-Land-Grant College Centennials (1962), IV, 210
    See also under specific subjects, offices, bureaus, and services.
Alabama Agricultural Experiment Station, 192
Albemarle Agricultural Society, 3
American Association of Agricultural College Editors, 155
American Association of Land-Grant Colleges. See Association of Land-Grant
    Colleges, American.
American Journal of Arts and Sciences
    founder and editor, 8
American Philosophical Society, 2
Association of American Agricultural Colleges and Experiment Stations
    Armsby Amendment to constitution, 67, 72, 78, 79
    Commission on Agricultural Research, 124
    Committee on Cooperative work between USDA and Experiment Stations,
      123
    Committee on Experiment Station Organization and Policies, 148
    Committee on Indexing Agricultural Literature, 147
    Committee on Uniformity of Station Publications, 146
    concerning administration of station research, 73, 82-86, 90
    concerning station-college relations, 63, 64, 66, 68, 69, 72-75, 78, 82
    development, 56-79
    early conventions, 33, 63, 69, 74
    establishment, 63
    functions, 63, 66, 71, 76
    impact of Johnson-Atwater-Cook report on station research, 65, 66, 73
    Joint Committee on Projects and Correlation, 113, 115
    Jordan report on teacher-investigator dualism, 75
    name change, 147
    new constitution, 147, 153
Association of Land-Grant Colleges, American
    centennial conference, 213
    change of name, 213
    Committee on Agricultural and Home Economics Publications, 152
    constitutional changes, 213
    Experiment Station Committee on Organization and Policy. See as separate
      heading.
    Joint Committee on Projects and Correlation of Research, 193, 194
    opposition to Cooley bill concerning marketing practices, 176
    See also Association of American Agricultural Colleges and Experiment
      Stations.
Association of State Universities and Land-Grant Colleges
    See Association of Land-Grant Colleges, American.

Association of Teachers of Agriculture
  annual meetings, 38, 44, 58
  Committee on Conjoint Experimentation. *See* Committee on Conjoint Experimentation.
  formation, 38
Atwater-Johnson-Cook Report on Station Work, 65, 66, 73, 209
Bankhead-Jones Act
  See Act of 1935 Providing for Agricultural Research and More Complete Endowment and Support of Land-Grant Colleges.
Bills of Congress
  bill, Adams
    provisions for further endowment of stations, 106
  bill, Carpenter
    advocacy of national experiment stations, 43–45
  bill, Christgau
    provisions for cooperative regional research, 193
  bill, Cooley
    provisions for marketing practices, 176
  bill, Cullen
    plan for organizing station as college department, 47, 48, 60
  bill, Flannagan
    proposed amendment of the Bankhead-Jones Act, 178, 179
  bill, Flannagan-Hope
    enactment, 178
  bill, Hawley
    proposal for federal support of college stations, 51, 52
  bill, Hope (H.R. 5925)
    provisions for a National Food Research Institute, 178
  bill, Hope (H.R. 6692)
    proposal for an Agricultural Marketing Administration, 178, 179
  bill, national stations (Knapp proposal), 44–46, 81, 116
Bureau of Agricultural Economics
  establishment, 175
California
  college-created station at Berkeley, 29, 41
Carpenter bill
  See under Bills of Congress.
Centennial lecture series, 210–213
Christgau bill
  See under bills of Congress.
"Classification of Agriculture," 147
Cooley bill
  See under Bills of Congress.
Colleges, agricultural
  Bureau of Education survey, 134
  college-created experiment stations, 24, 29, 41
  establishment of land-grant, IV, 11–13
  legislation affecting land-grant, 13, 15
  principal departments, 153
  relations with stations, 66, 73, 74, 77, 78
  relations with USDA, V, 122
  role of research, 62, 153
  roles of USDA and states in establishing college stations, 45–52
  See also under names of states.
"Colleges for Our Land and Time," 126
Colleges, land-grant
  See Colleges, agricultural.
Committee on Conjoint Experimentation
  establishment of stations recommended, 38
  station features outlined, 39
  state subsidy of stations recommended, 39
  See also Association of Teachers of Agriculture.
Committee on Experimental Stations
  stimulus to early station-founding, 35–37
  See also Experiment stations, state.
Connecticut
  Agricultural Experiment Station, 14, 22

Connecticut—Continued
    state-subsidized station, 22
    Storrs Agricultural School, 152, 153
    Wesleyan University, 22
    Yale (Sheffield Scientific School), 8, 11–14, 30, 152, 153
Connecticut Agricultural Society, 21
Connecticut Society for Promoting Agriculture
    founding in 1794, 2
Connecticut State Board of Agriculture (1875), 21, 22
Consolidation Act
    See Act of 1955 Consolidating the Hatch Act and Laws Supplementary
        Thereto.
Cooperative State Experiment Station Service
    establishment, 138
    functions, 138
Cornell University
    Agricultural Experiment Station, 37, 147
Cullen bill
    See under Bills of Congress.
Dabney Report
    Hatch funds, 64, 90
    standards for research, 94
    station-college relationships, 64
    See also Association of American Agricultural Colleges and Experiment
        Stations.
Department of Agriculture
    See Agriculture, Department of.
"Elements of Scientific Agriculture and Geology," 7
ESCOP
    See Experiment Station Committee on Organization and Policy.
Experiment Station Committee on Organization and Policy
    centennial activities, IV, VI, 210
    Committee on Distribution of Agricultural Literature Abroad, 152
    ESCOP–ECOP Committee on Agricultural and Home Economics Publica-
        tions, 152
    establishment, 106
    Experiment Stations Marketing Research Advisory Committee (ESMRAC),
        180–186
    function, 106
    Joint Committee (ARS–ESCOP) on Cooperative Research, 131, 132
    recommendations concerning Bankhead-Jones amendment, 178
    recommendations concerning marketing legislation, 176, 195, 196
    recommendations concerning station research and regulatory activities, 111–
        116
    recommendations for consolidated research funds, 170–173
    recommendations for station fiscal reporting, 118, 119
    recommendations for USDA-station cooperation, 126, 128–132
    Subcommittee on Federal-States Relations, 130, 131
    Subcommittee on Reorganization of USDA, 137
    Webber plan for federal-state research cooperation, 116, 117
    See also Association of Land-Grant Colleges, American.
Experiment Station Record, 145, 146, 149
Experiment stations, national, 43, 44
    See also Experiment stations, state.
Experiment stations, state
    administration and organization, 65, 69, 93–95, 103, 107
    Atwater research formula, 82–85
    basic research, 81, 86–89, 93–104, 119, 153
    college sponsorship, 29, 38, 41
    definition, 35, 38
    dissemination of information, 65, 82, 95, 113, 143, 144, 150, 152, 155
    documents for administering cooperative research, 132
    duplication of research, 194, 202
    early establishment, V, 14, 30, 33
    European precedents, 5–17
    Farrell appraisal of regional research programs, 202, 203
    fiscal accountability to USDA, 118, 119

Experiment stations, state—Continued
  growth of cooperative regional research, 191–194
  Hatch Act principle of research responsibility, 207
  introduction of project system, 162, 164–167
  Johnson-Atwater organization formula, 21–24, 35, 36, 39
  joint experimentation with USDA, 123
  limitations of Hatch funds, 90–93
  original research under Adams Act, 106, 107, 159, 207
  public relations, 121, 153, 154
  relations with colleges, 24, 66, 69, 73, 74, 77, 78
  relations with USDA, 89, 104, 105, 107, 126–128, 131, 139
  report of Committee on Experiment Stations, 35–37
  subsidies, 17, 35–38
  teaching-research function, 65, 76
  teaching-research-extension function, 114
  training function, 30, 31, 192, 207, 208
  See also under names of individual stations and specific subjects.
Extension service, federal, 184
Extension services, state, 184
Farm Foundation, 194
fertilizer
  misrepresentation of composition, 9, 14, 21
Flannagan bill
  See under Bills of Congress.
Flannagan-Hope bill
  See under Bills of Congress.
Forestry, 195
Friends of Agricultural Education
  Gregory-Flag convention of 1871, 30, 33, 38, 55
German station movement, 14, 23, 24, 76, 77
Hatch Act
  See Act of 1887 Establishing Agricultural Experiment Stations.
Hawley bill
  See under Bills of Congress.
Highland and Agricultural Society of Scotland, 5–7, 11, 12, 15, 30
Home economics, 152
Houghton Farm Experiment Association, 60
Hope bill (H.R. 5925)
  See under Bills of Congress.
Hope bill (H.R. 6692)
  See under Bills of Congress.
Illinois
  Industrial University, 30, 55
  University of Illinois, 38
Interior, Department of, 25
Iowa State University
  Ames Conference, 169
Journal of Agricultural Research, 148, 149
Kellogg Foundation, 155
Kentucky
  college-sponsored station, 29
Knapp bill
  See under Bills of Congress.
Land-Grant College Act
  See Act of 1862 Donating Lands for Colleges of Agriculture and Mechanic
    Arts (Morrill Act).
Land-grant colleges
  See Colleges, agricultural.
"Lectures on Agricultural Chemistry and Geology," 7
Legislation
  achieving federal support for college stations, 29–50
  affecting agricultural colleges, IV, 3, 13
  affecting establishment and functions of USDA IV, 3, 25–27
  consolidating federal payments to stations, 170–173
  recommendations of Abraham Lincoln, 210
  relating to conference travel, 194, 196

Legislation—Continued
  relating to original research at stations, 159
  relating to regional research, 195, 198
  supporting market research, 175
  See also under specific Acts and Bills of Congress.
Livestock council, 191
Maine Agricultural Experiment Station, 150
Marketing research
  coordination of programs, 184
  definition, 182–184
  economic value, 187–189
  expansion following Act of 1946, 186, 187
  history at stations (1940–1960), 175
  influence of depression, 175, 176
Massachusetts
  Agricultural College, 37
  Massachusetts Institute of Technology, 3
Massachusetts Agricultural Society, 3
Michigan Agricultural College, 29, 38, 44, 55, 58
Minnesota Experiment Station, 151
Moeckern experimental station, 16, 17, 20
Morrill Act
  See Act of 1862 (July 2) Donating Lands for Colleges of Agriculture and
    Mechanic Arts.
National Agricultural Convention (1872)
  promotion of conjoint experimentation, 33, 36
National Livestock and Meat Board, 194
National Project in Agricultural Communications, 155
New Jersey Experiment Station, 40
New Jersey Society for the Promotion of Agriculture, Commerce, and Art, 2
New York
  Agriculture Experiment Station, 37, 143
  Cornell Experiment Station, 37, 147
New York State Agricultural Society, 2, 19, 20
North Carolina Experiment Station, 60
Office of Experiment Stations
  activities under different departmental reorganizations, 117, 118, 137
  administration of project system, 160–164
  administration of publications, 134, 147, 148
  cooperation with Association of Land-Grant Colleges, 112
  establishment, 66, 111
  fiscal review of station grants, 82, 89–91, 112, 159–164
  included in States Relations Service, 113, 114
  name change to State Experiment Stations Division, 139
  role in USDA-station cooperative research, 122, 123
  transfer to office of the Director of Scientific Work, 117–119
Office of Extension Work in the North and West
  included in States Relations Service, 113, 114
Office of Extension Work in the South
  included in States Relations Service, 113, 114
Office of Home Economics
  included in States Relations Service, 113, 114
Patent Office, United States, 25
Pennsylvania
  Philadelphia Society for the Promotion of Agriculture, 2
  University of Pennsylvania, 3
Policy letters, USDA, concerning federal grant payments to states programs
  administration of the Adams Act, 236, 237
  administration of the Bankhead-Jones Act, 238–243
  administration of the Hatch fund, 237
  administration of the Purnell Act, 237, 238
Policy recommendations of directors of agricultural experiment stations
  administration of the Purnell Act, 248, 249
  cooperative research with commercial enterprises and interests, 250
  outline of essentials of an experiment station project, 249, 250
  report of the Joint Standing Committee on Projects and Correlation of Re-
    search, 247, 248

Policy statements, USDA, concerning departmental organization affecting relations with experiment stations
  administration of the Research and Marketing Act, 245
  coordination of research activities of the Department, 243, 244
  designation of agencies to administer functions transferred under reorganization plan of 1947, 244
  establishment of Agricultural Research Administration, 243, 244
  establishment of Cooperative State Experiment Station Service, 245–247
  reorganization of USDA (1953), 245
  USDA-states relations in research extension and regulatory work, 243, 245
"Progress in Agriculture by Education and Government Aid" (1882), 41
Publications
  debates on publishing policies, 147, 148
  emphasis of Associations, 143–155
  emphasis of ESCOP, 113, 143, 148, 152, 154
  foreign exchange and distribution, 151, 152
  improvement of public relations, 154
  manual on cooperative regional research, 198
  number published by stations, 147
  recommendation, bureau of public information in USDA, 143
  Report on Experiment Station Annual Reports (ESCOP), 150
  Report on Publishing the Work on the Experiment Station (1917, ESCOP), 143
  types, 143–145, 151
  USDA activities, 143–148
  See also under titles, reports, and journals.
Public Law 733
  provisions for marketing research, 179
  See also Flannagan-Hope bill and Research and Marketing Act of 1946.
Purnell Act
  See Act of 1925 for the More Complete Endowment of the Agricultural Experiment Stations.
Regional conferences
  development of regional research concept, 191–194
  Joint Committee on Cooperative Research, 201
  work of Committee of Nine, 197, 198, 201–203
Regional research fund
  use, 195, 196, 202, 204, 207
  See also Act of 1955 Consolidating the Hatch Act and Laws Supplementary Thereto.
Research and Marketing Act of 1946.
  See Act of 1946, Agricultural Marketing.
Rhode Island Experiment Station, 155
Royal Academy of Agriculture and Forestry (Tharand), 16
Royal Agricultural Society (British), 15
Royal Society of London, 2
Scotland, 5–11, 15
  See also Highland and Agricultural Society of Scotland.
Societies, agricultural
  beginnings, 2, 8
  British, 15
  importance to station movement, 3, 6, 15
  See also under names of societies and associations.
Soil analysis, 9, 12
South Carolina Society for Promoting Agriculture, 2
State Experiment Stations Division, 180–184
  See also Office of Experiment Stations.
States Relations Service
  establishment, 113, 126
"Suggestions for Experiments in Practical Agriculture," 7
Tennessee
  college-sponsored station, 29
United States Agricultural Society, 27
"Western Stock Farmer and Journal," 43
Wisconsin
  Agricultural Experiment Station, VI
  college-sponsored station, 29
"Workers in Subjects Pertaining to Agriculture in the Land-Grant Colleges and Experiment Stations, List of," 147

NAME

Abbot,
Adams,
  107, 1
Allen, 1
  139, 1
Alvord,
  79, 9(
Anderso
Armsby
  70, 71
  124, 1
Atherto
  72, 73
Atwater

  76, 7(

Auchter
Bacon, 1
Bacon, 1
Bailey,

Bailey,
  147, 1
Barre, 1
Baver, 1
Benson,
Bessey,
Borjka,
Boss, A
Bonasit
Branna
Brewer
Bryan,
Buchan
Buchar
Burgess

Caldwe
Call, L.

Carpen
Carpen
Carrier
Carstei

Clark,
Clark,
Colmai

Coke, I
Conove
Cook,

Cooke,

Cooper, Tom, 193, 205.
06, Coville, Frederick V., 127.
Cronemiller, F. P., 141.
36, Crusius, 16.
Cullen, William, 47.
66, Cutter, W. P., 147, 156.
. Dabney, Charles W., 60, 63, 64, 70, 71, 73, 84, 90, 107.
69, Davenport, Eugene, 88, 106, 108, 126,
94, 139.
Davy, Humphrey, 2.
71, Dickins, Dorothy, 181.
Dixon, H. A., 173.
25, Dodson, W. R., 173, 248.
75, Dorman, C., 195.
95, Doten, S. B., 151.
44, Dupree, A. H., 28.
Eddy, E. D., 3, 4, 126, 139.
Elting, E. C., 131, 132, 136, 139, 197, 202, 205.
Farrell, F. D., 153, 154, 156, 249.
Farrell, M. A., 195, 202.
Flagg, Willard C., 30, 31, 32, 33, 38, 55,
24, 56, 57.
Flannagan, John W., 177, 178.
Fletcher, S. W., 127, 128, 140.
Foster, L. S., 28.
Franklin, Benjamin, 2.
Freeman, Orville L., 138, 212, 246, 247.
Fulmer, Hampton P., 177.
Funchess, M. J., 127.
George, James Z., 50, 51, 52, 53.
Gilbert, B. E., 151.
Goessmann, C. A., 60.
Goodell, H. H., 123, 147, 156.
Gregory, John M., 30, 33, 34, 35, 36, 38, 50, 55, 56, 57, 58.
Grey, Dan T., 192.
Griffee, Fred, 150, 156.
Grout, W. W., 44, 53.
Guterman, C. E. F., 170, 173, 195.
Hardin, C. M., 181.
Harris, Abram W., 89, 145, 146, 157.
Hatch, William H., 50, 108.
Hawley, Joseph R., 51, 52, 53.
Henke, L. A., 152.
Henry, William A., 63, 74, 75, 76, 79, 85, 86, 88, 89, 94, 96, 97, 108, 123, 144, 145, 146, 157, 159, 166.
31, Hilgard, Eugene Woldemar, 41, 42, 43, 44, 53, 98.
Hills, J. L., 134, 135, 140.
Hilton, James H., 211.
79, Hope, Clifford R., 178, 189.
Houston, D. F., 113, 114, 140.
Hubbard, R. D., 28.

GRAIN EXPORTS

Ingalls, John J., 51, 53.
Jardine, James T., 127, 128, 135, 136, 137, 151, 249, 251.
Jardine, W. M., 238.
Jefferson, Thomas, 2, 3.
Jehlik, P. J., 157.
Jenkins, Edward Hopkins, 21, 152, 153.
Johnson, [A. A.], 146.
Johnson, E. C., 127.
Johnson, I. B., 152.
Johnson, Samuel William, 14, 15, 16, 18, 19, 20, 21, 22, 23, 24, 25, 27, 28, 30, 32, 33, 35, 36, 39, 41, 43, 53, 65, 67, 75, 76, 79, 82, 86, 94, 107, 108, 143, 145, 146, 147, 152.
Johnston, James F. W., 6, 7, 8, 9, 10, 11, 12, 13, 14, 17, 18, 62, 84.
Jordan, David Starr, 124, 140.
Jordan, Whitman Howard, 75, 76, 79, 86, 87, 88, 89, 94, 101, 102, 103, 104, 106, 108, 124, 163, 166, 170, 174.
Judd, Orange, 22.
Kellerman, K. F., 128, 157.
Kemp, W. B, 178, 195.
Kendall, J. C., 251.
Klein, Arthur J., 134, 140.
Knapp, Asahel, 43, 44, 45, 46, 47, 51, 52, 59, 60, 61, 73.
Knight, H. G., 128, 249.
Knoblauch, H. C., 136, 139, 170, 202.
Krauss, W. E., 214.
Larned, W. A., 18.
Lavoisier, 2.
Law, Ernest M., vi, 22, 153.
Lawes, John Bennet, 23.
Lazenby, W. R., 60.
Leach, J. G., 151, 157.
Ledoux, A. R., 60.
Lee, Stephen D., 61, 62.
Lemmer, G. F., 53.
Lewis, R. D., 213.
Lincoln, Abraham, iv, 210.
Lininger, F. F., 181.
Lipman, Jacob G., 192, 248.
Logan, James, 1.
Loring, George Bailey, 40, 41, 45, 59.
Macy, H., 137, 138, 151, 157.
Mann, A. R., 205.
Martin, William H., 137.
McCormick, Cyrus, iv.
Merrill, M. C., 149.
Meyer, W. P., 157.
Miles, Manly, 30, 55, 56, 57, 58.
Miller, Paul A., 213, 214.
Mohler, J. G., 248.
Money, H. D., 44, 53.
Mooers, C. A., 251.
Morrill, Justin, 32, 34, 37, 52, 53.
Morrow, George E., 86, 94, 108.
Morton, J. Sterling, 91, 92, 108.
Mumford, F. B., 140, 205, 248.
Norton, John Pitkin, 9, 10, 11, 12, 13, 14, 15, 18, 21.
O'sen, Nils, 128.
O'Neal, Edward A., 176.
Osborne, E. A., 18, 28, 53.

Penn, William, 1.
Peterson, Ervin L., 138.
Pinchot, Gifford, 124.
Plumb, Preston B., 52, 53.
Priestly, Joseph, 2.
Pugsley, C. W., 117, 140.
Redding, (R. J.), 146.
Riessner, Friedrich, 16.
Roberts, Isaac P., 60, 87, 101.
Roosevelt, Theodore, 106, 160.
Ross, E. D., 28.
Rummell, L. L., 154, 157.
Rusk, H. P., 137, 140.
Sanborn, J. W., 60.
Selke, George A., 138, 246.
Shaw, B. T., 131, 136, 138, 141, 205.
Silliman, Benjamin, Jr., 9, 11, 12.
Silliman, Benjamin, Sr., 8, 9, 11.
Smith, E. V., 130.
Spielman, A. A., 201, 205.
Stockhardt, Adolph, 16, 23.
Sturtevant, E. L., 60, 143, 157.
Talbott, M. W., 141.
Tapp, Jesse W., 211.
Taylor, W. A., 248.
Thatcher, R. W., 141, 205, 249.
Thorne, Charles E., 63, 98, 140, 156.
Thorne, D. W., 201.
Townshend, N. S., 53, 60, 79.
True A. C., vi, 18, 28, 53, 89, 91, 92, 94, 95, 96, 97, 108, 112, 113, 114, 123, 126, 135, 139, 141, 144, 145, 147, 148, 157, 159, 160, 161, 162, 164, 165, 166, 167, 168, 174, 205, Trullinger, R. W., 1, 4, 119, 120, 136, 200.
Truman, Harry S., 178.
Tull, Jethro, 1, 4.
Volk, N. J., 130.
von Liebig, Justus, 2, 6, 15, 18, 23, 76.
Walker, Eric A., 141, 208.
Wallace, Henry, 243.
Wallace, Henry A., 211, 243.
Wallace, Henry C., 114, 117, 141.
Washington, George, 2, 210.
Waters, H. J., 123.
Watts, Frederick, 34, 35, 36, 37, 40.
Weber, A. D., 138.
Webber, H. J., 116, 141.
Welch, Adonijah S., 57.
Welch, Frank J., 135, 181, 210.
White, Henry Clay, 99, 100, 101, 104, 105, 106, 109, 163.
Whitney, Milton, 248.
Whitten, (Jamie L.), 199, 200.
Wickard, Claude R., 244.
Williams, S. P., 132.
Willits, Edwin, 61, 62.
Wilson, James, 96, 104, 105, 106, 122, 123, 160, 161, 237.
Wilson, M. L., 206.
Wright, Carroll D., 124.
Wright, J. A., 28.
Young, Harold, 206.

· U.S. GOVERNMENT PRINTING OFFICE: 1962   O—634244

Lightning Source UK Ltd.
Milton Keynes UK
UKHW041424180219
337528UK00013B/873/P